D0288836

# THE MEXICAN POLITICAL SYSTEM

# THE MEXICAN POLITICAL SYSTEM

SECOND EDITION

## L. VINCENT PADGETT

SAN DIEGO STATE UNIVERSITY

HOUGHTON MIFFLIN COMPANY BOSTON

ATLANTA DALLAS GENEVA, ILLINOIS
HOPEWELL, NEW JERSEY PALO ALTO LONDON

Figure 7 from Adolfo Orive Alba, "La irrigación como factor del bienstar campesino," in Ifigenia M. de Navarrete, *Bienstar campesino y desarrollo económico,* published by Fondo de Cultura Economica, México, 1971.

Figure 8 from Ifigenia M. de Navarrete and Arturo Cardenas Ortega, "Un modelo de desarrollo agropecuario y bienstar campesino 1970–1980," in Ifigenia M. de Navarrete, *Bienstar campesino y desarrollo económico,* published by Fondo de Cultura Economica, México, 1971.

Printed in the U.S.A.
Library of Congress Catalog Card Number: 75-27497
ISBN: 0-395-20364-3

*To Edna, Beth, Donna, and Nancy*

# CONTENTS

# FIGURES

# TABLES

# PREFACE

Since publication of *The Mexican Political System* in 1966, both the course of events and continued observation have led the author to modify some of his earlier underlying assumptions, which governed the writing of that volume. The first assumption was that industrialization was fundamental to modernization. Modernization meant the reduction of want and the increased opportunity for wider citizen participation. Industrialization and modernization would interplay to reduce stress in the political system and provide a more affluent and "open" society.

Such conceptions were ascendant in the post–World War II era, and governed much of the social science writing of the 1950s and 1960s. They exert influence today. In this volume, however, the author feels it more useful to seek another perspective. This emphasis centers on political tradition and the continuity of culture as factors strongly affecting the way the Mexican people conduct their politics.

The present Mexican political *style* is based on Hispanic and indigenous cultures, and yet present political *forms* are derived from Anglo and French sources. The remarkable long-term stability (for an Hispanic-American regime) of Mexico since the Revolution of 1910–1917 is based on a unique and distinctively Mexican marriage of these cultures and political experiences. This volume examines the reasons for this stability, but soberly notes the storm signals that have appeared on the political horizon in recent years.

The author does not make the assumption that stability is intrinsically valuable but adopts rather the view that stability can be instrumental in serving, whether for good or ill, the interests of Mexico. The Mexican leaders in the Revolution of 1910–1917 set ambitious goals and initiated far-reaching reforms. Governments of the present regime are still avowedly progressing toward these goals, and legitimacy is predicated on their realization. But the "final judgment" is not in as yet; vital questions are still being resolved. Will Mexico continue its "new" tradition of stability? Will the present elite continue to rule? Will the Revolutionary goals be actively striven for, or will they be dismissed as empty rhetoric? Will the problems arising from widespread political apathy and ignorance among most of the people be resolved? Finally, and perhaps most important, will the challenges posed by rapid social change and population growth be met?

A major difficulty in writing about the Mexican government is that so few who have experienced Mexican politics leave a written record of their political careers. Moreover, Mexican scholars and commentators still spend relatively little time writing about present-day political developments although their output in this area is greater than before. Because politicians tend to maintain an attitude of distrust toward all outsiders, the foreigner is even more hard-pressed to obtain an accurate picture of the system at work. Moreover, since most Mexicans must know the observer very well before silence is broken, it is frequently the case that the academic scholarly observer from abroad does not possess the resources necessary to surmount the cultural and interpersonal barriers so that information can be exchanged. For these reasons, much about Mexican politics remains either entirely unknown or very much in the realm of conjecture. Only with time do the underlying patterns emerge.

It is also difficult to write about Mexican politics because of the changing significance of language and meanings related to the ideology of the present regime. The author capitalizes the words *revolution* and *revolutionary* whenever they refer to the Revolution of 1910–1917 or whenever linear identification is sought with that Revolution. The word *president* is capitalized whenever it refers to the President of the country, but not when it refers to the president of a political party. More difficult to understand and relate are differences in meanings. The words *Revolutionary, continuity, continuism,* and others have special significance because of the connotations attached to them. The "flavor" of these and their impact in Mexican politics is difficult to relate, and yet the author feels justified in using them because of their importance in the political symbolism of Mexico.

That this volume exists is a tribute to many people whom the author has not forgotten. The author developed an interest in Mexico in large part through the efforts of Professors Howard F. Cline and George I. Blanksten. Indispensable encouragement in academic endeavors was provided by Charles S. Hyneman and Kenneth W. Thompson. It was through Kalman Silvert's efforts that the author undertook the first edition of *The Mexican Political System.*

When the author was first researching in Mexico, Lic. Hugo Cervantes del Rio, Lic. Manuel M. Moreno, Ing. Vicente Salgado Páez, Lic. Gilberto Loyo, Conrado Magaña, and Robert C. Jones all contributed to a better understanding of Mexican politics. More recently, members of a newer generation of Mexicans have substantially furthered the author's knowledge. A special debt of gratitude is owed to both Lic. Sergio Noriega Verdugo and Lic. Rafael Padilla Ibarra. The author feels especially fortunate to have had both their friendship and their advice.

In past years assistance from the Institute of Latin American Studies at Tulane University, the Doherty Foundation, the Social Science Research Council, and the Rockefeller Foundation provided aid at critical times. Without these resources it would have been impossible to maintain involvement in the study of Latin America and especially Mexican politics.

In substantially revising both material and perspective for this volume, two individuals were indispensable. In the initial stages the author was particularly fortunate in having a brilliant young colleague, Professor Brian Loveman, who gave generously of his own time, knowledge, and insight. The author considers that the lengthy discussions and work sessions with Dr. Loveman were some of the most profitable of a lifetime. In the latter stages of revision, it would be impossible to overemphasize the contribution in creative thought, editorial skill, and self-sacrifice that was made by my good friend and former student Robert G. Benson. Professor Susan Kaufman Purcell of UCLA generously offered assistance by providing a manuscript of her forthcoming book, *Public Policy and Private Profits*. Also, the author wishes to acknowledge the understanding and encouragement of Charles Andrain and Louis Terrell, chairpersons of the Department of Political Science, during this period. The clerical assistance of Karen Schnaubelt and Maureen Robison and the intellectual curiosity of two other students, John Tosello and Jaime Mohr, were exceedingly valuable.

Three professors reviewed this book in various stages of completion: Philip B. Taylor, Jr., of the University of Houston, Edward J. Williams of the University of Arizona, and Richard D. Baker of the University of Oklahoma. Professor Taylor provided indispensable criticism as well as suggestions at all stages of work and, whatever its defects, this is a better book because of his efforts. Both Professors Williams and Baker contributed constructively and generously in the earlier stages of the revision. The author is deeply indebted to these gentlemen. And, just as the author was grateful to Dayton McKean for his editing assistance in the first edition, so also he thanks the present staff of Houghton Mifflin Company who provided much assistance and encouragement for this volume.

Finally, and most importantly, this study simply could not have been undertaken and completed without the understanding and support of my family, my wife, Edna, and my daughters, Beth, Donna, and Nancy. To them I dedicate this book.

*San Diego State University*                                    L. VINCENT PADGETT

# GLOSSARY OF ABBREVIATIONS AND ACRONYMS

Definitions provided here are skeletal. Refer to the text for complete information.

| | |
|---|---|
| ABM | Association of Mexican Bankers |
| AMIS | Association of Mexican Insurance Institutions |
| AOCM | Workers' and Peasants' Alliance of Mexico |
| ARMO | National Vocational Training Service for Industry |
| BUO | Workers' Unity Bloc |
| CCI | Independent Peasants' Confederation. A group in competition with the CNC, which like the CNC is progovernment. |
| CCM | Mexican Peasants' Confederation |
| CEN | National Executive Committee (of the PRI). The most important decision-making body in the PRI. |
| CGT | General Labor Confederation. A confederation of workers that began with a strong leftist orientation, somewhat mitigated today. |
| CNC | National Peasants' Confederation. An official organization articulating peasant interests. |
| CNED | National Confederation of Democratic Students |
| CNIT | National Chamber of Manufacturing Industries. An organization of manufacturers within CONCAMIN. |
| CNOP | National Confederation of Popular Organizations. An organization representing a wide variety of groups within the PRI and the government. |
| CNP | National Proletarian Confederation |
| CNPP | Owners of Small Agricultural, Livestock, and Forestry Property |
| CNRU | National Committee for Participation of Workers in Profit-Sharing |
| CNTM | National Confederation of Mexican Workers |
| COCM | Confederation of Workers and Peasants of Mexico |
| CONASUPO | National Popular Subsistence Corporation. A government-owned corporation to guarantee lower prices of basic foodstuffs to lower-income citizens. |
| CONCAMIN | Confederation of Chambers of Industry of Mexico. The organization containing most industrial concerns. |
| CONCANACO | Confederation of National Chambers of Commerce. The organization containing most commercial concerns. |
| COPARMEX | Mexican Employers' Confederation. A business-oriented service organization. |

|  | Revolutionary Confederation of Workers and Peasants. The confederation which provided competition to the CTM in the 1950s. |
|  | Regional Mexican Workers' Confederation. The first great post-Revolution labor confederation. |
| CRP | Revolutionary Confederation of Workers |
| CTAL | Confederation of Latin American Workers |
| CTM | Confederation of Mexican Workers. The major labor confederation, headed by Fidel Velázquez. |
| CUT | Single Workers' Confederation |
| DAAC | Department of Agrarian Affairs and Settlement (Colonization) |
| F de PPM | Federation of Mexican Peoples' Parties |
| FEP | Popular Electoral Front |
| FOGA | Fund for the Guarantee of Housing Credits |
| FONACOT | National Fund for the Promotion and Guarantee of Workers' Consumption |
| FOVI | Banking and Discount Housing Fund |
| FOVISSSTE | Housing Fund of the ISSSTE |
| FROC | Revolutionary Confederation of Workers and Peasants |
| FSTSE | Federation of Unions of Employees in Service to the State. The powerful interest organization of national government employees. |
| FTDF | Federation of Workers of the Federal District |
| IMSS | Mexican Institute of Social Security. The primary agency for social security and related welfare programs. |
| INDECO | National Institute for Development of Rural Communities and Popular Housing |
| ISSSTE | Institute of Social Security and Services for Public Employees. The primary agency for social security and related programs for national government employees. |
| LCE | Sparta Communist League |
| LNC | National Peasant League |
| MLN | National Liberation Movement |
| PAN | Party of National Action. The major opposition party to the PRI. |
| PARM | Authentic Party of the Mexican Revolution. A political party related to the PRI composed mostly of older generations of revolutionaries. |
| PCM | Mexican Communist Party |
| PDM | Mexican Democratic Party |
| PNA | National Agrarian Party |
| PNM | Nationalistic Party of Mexico |
| PNR | National Revolutionary Party. Forerunner of the PRI. |
| PPS | Popular Socialist Party. Related to the PRI but leftist in orientation. |

| | |
|---|---|
| PRI | Institutional Revolutionary Party. The d since 1929. |
| PRM | Party of the Mexican Revolution. Forerun PRI. |
| PRUN | Revolutionary National Unification Party |
| SNTE | National Union of Workers in Education |
| STFRM | Union of Railroad Workers of the Mexican Republic. The government-sponsored union for the nationalized rail system. |
| STPRM | Union of Petroleum Workers of the Mexican Republic. The government-sponsored union for the nationalized petroleum industry. |
| UGOCM | General Union of Workers and Peasants of Mexico |
| UNAM | Autonomous National University of Mexico. The most prestigious nationally funded university, and the center of greatest student radicalism. |
| UNS | National Sinarquista Union |
| USEM | Social Union of Mexican Businesses |

# 1

# The Bases of Legitimacy

## Politics and Political Culture

The chairman had offered me a place beside his desk with the promise that I would learn more by observing what happened in that office than he could possibly tell me about politics in the state of Puebla. This was the headquarters of the state committee of Mexico's dominant political party, the *Partido Revolucionario Institucional* (PRI). It was an old two-story building close to the center of the city. On the first floor were offices for the state chapter (*liga*) of the National Peasants Confederation (CNC). There was also a medical center for the needy supported by the PRI committee and a room at the back of the courtyard where corn acquired at special prices through government cooperation was sold to the poor.

On this particular day the headquarters were much livelier than during my earlier visits, for this was the last day before the party municipal nominating assemblies were scheduled to meet throughout the state. The chairman of the state committee had been out of town making arrangements for these conventions and now was perpetually in demand. His outer office was crowded to capacity with long lines of peasants and workers waiting to see him. Party employees scurried in all directions through the throng, and self-important looking men in business suits pushed past the patient queues of people in work clothes in order to gain a word with the "chief." These were smaller-scale political bosses from the surrounding regions. In a single hour between eleven and twelve o'clock Ignacio Morales, the chairman of the committee, was confronted with groups from four *municipios*

## Figure 1

### Mexico and Its States

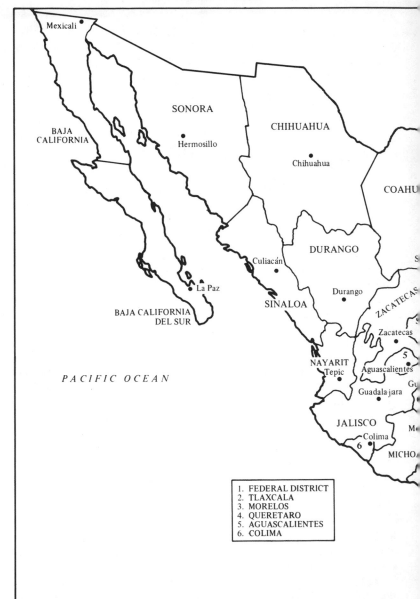

(basic units of local government which roughly correspond to counties in the United States) in each of which two or more lists for town council posts had been proposed by rival factions. Each faction had petitions in support of its lists, and the decisions were so close that it was necessary to hold informal assemblies in the room adjacent to the office. Some of Puebla's most important politicians were on hand to observe and help Morales in resolving the controversies. The head of the Mexican Workers Confederation (CTM), who was also a federal deputy, was there. Another important figure, a close friend of the governor, was a federal senator and a leader in one of the PRI-affiliated organizations, the National Confederation of Popular Organizations (CNOP). Several members of the state committee of the CNC were on hand.

The politicians listened carefully to points made by each side in

*Table 1*

**Presidents of Mexico Since 1900**

| | |
|---|---|
| December 1, 1884–May 25, 1911 | Porfirio Díaz |
| May 25, 1911–November 6, 1911 | Francisco León de la Barra |
| November 6, 1911–February 19, 1913 | Francisco I. Madero |
| February 19, 1913 | Pedro Lascuraín |
| February 19, 1913–July 14, 1914 | Victoriano Huerta |
| July 15, 1914–August 13, 1914 | Francisco Carvajal |
| August 20, 1914–May 21, 1920 | Venustiano Carranza |
| November 3, 1914–January 3, 1916 | (Conventionist Presidents) |
| | Eulalio Gutiérrez |
| | Roque González Garza |
| | Francisco Lago Chazaro |
| June 1, 1920–November 30, 1920 | Adolfo de la Huerta |
| December 1, 1920–November 30, 1924 | Álvaro Obregón |
| December 1, 1924–November 30, 1928 | Plutarco Elías Calles |
| December 1, 1928–February 5, 1930 | Emilio Portes Gil |
| February 5, 1930–September 2, 1932 | Pascual Ortiz Rubio |
| September 3, 1932–November 30, 1934 | Abelardo L. Rodríguez |
| December 1, 1934–November 30, 1940 | Lázaro Cárdenas |
| December 1, 1940–November 30, 1946 | Manuel Ávila Camacho |
| December 1, 1946–November 30, 1952 | Miguel Alemán Valdés |
| December 1, 1952–November 30, 1958 | Adolfo Ruiz Cortines |
| December 1, 1958–November 30, 1964 | Adolfo López Mateos |
| December 1, 1964–November 30, 1970 | Gustavo Díaz Ordaz |
| December 1, 1970– | Luis Echeverría Álvarez |

support of its case. After each group had listed the major points of its argument for the respective candidates, the leaders attempted to formulate a balance sheet from which they suggested possible compromise arrangements on the basis of the virtues, faults, and local political support of each candidate. When the moment for decision came, Morales and his associates did not try to hide their preference but at the same time made a genuine effort to secure a compromise satisfactory to all parties. Positions and candidates were juggled persistently in search of a formula. Once agreement had been negotiated, it was clear that all factions were expected to return to their homes and unanimously endorse the ticket when the election assembly met on the following day.

A particularly difficult case involved the *municipio* of San Martín from which a group had come to protest the preassembly understanding that had been reached with regard to town council offices. Included in the group from San Martín were elements from three affiliated sectors of the party — Popular, Agrarian, and Labor. The most effective spokesmen were from the middle class, or Popular Sector — a primary school teacher and the local doctor. Although these men carried the burden of the argument, there were also representatives from the two other sectors, presidents of local peasant (*ejido*) communities and officers of local unions, who took part from time to time.

The complainants formed a noisy and belligerent semicircle around the chairman. Morales stood facing them. He was taller than most Mexicans and very broad shouldered. When everyone had positioned himself in the office, Morales opened the discussion by asking the nature of the trouble. From somewhere came an angry voice. "We are completely dissatisfied with the situation at San Martín." Morales shrugged his shoulders. "All right, you aren't satisfied. I can't help that. This is no way to further your case." The group became quiet, and the school teacher, the doctor, several union officials and some of the *ejido* presidents spoke in turn for their people. They outlined a situation in which the municipal president was the prime offender. He had arranged a convention of the Popular Sector in which he had used outside help to win the endorsement of the assembly for his chosen successor. Neither the peasant leaders nor the union officials had been notified of the assembly. Despite these procedural irregularities the municipal president with his chosen group had proceeded to form the entire list of PRI candidates for municipal office. The list had then been presented to Morales who had given his approval since the minutes of the assembly had made it appear that all was in order.

The result was that both labor and agrarian sectors were incensed because of the manner in which their strength had been ignored, and the majority of the Popular Sector also felt cheated. Morales argued that on the basis of the convening order for municipal assemblies he could not receive complaints until after the official assembly had been held the next day. His general secretary spoke up. "Look here! There are many factors involved in this situation. If you don't like the man your municipal president has selected as his successor, remember at least that he is a well-known businessman and well prepared to talk with government officials about the financial problems of your *municipio*. Moreover, the present nominee has close ties of friendship with various people in the federal government. It is necessary at least to give such a man a place on the ticket." In reply, the spokesmen for the delegation from San Martín pointed out that they clearly had an "absolute" majority and invited the party officials to come to the *municipio* and see this for themselves. "Don't tell us the party has to wait until after the municipal convention to act on a complaint!" they said. "You can act now if you want to! If you don't we will not have nearly so good a chance." Those from San Martín then pointed out that if the party persisted in the arrangement it would be responsible for putting an undesirable man in the municipal presidency, a man disliked throughout the *municipio*. One spokesman said with conviction, "The *municipio* will be seething with discontent. Do you like that kind of picture? Do you want to be a party to such an arrangement?" Several of the San Martín leaders pointed to sections of the party statutes which supported their argument.

When the delegation showed no signs of leaving until satisfaction had been obtained, Morales capitulated. He gave the following instructions. "Doctor, professor, and other members of the Popular Sector, hold your convention at eight o'clock this evening. I shall be there or shall send a trusted representative. The agrarian and labor sectors will meet beforehand to select nominees for the municipal ticket and delegates to attend the popular sector convention."

After the San Martín episode the excitement became less intense, and the number of people waiting grew steadily smaller. Finally, at four o'clock Morales left the office and took me along with some of his associates to a nearby cafe. There it was decided that the candidate for the state legislature from San Martín should preside over the assemblies that evening. The outcome, as I later discovered, was a victory for the delegation that had visited Morales.

Mexico is a country of great contrasts and deep emotional involvements, with a political history characterized by shattering revolutions and much bloodshed. Paternalism and personalism have been much in evidence. Until recently these tendencies existed in a milieu of backward economic institutions and an underdeveloped social stratification arrangement, i.e., one in which discernible strata are few and the distance between them great. All these patterns are evident or implied in the political behavior observed at Puebla. Their roots are ancient.

Bloodshed and paternalism were evident at the beginning of colonial times with the arrival of the Spanish, although these characteristics were also part and parcel of the native principalities and aboriginal empires which the Spanish overcame. The period of colonial rule was marked by an effort to transfer European institutions and adapt them to Mexican conditions under the sponsorship of a Crown that claimed to be omnipotent in all matters. Royal representatives were at first conquerors who killed Indian warriors and later viceroys who symbolized the paternalism of the Crown. Everything was done through personal contact with the paternalistic representative of a paternalistic power.

Independence replaced the Crown and the viceroy with the successful military leader as the paternalistic symbol of personal rule. The paternalistic pattern of the Crown's agent and his intimate personal way of dealing with the problems of the people, a pattern of centuries, is reflected in the political style of Ignacio Morales, the party committee chairman in Puebla, in his role as representative of the viceregal presidential power in Mexico City.

A tradition of revolution accompanied by an intense sense of personal pride exists together with the tradition of paternalistic rule. The concept of rebellion was not unknown in colonial times, but with the advent of the spirit of independence revolution became endemic to Mexico. For this reason the politician's personalistic interpretation of the existing system of rule must be "just," or he will be confronted with dangerous dissatisfaction among those he would govern. Octavio Paz has summed up Mexican rebelliousness and intransigence in a brilliant passage:

> All our anxious tensions express themselves in a phrase we use when anger, joy or enthusiasm cause us to exalt our condition as Mexicans: *"¡Viva México, hijos de la chingada!"* This phrase is a true battle cry, charged with a peculiar electricity; it is a challenge and an affirmation, a shot fired against an imaginary enemy, and an explosion in the air. . . . When we shout this cry on the fifteenth of September, the anniversary of our independence, we affirm ourselves in front of, against and in spite of the "others." Who are the "others"? They are the

*hijos de la chingada:* strangers, bad Mexicans, our enemies, our rivals.[1]

Not only does the San Martín episode reflect personalistic and paternalistic tendencies and the capacity for rebellion, it also calls attention to other aspects of the Mexican scene. There is the question of social class. The people who came from San Martín were among the "articulate" in Mexican society. When they said they had the "absolute" majority, they meant that they had a majority of the articulate group on their side. This would automatically exclude the large number of people found in nearly any Mexican *municipio* who are part of the "culture of poverty," as described by Oscar Lewis. "A critical attitude toward some of the values and institutions of the dominant classes, hatred of the police, mistrust of government and those in high position . . . gives the culture of poverty a counter quality and a potential for being used in political movements aimed against the existing social order." [2] Although the potential for power exists among the poor, the limitations on its expression are formidable. The hatred, distrust, and sense of violence of the group are offset by the political submissiveness and apathy they express.[3]

The San Martín episode also raises questions relating to the undiluted desirability of economic and social change. From one point of view, modern means of transportation and communication are desirable because they facilitate the presentation of demands from more remote *municipios*. But modern communication and transportation systems may present another side. When the previously isolated rural poor are given access to governmental decision-makers, they place new demands on a political system that is already hard put to effectively meet existing commitments. The regime's commitment to public education and health services, as in the case of modern communication and transportation, also can produce unintended consequences. The improvement of educational and health services brings urban-educated professionals and paraprofessionals to the village community or urban slum. These professionals raise the aspirations of the poor and serve as advocates for them before the modern bureaucracy.

[1] Octavio Paz, *The Labyrinth of Solitude,* Lysander Kemp, trans. (New York, 1961), pp. 74–75.

[2] Oscar Lewis, *The Children of Sánchez* (New York, 1961), p. xxvii.

[3] See Robert E. Scott's modal typology for distinguishing population segments within the "culture of poverty." Robert E. Scott, "Mexico: The Established Revolution," Pye and Verba, eds., *Political Culture and Political Development* (Princeton, N.J., 1965). Roger Hansen also finds the typology useful and applies economic analyses to the groups. See especially his Chapters 4 and 7. Roger D. Hansen, *The Politics of Mexican Development* (Baltimore, 1971).

The potential for an increasing awareness of a gap between the regime's promises and performance and the new aspirations of rural workers and the urban poor provides fertile ground for would-be politicians to become spokesmen for the disaffected. Sometimes such spokesmen are co-opted successfully. But unless the overall capability of the system to deliver goods and services improves, co-optation or inclusion of new elites and their clients only stretches thinner the bonds holding together the political system. The speed of change thus becomes an important factor from the standpoint of both stability and instability.[4]

## History and Political Socialization

Certain aspects of Mexican history cluster together to provide the basis of an ideology for the Mexican political system and the "national order" of today. *Ideology* is used loosely in this chapter to refer to a set of norms, goals, and principles for which many Mexicans have developed strong emotional ties and which, in this case, have the official blessing of the governing group. It is in terms of these goals and norms that political experience becomes meaningful and the system worth struggling to maintain. Accordingly, the purpose of this chapter is not to provide the most objective statement of Mexican political history. Instead its aim is to present the key events and official interpretations that form the basis of the present myth of legitimacy. A knowledge of these events is necessary in order to understand both the maintenance of the existing political system and the occurrence and direction of change. The official interpretation of Mexican history is widely disseminated within the country through speeches and actions of community leaders and high officials at all sorts of public events and festivities from the opening of an electric plant in an obscure village to the elaborate celebration of Independence Day in Mexico City. Newspaper editorials, official and semi-official pronouncements, literary figures, and many other persons and groups vital to the communications function make constant reference to familiar heroes and events.

Particularly important is the interpretation of history as presented to most Mexican school children and young people. It is primarily during the formal schooling process that the basis of political socialization is established. Herbert Hyman has written about "political behavior as *learned* behavior." He points out that norms of participation

---

[4] Ivo K. Feierabend, Rosalind I. Feierabend, and Betty A. Nesvold, "Correlates of Political Stability." Paper presented before the American Political Science Association (September 1963).

and goals of action as well as the directions of those action goals that are learned by the populace are vital to the characteristics of politics in a system. It is in relation to this socialization that the official Mexican ideology of history is treated as a vital aspect conditioning political behavior in the system.[5] Particularly we are interested in an explicitly taught set of norms and goals based upon an historical interpretation that is part of nearly every primary and secondary school curriculum in the country and is integral to most interpretive commentary in the media of communication. The emphasis upon education is important in this connection, as has been stated by James S. Coleman:

> Increased awareness of this functional interdependence between education and polity has stimulated social scientists and educators to concern themselves with a more comprehensive array of variables. Such broadening is essential if we are fully to understand and interpret the particular facet of the multidimensional development complex which engages our specialized training. As holists, conscious of this interdependence and interested in the maintenance, integration, and transformation of total societies, political scientists are particularly affected by this new challenge. It is the holistic imperative that enjoins political scientists to search for what has been termed "a more complete and systematic conception of the political process as a whole." The same imperative directs our attention to the study of the role of education in the political process and in political change.[6]

Mexican history has generated a legacy that raises a number of problems for political socialization, including the question of what Mexican children should learn concerning the relationship between past events and the present system. The Mexican political culture is a fragmented one in which the violence of internecine struggle has appeared again and again in the absence of consensus on fundamentals as to the way government should operate — its relationship to citizens, their relationship to government, and the overall goals toward which policy should be directed, that is, the basic purposes of government. All these matters have been much disputed, leaving in various sectors of society residues of commitment to values regarding proper uses of governmental power and reasons for existence of government which are at variance with major characteristics of the present system. These residues of allegiance to values of other periods have raised more

[5] Herbert H. Hyman, *Political Socialization* (Glencoe, Ill., 1959), pp. 15–17.

[6] James S. Coleman, "Education and the Political Scientist," *ITEMS*, Social Science Research Council (March 1965), p. 5.

questions of social adjustment because the dominant groups in the present situation cannot fall back upon some distinct philosophical system, such as Marxism, which can be treated as revealed truth for justification of the present political arrangements. Fragmentation of political culture is related to many questions. A partial list of these explosive conflicts would include ethnic differences *versus* desire for a unified, national community, absolutism *versus* representative democracy, a political church *versus* an essentially apolitical one, and distribution of opportunity among a few *versus* its distribution among the many. Any single one of these issues represents a source of conflict; so many sources of ill will in combination made bloodshed inevitable.

In the case of ethnic differences involving Spanish and *criollo, mestizo,* Indian, and others, the problem is not only that of physical appearance but also of status differences ascribed in terms of birth which prevented integration of all groups in terms of a national identification common to all. Spanish refers to those who were native-born in Spain, while *criollo* refers to pure-blooded, Mexican-born Spanish descendants. The mixture of Indian and Spanish or *criollo* is termed *mestizo.* Indian refers to pure-blooded native Indians. Colonial law recognized many more racial categories than these.

Three centuries of Iberian absolutism and paternalism overlaying an earlier tradition of despotic Indian tribal rule provided little basis for placing in operation some form of representative democracy, a concept that has had much theoretical appeal for many Mexicans from the beginning of the nineteenth century. Efforts to establish representative institutions and a liberal approach to human freedoms have floundered repeatedly on the shoals of inexperience, a feudalistic class structure, and the determined commitment of the conservative coalition to its particular concept of order and the social status quo. Reaction to unsuccessful liberal political experiments have resulted in conservative dictatorships, which the liberal group could dislodge only by another resort to violence. Military leaders with their access to arms and men found political activity and internal strife a riper field of endeavor than routine preparation for the defense of national boundaries. A clergy with established privileges interpreted religion for its own ends, holding its position above civil law by exercising its vast influence in education, the economy, and spiritual concerns, and by steering politics toward maintenance of the colonial status quo with regard to clerical secular interests.

Distribution of wealth and opportunity among a few great landholders and leading merchants fitted so well with the determination of many military leaders and the clergy to maintain privileges above law in the colonial tradition. Privilege was thus the basis of the conservative coalition, which kept rising like a phoenix from the ashes of defeat all during the nineteenth century. This Mexican brand of conservatism was repeatedly able to overcome, or at least subvert, as in the years after the Reform, hard-won victories of those who sought wider distribution of opportunity through expansion of popular participation, wider access to learning, protection of individual rights, application of one body of law to all persons, suppression of monopoly privileges, more equitable division of wealth in land, and pride in nationhood and national sovereignty. These liberal goals and the leaders who struggled for them form the core of the current legitimizing myth.

However, in a real sense, this myth is not so much philosophy as it is fictionalized historical experience. It has been successfully appropriated by individuals and groups who have had a common concern with maintaining a unique relationship with it, by invoking the image of an ongoing family line. On this basis there is a metaphorical mantle of legitimacy to which only those of the appropriate ideological lineage can claim possession. It was in this context that President Calles formulated the phrase *Revolutionary family,* a phrase used by both Mexican and American writers.[7] The phrase recalls important differences between the Latin and North American conceptions of family. The emphasis upon extended family rather than nuclear family, upon lineage and familial continuity rather than procedural norms, upon patriarchal hierarchy rather than relatively equal roles — all are interlocking concepts in Latin cultures. The extended family, serving as the primary reference for its members and as the focus of primary loyalty, forms a politically functional value and norm set which Charles Andrain extensively analyzes as "primordial" political culture.[8] Also used in the metaphor are the concepts of fertility (both male and female) and bloodlines. Lineage is one of the strongest unifying elements in the Revolutionary tradition, even to the point where physical lineage becomes comingled with ideological lineage. Hansen notes that familial lineage has become a part of Revolutionary legitimacy.[9] The family myth is promulgated for consumption by the general population and not the Revolutionary elite. However, the ruling elite attempts to maintain its patriarchical character, as evidenced by the title of the Second State of the Union Address

[7] See Frank Brandenburg, *The Making of Modern Mexico* (Englewood Cliffs, N.J., 1964), p. 3.
[8] Charles Andrain, *Political Life and Social Change,* 2nd ed. (Menlo Park, Calif., 1974), p. 59.
[9] Hansen, p. 129.

(*Informe*) of Luis Echeverría: "The policy of government is unified with one ideology and one plan of action." [10]

## The Indian

Indianism is one important thread of the nationalist revolutionary tradition. Indianism is regarded as the antithesis of the Spanish heritage. The Indian is conceptualized as the basis of the truly national tradition and the Spaniard as the epitome of antinationalist, colonialist forces working against Mexican self-determination and the progress of Mexicans as a national group. For this reason the Indian leaders who sought to stave off the Spanish Conquest have been elevated to the status of national heroes. The glories of pre-Conquest cultures as well as Indian heroes of those times play a part, but the abuse of the Indians by the Spaniards and in later periods is not insignificant.

The cultural achievements of the Maya of Yucatán and of the Aztecs and other tribes of the Central Plateau are taught to school children from the first grade on. And just as school children in the United States learn the facts and legends about the fathers of their states and their nation, so Mexican children learn of the Aztec heroes who struggled against the Spanish. Heroes are legion: an outstanding one was Cuitlahuac, who organized the rebellion against the Spaniards under Cortés and drove them from Mexico City (Tenochtitlán). Another figure, all the more heroic because of the tragedy and futility of his struggle, was the nephew of the Emperor Moctezuma, Cuauhtémoc, who led the last desperate stand of the Aztecs against the Spaniards. Still another was General Tomas Mejía, a leader of conservative forces in the War of the Reform. But there are no statues of Mejía in Mexico today because he regarded Spanish tradition as benevolent and joined with antinationalist forces. His death on the Hill of Bells east of the town of Querétaro in company with the Hapsburg prince, Maximilian, pretender to the mythical Mexican throne, left Mejía far outside the accepted group of Mexican Indian heroes.

From the Indian cultural heritage are drawn (with or without justification) certain contemporary Mexican ideas concerning communal life and collectivism. The extent to which Mexican leaders of today lean toward the patriotic significance of the Indian and the Indian heritage of collectivism — as much or more than dedication to more recent collectivist ideals ——marks them as leftist or rightist within the framework of revolutionary experience.

[10] *Hispano Americano* (September 11, 1972), p. 20.

The heroism and tragedy of Indian groups and leaders who rose against the Spaniards or who stood against the efforts of *criollos* and *mestizos* to overrun their lands during the nineteenth century also receive attention from teachers and pupils. Perhaps more important, however, is the instructional emphasis placed upon the abuses suffered by the Indians in the colonial period and in the first century of independence, the lesson being that these abuses were suffered at the hands of exploiters, aliens to the national tradition. However, Indianism is only one of several important themes of the nationalist, revolutionary tradition that serves as the basis for legitimizing today's political system.

## The Generation of Independence: Hidalgo, Morelos, and Others

The revolutionary ideas of the latter eighteenth and nineteenth centuries led toward national self-consciousness and pride. The aspirations involved formed the basis for repeated revolutionary efforts against the hardy, exclusive colonial status quo, which continued to appeal to various segments of the Mexican population long after independence from Spain was an accomplished fact. Those who supported in one form or another the ideas which led logically to emphasis upon integration of all Mexicans in a coherent national group created the nationalist, revolutionary tradition and provided the stuff of Mexican patriotism as it operates today. The others represented the Mexican style of conservatism which lost out because, above all, its exclusiveness logically worked against integration of a variety of ethnic types and was essentially anti-nationalist.

The revolutionary struggle of the nineteenth century fluctuated both in its intensity and in its success. Historical phases may be distinguished in various ways — according to key personalities, constitutions, battles, or the composition of governments. Because the revolutionary tradition as an ideology relies so heavily upon the ideas and exploits of heroic figures, it may well be that the most fruitful approach is to trace the course of the revolutionary contest with the conservatives in terms of those who played the leading roles.

Our first protagonist is the father of Mexico's Independence Day celebration. Padre Hidalgo issued his cry of rebellion, the *Grito de Dolores,* in September 1810. Hidalgo, a parish priest, had plotted with others to organize a *criollo* rebellion against the Spanish, but the plot was discovered and instead of appealing to the *criollos* Hidalgo called his Indian and *mestizo* parishioners to arms to protect the Spanish throne against the Bonapartes and to prevent betrayal of their religion to the French. The most prominent notes sounded by Hidalgo had little to do with the Enlightenment philosophy he had been studying secretly, but they did arouse the feelings of the rural poor who had been the objects of domination by both wealthy Spaniards and *criollos*. The rebellion that had been planned as a *criollo* war for independence from Spanish colonialism became instead a class war of the lower strata against the upper, driving the *criollos* into alliance with the Spaniards. Great success greeted the first efforts of Hidalgo's motley band. Thousands joined his standard, and all resistance was swept away in the initial stages of the rebellion.

The conflict that followed was truly a civil war, since most of those fighting under the Spanish emblem were, in fact Mexicans, as were Hidalgo's troops. Dissension in Hidalgo's command, coupled with his own vacillation in the face of stiffening Spanish opposition at Mexico City and Guadalajara, brought about the defeat and decimation of his forces as well as the capture and execution of Hidalgo and his lieutenants.

Hidalgo's rebellion was carried on after his death by another parish priest who had once been a pupil of Hidalgo's, José Maria Morelos. While Hidalgo died in a Spanish prison repudiating his rebellious acts in an effort to escape from the onus of excommunication which the church had placed upon him, Morelos, also under the shadow of excommunication, carried on the war. With him were Matamoros, another village priest, and the *mestizo* peasant's son Vicente Guerrero, who, like Morelos, has a state of modern Mexico named for him.

Morelos' military leadership was more successful than Hidalgo's, and he was encouraged to set about organizing a government. His ideas for Mexican political organization, first expressed at Chilpancingo in 1813 and formalized as a constitution at Apatzingán in 1814, became an important source of revolutionary thought during the following century. The fundamentals included such revolutionary ideals as racial equality, abolition of clerical and military *fueros* (special privileges), abolition of compulsory tithing, and seizure of church lands. Morelos believed in partition of the great landholdings to provide small farms for peasants. Universal suffrage was endorsed, but was offset by a method of indirect elections. There was to be a plural executive.

Morelos represented a familiar Mexican paradox: a devout Catholic who espoused anticlerical measures, and a product of the Spanish tradition of government who sought to formulate a synthesis of that tradition with the Anglo-Saxon and French ideals of democracy. But Morelos was never to have an opportunity to see his ideas tried in practice, for the Spanish forces defeated him in Michoacán and elsewhere. He was eventually betrayed to the Spanish and executed.

Along with Hidalgo the stories of the exploits of Morelos adorn the texts of the early grades in Mexico's elementary schools. It is difficult for Mexicans to have attended school even for a short time and not know that Morelos and Hidalgo stood for equality, the poor, and the *patria*. Their names are immortal in the revolutionary tradition.

## Beginning of Independence: Villains and Heroes

It is a paradox of Mexican history that independence was brought about by conservatives reacting against the liberal Spanish rebellion of 1820. The key step involved an agreement between Agustín de Iturbide, a *criollo* officer in Spanish service, and the perennial rebel, Vicente Guerrero. Iturbide's Plan of Iguala provided the basis for independence and at the same time sounded keynotes for the conservative programs of the ensuing years. Central to Iturbide's program were Roman Catholic supremacy and the principle of monarchy with a dynasty other than that of Spain to govern a sovereign Mexico where Spaniards and *criollos* were equal. For a moment liberals and conservatives agreed. For the liberals there was independence; for the conservatives there was a monarch. There was also release from the control of the Spanish government which the conservatives perceived as dangerously liberal under the Constitution of 1820. Iturbide soon tried to make himself emperor and succeeded for almost a year until rebellion drove him from the country.

The leader in the rebellion against Iturbide was a young army officer, Antonio López de Santa Anna, known simply as Santa Anna. Iturbide and Santa Anna had in common a military background and a driving ambition. Also common to both is their connection with nineteenth-century conservatism and their place in the gallery of Mexico's villains, fools, and historical mishaps. Iturbide and Santa Anna are two of the "bad guys" of Mexican history. Only the dictator of a later period, Porfirio Díaz, is more universally condemned by the custodians of the Revolutionary tradition.

Santa Anna burst into the arena of Mexican politics as a republican and a liberal. Later, in a seemingly effortless about-face, he became the leader of the conservatives. With Santa Anna there came to power in the spring of 1823 the old revolutionary element composed of such people as Guerrero, Guadalupe Victoria, and Juan Álvarez, as well as a newer group dedicated to independence and liberal principles. The latter included Miguel Ramos Arizpe, Valentín Gómez Farías, and Manuel Crescencio Rejón. Also on the scene was a former soldier and comrade of Morelos, Nicolás Brava, and a new personage, who was later to be aligned with conservative causes, Lucas Alamán. From the deliberations of these men there emerged a method of selecting a president based upon votes of the Mexican states. In such voting under the provisions of the Constitution of 1824, General Guadalupe Victoria became the first President of Mexico.

The discussions and arguments involved in the framing of the Constitution of 1824 raised most of the substantive questions which were to affect the fortunes of liberal reform in Mexico over the next ninety years. Symbols such as rationality, equality, freedom, and progress were to be important. These words, however, had different meanings for different people. For some, the meanings added up to relative regional autonomy; for others, free ports and free enterprise. Some saw expanded educational opportunities as the core of liberal reform. Others felt reform meant principally a clear separation of church and state. The developing revolutionary tradition could not accept the idea of monarchy, nor tolerate the notion of any operation similar to the Spanish Inquisition. Free speech became a major goal. Freemasonry provided a basis for liberal thought and organization. There was emphasis upon rational approaches to natural sciences and to the study of social phenomena.[11]

In the years that followed 1824, the conservative position emerged as one which was proclerical in the sense of wishing to help the clergy maintain its dominant position in the society both economically and politically, promilitary in the sense of supporting the privileges and special courts of military officers, and procentralization in the sense of supporting the continued control of the core area of Mexico over the peripheral regions. Conservatives were against Freemasonry, which they regarded as anticlerical, and felt that Freemasonry was connected with other revolutionary, conspiratorial, and undesirable ideas such as political democracy and egalitarianism.

A generation committed to reform dominated the period from 1824 to 1834, but it was an uneasy supremacy, with Santa Anna and the conservatives causing more than one government to fall. The leading liberal of the period was Valentín Gómez Farías. Through the efforts of Gómez Farías and his colleagues, the thought of the revolutionary

[11] The reformers saw the Indian as a symbol of freedom. Their model, however, was the idealized Indian of pre-Conquest times. They were ambivalent; there was the glorious Indian, and then there was the Indian who seemed somehow to stand in the path of progress. Liberals did not look to the Indian for their philosophy, but rather to Europe and to the United States.

liberal tradition became more clearly defined. Basically it was nine-teenth-century economic and political liberalism molded to the Mexi-can context. Legal reform, civil controls over the army and the church, as well as progress in education were stressed. More attention was given the concept of nationality. It was pointed out that no truly united nation could have specially distinguishable and privileged bodies above law or with special legal privileges such as existed under Spanish colonialism.

The clergy, the military, and the aristocracy in general could not tolerate the revolutionary demands for change in Mexico. Issues ran all the way from the general question of the clergy's and the church's relation to the government to rather narrow ones having to do with plans for improvement of transportation and development of new ports. In the end the reaction to the program for change overwhelmed the Gómez Farías government. Santa Anna came back to assume the presidency and Gómez Farías fled into exile. On assuming power, Santa Anna completed his change from liberal to conservative. The clergy, the military, and the great merchants and landholders became domi-nant and were able to control the central governing machinery in Mexico City. Liberals fought back from the outer provinces, but Santa Anna succeeded in building an alliance of the interests of Mexico City, Puebla, and Veracruz which was strong enough to resist liberal efforts from the periphery. There was an effort on the part of liberals in Yucatán to wed their cause to the Yucatecan caste war which broke out in 1839. There was unrest in Jalisco and elsewhere. This was also the time of Mexico's great territorial losses to the United States in the Mexican War of 1846–1848. Santa Anna and the conservatives domi-nated the destinies of Mexico for about twenty years after 1834, but were never able to wipe out the ferment of liberalism and the revolu-tionary tradition.

Liberal ideas drew wider attention as various interests reacted nega-tively to special privileges given to concessionaires. Those adversely affected by monopoly privileges granted by conservative governments embraced the liberal program of free competition and individual enterprise with the hope of more equal opportunity. Men attempting to begin manufacturing enterprises particularly resented the monopoly privileges of the import-export interests of Veracruz and Mexico City. A new generation came forward to press for change in accord with the basic ideals of liberalism. For the rising generation of liberals the overriding issue was change and progress. Nationalism, liberty for the individual, popular representation, and the destruction of the old privileged military and clerical cliques were considered by the new revolutionary generation to be the necessary instruments of progress toward a genuinely prosperous nation-state.

## The Reform: Juárez, Lerdo, and Others

Santa Anna was driven from power by the old *mestizo* warrior, Juan Álvarez, who had fought the Spanish and the conservative coalition since the time of Morelos. The names of the men whom Álvarez brought to power in the mid-1850s have become familiar to all Mexican school children. This generation of outstanding leaders included Benito Juárez, an Oaxaca Indian who had been trained in the law, Melchor Ocampo, and the Lerdo de Tejada brothers. There was also the tragic Ignacio Comonfort who had demonstrated his military talents in support of Álvarez and then, as President, lacked the will necessary to make the Reform a reality in the face of bitter conservative opposition. Comonfort was replaced by the indomitable Juárez, who led the supporters of the Reform to victory first against the conservatives and then against intervention by the French.

Aims of the Reform reached a high point with the laws of Juárez and Lerdo. The Juárez law of 1855 reflected liberal revolutionary concern for unification of the nation under one law by abolishing ecclesiastical and military courts. The Lerdo law of 1856 attacked the material holdings of the church in such a way as to force large amounts of land controlled by the clergy onto the open markets for purchase and use. The Juárez and Lerdo laws were incorporated into the Mexican Constitution of 1857. When that happened, conservative resistance widened into full-scale civil war. This was the War of the Reform or the Three Year War, 1857–1860.

In 1859, as the struggle became ever more difficult, Juárez moved once more against the clergy by decreeing that all their real property belonged to the nation, abolishing tithing, and dissolving monastic orders. Further decrees established civil marriage and freedom of religion. Juárez' clear policy was that church and state were to be separated.

No sooner had the Reform triumphed in January 1861 than intervention threatened from the outside. Mexico's delinquency in paying foreign debts was the immediate cause. First came Spanish troops, shortly followed by English and French forces. Although the English and Spanish withdrew their soldiers when Juárez promised renewed efforts to make payments on Mexican debts, the French increased their strength and began to move inland from Veracruz. The French purpose was the establishment of a Mexican kingdom with Prince Maximilian of Hapsburg on the throne. Thus the bitter domestic hatred already engendered by the long struggle between generations of conservatives and liberal revolutionaries was compounded by the alignment of the conservatives with the French forces and the establishment of Maximilian as Emperor of the Mexicans. In the face of international developments from 1865 on, Napoleon III of France withdrew his forces, and with them went the conservative cause. By 1867 the liberals were strong enough to surround Maximilian's forces at Querétaro. Maximilian was forced to surrender and died before a firing squad with his Mexican generals, Miguel Miramón and Tomas Mejía.

Thus ended Mexico's second monarchist experiment, a more serious and bloody one than that of Iturbide's. But unlike the situation when Iturbide fell, there was by this time a sense of nationhood. Moreover, the liberal principles and the leaders who had fought for them over the years after September 16, 1810 had emerged as a national revolutionary heritage capable of embracing all Mexican ethnic groups, one that all Mexicans could perceive as the basis for a new, inclusive patriotism. It is this tradition and these heroes and heroic events that form the basis for the national myth evident not only in textbooks, but in official speeches, in newspaper editorials, and generally in all channels of communication in present-day Mexico. In taking his stand Juárez was able to achieve a clearer synthesis of liberalism and national identity and thus become a "father of the nation" in the Mexican pantheon.

### The Reaction: Neo-Conservatism and Porfirio Díaz

In 1971 Juárez announced that he would again run for President, and was elected. Criticism of this fourth term was quite bitter in some sectors. The liberals split into three groups, Juaristas, Porfiristas, and Lerdistas. Porfirio Díaz, military hero of the wars against the conservatives and the French, attempted to bring off a coup directed at the government in the city of Mexico, but was defeated. Then, just as Juárez had demonstrated his mastery, he died in July 1872. After Lerdo governed five years, Porfirio Díaz rebelled again, and this time succeeded in taking office in the name of "effective suffrage and no re-election."

In order to understand the development of the revolutionary nationalist tradition in the twentieth century it is necessary to touch on selected characteristics of the regime of Porfirio Díaz (known as the *Porfiriato*), which began in 1876 and lasted until 1910. The *Porfiriato* gradually developed into the neoconservative reaction to the Reform of 1857.

The philosophical basis of the Díaz regime became the positivist philosophy of Auguste Comte. Juárez chose a French-trained Mexican, Gabino Barreda, to head the national preparatory school, a school created to give a new focus to Mexican education. The positivist orientation was originally intended by Juárez and his colleagues to weaken ecclesiastical influence through emphasis upon science and scientific method as distinct from theology, metaphysics, and philosophy. Positivism itself, however, became a very important philosophical influence. It stressed rational processes to bring about order, progress, and stability so that there could be evolution, change, and economic advance.

At first positivism seemed clearly in conflict with the old conservatism, since positivists attacked reliance upon tradition as a basis for making judgments. In the end, however, the new philosophy became an instrument of the conservative reaction in Mexico. In fact, the new education became the property of a select few, much as had been the case with education throughout the entire history of Mexico. Positivism had an inherently elitist character, and its emphasis upon order and progress, particularly in the material realm, substantially altered the outlook of the Reform. Principles of freedom and progress toward democratic institutions were de-emphasized, while attention was increasingly focused upon the principle of order and the goal of material prosperity. Gradually the Reform was pushed aside to make way for a new idea, that of internal peace and prosperity at any price.

Concern was lost for individual freedom and the principle of equality before the law. Also lost was the ideal of building a large rural middle class of small proprietors. The whiter Mexicans, the *criollos,* tended to place greater social distance between themselves and the *mestizos.* *Mestizos* once again began to be faced with the problem of upward social mobility, the same problem that had aroused them in times past. A new generation of officeholders, indoctrinated in positivism, created their own strange synthesis to justify the Porfirian regime. The value of material progress was harmonized with the old conservative ideals of clerical privilege, distribution of opportunity among the few, and political dictatorship. Progress in an egalitarian sense tended to be written off.

Industrialization and scientific progress became norms to which many people closely connected with government were deeply devoted. The idea that much could be done for Mexico if only foreign capital could be imported was interpreted in practice to provide legislation leading to a great railway boom and to the acquisition of rich oil lands by foreigners at incredibly low prices. The government took the position that foreign capital was enough in itself, that no control or planning needed to be imposed by the government. In the case of railroads the result was a series of large and small railway lines without any system or key terminals except in Mexico City. Most of the roads were built for short-term gain, sometimes for no other reason than to serve large plantations. There was very little in the way of railroad service east and west in Mexico. The fact that most of the traffic moved north and south considerably limited the benefits the nation might have enjoyed from railway expansion.[12] Mexico under the dictatorship of Porfirio Díaz was a rewarding place only for those few who were able to command great economic resources or who had political favor, or both.

Politically, Porfirianism operated on the principle that politics should be minimized to achieve orderly economic prosperity. The tools of political stagnation were assassination, imprisonment, and bribery. There was always scrupulous attention to the form of elections, although it became clear before long that there was very little point in participating, since the decisions were made in other ways. As prosperity returned and order was established, Díaz found that the clergy was not the same enemy that as a military leader he had once believed it to be in the generation of the Reform. Anticlerical moves by the government diminished. The clergy was encouraged to expand its activities once again.

One of the keys to the success of the *Porfiriato* was the elite core of rural police known as the *rurales*. The backbone of this rural police was composed of ex-bandit chieftains who had been reconstituted as a group to hunt down anyone who threatened the rights of property in the countryside.[13] Another key to success was the practice of playing off state governors against each other. Of particular importance in maintaining the regime (from the standpoint of today's perspective) was the tendency to forget Mexican nationalism in an effort to bring in foreign capital and to import foreign culture. As a result of all these efforts, the people who were supposed to be the custodians of the nationalist revolutionary tradition became eminently conservative in the worst sense.

Four major tendencies of the *Porfiriato* are worth noting. One, poverty of the rural masses increased. Two, there emerged the beginnings

---

[12] Harry Bernstein, *Modern and Contemporary Latin America* (New York, 1952), pp. 98–99.

[13] The *rurales* seldom took prisoners, as they employed the *ley fuga,* which was simply the right to shoot anyone in the back who happened to be running from them. The success of the *rurales* made it less necessary to maintain a military establishment. The army under Díaz declined both in numbers and in effectiveness. This condition was regarded by many as a sign of progress.

of an urban proletariat that was forced to live at a subsistence level. Three, great landholding companies were formed and frequently kept the land out of production in order to be able to speculate on land values at a later date. There was, finally, the growth of the economy and of political self-consciousness in the north from which eventually came much of the impetus for the rebellion against Díaz.

As the number of those who benefited from the Díaz regime became smaller, and as wealth was concentrated in ever fewer hands, dissension became evident. The protest was both intellectual and political. In the intellectual arena disagreement was reflected most clearly in the writing of Justo Sierra, who advocated returning to the political aims that had stimulated the generation of the Reform. Moreover, an increasingly negative reaction to positivism and the regime it justified was manifest in the occasional writings that emphasized the worth of the Indian instead of the positivist position that the Indian was simply a force of inertia and a barrier to progress.[14] There was also the writing of the Flores Magón brothers and others, embracing anarcho-syndicalism and demanding betterment in the lot of the industrial worker.[15] In addition, there began to appear more groups or clubs dedicated to discussion of democracy and representative government. Disenchantment was also manifest in the speaking and writing of one of the sons of the wealthy Madero family, Francisco I. Madero. As these evidences of discontent began to emerge, there were, at the same time, marks of senility in the Díaz government. The old dictator himself was more and more out of touch, and he distrusted some of his most important colleagues and aides. It was nearly impossible to get an appointment with Díaz. A split developed in Díaz' official family, since there were still some military men of importance such as Bernardo Reyes, governor of Nuevo León, who were disliked and distrusted by the *criollo-científico* elite. Perhaps more than any single factor in the growing discontent was the constant dominance by the tiny number of *criollo-científicos* and the seeming perpetual occupation of the places at the top, leaving room for no one else — what Howard Cline calls "the full car."[16]

---

[14] Bernstein, p. 102.

[15] For contrasting views on the philosophical approach of the Flores Magón brothers see: Howard F. Cline, *The United States and Mexico* (Cambridge, Mass., 1953), p. 117, and Daniel James, *Mexico and the Americans* (New York, 1963), p. 125.

[16] Howard F. Cline, *Mexico, Revolution to Evolution, 1940–1960* (London, 1962), p. 22. "The Díaz regime was not only a government of the privileged but also of elderly men who could not resign themselves to giving up power." For a similar statement see Octavio Paz, *The Labyrinth of Solitude* (New York, 1961), p. 137.

**Madero and "No Re-election"**

The first major statement of determination to end the *Porfiriato* and re-establish the tradition of liberalism and the revolutionary struggle for Mexican nationalism and progress for all Mexicans came from Francisco I. Madero. His emphasis was primarily political; he wanted wider participation and more democratic processes in politics in an effort to end the *continuismo* of the Díaz regime. *Continuismo* is that phenomenon in which one person determines to maintain himself in power by any means on the grounds that he is essential to the welfare of the state. In 1908 Madero wrote a book, *The Presidential Succession of 1910*, for some of the newly formed clubs interested in democracy. The book was squarely in the political tradition leading up to the Reform.[17] Madero's slogan was "effective suffrage and no re-election," and differed only slightly in its emphasis from many aspects of the Plan of Tuxtepec once announced by Porfirio Díaz in the days when he was still a reformer-liberal and not a dictator. The ideals of political liberalism, which had survived so many reverses, were reflected in the wide popular response to Madero's appeal. There was also a quality of mysticism in his writing, which helped to give authenticity to his plea for moral and political reform. It is one of the paradoxes of Mexican history that this man, so small of stature, with his high-pitched voice and his essentially moderate views — so unlike the usual political agitator or the stereotype of the Latin American *caudillo* — became the symbol of the anti-Díaz movement and the spark that touched off the first great social revolution of this century.

A number of key events fanned flames of discontent with the *Porfiriato*. A bad harvest in 1909 took the rural population in some parts of the country to the brink of starvation. An interview given by Díaz to the American journalist James Creelman turned out to be a disaster because it raised hopes for a free election in 1910. Efforts of Bernardo Reyes, wealthy politician of Nuevo León, to mobilize personal support, and the publication of Molina Enríquez' book, which presented a devastating critique of Díaz' agrarian policy, all worked to undermine Díaz. Reyes stepped out of the picture in 1909, and more anti-Díaz factions flocked to support Madero. These factions selected Madero to run for President against Díaz with a *reyista* as vice-presidential candidate. Madero was imprisoned but was later released

---

[17] In 1909 another important book appeared, Andres Molina Enríquez' *Los grandes problemas nacionales*. Molina Enríquez tied together the liberal-nationalist tradition and the contribution of the heroes of the revolutionary struggle much better than did Madero. See James, pp. 136–143.

through the influence of his family and crossed the border into Texas. There he issued his celebrated Plan of San Luis Potosí. Sporadic uprisings followed Madero's *pronunciamiento,* but they were put down easily, as was Madero's own first effort. The rebels then began to have success in Chihuahua under Pancho Villa. Rebel efforts under Emiliano Zapata in the south were also successful. The aged, feeble character of the governing group and the Díaz' policy of weakening the army were good fortune for the rebels. Díaz was forced to resign in May 1911.

No sooner had Madero gained control with massive popular support than the factions that had for the moment united behind him began to quarrel. With the revolutionary forces divided, the leaders of the reaction were able to carry off a counterrevolutionary coup which resulted in Madero's imprisonment and eventual assassination. At the head of the counterrevolution was General Victoriano Huerta. He had himself made President, but was beaten by the revolutionaries hammering at him from north, west, and south. He resigned July 15, 1914.[18]

And what of the man who died so ignominiously? This man, Francisco I. Madero, was a great symbol, and his political failure could not obscure the fact. He epitomized opposition to the continued tyranny of the neoconservative regime. As a symbol he did not need an extensive program to become immortal. All he needed was a principle that seemed to fit the times. This he had — "no re-election." The reign of the dictator must end. It is for this conviction and this insight that he is known as the "Apostle of the Revolution." He opened the way for the tides of social change, and for so doing he enjoys an undisputed place among the heroes of Mexico's revolutionary tradition. "A new generation had risen, a restless generation that desired a change. The quarrel of the generations became a part of the general

---

[18] The Constitutionalist Army swept the federal troops of Huerta from the north while Zapata closed in on Mexico City from the south. By the end of 1914 victories by the Constitutionalists had opened the way to Mexico City, but there had arisen a split between Villa and Carranza which prolonged the Revolution. The situation was further complicated when the United States Marines, on orders from President Woodrow Wilson, landed in Veracruz to help in the overthrow of Huerta. Nationalist sentiment, already heightened by events, reacted violently to this intervention by the United States. Even the Constitutionalists, who stood to benefit by the Marines' presence, took the position that the United States was violating Mexican sovereignty. The Marine occupation of Veracruz took place at the expense of many Mexican lives; it lasted about seven months and made it very difficult for the United States and anti-Huerta forces to reach any satisfactory relationship after Huerta was defeated.

social discord . . . the Revolution, without any doctrines (whether imported or its own) to guide it, was an explosion of reality and a groping search for the universal doctrine that would justify it and give it a place in the history of America and the world." [19]

## Carranza, Villa, and Zapata

Another hero was added to the revolutionary tradition when Venustiano Carranza of the northern state of Coahuila, once a senator under Porfirio Díaz, pronounced the Plan of Guadalupe, challenging Huerta's legitimacy in March 1913. Carranza was a large landholder in Coahuila and had gathered a private army about him even before Huerta completed the coup against Madero. When the news of the Huerta coup reached him, it did not take long for Carranza to assume the role of Madero's avenger under the title of First Chief of the Constitutionalist Army and thus become a part of the revolutionary nationalist tradition.

Two facts assure Carranza a place in the revolutionary tradition. He was, in the first place, an avenger of Madero and a powerful enemy of the counterrevolution. Secondly, he was an adamant nationalist in dealing with the United States and other foreign powers even when his victory in the revolutionary effort seemed very much in doubt. Thus, he symbolized Mexican nationalism when he entered a formal objection to the landing of United States Marines in Veracruz in April 1914, even though the landing benefited *carrancista* forces. Among other nationalist stands were his refusal to allow Argentina, Brazil, and Chile to mediate differences between Mexico and other foreign powers and his determined protests against the Pershing expedition into Mexico in pursuit of Villa after Villa attacked a small town in New Mexico in 1916.

Carranza and Villa, allies at first, finally quarreled. Zapata, whose personality and general view of the revolution as a social movement came closer to Villa's than Carranza's, joined Villa in operations against the First Chief. It was not until the battle of Celaya in the state of Guanajuato in April 1915 that Carranza's forces were clearly in the ascendant. This defeat of Villa by Carranza's great general, Obregón, was clearly the turning point. Other *carrancista* victories followed until Villa's operations were confined to his home state of Chihuahua and Zapata to his stronghold in the southern state of Morelos. By October 1915 Carranza and his lieutenants were so clearly in command that it was possible to gain recognition from the United States while at the

[19] Paz, pp. 137–140.

same time rejecting all efforts of the Wilson governments to play a part in arranging a new constitutional regime for Mexico.

Carranza's revolutionary bent reached no farther than a few vague notions relating to political liberalism and an uncompromising nationalism. His personality, however, did not overshadow those about him as was the case with Villa and Zapata. Consequently, the intellectuals and persons with statesmanlike qualities who for one reason or another attached themselves to Carranza could make their influence felt on his revolutionary activity. Thus, Carranza's narrow conception of the Revolution did not limit him to policy pronouncements of the same narrow scope. At the urging of Luis Cabrera, Carranza promulgated an agrarian reform decree similar to Zapata's proposals, and yet better thought out. As the same time, on the urging of his best general, Álvaro Obregón, who was also a gifted politician, the fundamental demands of organized labor were granted. As a result, battalions of workers joined the *carrancista* armies and labor leaders set up headquarters behind *carrancista* lines.

Thus, Carranza, the "limited" revolutionary, became for a time a symbol of leadership to those groups for whom the revolutionary struggle was basically an effort for social change. In a great paradox of history, Carranza, the *hacendado* and former senator under Díaz, became a full-fledged member of the nationalist revolutionary tradition, avenging Madero and supporting the principles of the Reform, defending Mexican nationalism, and sponsoring however unwillingly, the goals of social reform.

Both at the time of the framing of the Constitution of 1917 and later, Carranza attempted to renege upon his social revolutionary commitments. He was opposed in this by most of the able men who had gathered about him during the revolutionary fighting. As President he grew continuously more isolated from those whose leadership had made possible the *carrancista* triumph over Villa and Zapata. When he attempted to name Ignacio Bonillas as his successor, Obregón, Plutarco E. Calles, Luis N. Morones, and Adolfo de la Huerta rebelled and brought him down.

Another leader who fought against Victoriana Huerta was Pancho Villa. He was already a hero of the Madero phase of the Revolution, and his movement represented a popular explosion in the north of Mexico. Villa was a northerner who was a legend as an outlaw before he turned revolutionary. He was an instinctive leader and tactician uninhibited by moral scruples. He was a child of the exploited class, and he found it natural to adopt a style which captured the imagination of the masses of the north. He was a man with whom the small *rancheros,* the range riders, the peons, and the town loafers of the north could identify. He was the man who had laughed at Díaz' police before it came time to defeat Díaz' soldiers.

Villa has a leading place in revolutionary mythology and in the nationalist tradition but not because of his role as a reformer. Intellectuals with him tried to make of him an heroic fighter for social justice, but it was Villa's genius to make Mexicans feel, not think. He was the epitome of the most crude aspects of the cult of virility, *machismo*. He helped pull down a dictator, and he raided into the United States. He inspired songs and legends. He was a warrior, not a statesman, but as a warrior figure he contributes essential zest and color to the nationalist revolutionary tradition.

Emiliano Zapata fought against Díaz, then took up arms against Madero in the south as the revolutionary alliance began to break up shortly after Madero took office. When the counterrevolution displaced Madero, Zapata grew stronger until he dominated south-central Mexico.

Zapata's *pronunciamiento* against Madero was the Plan of Ayala. Its demand for "land and liberty" became one of the great pillars of the revolutionary tradition. Almost all the programs advanced by revolutionary leaders referred to the agrarian problem sooner or later, but only Zapata, leading the Revolution of the South, gave top priority to reform in this area of affairs. The program of Zapata was simpler than most. The whole message was summed up in the demands for redistribution of land to Indian villages and expropriation of the great landholdings. Though simple, the message meant a great deal, for it spelled the end of feudal Mexico and opened the door for modernization.

Zapata and the intellectuals around him, who attempted to make explicit his intuitive approach to the Revolution, were essentially traditionalists. They believed their role was to return Mexico to its origins, to the pre-Conquest communal farming units. There was no place for futuristic dreams in their plans.

The *zapatista* explosion of the south, like Villa's in the north, never succeeded in making its intuitive truths into an organic plan, despite the efforts of attendant intellectuals. The *zapatistas* were a wind of violence across the land. They did not bring organization in the wake of the chaos they created, but they did raise up an idea too powerful to be denied because it stemmed from the most fundamental realities of the Mexican situation.

## Álvaro Obregón

Nearly devoid of popular support, Carranza still insisted on naming his successor. He passed over Álvaro Obregón for a man with little standing, Ignacio Bonillas. This was the last straw for those leaders of the north who had engineered Carranza's victory. Armies were recruited, and the move on the capital began in April 1920. Carranza gave up and fled. Supposedly friendly officers betrayed him, and he was assassinated, whether on orders from the top leaders is not clear. The leaders from Sonora entered Mexico City in May. Adolfo de la Huerta was named provisional president by the *carrancista* Congress, and the stage was set for Obregón's ascent to the presidency later in the year.

Obregón was a man with great popular appeal, and a systematic, pragmatic turn of mind. He believed in the social ideals of the Revolution, but he recognized the barriers to their rapid achievement. He displayed an unusual capacity to win popular applause while moving forward slowly and methodically toward limited goals. Obregón was the kind of man Mexico needed at the time. He proved to be a clever and ruthless politician who was able to play off one group of revolutionaries against another, and he knew how to crush his enemies if the occasion demanded. At the same time his policy was a careful mixture of nationalism with the revolutionary social change for which he had fought so many years. His task was to consolidate and pacify the nation without abandoning the Revolution.

The focal points of Obregón's presidency involved four areas of revolutionary ideals: expansion of educational opportunities, concrete recognition of agrarian reform, support of labor, and maintenance of a strong nationalist position in international affairs, especially toward the United States and foreign capital.

For the task of pushing education, particularly the problem of bringing literacy to the rural areas, Obregón chose José Vasconcelos, whose political views were a strange composite of nineteenth-century conservatism and the *maderista* emphasis upon the essentially political and legal aspects of liberalism. But there was no doubt about Vasconcelos' commitment to the goal of education for the masses. His measures laid a firm foundation for the expansion of rural schools under succeeding administrations.

Agrarian reform first gained momentum under Obregón. However, his course was carefully plotted to avoid the twin dangers of serious disturbance of agricultural production through excessive distribution of land to peasants as well as the wrath of United States landowners in Mexico which might worsen already difficult diplomatic problems.[20]

---

[20] The basis of Agrarian Reform was *ejido* land grants to peasants. An *ejido* is land set aside by the government as a trust for the use of a group of individuals in some kind of agricultural, pastoral, or related activity. Those with primary rights of usufruct under the government grant are called *ejiditarios*. The original grant could be broken into smaller parcels for individual family use, or worked collectively, or a combination of the

At the same time, land was judiciously distributed in those rural areas of greatest discontent.[21] A good deal of the distributed land went to make peace with militant followers of the deceased Zapata in the state of Morelos. Obregón was active enough on agrarian reform to win some support from agrarian leaders. This kept him less dependent upon militant organized labor groups and military chieftains than would otherwise have been the case. Obregón's determination to support labor was clear enough. Out of the young labor movement there emerged one organization which wielded great power through government support. This was the *Confederación Regional de Obreros Mexicanos* (CROM) which was organized before the end of Carranza's presidency. The size of the organization grew rapidly with Obregón's aid. CROM unions were the only ones that could strike with government support. The CROM was organized along the lines of the AFL in the United States, and it was both nationalist and anti-communist in orientation. Labor became a serious force in Mexican politics in these years, and even though the CROM declined at a later date, organized labor continued to be a vital part of the political system and an important factor in the economy. Through the CROM Obregón provided the urban wage-earning groups with an important place on the Mexican political scene.

A major problem area for Obregón involved foreign capital and United States diplomacy as these might affect his position in the nationalist tradition and his hopes of creating a stronger and more stable

---

two. Secondary categories such as *colono* were legally established, but in no case could the land be held as private, "sellable" land in the Anglo sense. Should the occupants depart, the land would revert to the government. *Minifundia* is a category of tiny, privately held (and usually secondrate) crop land. *Latifundia* is a category of extensive (and often immense) private property. Currently, small *ejido* parcels and *minifundia* are often referred to as *minifundia,* and their occupants as *minifundistas.*

Under the Agrarian Code the category of *pequeña propiedad agrícola* (literally "small private property") has been of increasing importance beginning with President Alemán. "Alemán . . . augmented the size of small properties in precisely the most remunerative crops. Dedicated agrarian reformers pointed out that legalizing 741 acres of choice land as a 'small farm' . . . ended the agrarian reform." Brandenburg, p. 106. The Alemán amendment to Article 27 permitted 247 acres of choice land and greater portions of less desirable land to be classified as "small private property." Brandenburg's reference to 741 refers to additional special allowances made for growing certain exportable plantation-type crops (bananas, henequen, etc.).

[21] See Eyler N. Simpson and Frank Tannenbaum for comparative views on Obregón's agricultural policy. Eyler N. Simpson, *The Ejido* (Chapel Hill, N.C., 1937), p. 87. Frank Tannenbaum, *Mexico, The Struggle for Peace and Bread* (New York, 1951), p. 147.

Mexico. The United States government at this time proposed recognition of Obregón on the basis of an agreement designed to make provisions of Article 27 of the Mexican Constitution of 1917 non-retroactive. The article states in part that "ownership of the lands and waters included within the boundaries of the national territory belongs originally to the nation." The nation at all times has the right "to impose on private property the measures that the public interest dictates." Most important under this article, the nation has ownership of all subsoil wealth. The proposal was refused, since Obregón feared such an arrangement would damage his standing as a nationalist and would produce far-flung political repercussions in Mexico that would endanger stability and the possibility of a peaceful presidential succession.

Obregón was able to negotiate a successful agreement with United States bankers concerning funding of debts and handling of railroads. The real difficulty centered around the question of subsoil rights under Article 27, and the uncompromising attitude of many American oil companies. Guarantees were demanded which were politically impossible for Obregón to grant. For example, Obregón was asked to promise tax relief and exemption from expropriation, in violation of both the spirit and letter of Article 27. The situation dragged on with feelings on both sides growing ever more intense until some people in the United States began to urge intervention. Not until 1923 was it possible to develop a satisfactory basis for talks to resolve the conflict. The famous Bucareli agreements followed. Both a General and a Special Claims Convention were signed with United States recognition of Mexico just preceding the event. The United States was temporarily satisfied, but various dissident groups in Mexico used the occasion as a pretext for challenging Obregón's legitimacy as protector of Mexican sovereignty. Obregón in fact gave up nothing of substance in relation to Article 27; nevertheless, the agreement to arbitrate claims worked in favor of anti-Obregón forces and aided them in their plan to oppose Obregón's choice for the presidential succession.

In retrospect, Obregón stands out as a definite contributor to the Revolution and its goals. His was the first in a series of efforts to go beyond ideal homage to the Indian of pre-Conquest times in order to effect a realistic educational program for integration of the Indian and indeed all rural Mexico as a participant in the Mexican polity. He provided labor with a strong political position as an articulator of the interests of the urban masses, and he was so firm in his dealings with the United States that it took him three years to obtain diplomatic recognition. He was thus an implementer of revolutionary goals and a nationalist in sufficient degree to place him securely in the revolutionary heritage. As such he has become an appropriate subject for study by school children, a reference for orators, and an artistic exercise for painters and sculptors in the revolutionary tradition. Had he lived to serve a second term instead of being assassinated immediately after re-election in 1928, the case might not have been as clear.

## Calles: A Controversial Figure

Plutarco Elías Calles was clearly a revolutionary and nationalist in orientation, but there is an air of doubt about his place in the tradition of events and heroic actions which constitute the legitimizing heritage of the regime. As President, many of his policies sought to realize revolutionary goals, but his determination to maintain his supremacy by directing Mexican politics from behind the scenes for several years after the termination of his presidency in 1928 has cast a shadow upon his historical image and has made it more difficult for succeeding generations to award him a place in the revolutionary pantheon. However, his role in developing the modern Mexican economy and political system can never be dismissed, for it was substantial. From the standpoint of the present, Calles remains a formidable figure who made a positive contribution to the existing system.

Calles came from Guaymas, Sonora, and his family was well known throughout the state. He had a revolutionary turn of mind, which demonstrated itself as early as 1900 when he had some trouble with *Porfiriato* officials. He was a man who knew a number of occupations and was for a time a school teacher. After the Revolution had gone into its second phase in 1913, Calles joined Obregón and became his most capable lieutenant. He was one of the Sonoran triumvirate with Obregón and Adolfo de la Huerta who brought about the downfall of Carranza and was a close collaborator of Obregón during the latter's presidency. As Obregón's term drew to a close, the question of the succession split the Sonoran triumvirate, and when Obregón chose Calles, his other friend and colleague, Adolfo de la Huerta, pronounced against the two, gathering strength from Obregón's enemies to the right and left of the political spectrum. The rebellion was serious, but the United States elected to help Obregón, whose government it had just recognized, and this help was an important factor in deciding the struggle. De la Huerta had to leave the country, and Calles took over the presidency.

Calles, like Obregón, was faced with several fundamental decisions when he entered the presidency, all of which directly related to the core ideas of the Revolution and the means of achieving revolutionary goals. First, he had to choose between emphasis upon labor support or agrarian support. Obregón had managed to walk a tightrope between them; Calles clearly chose labor. Labor, for all practical purposes, meant the small coterie of leaders grouped around Luis N. Morones called *Grupo Acción,* who ran the CROM, with its million members, and the Labor party. Morones' record as a key member of Calles' cabinet was not as clean as it might have been. On the positive side, the overall wage level of CROM membership continued to rise, and indemnification of injured workers, as well as those dismissed without "adequate" cause, increased. The course begun under Obregón of adapting both ideology and practice to a policy of coexistence with employers was continued. Other items do not read so well. Strikes declined, and labor leaders grew rich on management kickbacks for help in maintaining peaceful labor-management relations. Government-supported attacks on independent unions increased. The privileged position of the CROM and its tolerant attitude toward factory owners fitted well with Calles' encouragement of the growth of a new class of Mexican capitalists centering their activities for the most part in consumption and construction industries, and the acceptance of these business leaders into the governing group.[22] Calles and Morones continued to style themselves "socialists," stressing the compatibility of socialism and capitalism as the money poured in, and all those at the top embarked upon a pattern of conspicuous consumption in fine houses, luxurious cars, clothing, and jewelry which marked them as something totally apart from the rank and file they professed to serve.

Meanwhile, agrarian leaders, concerned with land reform, found their influence and access to the President on the wane in the cabinet and in the Congress. A sense of frustration and neglect developed among the leadership and rank and file of the Agrarista party, causing a swing away from Calles and closer ties with Obregón. Calles' constructive policies in agrarian reform were obscured by his close personal ties with labor and the new business groups among the "revolutionaries." Procedures to clarify land distribution were written into the law in 1925 and these were followed by sweeping changes in 1927 which gave greater clarity to the procedures for acquiring land and delineated more clearly the rights of private landowners. The result was a relatively coherent basis for future reforms and an expansion of land distribution.

In a second fundamental decision Calles took the position that modernization was vital to the realization of all revolutionary goals. A systematic road-building program was launched, setting a precedent for Mexico's relatively modern and constantly expanding highway

---

[22] Henry Bamford Parkes, *A History of Mexico* (Boston, 1938), p. 381.

network of the present. He also realized that a sick population can never be industrious and productive, and provided for programs of sanitation and wholesale vaccination that set precedents for continued efforts in public health on the part of succeeding administrations. Calles pursued modernization by expanding the amount of arable land through the establishment of an irrigation program. Subsequent improvements in this field have made possible the increasing agricultural production of modern Mexico. Finally, the former school teacher did not overlook the importance of literacy, and carried forward the policy begun by Obregón of lifting Mexico's educational level.

A third problem confronting Calles was the attitude of the Roman Catholic clergy, which had not changed much despite reverses in fortune dating back to the Reform. The old alliance between the higher clergy and the traditionally privileged groups among large landholders and old mercantile families still existed. Calles mounted an all-out attack. In 1926 leaders of the clergy published a political advertisement in a number of leading newspapers denouncing various portions of the Constitution of 1917. Calles reacted by enforcing one of the Constitution's anticlerical provisions that had previously lain dormant, and a number of alien priests and nuns were deported. The clergy then refused to conduct services anywhere in Mexico. Subsequently, proclerical groups raised the standard of rebellion in the western states of Michoacán, Jalisco, and Colima. Violence mounted, and outrages were perpetrated by both sides. The outcome was a definitive victory for Calles.

Mexican nationalism in relation to the United States constituted a fourth area of decision for Calles. Here the crux of the matter was foreign oil holdings just as it had been for Obregón. Toward the end of 1925 the Mexican Congress passed two laws jeopardizing the position of the American oil companies in regard to subsoil rights. President Coolidge attacked the Mexican position in a public address, and a rupture in relations and intervention seemed imminent. With the situation at an impasse and neither side ready to give ground, Coolidge changed ambassadors, and Dwight W. Morrow, an outstanding financier, went to Mexico to see what could be done. Morrow's approach was unpretentious and friendly. Calles liked him and so did a good many other Mexican leaders. Thus it is not difficult to understand the subsequent decision of the Mexican Supreme Court to rule out the most controversial provisions of the oil legislation. This decision paved the way for a period of more amicable relations between the two countries, though the conflict between the companies and Mexican nationalism remained.

Finally, Calles had to solve the problem of the presidential succession. Involved were such sensitive issues as "no re-election," *continuismo,* and Caesarism. Madero had made "no re-election" an effective symbol of the revolutionary tradition. Calles' actions in this connection did much to confuse his claim to a place in the revolutionary pantheon.

As the time for succession drew near, Calles supported Obregón's desire to become President once again. Two constitutional amendments were pushed through, permitting Obregón to be re-elected and lengthening the presidential term to six years. Obregón rolled over his opposition, including the formidable CROM, and with Calles' support was declared candidate-elect in July 1928. Then, two weeks later at a great victory banquet, the whole political arrangement was thrown into disarray when a young fanatic approached the great *caudillo* on the pretext of sketching him and shot him to death.

*Obregonistas,* especially leaders of the Agrarista party, who had expected cabinet posts and a generally more favorable political situation once their leader took office, began hunting for a scapegoat. They found him in Luis Morones and the labor leaders around him, the *Grupo Acción.* To the *obregonistas,* it was even possible that Calles himself was implicated. Any attempt by Calles to retain power seemed impossible in the face of these suspicions.

Rather than risk civil war among diverse groups of the revolutionary camp, Calles took himself out of the presidential picture, and at the same time offered an organizational substitute for the personalism that had characterized revolutionary presidents up to that time. In so doing, he demonstrated a high degree of statesmanship. The new concept of machinery for the succession was mentioned in his annual State of the Union message with the Congress, state governors, and high military assembled. Then to satisfy the disappointed *obregonistas,* one of their number, a lawyer named Emilio Portes Gil from Tamaulipas, was named provisional president by the Congress. After thus preparing the way, Calles set about organizing a Revolutionary party encompassing all factions, to which they would swear loyalty and through which procedures for institutionalizing peaceful succession to public office at all governmental levels could be adopted and made workable. Nearly all organized "revolutionaries" swore loyalty to the new party, its program, and procedural rules — thus emerged the *Partido Nacional Revolucionario* (PNR). This was the forerunner of the *Partido Revolucionario Institucional* (PRI) which dominates present-day Mexican politics.

Calles ran the party, the presidency, and the legislature from behind the scenes after 1928. He picked a relatively obscure man, Pascual Ortiz Rubio, as the PNR's candidate to succeed Portes Gil at the end of the provisional presidency, and arranged a lopsided victory over the PNR's popular opponent, José Vasconcelos. Vasconcelos was credited with only 20,000 votes against 1,000,000 for Ortiz Rubio in an election race that was clearly not that uneven.

Ortiz Rubio never finished his term. He had to consult Calles on the slightest question of policy. At the same time he had to work with Portes Gil, president of the PNR. Gil's egalitarian bias did not fit with Ortiz Rubio's political leanings, which were to the right of the increasingly conservative Calles. Portes Gil had been able to influence the composition of the Congress, which was essentially from the left-wing faction of the PNR. In a series of moves against agrarian and labor leaders, Ortiz alienated large sections of both Congress and party. Confronted with an opposition that ended his usefulness as a political instrument, he resigned, and Calles turned over the presidency to one of his close friends and business associates, General Abelardo Rodríguez.

Rodríguez, who had become one of the great Mexican capitalists, also had a flair for politics which Ortiz never possessed. He paid attention to Calles' dictates, gave the PNR its due respect as Calles' organ, promoted business, encouraged foreign capital, kept labor prostrate, put the lid on agrarian reformers, tolerated public graft and corruption in which Calles' associates were involved, and still managed to keep an air of presidential dignity.

Rodríguez brought a number of younger men into the government, an action which in itself helped allay the resentment against the existing situation. It was some of these younger men who improved on the Calles agrarian legislation and provided the legal framework used in the vast agrarian reforms of the next president, Lázaro Cárdenas. Just at the time that Calles and his conservative friends seemed most powerful, Rodríguez was presiding over a government and working with a political party in which younger men were rekindling the zeal of the revolutionary tradition.

In summary, the contribution of the Calles period to the revolutionary tradition is obscure. His recognition of the needs of his day and attempts to inaugurate relevant programs set useful precedents for subsequent governments. His contribution to the revolutionary fighting is not in dispute. However, his affinity for newly rich labor leaders and businessmen and his inability to avoid great waste and corruption make his standing ambiguous. Further, his organization of the Revolutionary party as a mechanism for undergirding the "no re-election" principle is weakened as an achievement by his determination to govern from behind the scenes after saying he would step down. His achievements are clear enough, but his Caesarism removes him from the mainstream of the revolutionary tradition which legitimizes the regime.

## Lázaro Cárdenas

The left wing of the Revolutionary coalition grew more powerful, and its central figure became Lázaro Cárdenas, whose star continued to rise in spite of differences with Calles, the paramount chief.[23] Cárdenas had been one of Calles' successful junior officers in the revolutionary fighting and had held many important posts during Calles' period of dominance, but Cárdenas had never become completely identified in his own mind with his powerful mentor. Nevertheless, Calles preferred Cárdenas to any other leftist he could select. Cárdenas' intentions were perhaps foretold in his extensive electoral campaign, when he visited even the most remote corners of rural Mexico to let the people know him.

Once in the presidency, Cárdenas began to build the political strength he would need to expand the drive toward revolutionary goals far beyond the limits marked off by Obregón and Calles. He began by moving simultaneously in a number of directions. He created an image of himself as a symbol of honesty and austerity by closing many of the gambling casinos and moving out of the elaborate presidential residence, Chapultepec Castle. At the same time he stepped up the distribution of land to a pace unequaled by any previous administration and thus assured peasant leaders of the sincerity of his promises. Labor was encouraged to strike with government support, and labor leaders quickly gravitated to the man whose zeal for bettering their power and economic position stood in marked contrast to the policy of the post-1928 *callista* presidents.

Calles' intransigent anticlericalism was turned against him as Cárdenas took a soft line toward the Church, and pro-Cárdenas military elements were quietly moved into key positions while *callistas* in the presidential cabinet were neutralized or removed in a complex set of political maneuvers. By June 1935 Calles felt it necessary to

[23] The selection of "coalition" as a term for the ruling elite and their immediate retinues should not be misunderstood as reflecting low valuation of the importance of the "family" metaphor for continued credibility of the legitimizing myth. I choose the term *coalition* because it reflects the fact of past and present disputes and disaffections among Mexico's political leaders, each of whom has his own entourage (*camarilla*). The situation that exists is one of individuals with loose rather than strict ties linking members of an extended family or clan. The Revolutionary coalition is not static; its membership varies. Continuity lies in the exclusive and unified claim to the Revolutionary mantle.

threaten Cárdenas openly, but his move came too late, and the overwhelming strength which Cárdenas had amassed forced Calles, the onetime strong man, to retire from politics and leave Mexico.

Along with his all-out drive toward achievement of revolutionary goals Cárdenas brought about organizational innovations which distinctly altered the Mexican political scene and continued to provide some of the distinguishing marks of Mexican politics. From a mammoth conclave of labor leaders in February 1936 there emerged the *Confederación de Trabajadores de Mexico* (CTM) which has continued to dominate organized labor to the present. Cárdenas was also determined that *ejidatarios* should have a unified national leadership. He encouraged the revolutionary agrarian leadership to combine in leagues at the state level and then encouraged the national affiliation of them all in the *Confederación Nacional Campesina* (CNC). The reciprocity of support between government and organized peasants and labor placed Cárdenas in a position to keep expanding the Revolution to which he had given new life both in agrarian reform and in labor-management relations. In addition, he was able to reorganize the old PNR to include the new militant elements and provide a basis for consolidation of his reforms by later governments. His instrument of unification was the *Partido Revolucionario Mexicano,* which was based upon the concept of four distinct political segments. These "sectors," as they were called, were considered to include the most vital political forces in *cardenista* Mexico. There were peasant and labor sectors as well as the military. A fourth sector was recognized but did not become effective until after Cárdenas' presidency. This was the so-called Popular Sector, which was conceived as a catchall for all those who did not fit in the other categories.

With regard to foreign-held property in Mexico, Cárdenas placed himself fully in the mainstream of the revolutionary heritage by pushing a bill through Congress in 1936 that made any property defined as having "public utility" subject to expropriation. The constitutional basis of the law was Article 27, and it was designed to fill in gaps in the Agrarian Code of 1934. The President was given nearly unlimited discretion to determine what property could be expropriated. The law was applied to industrial and commercial as well as agricultural property. Where labor was involved, there were strikes for benefits under Article 123 of the Constitution, and if foreign capital was involved, it faced intervention by the government if labor's demands were not granted. Some Mexican owners fell before labor's onslaught, but foreign enterprises were worse hit. In the countryside as well, foreign owners felt the pressure as the government moved to distribute more and more of the available arable land. Foreign-held stock in the National Railways of Mexico was taken over by the government with promise of indemnification. The promise was honored. There remained the question of oil. This was a major resource dominated by foreign capital, and it was impossible for Cárdenas to overlook it in light of the strong nationalist bias of his government. Cárdenas' solution to the perennial oil question made him a national hero, almost a folk hero before he left office.

A labor dispute set off the series of events leading to Cárdenas' final decision to expropriate all major foreign oil holdings. There were between 13,000 and 19,000 Mexican petroleum workers.[24] Before Cárdenas' time these workers had been organized in a multitude of small, weak unions. Cárdenas brought about their unification under a single leadership which in its turn affiliated with the expanding power of the CTM. The new and powerful petroleum workers union made numerous demands, some realistic and some not, for higher pay and fringe benefits. When the major companies turned down key demands on wage increases and inclusion of Mexican office employees in the union, a strike was threatened. Cárdenas intervened to arrange a six months' period for further talks. Bitterness increased instead of lessened, and the union called a general strike when the "cooling-off" period ended late in May 1937.

To strengthen its position the union petitioned for government intervention under a provision of the Labor Code of 1931, which distinguished between an ordinary strike situation and an "economic conflict" involving an imbalance in the industry detrimental to the national interest. The Federal Board of Conciliation and Arbitration granted the union's request and set up a commission to study the conflict while workers returned to their jobs. The report that ensued was fair or unfair, depending on one's choice of statistics, accounting procedures, and bias. The report, in any case, was not favorable to the companies, since it rejected their position on both wage increases and union jurisdiction over white-collar personnel as well as on many lesser questions. The Board accepted the recommendations of its investigating committee and ordered the companies to comply. The companies then made a concrete offer for wage increases which brought a favorable response from the government, but they lost their momentary advantage by demanding that Cárdenas formally swear to support the deal offered by the companies. The demand put them in a position of impugning the honor of Mexico's President and, indeed, of Mexico itself. The demand for a sworn statement was turned down,

---

[24] Numbers vary according to what types of jobs are included. James gives the higher figure and Cline the lower. James, p. 281, and Cline, *The United States and Mexico,* p. 231.

and the companies then refused outright to comply with the Board's order. National honor and national sovereignty were clearly at stake from the official Mexican point of view. In this situation Cárdenas switched from what was apparently his earlier position, to get the most from the companies short of expropriation. The final acts of the major producers, in addition to the blustering attitude maintained by their representatives both in Mexico and the United States throughout the dispute, constituted an unforgivable offense to Mexican pride. Discarding considerations of economic and diplomatic repercussions, Cárdenas went the whole way for nationalism. A presidential decree of March 18, 1938, based on the expropriation legislation of 1936 brought Mexican control of the major British and United States oil properties and shouts of jubilation from the people. Historians seem to agree that the move was supported by nearly all articulate elements in Mexican society; this was unquestionably one of the most widely supported policies ever promulgated by a Mexican President.

The expropriation decree did not end the matter. Negotiations with the United States government dragged on into the administration of Cárdenas' successor. However, the bitterness that had characterized diplomatic interchange between the two countries in similar crises of earlier times was less intense than before. Neither withdrawal of recognition nor intervention was threatened by the United States. Mexicans for their part maintained a courteous and open attitude, and the moderation of both sides made possible settlement of agrarian claims before Cárdenas left the presidency and paved the way for settlement of the oil claims during the second year of Cárdenas successor, Ávila Camacho.

Cárdenas' nationalism would have placed him as a direct lineal descendant in the revolutionary tradition of Hidalgo, Morelos, Juárez, and the leaders of the conflict of 1910–1917 without much other action on his part. But his other policies formed the essential background for the oil expropriation. Had there not been a new drive toward the goals of agrarian reform and improvements for labor, the organized and militant political force necessary for the oil expropriation might have been lacking. In the agrarian field, Cárdenas not only distributed twice the total amount of land distributed by his predecessors since 1915, he approximately doubled the number of beneficiaries of land distribution.[25] Along with the physical fact of land distribution went a new and expanded conception of agrarian reform which affected for the first time large numbers of rural wage laborers in northern Mexico. The old concepts of land reform primarily referred to restitution of

[25] Nathan L. Whetten, *Rural Mexico* (Chicago, 1948), p. 127.

Indian lands taken from villages under Díaz, and included grants to certain other types of villages with the net result that in many areas of the north and north-central region the *hacienda* as a traditional social and economic institution had continued to dominate the rural land tenure arrangement. Cárdenas changed this situation by pushing distribution of *hacienda* land to groups of landless rural wage earners who could claim no village land rights.

Moreover, kinds of agricultural enterprises to be affected by the land distribution program were expanded to include areas involving large-scale cultivation of commercial crops such as cotton, henequen, wheat, and coffee. Expropriation of many rich Laguna region cotton properties in southwestern Coahuila and northeastern Durango in 1936, the organization of formerly landless peasants into cooperatives to run the new *ejidos* and the collectivization of the henequen industry in Yucatán dramatically illustrated Cárdenas' determination to attack the *hacienda* system in all its forms. In addition there was expropriation of coffee properties in Chiapas and American-owned wheat lands in the Yaqui Valley of Sonora. Whether it was a rural *mestizo* group as in La Laguna or Maya Indians as in Yucatán, Cárdenas was set on expanding the agrarian reform for their benefit. By the time he finished his term, half the rural peasantry was organized in an *ejido* of some type.

Hand in hand with the wholesale distribution of lands went a renewed drive to educate the peasantry, and thousands of young people went out into the rural areas, inspired by an awakened educational evangelism reminiscent of the days when José Vasconcelos was Secretary of Education in the Obregón cabinet.

Realization of revolutionary goals was also pushed in the urban areas as labor unions affiliated with the CTM struck again and again in all types of industries to push for collective bargaining contracts based on the guarantees of Article 123 of the Constitution. The demands for an eight-hour day, higher wages, and recognition of benefits relating to sickness, unemployment, and recreation facilities were most dramatically illustrated in the great petroleum workers dispute; but other labor-management conflicts followed much the same lines, though with less at stake for the nation.[26]

Mexico's political system has evolved through the influences of many, but Cárdenas more than any other president since the Revolution provided the basis for Mexico to meet successfully the challenges of the latter part of the twentieth century. In his presidency, socialist ideals and egalitarian tendencies were given new vitality, and were combined with a definition of the role of private property that has

---

[26] See Albert Michaels, "The Crisis of Cardenismo," *Journal of Latin American Studies* (May, 1970), for a discussion of this revolutionary period.

since been a guide for the relations of the public and private economic sectors. A durable coexistence was created between private-enterprise management and the representatives of the large, centralized industrial labor unions. In a parallel vein, the peasants of the *ejido* communities — the beneficiaries of land distributed under the *Reforma Agraria* of the Revolution — formally acquired status in the political system, their leadership was centralized, and their structure permanently institutionalized in the agrarian code. Parameters and guiding orientation were given to industrial and agricultural development in financing from both the public and private sectors. Public support was mobilized for industrial development so that the competing claims of labor demands, managerial aims, and investment policy could be balanced. In agriculture the government had undisputed authority to eliminate the pre-Revolutionary semi-feudal *hacienda*. Any large-scale agricultural operation had to justify itself as a modern enterprise producing needed agricultural products efficiently. These farms, however, had to co-exist with *ejido* communities as well as to be responsive to decisions made by federal policy-makers.

These accomplishments were juxtaposed with the establishment of a policy that did not permit foreign capital — invested either in urban or rural areas — to influence decision-making, as it had prior to Cárdenas. A principle was formulated that neither foreign owners nor foreign investment in either the public or private sector could expect their interests to be treated as legitimate unless congruent with Mexican public policy. "Mexico for Mexicans" was the guideline for policy toward foreign business investment.

Congruence with the public good did not apply to foreign investors alone. The private sector, whether industrial, agricultural, Mexican, or foreign, had to meet the same essential requirement. Capitalism was directed to produce on a competitive basis, a departure from the traditional orientation of monopolistic concessions. The collective good in both nationalistic and technological terms legitimized the private sector, and was concomitant with a strengthening of the ideological antiimperialism characteristic of post-Revolutionary Mexico. Antiimperialism, in turn, was the cornerstone of Mexico's diplomatic relations with the weaker, newly emerging nations. Modern Mexico was able to step forward as a sovereign state based on the twin values of nationalism and technological progress.

Cárdenas was able to perform major surgery on long-standing economic and social institutions in a time of worldwide ideological struggle without resorting to any nonindigenous ideology. The overriding theme of his presidency was always Mexican nationalism, and his political sagacity permitted the accomplishment of extensive social change for the national good without provoking a civil war, a military coup d'état, political terrorism and violence, or rule by force.

Perhaps most important from the standpoint of Revolutionary legitimacy and political stability as well as the liberal principles for which so many had died was Cárdenas' decision to step down at the end of his term. Thus the *maderista* tradition was maintained and strengthened. The "no re-election" principle triumphed, and Cárdenas became a legend in his own lifetime. How he will be treated in official accounts and public-school textbooks over the next few years remains a matter of conjecture. But it seems likely that his deeds in the 1930s will stand the test of time, and that he will become part of the nationalist, revolutionary tradition and the national myth. Although he did not do battle in the field on a scale comparable with Zapata, Villa, and Carranza, he appears to qualify as one of the true revolutionaries, deserving his own niche in the pantheon of Mexico's legendary heroes. Barring a civil war in which the traditional conservatives come out on top, future leaders and governments will no doubt attempt to strengthen their claim to legitimacy by linking themselves with Lázaro Cárdenas.

## Post-Cárdenas Revolutionaries:
## Ávila Camacho, Alemán, and Others

The Presidents succeeding Cárdenas have been essentially "gradualist" within the framework established by the end of Cárdenas' presidency in 1940. Beginning with Manuel Ávila Camacho, each new President has left some distinguishing work of his own without abandoning the economic and social philosophies that have shaped the Revolutionary regime. It was in Cárdenas' presidency that the political culture of the regime was finally established out of the ideological and personal conflicts of the post-Revolution. With each succeeding six-year presidential term, each passing decade, each victorious candidate of the Revolutionary coalition, it has become clear that short of the most desperate circumstances there will be no deliberate initiation of mass political mobilization and conflict such as occurred during Cárdenas' presidency. Moderation, political stability, and *continuismo* of the Revolutionary regime take precedence over demands for sweeping change. The *cardenista* legacy was the last major contribution to the legitimizing myth, the claim of direct lineage in a mythical familial line of revolutionary nationalist heroes.[27]

[27] Great insight can be gained through reading the free textbooks distributed by the national government through the National Commission for Free Textbooks. See especially Concepción Barrón de Morán, *Mi libro de cuarto año* (México, D.F., Comisión Nacional de los Libros de Texto

It should not be imagined that Cárdenas' accomplishments on behalf of the regime guaranteed an untroubled succession for him. In fact, the country was badly divided at the time of the succession, and so was the Revolutionary coalition. Cárdenas chose General Manuel Ávila Camacho, whose candidacy was bitterly opposed by another of the high-ranking officers in the Revolutionary coalition, General Juan Andreu Almazán. Cárdenas' efforts at political mobilization of the urban and rural proletariats paid off. The coalition of military officers, northern peasants and traditional proclerical elements was unable to control the succession.[28]

Ávila Camacho appeared mild-mannered but had enough determination and political acumen to rise to the rank of general in the army during a period of considerable turbulence. One important factor which helped him was the political strength of his older brother Maximino who was Governor of Puebla during Cárdenas' presidency and who had close ties with the wealthy Jenkins enterprises. Maximino had worked closely with Vicente Lombardo Toledano, Cárdenas' major urban labor organizer, to strengthen the *cardenista* labor organization, *Confederación de Trabajadores de México* (CTM). Ávila Camacho's closest familial and friendship ties were centered in the Federal District–Puebla–Veracruz area, traditionally the politically dominant area of Mexico. Further, Manuel, Maximino, and Rafael (a younger brother and subsequent Governor of Puebla) all had close ties with the politically successful army leaders of the Revolution and post-Revolution period. Ávila Camacho was the head of the Ministry of the Interior (*Gobernación*) and had proven his political skill and responsibility in government. His declaration that he was a "believer" in Catholicism made him acceptable to most clerics and the proclerical laity. Most important, though, was his strong claim to membership in the coalition of revolutionaries: his own unimpeachable revolutionary commitment and the strength of his family's association with the Revolutionary coalition.

With his base of power Ávila Camacho was able successfully to formulate policy in several areas of major concern. First, he was able to contain the Mexican version of fascism, known as *sinarquismo*. He was strong enough to steer a middle course between the Fascist and Communist extremes which threatened Mexico during World War

---

Gratuitos, 1960), pp. 170–177. The presentation of all Presidents since the Revolution of 1910–1917 as "revolutionary" is to be clearly observed in this and other similar elementary texts.

[28] Virginia Prewett, *Reportage on Mexico* (New York, 1941), and Betty Kirk, *Covering the Mexican Front* (Norman, Okla., 1941). Both give vivid accounts of the conflicts in this presidential succession period.

II, and he was able to ally Mexico with the United States during the war without alienating groups essential to his support. Second, he initiated policies designed to heal the still-open wounds in Mexican society left by the revolutionary policies of Cárdenas. Third, he began to rebuild agricultural and industrial productivity which had suffered serious setbacks under the wholesale land redistribution and waves of strikes used by Cárdenas to effect his revolutionary goals. Using the *cardenista* legacy creatively, an expanding Mexican middle class grouped around bureaucrats, professional men, and the new industrialists began to increase its political influence through the *Confederación Nacional de Organizaciones Populares* (CNOP) and the national chambers of industry and commerce. The role of the middle class was guaranteed and strengthened for the future.

Ávila Camacho's successor, Miguel Alemán Valdés, became President in a manner that had become institutionalized. He was governor of Veracruz (a key state); he was Interior Minister; he was closely tied to the man he succeeded — in fact was his "campaign manager." But his selection indicated a shift in emphasis by the Revolutionary coalition. Instead of being a general or an "old revolutionary," he was a lawyer (*licenciado*) and had been too young to participate in the Revolution. He was a symbol of new times and of the new generation which would take Mexico into rapid social change and economic growth.

By the time Alemán became President, the stage was set for an unprecedented expansion in business activity based on an influx of foreign capital and the growth of Mexican-owned industrial enterprises. This was accompanied by an extensive public-works construction program — expanding transportation and communication networks and building a completely new campus for the national university, *Universidad Nacional Autónima de México (UNAM)*. Related to this expansion were two key policy decisions. First, Mexico's foreign exchange was to be directed away from food importation and towards importation of capital equipment and materials, especially those critical to the expansion of the economic infrastructure. To accomplish this, agricultural self-sufficiency was essential despite rapid population growth and increasing concentration of the populace in urban areas. It was decided that the "small private property" classification of the agrarian code should be the center of programs to increase agricultural productivity. A second decision to accomplish these goals was the construction of extensive and costly tropical lowland river basin dams, power plants, and water distribution systems. These were to allow for intensive settlement and cultivation of hitherto under-utilized territory. The key to such aims was the construction of massive dams, such as the Alemán Dam in the Popaloapan River Basin centered in Oaxaca, Puebla, and Veracruz.[29] Similar projects were to follow. These would all increase employment, shifting some urban population to cities in the lowlands, spur agricultural production in the lowlands (through irrigation systems), and reduce pressures on the other agricultural land, thus allowing current needs to be met and increasing mechanization and productivity of small private holdings in the future.

Not surprisingly, Alemán's large-scale, free-wheeling program for economic expansion with its emphasis on extensive expenditures in the public sector produced dissension within the Revolutionary coalition and major support groups. (One highly placed politician said to the author, "We can't afford another Miguel Alemán for awhile.") Widespread and well-founded charges of corruption were also levelled at his administration.[30]

Accordingly, the presidential succession of 1952 was more troubled than that of 1946, although Adolfo Ruiz Cortines, the candidate of the Revolutionary coalition, won easily. His greatest opposition, however, was from General Miguel Henriquez Guzmán, once a member of the inner circle of the coalition. Ruiz Cortines was the compromise candidate of the *cardenista* and *alemanista* factions. For the *alemanistas* it was necessary that the vindictiveness felt by other Revolutionary factions towards them not become governmental persecution or revenge. To other elements of the Revolutionary coalition, Ruiz Cortines' long record of government service indicated his reliability at a time when it was needed. He had been both Governor of Veracruz and Interior Minister, and his roots in the regime went back far into his past. The *cardenistas* considered him in tune with the needs of the country and of the people. Both sides knew him to be a good, honest, and competent administrator, as well as moderate in his views and conciliatory in his political style.

Ruiz Cortines' most onerous burden was to preside over a 50 percent devaluation of the peso necessary for restoring depleted dollar reserves caused by his predecessor's policies. To accomplish this without causing widespread loss of support for the regime, Ruiz Cortines had to restore and maintain confidence in the continued commitment of the leadership to the values and symbols of the revolutionary tradition. His personal example of integrity and relatively frugal life style (in contrast to his predecessor's lavish one) were important. He produced a steady stream of official acts emphasizing important Revolu-

[29] Thomas Poleman, *The Popaloapan Project* (Stanford, Calif., 1964).
[30] A more extended discussion of the ferment of the period can be found in Brandenburg, pp. 106–107.

tionary promises to rural and urban workers and the nation as a whole. These included commitments to labor, antiimperialism, anticorruption in government, universal literacy, and the growing unity and strength of the Mexican nation.[31] He succeeded in restoring much of the credibility lost by Alemán, although not enough to insure an untroubled succession in 1958.

While Ruiz Cortines faced these difficult tasks, emphasizing hard work and austerity, he did not abandon the goals of Alemán. Ruiz Cortines continued to build up the economic infrastructure, basic industries (especially steel), and the elaborate tropical lowland river basin development program. Many of his programs focused on more direct aid, such as schools, feeder roads, and technical assistance.

At this time the Revolutionary coalition was beginning to change. The bureaucrat, the professional, the businessman were all growing in importance, while the peasant and worker were in relative decline. CNOP (the Popular Sector) was gaining strength as more and more government personnel claimed Popular Sector affiliation (rather than Labor or Agrarian Sector affiliation) within the Revolutionary party.

Adolfo López Mateos became the next President. He fit into the developing pattern of presidential requirements well. His family had a notable revolutionary background, including the distinguished writer Ignacio Ramírez and Benito Juárez' foreign affairs minister, Francís Zarco Mateos. López Mateos had the right mix of educational background, governmental service, and political experience. He was unique in being chosen as presidential candidate while serving as Minister of Labor, rather than Interior. He was a civilian, not a soldier, and was part of the Revolutionary coalition.

When López Mateos became President in December 1958, he became the helmsman of Mexico's system of rule which had developed under the guidance of the Revolutionary coalition as well as the machinery and symbolism of the Revolutionary party. In his new role he was heir to numerous legacies. First of all, he inherited the mythical mantle of legitimacy based on the nationalist, revolutionary tradition. As a President who had long apprenticeship in service to the regime and its ruling elite, López Mateos effectively used the valuable asset of the myth to further the policies already charted by his predecessors. Another asset was Mexico's record of economic growth. Its extensive development of infrastructure — transportation, telecommunications, and energy — was outstanding. Its industrial

[31] The growing burden of population growth on revolutionary goals, such as universal literacy, was emphasized in the Sixth State of the Union Address by Ruiz Cortines on September 1, 1958. *Hispano Americano* (September 8, 1958), pp. 8 ff.

expansion was not surpassed among third-world countries. Its pioneer projects for river-basin development and integrated urban-industrial centers were notable among developing countries. The increasingly "modern" life-style enjoyed by the advantaged and upwardly mobile groups in the cities, especially those of *mestizo* ancestry, was widely known in other countries and regarded with pride by beneficiaries of this new life. These combined assets could appropriately be viewed, as Professor Cline pointed out, as the basis for a new approach to governing and legitimacy. Cline felt that the phrase "Institutional Revolution" described well this unfolding phenomenon, that as the "unity" drive began under Ávila Camacho "the fundamental Cárdenas concept of class struggle as a basis for policy was changed to 'harmony for the common Mexican cause.' " [32]

However, it could not be said that the inheritance of López Mateos was without negative elements. One of the policies of the Revolutionary coalition had been to feed population growth at both ends, that is, by increasing sanitation, innoculation, and the general availability of medical services while simultaneously refusing to take measures to reduce fertility. The official position had been that Mexico's greatness could only be achieved through population expansion. The doctrine was quite old: the great Mexican demographer Gilberto Loyo made the best statement of this idea, and it continued to be the "prescribed formula" of the Revolutionary coalition long after Loyo himself recognized the danger of its continued application.[33] The consequence was a rate of population growth from 1940 to 1954 that averaged 3 percent. In common-sense terms this meant that the government would be hard put to meet its commitments under the regime's values. It meant that the land appropriated by the government for landless rural workers could not fill the growing pressures for still more land appropriations from the new generations for whom there were as yet no *ejido* parcels. Further, there was an excess population increase that could not be absorbed by industrial and technological progress, which by definition were oriented towards capital-intensive production rather than the labor-intensive production of traditional times. In addition, during the 1950s the government allowed inflation to run its course unchecked following the peso devaluation, and this worsened the situation of lower-income groups in

[32] Howard F. Cline, "Mexico, Fidelismo and the United States," *Orbis* (Summer, 1961), p. 157.

[33] Gilberto Loyo, *Las deficiencias cuantitativas de la población de México y una política demográfica nacional,* 3rd ed. (México, D.F., 1934). Also see his later work. Gilberto Loyo, *Población y desarrollo económico* (México, D.F., 1962).

both urban and rural areas. Finally, the focus of public policy and the attention of the governing circles had shifted away from even the most advantaged of the rural and urban labor force, the *ejidatarios* and members of industrial labor unions. "The privileged place of the proletariat was suddenly challenged by equally vocal middle and upper class bodies." [34]

This last factor is important in underscoring the turbulence of the time. In large part, this was caused by the policies of the Revolutionary coalition itself. It was not responding well enough to the demands of the labor and agrarian leaders, due to the changing nature of the coalition's clientele and the relative economic decline of the urban laborer. Real wage levels declined during the later 1950s. However, the downward turn would not necessarily mean that labor disputes could not be handled without resort to the military, as Alemán successfully dealt with a similar problem in 1950–1951.[35] The labor and agrarian groups had been so strengthened by the *cardenista* reforms that alienating some of their more active members proved to be a serious matter.

Philip B. Taylor Jr. carefully monitored the course of events during this time, and discussed in detail the factors that most overtly contributed to the unrest.[36] He cautioned that the government's widespread use of the military to contain the violence of 1958–1959 might prove an insufficient force in the long run if the urban and rural workers' demands could not be satisfied.

Some of the most violent conflicts seen in Mexico in years took place during this time. There were several serious strikes. Perhaps the most notorious was led by Demetrio Vallejo of the railway workers union. But troubles were not confined to the unions. Disaffected rural workers and peasants in the northwest were led by Jacinto B. López and others on a wave of squatter (*paracaidista*) raids. The government responded with military repression to any popular resistance. Squatter leaders, including Jacinto López, were imprisoned, but they had some successes.[37]

The northwest was not the only area affected. Rosa Tirado de

[34] Cline, p. 157. Roger D. Hansen has carefully documented the change in income distribution which accompanied the shift in governmental focus to the needs and demands of "white collar" workers. Hansen, p. 180.

[35] James W. Wilkie, *The Mexican Revolution: Federal Expenditure and Social Change Since 1910* (Berkeley, 1967), p. 185.

[36] Philip B. Taylor, Jr., "The Mexican Elections of 1958: Affirmation of Authoritarianism?" *The Western Political Quarterly* (September 1960), pp. 722–744. This article has become a classic because of its insight into the possibility of spiraling violence in later years.

[37] Hacienda Cananea in Sonora lost much of its land to the squatters.

Ruiz reported on the growing plight of the rural worker.[38] Because of the rapidly growing rural population and increasing farm mechanization, the rural employment problem was becoming serious. Groups of homeless, unemployed rural youths (*golondrinas*) wandered the countryside. Without education or experience they were poor prospects for becoming productive urban workers.

In addition to labor and agrarian disaffection, a new phenomenon appeared. The university students at UNAM, instead of remaining quietly on the extravagant and colorful campus built by Miguel Alemán, began to demonstrate in an even more violent and extensive fashion. These demonstrations reached their peak after the July elections.

Taylor has summarized this period of succession including the resumption of labor violence under Vallejo:

> The conclusion is inescapable that the PRI was in trouble in 1958. López enters office confronted by problems which indicate the recognized functional groupings are dissatisfied. Although the suppressions of the disorders . . . had the effect of giving López a breathing spell in formulating his policies, he will have to move, expeditiously and forcefully, to preserve the system of control. . . . The summer of 1958 demonstrated the maturing of the political and social situation. . . . But the period also saw a revival of the spirit of Revolution and expectation.[39]

If disaffection increased due to these economic and social factors, revolutionary spirit was also increased by an external factor, the triumph of the Cuban revolution. This was significant for several reasons. First, Mexico and Cuba traditionally have enjoyed especially friendly relations and close ties between their peoples. "Peoples' revolutions" are highly significant to Mexicans. They bring about an immediate identification with the oppressed revolutionaries and the reinvocation of the trauma and triumph of the Mexican revolutionary myth. Thus the revolutionary sympathy and fervor of the nation increased.

The situation was complicated because of the interaction of domestic and foreign policies. Mexico had usually extended its moral support to foreign revolutionary regimes. This policy tended to increase popular support for the government. Cuba, accordingly, received routine expressions of warmth and congratulations. But along with

---

[38] Rosa Tirado de Ruiz, "Desarrollo histórico de la política agraria sobre tenencia de la tierra, 1910–1970," Ifigenia M. de Narvarete, ed., *Bienestar campesino y desarrollo económico* (México, D.F., 1971), pp. 36–59.
[39] Taylor, pp. 740, 744.

these went (again, routinely) invitations to the Cuban leaders to visit Mexico. Thus the Cuban leaders appeared several times before enthusiastic Mexican crowds. At the same time disaffection with the Revolutionary coalition moved many Mexicans, ranging from simple reformists to violent revolutionaries, to see in *fidelismo* an important aid.

In order to deal with this difficult set of problems López Mateos first did as his predecessors. He toured the country before his term began, identifying himself with the symbols of revolution. He pledged agrarian reform, the rights of organized labor, and the rights of all Mexicans to education (in the spirit of Articles 27, 3 and 123 of the Constitution of 1917).

When he became President, it was clear that his pronouncements were not empty rhetoric, for he emphasized distribution of *ejido* land more than any of his predecessors except Cárdenas. He initiated a "free textbook" program for poor children, greatly enlarged school facilities, and expanded the literacy program (*alfabetización*). He also increased urban worker benefits through profit-sharing and expansion of the Mexican Institute of Social Security (IMSS). He benefited both poor rural farmers and poor urban consumers by buying agricultural staples at guaranteed prices and selling them at low prices. This was an expansion of an older agency which was renamed the National Popular Subsistence Corporation (CONASUPO). Thus López Mateos did attempt to increase the rewards of the system given to its people.

By no means did he abandon the long-range goal of the Revolutionary coalition for modernization and industrialization. He continued plans for river-basin developments, opening new lands to more intensive settlement, and furthered irrigation projects in more heavily settled areas. The telephone system was placed completely within the public sector. A strong record of growth was maintained while inflation was controlled. United States private investment increased steadily, and the Mexican government expanded the lending capacities of the national banks.

Due in part to improved economic factors, and a change in the supporting bases of the Revolutionary coalition, López Mateos was able to cope with the turbulence of the early years of his administration, and the remainder of his term was relatively stable. His approach to the problems facing the nation was clearly an "evolutionary" one. He attempted to correct labor and agrarian dissatisfaction. He actively sought peaceful cooperation between the different sectors. But he was not above using physical force to maintain stability. His attitude toward radical change was not favorable, as exemplified in his government's policy reversal to guarded neutrality as Castro moved Cuba into the Soviet orbit. Similarly, radicals (especially Communists) such as the famous artist David A. Siquieros faced long imprisonment or suppression for their political activities. The effectiveness of the "official" Revolutionary party was preserved. Revolutionary symbolism continued to be appealing in many sectors, especially where material benefits of policy were evident. Yet the balance achieved was marred by two factors. First, over the years a new class had been formed of those who were benefiting from the policies of the regime.[40] As a consequence they were aligning together in the Popular Sector at the expense of *agrarista* and laborite radicalism. So, although middle and upper groups supported the regime as never before, it remained questionable whether these groups provided sufficient support to balance labor and agrarian disaffection. Second, when dealing with dissidence, the government strengthened its support for and active use of the military. In short, although Revolutionary symbolism was invoked and serious attention was paid to satisfying demands for greater rewards, use of the military became more evident in dealing with those who questioned the regime.

These policies were essentially effective. However, realistically they can be viewed as part of a process of change which was a natural consequence of the historical success of the regime. Gustavo Díaz Ordaz, the next president, inherited this situation. He again closely fit the preceding pattern of presidential choices made by the Revolutionary coalition. He had antecedents reaching back to Juárez' time when an ancestor served as a general in the *juarista* army. He was from the key, centrally located state of Puebla. He was a lawyer who had worked his way up through the government, becoming finally administrative head (*oficial mayor*) of the Interior Ministry. He was selected by López Mateos as Minister of the Interior. The "familial" continuity of the Revolutionary coalition was also invoked (as usual) in the nominating speeches. Díaz Ordaz was described as having the "clearest promise of [linearly] unbroken Revolutionary ideas." [41]

Ideologically his administration stressed important Revolutionary themes. These included agrarian land distribution, increasing union labor benefits, and educational improvements. The heavy emphasis upon economic growth and political stability continued while the

---

[40] "Upper and middle class Mexicans constituted less than 17 percent of the total Mexican population in 1940. By 1963 that figure had approximately doubled." Hansen, p. 180.

[41] Comments by sector leaders reported in *Hispano Americano* (November 11, 1963), p. 10, translated by author.

government also tried to deliver what material benefits it could. But a subtle shift was emerging in the meaning attached to the traditional revolutionary themes. For example, although Díaz Ordaz made sweeping land distributions, at the end of his administration he announced that all of the land remaining for such purposes totaled less than half of what he had distributed. The gravity of this pronouncement was underscored by the most extensive aerial surveys yet attempted cataloging the nation's land resources. Another sign of change in traditional agrarian reform was the government's attempt to settle its existing large backlog of land-distribution appeals. The Department of Agrarian Affairs and Settlement (DAAC) quickly dismissed many cases at lower administrative levels. Those remaining were decided with unprecedented speed. The minister of DAAC announced that "we wish to convince the rural workers that their destiny is not inevitably linked to agriculture." [42] Thus agrarian reform could not mean principally land distribution as it had in the past, just as *revolucionario* could no longer mean what it had in the past.

Other aspects of agrarian policy including continued irrigation expansion, the emphasis on private agricultural properties as major producers, and feeder road systems remained essentially unchanged.

With respect to organized labor programs, Díaz Ordaz emphasized extensive public housing in major urban centers. The public sector, meanwhile, continued to show a marked increase in lending and investment. All aspects of the infrastructure were expanded. However, to pay for these programs a shift was seen from the traditional dependence on private foreign investors (especially from the United States) to extensive use of international lending agencies. Some of these, such as the World Bank and Export-Import Bank had previously been used by Mexico from time to time. But newly used major sources of credit were the International Monetary Fund and the Inter-American Development Bank. Also European sources of private capital were increasing in importance. Tourism, the usual source of Mexico's foreign currency, was clearly inadequate in meeting the nation's need. The revolutionary goals of national self-determination and self-sufficiency were proving increasingly difficult in light of the above trends. Left-wing elements used this fact in political attacks against the Revolutionary coalition.

The increasing costs of development were closely tied to population. Mexico's rapid population growth was placing heavy demands on the system's ability to provide adequate public services. For ex-

---

42 Norberto Onine Palancares, "Síntesis de la obra agraria de Díaz Ordaz," *Hispano Americano* (November 30, 1970), pp. 26–27.

ample, a nearly geometric increase in education expenditures (for all levels) was observed during Díaz Ordaz' administration. Basic services such as water, sewer, and power severely strained government resources. Repeatedly, actual population outran the population estimates of the Social Security Institute (IMSS), thus causing the Institute's operations to be continually under-supported. Both public policy for increasing economic activity and population growth helped spur an unprecedented domestic demand for credit. Public banks, savings and loan agencies, and other specialized credit outlets saw their most active period yet. The number of these agencies as well as the total amount out in loans increased substantially. The entire banking system, including public as well as private banks, reported an increase of 38 percent in the total of loans outstanding.[43]

Despite significant economic successes, the country continued to be plagued by a weak national income policy and a low rate of return on public investments. Balance-of-payments problems were mounting, and a large part of the government's expenditures went towards interest on the national debt.[44] One critical economic sector, agriculture, was not keeping pace with the overall expansion of the economy, despite the heavy infusion of capital given this sector since the days of President Alemán. The *ejidos* and *minifundios* were particularly ineffective because they were not the prime beneficiaries of this capitalization. The "small private farm" category, which was the prime beneficiary, was also not living up to expectations. Here, once again, the Revolutionary program was in apparent conflict with increasing national need.

On the surface these were only a few dark clouds in a sunny sky of growth and stability. Increasing numbers of textbooks distributed under the free textbook program painted a glowing picture of the Revolution and its myth. To the world at large Mexico seemed to be successfully emerging as a modern industrial nation and regional leader. But in fact the deeper discontents were not alleviated.

One growing newer group particularly dissatisfied was the university students. They believed their expectations for employment were thwarted by the government elite. They saw revolutionary liberalism as dead in the higher government councils. As Mexico City was preparing to host the Olympic Games, waves of student protests,

---

[43] Díaz Ordaz, "Sexto Informe," *Hispano Americano* (September 7, 1970), p. 29.

[44] Public debt service as a percentage of expenditures doubled between 1960 and 1966 and continued to climb. In 1967 it was 10.2 percent of federal government expenditures. See Table 10 in B. Griffiths, *Mexican Monetary Policy and Economic Development* (New York, 1972), p. 24.

demonstrations, and even violence provoked the government to use unprecedented force against students in the Plaza de Tlatelolco on October 2, 1968. The official mortality figures initially ranged from 75 to 200. After the incident, some student organizations claimed figures in the thousands. One high-ranking government official said to the author speculatively that the truer figure might be much higher than the official figures. The rather high fatality figure is, according to informants, due in part to erroneous timing in military action. When heavy weaponry was brought in, the square and surrounding areas held not only protesting students, but also heavy evening traffic (theatre crowds, shoppers, etc.). Unknown numbers of innocent by-standers were fatally injured, but the use of such heavy weapons in crowded conditions could only cause serious consequences. According to informants, the figures released reflected estimates *prior* to the incident. Carlos Monsiváis describes the incident in graphic and detailed language.[45] Not surprisingly, official oratory reflected increasing effort to vindicate the Tlatelolco action as legitimate and necessary. "Order" was emphasized as essential for the continued progress toward revolutionary goals. Clear attempts were made to alter the legitimizing myth by having "social peace" (*paz social*) replace "social justice" (*justicia social*) in the hierarchy of values. " 'Social peace' is the reality and symbol of modern Mexico. This is one of the greatest victories of the Revolution. . . . [To] pursue the peace is an irrevocable obligation and a solemn responsibility for Mexicans. The maintenance of 'social peace' . . . is the greatest challenge which the Revolution has in the coming years." [46]

The choice of the next President by the Revolutionary coalition represented a marriage of diverse interests, although it was still a choice by center elements of the coalition. Luis Echeverría Álvarez was a lawyer and an educator. He had been politically involved as a student at UNAM in the early 1940s and had joined the party. While teaching at UNAM he worked his way up through the party and on into the government. In 1957 he was the chief administrative officer of the PRI. In 1963 he held an important post in the Interior Ministry, and became Minister of the Interior in 1964.

Echeverría, although a native of the Federal District, was married to the daughter of an extremely important politician from the west of Mexico. Thus his selection represented a political marriage of the

[45] Carlos Monsiváis, *Días de guardar* (México, D.F., 1970), 300 ff.

[46] An address by the President of the Supreme Commission of the Senate of Mexico, Professor Enrique Olivares Santana, "Official Address: Twenty of November Celebration of the XL Anniversary of the Revolution," *Hispano Americano* (November 30, 1970), pp. 8–10. Translated by author.

core region with a region hitherto underrepresented. Moreover, his father-in-law was a liberal, which helped satisfy liberal factions in the party. Echeverría developed extensive international contacts while in the government. His experience in the party, experience with university youth, and his law background were also undoubtedly helpful to his being selected.

The Echeverría administration clearly was concerned with political stability to the same degree that it was concerned with national development. However, Echeverría showed markedly greater accessibility than his predecessors. He declared that "to govern is to coordinate," and began with a clear effort to demonstrate responsiveness and responsibility through his personal style of governing. To Echeverría "social peace" meant more than just maintaining political stability. It was the duty of the government to insure the achievement of the Revolutionary program, and while pursuing this, to attempt to maintain "social justice." [47]

Echeverría's political style was unique among modern Mexican presidents. With little or no announcement he would suddenly go to conduct personal investigations behind the scenes. He mingled freely in crowds and conversed openly with the press. He visited all parts of Mexico, even remote rural areas. In this way he helped enhance his credibility of being a "different president," one who could truly reconcile what appeared unreconcilable.

Agrarian reform had to change. And to reflect this, the DAAC was reconstituted as the Department of Agrarian Reform. Echeverría told the peasants that they must increase production on the land they had because there was so little which was eligible for redistribution. Instead of emphasizing *Reforma Agraria,* he emphasized "integral development." Although this concept was not new, Echeverría now made it a cornerstone of public policy. "Integral development" is many things, but most importantly it means that the rural areas are to be an essential part of the nation and must develop as the nation develops. Programs such as expanding rural electrification, agricultural storage facilities, and feeder roads received mounting emphasis, as did model collectives, called *calpulli.* These model collectives were often formed with the assistance of high-level politicians, agricultural specialists, and urban intellectuals who used special loans granted for specific purposes such as bee- or poultry-raising to ameliorate the stark reality of the effects of rural overpopulation  One *calpulli,* a

[47] Claudio Brun Martínez, "Algunos aspectos importantes del pensamiento político de Luis Echeverría," *Tesis Professional* (Universidad Nacional Autónima de México, México, D. F., 1972), p. 41.

community cooperative on the *ejido* of El Rosal in the state of México, possessed 145 heads of families living on 140 hectares. Rural unemployment of the nation's youth was a continuing severe problem. In the past, the solution to this would have been to provide (or at least promise) farm land. Now with a shortage of land, another substitute had to be found: a rural employment program integrated with the aims of overall national development. The program was largely based on establishing relatively labor-intensive jobs, such as earthen dam and road construction, and jobs relating to agricultural food processing. Rural diversification was considered a viable long-term goal which could be assisted by this program. Improved means of transportation would bring financial benefits to all Mexicans, and relieving unemployment would help mitigate rural unrest.

Rural diversification had a counterpart in the government's plans. Mexico had been developing in a lopsided manner. A disproportionate amount of governmental economics and urban activity was centered in the Federal District and a few neighboring states. Up to a point growth in this way is desirable. However, matters had progressed beyond that point. The problems of providing basic services for Mexico City's newly arriving inhabitants had become a nightmare. Governmental offices were likewise so concentrated in Mexico City that virtually all serious decisions were made there. Decision-making as a result was unnecessarily time-consuming as well as inefficient. And too great a concentration of economic activity invited population influx which contributed to unbalanced development. To relieve these problems the government instituted programs to reduce immigration to Mexico City, dispersed governmental offices to the states, and encouraged business activity in the states — the application of the principle of "integral development."

Labor policy continued in the direction of more benefits for more union workers. The main effort was a low-cost housing program, although social security benefits were further extended. One and a half million workers were added to the rolls of the Institute of Social Security for Public Employees (ISSSTE). Two other changes are worth noting. CONASUPO continued extending its benefits to many more poor people. A new agency was founded, known as the National Fund for the Promotion and Guarantee of Workers' Consumption (FONACOT) to establish credit to unionized labor for durable consumer goods purchases. To finance all of these and still other welfare programs and agencies the government was forced into a heavier level of borrowing.

Another change in government policy had been the official attitude toward population growth. When Echeverría entered office, exploding population was not seen as the severe problem that it really was. In 1970 confidence was still expressed in the ability of the nation to continue supporting adequately all population increases.[48] But by 1973 the truth was becoming all too clear, and a population growth law was passed. Still another problem area received attention. The university graduates (primarily the 25–35 age group) who were discontented with employment opportunities found that Echeverría, unlike his predecessors, seemed more willing to use them to fill posts on federal commissions and in second-level management. Thus, a crucial group which had too often been ignored was given a place in the system. The inflation problem worsened. Emerging as a world-wide problem, it was seriously affecting the Mexican economy. The poorer classes were seriously hurt. In 1973 alone, a 10 percent increase in the cost of living was reported by the government. That summer, strikes spread across the country. The government responded by wage raises ranging from 10 to 20 percent.[49] In moves similar to López Mateos and Díaz Ordaz, Echeverría increased military benefits and ceremoniously distributed honors in this critical sector.

But like his predecessor, Echeverría did not really succeed in unifying the nation and assuaging discontent. Many extreme leftists went "underground" even as Echeverría attempted to modify the authoritarian, coercive stance of the regime. Terrorist groups spread throughout the country. Guerrilla bands operated in Guerrero and other states. Acts of violence, including kidnapping and assassination, spread fear of terrorism in the major cities. The highest levels in society were affected. A United States diplomatic official was kidnapped and ransomed for the freedom of 30 leftist prisoners. Even the highest levels of the Revolutionary coalition were touched when the future governor of Guerrero was kidnapped, as was Echeverría's father-in-law. The right-wing was also affected when Eugenio Garza Sada, a notable and wealthy *Monterreño*, was murdered as he left a bank on a busy Monterrey street.

The uneasy political situation was reflected in the government's sensitivity to criticism. Since 1968 the government had claimed that it was dealing with common criminals and not politically motivated guerrillas. But as terrorism grew so too did protests from the right.

---

[48] Luis Echeverría, Inaugural Address, *Hispano Americano* (December 7, 1970), p. 12. "I have said on various occasions that the demographic increase is not a threat but rather a challenge that puts to the test our creative potential." (Translated by the author.)

[49] Francis B. Kent, "The Growing Menace of Revolution in Mexico," *Los Angeles Times* (November 11, 1973).

The president of the Monterrey Bar Association charged that "no effective action . . . had been taken against the terrorists." [50] Wealthy Mexicans, who had previously refrained from publicly criticizing the Echeverría administration, now were loudly complaining. And criticism levelled at the government by outsiders was fraught with danger. Dr. Kenneth F. Johnson had published a book containing scathing criticism of the Revolutionary regime. In the early summer of 1972, he wrote a devastating polemic on the regime for the Mexican periodical, *¿Por Que?* He was arrested and held by Interior Ministry agents after spending a weekend with an official of the rightist National Action Party (PAN). Upon arrival in the United States after his expulsion, Johnson told newsmen that he had been held incommunicado with his wife and child for two days, that he had been accused of being an agent of the CIA, and that his captors had threatened to "throw our four-month-old baby out of a window and say it was an accident." This threat forced him, he said, to sign a statement "admitting to interfering in their [Mexico's] political affairs." The whole incident was reminiscent of the interrogation and expulsion from the United States of the well-known Mexican professor, Daniel Cosío Villegas, during the anti-Communist hysteria of the early 1950s.

The situation grew worse as counter-terrorist actions were undertaken by extreme rightist groups. Resolution of these problems was a growing national necessity. However, it was not clear if Echeverría's policies were going to accomplish this. Terrorist attacks seemed never entirely to stop — though only occasional strikes against wealthy or politically important persons merited notice in the mass media. Rural guerrilla bands were apparently crushed only to be succeeded by others. The status of the military in handling political violence remained crucially under the control of the Revolutionary coalition. And as the era of the old revolutionary generals and their immediate successors drew to a close, the attitudes and the problems of sufficient incentives (both material and psychic) of officers for junior rank became important to the stability of the Mexican political system.

### Ideology and Political Socialization

The nationalist, revolutionary tradition composed of ideals and heroes reaches back through time. The roots lie in the periods of Cárdenas and Zapata, and further, in those of Juárez, Hidalgo, and Morelos, and even stretching back to Cuauhtémoc and the days of Indian greatness. All of this has been shaped into an historical synthesis which focuses on the identity of the people and forms the basis

[50] *Los Angeles Times* (September 22, 1973).

of the existing national order. "Mexicanism" (*Mexicanidad*) is used to justify the present and the future. The Revolutionary coalition has found it a valuable means of subordinating the deep schisms in Mexican society to the implementation of policy and the stability of government. Many of the divisions which afflicted the Mexican people originated in pre-Conquest times, the Spanish legacy, and the turbulent periods beyond. The "formula" has clearly worked for a long time because the primary values and associational symbols have remained much the same since the Revolution. Underlying Mexicanism and the Revolution there is still a tremendously strong emotional appeal used by the Revolutionary coalition.

> Villa still gallops through the north, in songs and ballads; Zapata dies at every popular fair; Madero appears on the balconies, waving the flag; Carranza and Obregón still travel back and forth across the country in those trains of the revolutionary period, causing the women to flutter with alarm and the young men to leave home. Everybody follows them.... It is the Revolution, the magical word, the word that is going to change everything.... By means of the Revolution the Mexican people found itself.... [Its superiority] compared with our nineteenth century movements ... resulted from the profound manner in which its heroes, bandits, and myths stamped themselves forever on the sensibility and imagination of every Mexican.[51]

More pragmatically, economic development, internal peace, removal of the military and clergy from political authority, expanding the sense of national identity, displacing *continuismo* and *personalismo,* and the continuity of the Revolution have all been fed into the formula for maintaining stability and legitimizing succeeding governments.[52] The primary ideological emphases are unchanging: commitment to the nationalist, revolutionary tradition and the establishment of a Mexican national order. However, it changes in its secondary emphasis all the time. Also notable is that over time a gradual evolution has occurred with the evolution of the nation and the Revolutionary coalition. Increasingly, governments have emphasized the national good (rather than attaining revolutionary goals), and identified the national good with economic progress and the welfare of the people. Gradually, the references in rhetoric to national self-determination, patience, and hard work have been joined by coequal declamations of the nation's edu-

[51] Paz, p. 148.
[52] Brandenburg, 8 ff. He discusses major themes of the "Revolutionary Creed."

cational, social, and economic successes. Symbols of economic accomplishments along with an increasing educational focus on continued national improvement have become integral in the political socialization of the young and the ideology used for the continuity of the regime.[53] But because there tends to be an inverse relationship between the benefits symbolized by economic progress and the deprivations called for by the drive for economic growth, the older appeals to frugality, patience and hard work tend to become weakened in their effectiveness. This means there will be greater demands on the system and the myth of legitimacy.

Among the general populace *Mexicanidad* has been the major unifying symbol and mainstay of the Revolutionary coalition. It has continued to provide extensive — though emotional and unfocused — support for the legitimacy of government through identification with the Mexican national order. Evidence indicates that the loyalty of Mexicans is directed much more toward the nation and revolutionary symbolism than toward the ruling elite. "Only a minority of the Mexicans (less than one-third) attributes significance to the government, and even among this third a substantial proportion either takes a skeptical position on the benefits of government or rejects it as largely harmful in its effects." [54]

Thus, the symbolism of *Mexicanidad* has proven useful in furthering peace and stability alongside economic progress and social change. Nevertheless, newer social and economic realities have generated new demands for which the solutions no longer appear as clearly as in the days subsequent to World War II. Departure in practice from the original precepts of the Revolution becomes increasingly necessary, but every inconsistency makes it harder to reconcile the divergence between the ideal goals of the Revolution and the internal and external pressures of the closing decades of the twentieth century. The widening gap threatens the unifying force of *Mexicanidad* and the future of the regime.

[53] See the references to these matters in such seemingly diverse sources of official thought as the presidential inaugural address of Gustavo Díaz Ordaz and the *Libros de Texto Gratuitos*. Such sources are not so diverse as they seem for there is an ideology which is called upon for all occasions and in all circumstances whether in educational orientation or political ceremonial address.

[54] Gabriel Almond and Sidney Verba, *The Civic Culture: Political Attitudes and Democracy in Five Nations* (Princeton, N.J., 1963), p. 82. Hansen, following Almond, Easton, and others, uses the terms "diffuse" and "specific" in discussing types of support, and the modal typology of Robert E. Scott and others to categorize the support groups. Hansen, pp. 174–175, 183 ff.

# ✢ 2 ✢

# The Political System:
# The Culture and the Parties

The characteristics of the political system reside in the culture of
the Mexican nation. In the words of Margaret Mead,

> "Culture" . . . is an abstraction from the body of learned
> behavior which a group of people who share the same tradition
> transmit entire to their children, and, in part, to adult immigrants
> who become members of the society. It covers not only the arts
> and sciences, religions and philosophies, to which the word
> "culture" has historically applied, but also the *system of tech-
> nology, the political practices,* the small intimate habits of daily
> life, such as the way of preparing or eating food or of hushing a
> child to sleep, as well as the method of electing a prime minister
> or changing the constitution.[1]

The view of normative sociology is that culture can be understood
on several levels. Highest is the level of values. "Values" are un-
observable goals, the definition of what is desirable or undesirable in
the broadest sense. "Norms" are the applications of values in the
definition of prescriptive or proscriptive behavior to fit assumed situations. "Roles" and "status" represent a pattern of norms which are
perceived to reside in an actor. "Organizations" represent a complex
pattern of norms and roles of which some apply to the organization
as a whole and some only to different actors. The complexity of these
concepts limits the usefulness of a more detailed description.

[1] Margaret Mead, ed., *Cultural Patterns and Technical Change* (New
York, 1955), pp. 12–13. Italics added.

Concerning the importance of values, however, Karl Deutsch explains their function by analogy with traffic signals, signaling "stop" and "go" to actors on traffic arteries in a community.[2] This explanation suggests the dependence of politics on the culture of a nation. Another explanation succinctly indicates the importance of political culture:

The demands made upon the system, the responses to laws and appeals for support, and the conduct of individuals in their political roles, will all be shaped and conditioned by the common orientation patterns. They constitute the latent political tendencies, the propensities for political behavior . . . and as such they are of great importance in explaining and predicting political action.[3]

To understand Mexican politics, then, it is necessary to understand Mexican political culture. "Political culture," however, is not an entity separate from the cultural values and norms of the Mexican culture.

The continuity of the culture occurs through the socialization process. Through this process, whereby certain values, norms, and roles are taught to the new generation, expectations and behavior patterns are given legitimacy. The importance of the socialization process is also pointed out by Margaret Mead.

The traditional behavior practiced between parents and children, for example, is systematically related to practices which pertain between employer and employee, audience and speaker or actor, teacher and pupil, et cetera. . . . This systematic or patterned quality of culture is a function of the integrated character of human beings, who, as they incorporate cultural traits, sometimes very diverse in origin, organize them into viable ways of life.[4]

## Mexican Political Culture

Many of the characteristics of Mexican political culture, as all cultures, owe their existence to events of the past. For example, the persistent character of authority relationships is notable. This can be traced at least as far as the era of the Spanish Conquest, with its emphasis on the clerical hierarchy, the leadership role of the warrior,

[2] Karl Deutsch, *Nationalism and Social Communication* (Cambridge, Mass., 1966), p. 89.
[3] Almond and Powell, *Comparative Politics: A Developmental Approach* (Boston, 1966), pp. 50–51.
[4] Mead, p. 14.

and the ability to endure any strain or setback. The conquest of the New World was based in part on the belief of the *conquistadores* that it was their destiny to conquer. Acts of force received the mantle of legitimacy through religious mystique, sacraments, and a special relationship to the Church. Thus the warrior over the centuries became interdependent with the Church. These were the ancient hierarchical bases of rule.[5] In the Americas there developed such institutions as the *encomienda*. The Spaniard as conqueror was blessed by the Church and charged by Church and Crown with "protection" of the Indian. He always felt morally superior to the Indian under his "protection," but it was his actual strength, supported by clerical organization, which kept the Indian subordinate and opened the way to exploitation. The Indian's woman was the Spaniard's as well. She was "taken," as Hernán Cortes took Malinche, the chieftain's daughter.

*Machismo* is a belief in strength and a determination to exploit weakness so that the superior position of the *macho* can be achieved. This action is seen in the language today in the use of the verb *chingar*. Octavio Paz describes the importance of this word in *The Labyrinth of Solitude: Life and Thought in Mexico*. Paz points out that the verb probably originated in certain Aztec words. Despite its distant origins, *chingar* and its derivatives are used today in most of America and parts of Spain.

> *Chingar* also implies the idea of failure. . . . In some parts of South America *chingar* means to molest, to censure, to ridicule. It is always an aggressive verb. . . . In Mexico, the word has innumerable meanings. . . . One may be a *chingón*, a *grán chingón* (in business and in politics, in crime or with women), or a *chingaquedito* (silent, receptive, fashioning plots in the shadows) . . . but in this plurality of meanings the ultimate meaning always contains the idea of aggression. . . . The verb denotes violence and emergence from one's self to penetrate another by force. . . . The idea of breaking, of ripping open, appears in a great many of these expressions. The word has sexual connotations but it is not the connotation of the sexual act: one may *chingar* a woman without actually possessing her. . . . *Chingar*, then, is to do violence to another. The verb is masculine, active, cruel: it stings, wounds, gashes, stains. . . . The person who suffers this action is *passive, inert,* and *open* in contrast to the *active, aggressive, enclosed* person who inflicts it. The *chingón* is *macho*; he rips open

[5] Américo Castro, *The Structure of Spanish History* (Princeton, N.J., 1954), Chapters 1 and 2.

the *chingada,* the female, who is pure passivity. . . . The idea of violence rules darkly over all meanings of the word. . . . The verb *chingar* — maligned and agile and playful, like a caged animal — creates many expressions that turns our world into a jungle: there are tigers in business, eagles in the schools and in the army, lions among our friends. A bribe is called a 'bite.' The bureaucrats gnaw their 'bones' (public employment). And in the world of *chingones,* of different relationships, ruled by violence and suspicions — a world in which no one opens out or surrenders himself — ideas and accomplishments count for little. *The only thing of value is manliness, personal strength, a capacity for imposing oneself on others.*[6]

But the role of the "victim" of the *macho* is not forgotten. In a broad sense, everyone is the *chingada.*

Who is the *chingada?* Above all she is the Mother. Not a Mother of flesh and blood but a mythical figure. . . . The *chingada* is the Mother who has suffered — metaphorically or actually — the corrosive and defaming action implicit in the verb that gives her the name.[7]

Carlos Fuentes in some ways picked up where Octavio Paz left off in the elaboration of the psychological, cultural, and social consequences and in the dimensions of the frame of mind which goes with the word *chingar* and the way it permeates Mexican society. In his book *The Death of Artemio Cruz* he has expressed the situation forcefully in an entire chapter, a plea to the Mexican people to abandon this word and all its connotations because it stands in the way of their becoming a better people.[8] The plea is all the more eloquent because the novel is about a man who has lived his entire life without great satisfaction, and who has even structured his existence around being able to *chingar* those around him, his enemies, and his friends. He is disloyal to everything, except to the idea of his own survival. Symbolically the man represents Fuentes' view of the generation of the Revolution and the world they have based on *machismo.*

The *macho* is able to prove his strength by overpowering the weak: if one is open, one gets "taken." Everybody admires everybody else's *maña* just as they admire everybody else's *macho. Maña* in a sense is the game, a game which ends suddenly with the *macho* "taking" his opponent. This manner of thinking about the weak, the "open," and

[6] Octavio Paz, *The Labyrinth of Solitude: Life and Thought in Mexico* (New York, 1961), pp. 75 ff. Italics added.

[7] Paz, pp. 75 ff.

[8] Carlos Fuentes, *The Death of Artemio Cruz* (New York, 1964).

women as being different categories is significantly different from the Anglo "male chauvinist" view. This is the historical basis of *machismo*.

Today in Mexico *machismo* is one of the essential characteristics of any authority relationship. It adds distinctive facets to other traditional values: family, paternalism, hierarchy, and order. Cultural values in authority-subject relationships are important in Mexican politics, and the commandment of *machismo,* that all males must manifest their virility through forceful, and even violent, competition with their fellows, is fundamental to the process of governance.[9] It affects the entire realm of politics as it is carried on under the Revolutionary regime.

The violence, guilt, excessive competitiveness and consequent distrust of others which form the essence of *machismo* in Mexico aggravate conflict on all levels from childhood on. The members of Mexican society view their situation as essentially conflict-oriented.[10] Violence is accepted and represents society's divided and hostile nature. No social structure is free from conflict; in fact some even seem to owe their existence to continuing hostilities. Interpersonal conflict can easily escalate to group conflict, and vice versa. Moreover, conflict situations are the usual characteristic of this society. The ways in which *machismo* aggravates conflict hardly need to be stressed further. In any case, conflict can be viewed as essentially a process of schism and dissolution which can eventually weaken or destroy any group or social structure, including a regime. The profundity of both interpersonal and intergroup conflict in reference to *machismo* amounts

[9] Many anthropological studies of Mexico offer crucial insight into these and other facets of political culture. These have included George M. Foster, *Empire's Children: The People of Tzintzuntzan* (México, D.F., 1948); Erich Fromm and Michael Maccoby, *Social Character in the Mexican Village* (Englewood Cliffs, N.J., 1970); Oscar Lewis, *Life in a Mexican Village: Tepoztlan Revisited* (Urbana, Ill., 1951); Elsie Clews Parsons, *Mitla, Town of Souls* (Chicago, 1936); Robert Redfield, *A Village That Chose Progress, Chan Kom Revisited* (Chicago, 1959); Robert Redfield and Alfonso Villarojas, *Chan Kom—A Mayan Village* (Washington, D.C., 1934); Lola Romanucci-Ross, *Conflict, Violence, and Morality in a Mexican Village* (Palo Alto, Calif., 1973); Octavio Paz, *The Other Mexico: Critique of the Pyramid* (New York, 1972).

[10] Lola Romanucci-Ross, *Conflict, Violence, and Morality in a Mexican Village* (Palo Alto, Calif., 1973), pp. 30 ff. In a recent study she has described many aspects of the Mexican political culture in a particularly vivid and insightful analysis. Many of the following observations are due in part to her study. She also presents an outstanding theoretical exposition of the role of conflict along with a most useful and interesting discussion of the forms of conflict in Mexican society.

to more than mere competition for scarce material resources, because in the end it involves competition for one's own personal dignity, a value far above material things since early Spanish times.

It remains to be seen whether the entrance of women into Mexican politics can alter very much what was presumed to be an arena for male contestants. Since the forceful image of *machismo* is necessary to political success, women involved in politics must find some way to conform to the culturally approved image of dynamic forcefulness.

In this conflict-oriented view of the world the individual is struggling for survival in a hostile *human* environment. Survival requires an ability to overcome or at least to weather crises usually instigated by others. Distrust, suspicion, and cheating are healthy. "To a certain extent, individual responsibility is submerged in the notion that everyone will steal given the opportunity. An individual most often regards this as true even of himself." [11] Because of this prevalent belief, everyone tries to establish a "security system," obtained essentially by adapting "primordial" orientations to real-life situations.

> Primordial values designate those first-order attachments based on biological (genetic) relationships and residence. People who are related to others through family ties and more inclusive ethnic affinities often perceive a solidarity based on shared beliefs about their historical origins and contemporary life styles. Similarly, those who speak the same language, live in the same geographic region, or show a deep reverence for the land may also share a common identity.[12]

If the necessary and proper attitude for demonstrating one's *macho* is distrust and suspicion of another's intentions, then it becomes clear why Mexicans in politics speak of the *maña* of an individual as a desirable, praiseworthy quality. *Maña* refers to the ability to formulate stratagems not easily discerned by others, to fathom another's motives and plans, which are always presumed "hostile" and which must be thwarted before they reach fruition. An individual's lack of *maña* means that he will suffer transgression of his virility, the loss of *macho*. In Mexican politics the loss of *macho* to other individuals or groups can mean a painful decline in personal dignity, a loss of fortune, removal from power, or from politics, or worse.

*Maña,* then, is the opposite of the quality of "openness" that presumably allows any actual or potential enemy to "take" one. To have

---

[11] Romanucci-Ross, p. 121.
[12] Charles F. Andrain, *Political Life and Social Change* (Menlo Park, Calif., 1973), p. 59.

*maña* is to be sly, adept at formulating stratagems, good at duplicity. It is a prerequisite to the real *machismo* so generally desired by Mexican males. Together *macho* and *maña,* as operative norms of the society, require the male — especially the male in political life — to present an image of decisive, aggressive assurance, an intuitive, closed, calculating mental orientation, and a subtle cleverness.

*Macho* and *maña* together give Mexico its own distinctive problems with *continuismo*. *Continuismo* refers to the established political practice of "continuing" an individual as close confidant or trusted lieutenant to the point that relying on his services tends to block information channels and undermine the morale of younger men. To some extent this practice exists in all countries at all levels of political activity. *Continuismo* has been treated as an institutionalized problem in Latin American countries by both Latin Americans and Anglo observers, though it is certainly not absent from the Anglo side: consider the committee chairmen of the United States Congress. Nevertheless the Mexican case has its own meanings. The prevalence of *machismo* with its corollary emphasis upon *maña* maintains and diffuses conflict throughout the society. This in turn necessitates a personal "security system" rooted in values and institutions that have their origins in Mexico's history. There reside in the figure of Malinche feelings that feed *machismo, maña,* and the conflict in society, feelings which give shape to Mexican *continuismo* and the need for a personal "security system." The system is grounded in the values of family, paternalism, and hierarchy so characteristic of the Hispanic legacy. They are maintained alongside the paraphernalia of modern technology and economic growth.

The security system of a Mexican in political life is typical of that in society generally. Everyone tries to establish such a system in which the major relationships are "primordial," associated with one's early commitments. The system is basically obtained by adapting these orientations to real situations, but to do this requires cultivation of every possible source of support, an impossible task.

The strongest ties in the system are to members of one's nuclear family (see Figure 2). For a male these are typically strongest in the order of brother, mother, father, and sister, although the situation determines the degree of reliance. Next come the ties to members of the extended family: first uncles and cousins, then *padrinos* (godfathers). A *padrino* need not be part of an actual godson-godfather pair: the godfather relationship can be between two unequal individuals, the senior "giving" to the junior because of personal reasons. The last group of primordial ties are those associated with childhood friends, especially "true" friends, and affections toward a certain

*Figure 2*

The Individual's Supporting Relationships

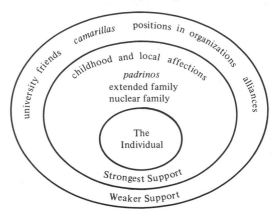

The closer the relationship to the individual, the stronger the ties. A "support system" is based on a unique set of ties used in defense against perceived threats.

locale. These are an individual's major resources. Other supports are used as the situation requires. Friendships from the university sometimes play a part. Alliances are basically linkages of *camarillas* and are often used in political situations. *Camarillas* are quasi-permanent, hierarchical, cooperative structures which are also crucial in the political arena. Lastly, an individual's own status and power resources in any organization he might be a part of are of great importance.

*Camarillas* perform a special function in the Mexican political system, transferring primordial ties to the conflict of the political arena. The *camarilla* is composed of a group of close collaborators centering on a "chief" with some position in the governing hierarchy. The more power he has, the more rewards come to his collaborators. This is the reciprocation for advancing the chief's position. It is the prime reason for the existence of the *camarilla*. The collaborators support the chief by supplying him with information and working for his goals. *Camarillas* are formed "vertically" across age levels as well as "horizontally" by peers. Each hopes to get its chief locked into a *camarilla* with a higher niche in the hierarchy. In this way one can speak of "*camarillas* of *camarillas*," wheels within wheels. *Camarillas* compete between themselves just as individuals do, forming still-larger circles or alliances. *Camarillas* do not make order out of the chaos of competition; their goal is attaining and maintaining control in the system. To do so, or merely to survive, a *camarilla* must link with higher positions in the hierarchy. While *camarillas* exist in all political situations, the only positions of real power are in the government, and posts in the Revolutionary party are sought as springboards for government positions.[13] In Figure 3 the social space has three dimensions: age, restriction in the number of collaborators (or participants) in the governing process, and position in the hierarchy. This typology exists in any nation, but these dimensions are particularly important here. There are other ways of transferring power in other cultures, but we are concerned with peculiarly Mexican features, such as the prevalence of conflict, extreme distrust, behavior patterns of withdrawal and arrogance, and doubt.

All these ties, so basic to an individual's security system, center on primordial values, whose function is to prevent destruction of the social fabric with its virulent hatreds and ceaseless struggles. Order and hierarchy were always closely intertwined in Church and Crown. Everything was viewed as having its natural, God-given order. The Church's order was a hierarchy of intercessors between man and God. The Crown's order was the king, through his hierarchy of nobles, providing for his subjects. The family's order had the head guiding and resolving conflicts and desires.

### Political Organization, Culture, and Continuism: Some Dilemmas

The emphasis upon family places an emphasis also on the status of its head. The family acquires status and prestige according to its lineage, and because the head has a special status, the prestige attached to the lineage is also connected with him and the continuity of his role. Each individual in the family acquires his or her sense of identity and status from this continuity, which is highly regarded in the deepest emotional sense, and therefore, as a basic notion, is legitimate. This legitimacy supports the individual's security system, and is critical to his personal identity and dignity (*dignidad*). Since the individual is brought up to value continuity it is natural for him to transfer or accept continuity in other structures than the family.

[13] See Kenneth F. Johnson, *Mexican Democracy: A Critical View* (Boston, 1970), pp. 67–76 for a working description of a *camarilla*.

*Figure 3*

## The Path to Advancement

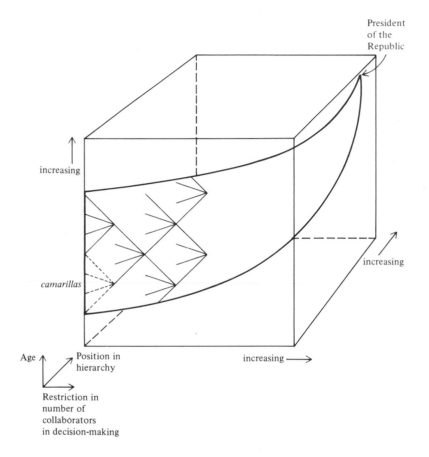

The dotted lines represent three camarillas which in turn form a larger camarilla. The best way to view this representation is as a cube containing a curved, triangular plane. The plane runs from lower age levels to higher, narrowing all the while. The plane also runs from broader participation to narrower, depending on position. However, in reality the shape is not a plane because it possesses depth. In fact, its shape is reminiscent of a pyramid. The position of the President of the Republic is only a symbolic representation; he is not usually the chronologically oldest individual in the hierarchy, but he is the titular head.

An arbitrary public deposition of an official who has held office for a long time may seem in bad taste to the general public and even be resented by many of them. Continuity in the family, paternalism, hierarchy, and order all extend easily to political organization.

If legitimacy is fostered largely through continuity, then continuism in a hierarchy is easily equated with something consistent with the Hispanic sense of order. But a person's continuity may also present many difficulties in a society where individuals rely most heavily on the primordial values of close friendships and alliances, because each individual assumes that others have interests which clash with his own, and in serving their interests he will be depriving himself. Dispersing to others a large share of the benefits coming from the system may eventually become threatening and reduce the value of continuity. Another dilemma is that continuing one's friends or allies over a lengthy period of time makes younger aspirants begin to see the promotion and information channels blocked. This can happen regardless of family connections, because the size of families means that some of the sons must make their own way in the hierarchy. Continuism in the hierarchy threatens an aspiring younger man not only with loss of distinction but also with the specter of downward social mobility for his branch of the family. Downward mobility is deeply menacing to the young man's dignity and brings with it such insults as pedestrian labor, small material returns, relatively mean surroundings in the home, the necessity of his wife having to do menial domestic chores or go to work outside at some low-prestige task. Worst of all is the prospect that his own sons will be deprived of opportunities, especially in education, and that his daughters will be unable to marry well. Continuism raises for the new generation the specter of denial of all the traditionally Hispanic values: dignity, wealth, leisure, and elegance, the style of the *hidalgo*. In this pattern the *macho* of the man moving downward is *chingado,* taken. Thus the "head chief" or the "highest *camarilla*" can bring down the entire political system by excessively continuing himself and his allies.

Individuals are continued because the paternal figure finds it difficult to remove men with long standing in a particular status. There is a tendency at all levels to equate continuity with legitimacy. Even more important, one's long-term associates become part of one's security system. In a society of conflict where trust is lacking, replacing key people in the hierarchy means painful personnel choices for the higher-ranking politicians.

In this milieu the change from personal continuism to political party continuism is one of the few plausible ways to maintain power. Some kind of continuism is expected by all members of the society, but over a period of time it results in progressively smaller circles of decision-makers and a growing disillusionment among younger aspirants. The body of discontented persons, potential rebels, increases while the circle of those holding control grows smaller. As in the *Porfiriato,* continuism threatens the leaders with moral and physical isolation from the main resources of the system and from the support of younger men, who might rebel because the system has become impossibly rigid and moribund.

In Mexico the characteristics of hierarchy, *machismo,* and *continuismo* pose serious dilemmas for the rulers, but at the same time facilitate suppression of possible rivals by the highest control group. They have only to co-opt the dissident leader by reward or threat and eliminate him from the arena. His followers are then left without a head, and become apathetic, ineffective, or directionless. However, real leaders are few. Consequently, it often pays the ruling group to co-opt a dissident leader and his personal following, especially when more extensive mass support is necessary to maintain control over the system.[14] Thus, the most promising manifestoes are likely to bring little reform. Even when there is a resort to violence and a revolution is successful, the new revolutionaries must maintain their own *macho,* their security system, and the old values of hierarchy and order if they are to legitimize themselves. Though they represent a new generation, if they promise changes which depart from the ancient core values, such changes will fail to materialize.

## PRI: The Institutional Revolutionary Party

Mexico's political system is frequently referred to as a one-party system, but there are in fact several parties. The one which wins the major electoral contests, however, is the Revolutionary party, which has been called PNR and PRM, and most recently, PRI. The organization of the PRI sets an example for organization of the other parties.[15]

The role of the PRI is the subject of controversy among observers. Robert E. Scott, for example, sees the PRI as a dominant, nonauthori-

[14] Romanucci-Ross, pp. 124 ff.

[15] The party has changed names three times and has undergone eight changes in organizational rules since 1929. When first organized at Querétaro in 1929 its title was *Partido Nacional Revolucionario* (PNR). In 1938 it was *Partido de la Revolución Mexicana* (PRM). Finally, in 1946 the party became the *Partido Revolucionario Institucional* (PRI). Changes in the party rules or "Statutes" occurred in 1933, 1938, 1946, 1950, 1953, 1960, 1971, and 1972.

tarian party, which functions as an aggregator of the various interests of its sweepingly inclusive rank and file.[16] Frank Brandenburg, on the other hand, regards the PRI as nothing more than an appendage of government, especially the executive branch of government. He views the existing arrangement as a benevolent despotism with the President of the Republic and a small coterie of trusted associates making the only significant decisions. In this latter view the constitutional limitation of no re-election provides the only deviation from an essentially authoritarian pattern of rule.[17]

While the author does not reject these assessments, his view differs in various ways. The Revolutionary party indeed dominates the legal opposition, is authoritarian in its structure, and is closely intertwined with the government. But the PRI cannot be dismissed as a minor office of the executive branch, nor can it be seen as the most vital source of demands on the system.

The PRI has three basic characteristics. First, it is both hierarchical and essentially authoritarian in nature, with decisions regarding party rules and personnel decided at higher levels and passed down. Second, the higher levels of the party are primarily composed of men who are also in the government, though they do not necessarily hold positions in the government corresponding to their high positions in the party. Because of this interconnection, the party acts in many ways as a ministry, capable of performing important functions that the formal channels of government cannot. Third, the structure and function of the lower levels of the party transmit information and citizen desires to the higher levels of party and government. The party is thus a significant element in the processes of governmental decision-making, and also forms one element of the hierarchical pyramid of control. The party came into being as a result of the need for stability among competing groups. The varying orientations within the normative framework espoused by the victors of the 1910–1917 Revolution produced thirteen years of post-revolutionary strife often marked by violence between divergent groups and their leaders. These difficulties culminated in the assassination of General Álvaro Obregón, the President-elect, in 1928. The assassination disrupted the presidential succession and raised the threat of an all-out civil war among the Revolutionaries who had established the constitutional norms and progressive goals that were designed to lead the country out of a situation of economic stagnation and backwardness.

16 Robert E. Scott, *Mexican Government in Transition* (Urbana, Ill., 1959), p. 146.

17 Frank Brandenburg, *The Making of Modern Mexico* (Englewood Cliffs, N.J., 1964), pp. 3–7.

The intense hostility between the Agrarista party, principal supporters of Obregón, and the groups supporting the outgoing President, Plutarco E. Calles, made it necessary to find some new solution to avert bitter civil strife. It was at this point that Calles introduced the idea of an inclusive single party which would incorporate all factions of Revolutionaries and provide established procedures by which these factions could work together to make decisions involving the succession to office at all levels.

Historians interpret in different ways Calles' motives in calling for the formation of a Revolutionary party during his State of the Union message in September 1928. One interpretation sees it as a clever, calculated move to achieve control of the presidency and all Revolutionary politics without violating the norm of no re-election.

> Calles emerged the full-fledged *caudillo* he had said Mexico would be well rid of. The chief difference between himself and Obregón was that he had the backing of a highly organized and united political party, which he ruled with an iron hand. He became, in short, the modern political machine boss so familiar in American politics. . . .[18]

Without entirely rejecting this view one can at least suggest that the innovation of Calles was a critical political decision. Calles made a choice which helped establish the basis for peaceful change in a country where violence was endemic. Rule by *caudillos* might otherwise have been easily perpetuated. If the Revolution has not terminated in another one-man rule as did the Reform, it is in part because of the decision made by Calles.

> He . . . use[d] this moment of tension and strife to attempt a bridge between the tradition of the *caudillo* and political democracy. The moment was tense with implicit tragedy, for the logic of political tradition required either a tyranny or a convulsion. That neither came to pass is to the credit of Calles, and it must be recognized as the beginning of that change in the political atmosphere which has since brought relative peace to the country.[19]

However, it probably would not have succeeded except for the advance toward the idea of a truly Mexican national order in the nationalist, revolutionary tradition.

[18] Daniel James, *Mexico and the Americans* (New York, 1963), p. 246.
[19] Frank Tannenbaum, *Mexico, The Struggle for Peace and Bread* (New York, 1951), p. 67.

The party which Calles brought into being was at first a loose coalition of regional parties and economically based groups. With the exception of the tiny Communist following and the labor leaders affiliated with Luis N. Morones, all other groups identified in some way with revolutionary ideals sent delegates to Querétaro in March 1929 to participate in the founding of the National Revolutionary Party (PNR). Not only was the new structure loosely knit in organizational terms, but its very inclusiveness presupposed an extensive range of views on agrarian reform, workers' benefits and treatment of the oil problem. Somehow these differences had to be resolved in terms of broad policy decisions. Calles was able to orient most of the choices in a generally conservative direction until after Lázaro Cárdenas became President in 1934. From that time on the views of the left wing of the party dominated Mexican government policy until Cárdenas left office in 1940.

The party was organized to unite the divergent revolutionary groups and reconcile personality differences among leaders. It was a political device created to provide the far-flung, leader-centered groups of the revolutionary tradition with a symbol of common interest. The *Pact of Union and Solidarity* which they signed at Querétaro provided a degree of moral pressure for conformity with newly established procedures in decisions concerning candidates.[20] The burden of proof morally — after March 1929 — rested upon any civilian or military leader who considered rebellion a viable alternative to party decisions.

The importance of the original purpose of unification cannot be emphasized too much. The Revolutionary party was organized to resolve crises that have recurred frequently in Mexican and Latin American history, crises of personal rivalry based on the primary loyalties of personal followings. Traditionally, leaders quarreling over the spoils of a victory carried their followers into the conflict. The ensuing violence undid the dream for which they had all struggled. The Revolutionary party was intended first and foremost as an institutional framework for dealing with this type of factional strife resulting from *personalismo*. It was only secondarily to serve as a way of eliminating personal *continuismo*.

## Evolution of PRI Structure

There have always been three principal organs of the party: National Assembly, National Executive Committee (CEN), and National Council. Formally speaking, the highest in rank has been the

[20] L. Vincent Padgett, *Popular Participation in the Mexican "One-Party" System* (unpublished dissertation, Northwestern University, 1955), p. 45.

National Assembly (or its replacement, the National Convention). The National Assembly has generally had the function of determining party statutes, statements of principles, and party programs. It has also selected the president of the party, and when doubling as National Convention, has nominated the presidential candidate. Whenever the statutes have provided for convention at the various levels, the conventions have formalized the party's candidates from President of the Republic through all the lesser public elective offices, while the assemblies have confined themselves entirely to internal party matters.

The National Assembly under the statutes of 1929 and 1933 functioned as the National Convention. It was composed of delegates elected indirectly through a series of conventions arranged in hierarchical order from the municipal level to the electoral district, the state level, and finally the national meeting. When the PRM was formed in 1938, a new arrangement for selecting delegates to the National Assembly emerged. Delegates were apportioned among four sectors which were titled Agrarian, Labor, Popular, and Military. Each sector included one or more groups for interest articulation. Each sector was to have a number of delegates assigned by another party organ, the National Council. In 1946, when the party became the PRI, the idea of a party primary based upon electoral districts as defined by federal law was introduced for selecting National Assembly delegates, but this was later abandoned.

The second of the three major organs at the national level has appeared under all the statutory arrangements from the conception of the party in 1929. It has been variously referred to as the National Directive Committee, the National Council, the Grand Commission, and once again, the National Council. Though this body has sometimes been able to select its own presiding officers, the most recent arrangement made the president and secretary-general of the National Executive Committee (CEN) its presiding officers.[21]

Presidents of the state committees are also on the National Council, as are 15 representatives from each of Agrarian, Labor, and Popular Sectors. The CEN decides which proportion of delegates the different associations within each sector should have, as was the case in many preceding years. The complexity of politics within the three sectors was indicated in the statutes of 1971 and 1972 in a special provision relating to numbers of dues-paying members, though there is no doubt that the CEN was the final arbiter in this case also.[22]

---

[21] *PRI Statutes, 1972,* Article 70.
[22] *PRI Statutes, 1971,* Article 17.

*Figure 4*

### The High Level Organization of the PRI (Formal Relationships)

Note: Solid lines indicate routes of authority or "control."
Dashed lines indicate routes of information flow to an authority.

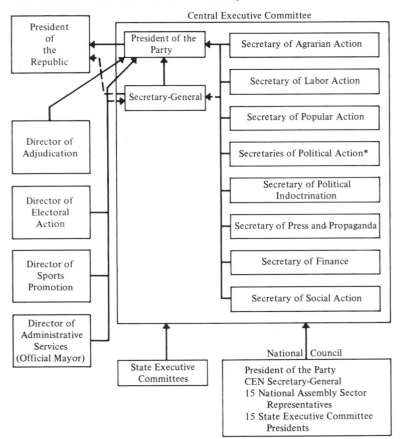

*One from the Senate, one from the Chamber of Deputies.

As in previous years, the only conceivable way in which the National Council could really affect decisions at the highest level of the party would be during a drastic rupture of relations among persons who constitute the top leadership of the Revolutionary coalition and the party. Only under such circumstances could some importance be attached to the National Council's powers of approval of orders for convocation of National Assemblies by the CEN, review of party

*Figure 5*

## The Low-Level Organization of the PRI (Formal Relationships)

Note:  Solid lines indicate routes of authority or "Control."
Dashed lines indicate routes of information flow to an authority.
Zig-zag lines indicate routes of personnel selection by election.
Specific limitations on an authority route are indicated by a one word description.

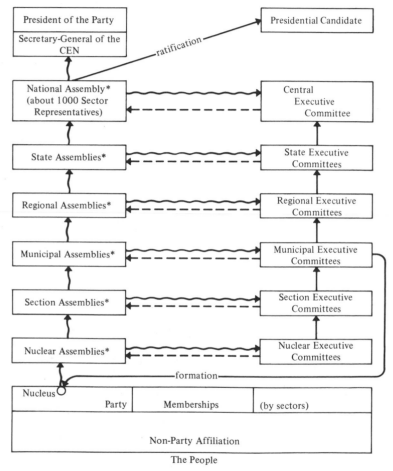

*Representation proportional by number of party sector memberships.

sanctions, re-establishment of party members in their rights, and the power to name a CEN president or secretary-general on an interim basis.

The CEN has always had more formal and substantive power than either the National Assembly or the National Council. It has convoked National Assemblies and established criteria for choosing delegates. It has convoked the National Council and specified how sector representatives to the Council should be chosen. It has been the center of disciplinary action taken against party members. Ultimately, it has been able to approve not only the minutes of the assemblies, but also the principles of the party's program and rules. It has appointed representatives to look in on party functions at all levels. In all the years since 1929, the statutes have gone through complex changes, but it is doubtful that the hierarchical order of control, centered in the CEN and its president, has been altered very much.

In the party structure the CEN president is the apex. He has the authority to call the CEN meetings, and he presides over its sessions as well as those of the National Council. He also implements the decisions reached in the sessions of the CEN and the National Council. Since his approval is necessary for all expenditures of the CEN, he controls the budget. He can by himself exercise the powers of the CEN in urgent situations. He acts as the representative of the party before all authorities and institutions in the country, or he can delegate this role to others. Formally, he is chosen along with the secretary-general of the CEN by the National Assembly; in fact, both these offices are responsible directly to the President of the Republic. The secretary-general monitors all activities related to the party and keeps the president of the CEN as well as the President of the Republic informed.

After 1946 there were three key offices in the CEN other than the president and the secretary-general. These were the secretariats representing the Agrarian Sector, the Labor Sector, and the Popular Sector. Secretariats of Agrarian Action and Labor Action were both formed in 1933.[23] Usually the person occupying either of these positions was the head of the most important organization in his sector.[24] After the Secretariat of Popular Action was established, it became the practice to appoint as its head the top functionary of the National Confederation of Popular Organizations (CNOP). This sector began to become very important after 1946.

The Secretariats of Agrarian Action and Labor Action reflected

[23] Padgett, *Popular Participation,* p. 30.
[24] Padgett, *Popular Participation,* p. 30.

the economic situation and initial priorities of the Revolutionary period of 1910–1917.[25] Agrarian Action was established to provide a link between the party structure and peasant organizations, especially at the state and national levels, such as the National Peasants' Confederation (CNC). Agrarian Action was formed to improve peasant life and to act as an investigatory agency for conflicts involving those connected with the peasant leagues. It was also intended to stimulate recruitment of rural workers into the party as well as to increase their party loyalty. In accord with the thrust of agrarian reform, the primary emphasis was upon *ejidatarios,* although other categories of rural workers and small property holders were sometimes included.[26]

Similar functions also existed for the other secretariats. The Secretariat of Labor Action was established to provide a similar linkage system between the party hierarchy and the affiliated organizations of industrial workers. Its function specifically included programs for the achievement of revolutionary goals, gaining benefits for the affiliated groups of the Labor Sector, and the investigation of complaints by workers and their organizations. The customary dominance of this secretariat from the late 1930s on by leading figures from the important Confederation of Mexican Workers (CTM) tended to isolate other labor groups from the services of the secretariat. Nevertheless for a time it provided an important channel of communication among elements of the Revolutionary coalition.[27] The Secretariat of Popular Action, which was similarly charged with representing the many diverse groups classified in the Popular Sector, promoting the party program, and expanding the party's membership in the Sector, was also linked to a major confederation.

It is important to note that these secretariats were explicitly charged with the political education of their memberships as a means of stimulating support for the regime. Emphasis was placed upon close coordination of the sector organizations in the interests of party unity and strength. An innovation of 1960 towards strengthening this — although not continued in later party statutes — was the provision for more consultation between the secretariats, reflecting the fact that they sometimes worked at cross-purposes.

Changes in Mexico's social and political environment were not adequately reflected in the functions of the formal party apparatus. Consequently, other aspects of the CEN altered. While Agrarian, Labor, and Popular Action were not de-emphasized, five new secre-

[25] Padgett, *Popular Participation,* p. 54.
[26] The development of the Secretariat of Agrarian Action is described in Padgett, *Popular Participation,* p. 30.
[27] Scott, p. 163.

tariats were established. The relative importance of each of these is indicated by the length and specificity of their definitions. Political Action Secretariat was headed by two congressmen, one from the Mexican Senate and one from the Chamber of Deputies. They functioned as liaisons with the national legislature and the party. Political Indoctrination Secretariat was charged with operating indoctrination centers in all jurisdictions, federal, state, and *municipio.* Press and Propaganda Secretariat was mainly concerned with party publications. Finance Secretariat collected dues from party members, took care of the accounting of party funds, and proposed a budget of expenditures to the CEN president. Social Action Secretariat was mostly concerned with community-development activities, campaigns to reduce illiteracy, and organizing festivities in honor of national heroes. There were also four subordinate offices created, some of which at times were more important than some of the secretariats. Electoral Action Directorate was responsible for organizing campaigns to register voters for the party and mobilizing party members for the public elections. Adjudication Directorate had existed for a long time without formal detailing in the statutes. It was the party president's organ for investigating the activities and conduct of party assemblies as well as potential candidates for public office. Sports Promotion Directorate sought to sponsor centers promoting sporting events and sports activities for youth. Administration Services Directorate was a housekeeping agency directly under the chief administrative officer, *oficial mayor,* of the CEN.[28]

Overall, these offices seem to point up rather well some of the priorities of today's PRI and of the Revolutionary coalition. Emphasis is less on sweeping reforms than on intraparty unity, recruitment, and mobilization of the rank-and-file. The party's greatest concerns have become effective communication among party and sector leaders, services for indoctrination of the rank-and-file, and institutionalized systems of record-keeping, an objective never characteristic of the party bureaucracy in the past. The author spent much time during the mid-1960s checking into the party practices of maintaining records of membership, dues-paying, basic biographical data, and activities and services of the party in relation to the frequently stated party concern for the militancy (*militancia*) of its members, and found that these were largely unimplemented. But form is one thing and substance another, and changes in some rules have never meant automatic, substantive change in the way the party functions.

It was clear by the late 1950s that the PRI and its affiliated orga-

---

[28] See, for example, Articles 87–102 of the *PRI Statutes, 1960.*

nizations badly needed overhauling to attract the newer generation of university students and neutralize the growing alienation caused by continuism.[29] The party's weakening popular image and the desirability of a loyal membership stood out as major concerns. Membership expansion was often urged, and was taken into account in the 1960 rule changes after student support of the violent strikes of the late 1950s, but not implemented. By the mid-1960s real change rather than rhetoric was needed. Selection of the veteran and dynamic Carlos A. Madrazo as president of the party in the mid-1960s marked the beginnings of important changes in party practices. The party's popular image and the necessity of a loyal membership were his major concerns. With regard to the former, Madrazo led the party forward on several fronts, particularly in an emphasis upon democratization of the choice of party municipal committees and party nominees for local government posts. The idea was to lessen the pre-assembly decisions made among sector organizations and reduce the influence of higher party levels which often resulted in unanimous votes in the municipal assemblies. Madrazo pointed out that the growing image of the party as the instrument of a few must be changed through actual expansion of popular participation at the grass-roots level of party organization. This was the meaning of the focus upon party nominations for municipal committees in most states during the first six months of 1965.

Moreover, attention was turned repeatedly to the problem of corruption within the Revolutionary coalition. Madrazo, who had distinguished himself by mid-1965 as one of the most dynamic and controversial presidents of the PRI central committee, supported the formation of a Commission of Honor and Justice to work with the Attorney General in order to clean up some of the racketeering among politicians. Pedro Vivanco, a leader of the Petroleum workers and Norberto Gómez Solis of the agrarian department (DAAC) were among the first singled out. Some enthusiastic younger politicians suggested that the great labor figures, Fidel Velázquez and Jesús Yurén, ought not to be overlooked.[30]

In still another move to provide more substance for the party structure and alter the party's character, Madrazo ordered the PRI and all its affiliated organizations to set up a record of all persons in their membership. The importance of providing independent finan-

---

[29] For various aspects of this problem see the monograph by William S. Tuohy and Barry Ames, "Mexican University Students in Politics: Rebels Without Allies," *Monograph Series in World Affairs* (University of Denver, 1969–1970).

[30] *Excelsior* (June–August 1965), *El Día* (June–August 1965).

cing for the party from the grass roots was recognized in the first systematic effort to record the "pledge" of each member for financial support. Madrazo said publicly that the party was in danger of losing the university students and that more must be done to recruit the able, politically articulate student leaders. In 1965 there were already plentiful signs of increased unrest among the university students, and it is to Madrazo's lasting credit that he was able to see this. He was, however, unable to convince the President and the powerful circle surrounding him that attachment to aging leaders and their methods should be changed in the direction of reform. Since it had become clear that change would take place in the directions that Madrazo had indicated if he remained president of the PRI, he was abruptly removed from the presidency in the fall of 1965.

In 1968 when the PRI's associated Popular Socialist party (PPS) lost its founder and onetime radical leader, Vicente Lombardo Toledano, there were some indications that Madrazo might be able to step into this slot. The left in Mexico had always needed some gifted person to bring together its many splinter groups, and Madrazo, if he had been able to do this, would have been in a position to oppose the PRI openly or force the top leadership of the Revolutionary coalition toward reform.

The flow of events strongly indicated the need for a shift in national policy and political strategy. Rural guerrilla activity and urban protests pointed to dissatisfactions unappeased by promises of future Mexican greatness and clear evidence of economic growth. The general bitterness of political divisions and the violence of student protests throughout the Western and third-world countries, in part a consequence of United States involvement in Vietnam, contributed additional aggravation. These world situations coupled with the signs of falling domestic support for Revolutionary coalition control set the stage for Madrazo to come forward in the role of political catalyst for unification of leftist reform in an effort to pressure alteration of revolutionary procedure and policy, but he was removed from the scene in 1969 when he died in an airplane crash.[31]

The *continuismo* which Madrazo had identified as a major problem was obvious to all but the vested interests of the Revolutionary coalition. The confederations which were supposed to be the vanguard of the Revolution in the fields of agrarian reform and labor rights were particularly notorious in this regard. Fidel Velázquez and Jesús Yurén, allied for decades with the Sánchez Madariaga brothers, had been the "Young Turks" of the Cárdenas "revolution" and lieu-

[31] Johnson, pp. 5–6.

tenants of the man who was regarded in the United States as the most notorious Marxist of all, Vicente Lombardo Toledano. Together they formed the mighty Confederation of Mexican Workers (CTM), which continued into the 1970s to dominate organized labor. In the 1940s they successfully dumped their old leader, Lombardo, and went on to dominate the Labor Sector. Yurén is now dead, but Velázquez has remained secretary-general of the CTM. A standing joke among younger Mexicans is that perhaps this year Fidel will really resign as he has indicated, rather than use a proposal to resign as a ruse to lure those with ambitions to succeed him into a vulnerable position where they can be eliminated.

Such classic cases of *continuismo* were also related to Madrazo's concern for opening up procedures of candidate selection, especially at the grassroots, to offset the sector leadership in the highest echelons that was beginning to decline through a developing political sclerosis.

When the author studied the party in the 1950s, it was still running on the energy provided by the change developed during the Cárdenas period. Even twelve years after Cárdenas had left office the only real politics in the country was within the Revolutionary coalition. Concern for the nature of political alignments within the Revolutionary coalition was then the major factor in evaluating the government and politics of the Mexican political system. The Revolutionary party in 1952 still depended for its rank-and-file support on organized groups within its three sectors. Most of these groups belonged to the Labor Sector or the Agrarian Sector. Cárdenas had organized them and got their loyalty to the regime. But by the mid-1960s the party committees depending upon these sector organizations and chosen by them were simply not capable of providing the political communication and responsiveness necessary for mass support from the party. The whole communications function among the sector organizations and committees up and down their respective hierarchies as well as their mass mobilization capability had become jeopardized by the retention of the same old men in the same old jobs.

Clearly neither the problem of communication of younger men with their elders nor the related problem of *continuismo* were being resolved by close-knit, extended families and *compadre-padrino* relationships. The life style of younger men differs from that of their elders. The emphasis on *macho* at all age levels aggravates competitiveness and makes it difficult for the older men to trust younger ones with responsible posts requiring effective communication. The older man who can maintain the level of vigorous activity necessary to keep his channels of communication open in hierarchical politics is just as rare in Mexico as elsewhere.

Madrazo thought that the way to solve the problem of *continuismo* was to move once and for all toward a defined party membership whose contributions to the party would be systematically evaluated. Substantial progress in this direction was simply not being made, and Madrazo's firm stand would have meant that a number of older revolutionaries at higher levels would have to step down. Yet in the early 1970s the party formally recognized Madrazo's earlier program for reform. The rubber-stamping by party assemblies was explicitly recognized as dysfunctional in the reform proposals of the Revisory Commission on Statutes to the National Assembly in March 1971. Principles of proportional representation and secret balloting were emphasized by the Commission as a cure to problems plaguing the political system:

> ... Democratization [will be guaranteed] in the municipal, district, and sectional assemblies through introduction of the requisite of proportional representation among delegates and elimination of any form of *"neo-caciquismo"* by secret vote of our "militants" in the municipal, district, and sectional assemblies.[32]

The key to the new reforms was found in the provisions of the rules relating to formation of "electoral sections" composed of "nuclei." [33] Sections (parallel structures to the existing sectors) were to have both their own assemblies and executive committees. Nuclei were to select delegates for the local municipal and district assemblies and elect the executive committee of the section. Section committees could be displaced by petition of section members to the National Executive Committee (CEN) of the party. The provision for nuclei took sector organizations (Labor, Agrarian, Popular) into account while providing for more direct contact of other public groups with the party organs.

Nuclei were supposed to have at least ten and no more than thirty members, but they could have less than ten members if the municipal party committees agreed. Nuclei were also to have their own committees and assemblies, and formally created the potential for handling the growing complexity of conflicting interests in Mexico. The nuclei provided the potential of better linkage to party and government hierarchies for the multitude of tiny organized groups that were not accommodated in the existing sector organizations. Perhaps more

---

[32] *General Proposal of Reforms to the Statutes, Sixth National Regular Assembly, 1971*, p. 7. (See also pp. 6–8.)

[33] *PRI Statutes, 1972*, Articles 4–9, pp. 8–10.

important was the fact that sector organization committees such as the National Peasants' Confederation (CNC) or the Confederation of Mexican Workers (CTM) no longer dominated the formal structure.[34]

Under the previous party rules, the labor union and peasant committees as well as the executive committee of the National Confederation of Popular Organizations (CNOP) formed the prime basis of party assembly and committee member selection. With this formal basis in the rules, the situation in practice developed as follows. Local organizational committees of the various sectors were responsible to memberships, which being controlled, ratified unanimously the slates of delegates to the local and state assemblies of the party according to the dictates of the national sector confederation executive committees. The sector executive committees had only to negotiate conflicts or differences of opinion in such matters with the chief executive of the governmental hierarchy at the level involved — the President, the state governor, or the municipal president.

Party committees were then composed of persons selected through negotiations by these two hierarchies, as were the party assembly delegates. Party assemblies rubber-stamped (*por unanimidad*) the decisions not only for internal party matters, but also in selection of party candidates who nearly always seemed to win elections to public office. The party committees' functions were principally those of liaison and communication between the two hierarchies, though there was unquestionably an important vertical channel of information going from the party offices up to the President.

Under the new arrangement, the sector hierarchies, although by the party rules the basis of party representation and action, no longer were the only channel for expression by rank-and-file members in local party activities. Instead, memberships of blue-collar unions, peasant organizations, and popular groupings were given an opportunity for formation of their own organizational units. These nuclei, sufficiently small for face-to-face contact and reinforcement, provided a manageable unit for assessment of membership activity by higher organs of the party and government. The new section committees, linking nuclei, were explicitly charged with maintaining various kinds of services: literacy, health, job-training, political indoctrination, and electoral activity.

The Revisory Commission report as well as the rules as amended in 1972 all emphasized two basic principles to provide substance for

[34] *PRI Statutes, 1972*, pp. 8–10. See especially Articles 4, 5, 6, 30, 40, 67, 82, 120, 135.

the structural additions of nuclei and sections. Specifically, the sections were given proportional representation in the municipal and district assemblies, which were then to select party committees at local and state levels. This was done proportionately by the number of persons which could be shown to be registered, dues-paying members of the party in that territory and section.[35]

The principle of proportional representation by size of section membership was given substance in the requirement that members of a section be recruited from the territorial jurisdiction of that section. This was true regardless of whether an individual who became a dues-paying member was placed upon the party rolls through presentation of his name by a sector committee or simply upon request of the individual himself. The executive committee elected by the assembly of a section's members was charged with keeping the roll and reporting to the party's municipal committee whether members were paying dues and performing the basic duties of registering and voting in public elections. Conflicts concerning accreditation of a member in terms of his sector organization affiliation were to be handled through the section committee reporting to the municipal and state committees of the main party hierarchy. In this way, still another step was taken away from the principle of functional representation introduced by Cárdenas, and away from the tyranny of *continuismo* in the old sector hierarchies.

Despite the party reform, the principles of hierarchy and discipline directed from above were maintained. Most importantly, the all-powerful role of the CEN was reaffirmed on every level. The reforms required a certain number of years of party membership for holding party posts, thus insuring that party regulars would hold these offices. An additional number of years were required for nomination to governmental or elective posts. Party membership requirements in order to hold various posts were as follows: for a nuclear committee, one year; for a section committee, two years; for all other committees and any public office, three years.[36] An executive office was attached to the CEN for the express purpose of checking on the electoral activity of members, making sure that they were registered and that they voted.

Another aspect of the Revisory Commission's report to the National Assembly of 1971 was an explicit attempt to deal with the

[35] *PRI Statutes, 1972*, pp. 8–10. This was also true of the 1971 Statutes. See articles 7, 8, 12, 13, 127 of the 1972 Statutes and 107 and 108 of the 1971 Statutes. Note that the main hierarchy executive committees can alter these principles at their discretion.

[36] *PRI Statutes, 1972*, Articles 118 and 148.

tragedy of Tlatelolco. The Commission asked the party to provide potential leaders among Mexico's youth with "more ample opportunities, rights, and responsibilities." The Revisory Commission stated that youth "constitutes . . . in this historical moment of Mexico, a political force whose opinion cannot be placed at the margin and whose participation is indispensable for completing and enriching our political process." [37] The Commission recommended in 1971 that the list of candidates (*terna de pre-candidatos*) for the local party offices of *regidor* and *síndico* should include a person aged 25 or under.[38] In 1972, the scope of the provision was expanded to include not only municipal offices, but the office of state deputy as well, along with the provision that not only a young person but also a woman should be included on the lists of pre-candidates.[39] The awareness of the increasing political importance of youth and women was reflected in the lengthy provisions describing their new formal status in the party structure. Two entire chapters of the 1972 Statutes were devoted to this subject. By contrast, the Secretariats of Agrarian, Labor, and Popular Action were limited to one section of one chapter and received no more notice than had been given them in the previous twenty years.[40]

The evaluation of the entire Mexican Revolution of 1910–1917 and the Constitution of 1917 made by James D. Cockcroft in *Intellectual Precursors of the Mexican Revolution,* described it as a "paper triumph." [41] At the end of the 1960s Manuel Velázquez quoted Jacques Lambert as follows:

At present, the official party system is able to appear as a tolerable procedure for resolving political contradictions. [but] . . . it has assigned more importance to political control than to the authentic militancy of the party; it has left its ideological image uncared for, which obliges it to run two risks: the loss from its

---

[37] *General Proposal of Reforms to the Statutes, Sixth National Regular Assembly,* 1971.

[38] *General Proposal,* pp. 7–8. With these exceptions noted above, the procedures for presenting the list (*terna*) of the three candidates that each sector is entitled to present to the party nominating assemblies (sometimes called "conventions") remained the same for approximately three decades. The procedures were first made explicit in 1960. The rules of 1972 took regional differences into account in a catch-all article (Article 120) and let the door open for use of the sections and nuclei. However, all decisions depended in the last analysis upon the CEN offices of Electoral Action and Legal Affairs.

[39] *PRI Statutes, 1972,* Article 123.

[40] *PRI Statutes, 1972,* Chapters 4 and 5, pp. 15–22.

[41] Quoted by Johnson, p. 7.

bosom of groups that are the most difficult to control through governmental channels and the disrespect of new generations upon not finding among its [the PRI's] members political objectives for which to struggle, when it has been reduced to just one more ministry of the government whose only function is of an electoral nature. [A third risk] . . . is to overlook the rebellion against traditional systems of political control.[42]

Velázquez then indicated areas critical to future successful use of the PRI as an instrument of political control: it should become "the ideological vanguard of the government"; it should become "the standard bearer of popular causes"; its objective should be to "struggle for the true interest of the people"; and its internal means of candidate selection should be changed by "implanting a method that carries the best of its men to power." [43]

Velázquez' prescriptions posed a dilemma for those in power, yet some real reform is fundamental to the mobilization of support necessary for the continued role of the Revolutionary coalition and the existence of the Mexican political system as it has developed since 1917.

The credibility of the regime was at a new low in the mid-1970s. However, even lower in credibility were the promises of the Revolutionary coalition to bring about reform within the political party which had been their tool for decades. Real reform unquestionably would involve the possibility that the party might grow stronger and become a political organism in its own right, less dependent upon the President of the Republic and other high persons in the coalition. The record of the past and the consideration of the central position always enjoyed by the President of Mexico in the political system seemed to argue that changes in the rules were unlikely to alter the customary situation.[44] In particular, the fate of Madrazo's effort to bring about substantive reform in ways other than formal rule-changes seemed to argue against the effective implementation of broader participation at the grassroots of the party. Time will indicate to what extent the new functions and structures for political reform have operated.

Nevertheless, the party has been a useful political mechanism. It

---

[42] Manuel Velázquez, *Revolución en la Constitución* (México, D.F., 1969), pp. 58, 59. Translated by the author. Quotation cited from Jacques Lambert, *América Latina* (Barcelona, 1964), p. 288.

[43] Velázquez, pp. 58, 59.

[44] Cline, Mexico, *Revolution to Evolution*, p. 159. Scott, p. 117. Manuel Ramírez Reyes, "El desarrollo histórico de los partidos políticos mexicanos," (*La Sociedad Mexicana de Geografía y Estadística,* unpublished manuscript, October 8, 1963).

has facilitated political communication and other functions. The key decisions in intraparty interest group conflict have been made by the president, but the party has provided a most important sounding board and listening device by which trial balloons can be released among the rank-and-file of power-seekers in the lower echelons of the Revolutionary coalition. The party has also been useful at all levels in assessing and reporting positive or negative sentiment and providing a buffer in conflicts between Revolutionary coalition elites. For decades the party was able to perform mediation and consensus formation sucessfully in many difficult situations. The most difficult situations were usually presidential successions. The position of the party always merited more careful consideration than would have been the case if the party were a mere appendage of government. The party continued to be an agency with its own personnel, procedures, and hierarchy of command, and possessed functions vital to the existing system of national control. The party offices always provided convenient meeting places for members of ideologically and occupationally diverse groups within the Revolutionary coalition. Also, party officials performed important liaison missions in communicating messages or making diplomatic representations to different factions.[45] Relevant also for consensus formation was the fact that the party officials, their political acquaintances, friends, and members of their families all were enabled to articulate arguments in favor of projected government policies in face-to-face gatherings among politically active individuals while planning strategies for the dissemination of propaganda to the masses.

The function of the party as a mediator of disputes and promoter of consensus within the Revolutionary coalition was also vital to the maintenance of the symbolic unity so useful to the coalition during periods of presidential succession. In fact, the party from its formation in 1929 provided a basis for cohesion of the diverse groups in some way identified with the symbol "Revolutionary." The presence of the party made the high-level decisions concerning presidential succession and the succession to lesser offices seem less arbitrary because there was a set of procedures for resolving disputes among the organizations and factions without recourse to violence. Moreover, the party provided the machinery for mobilizing the extensive support for its *inclusive* ideological position, public policy program, and its candidates for public office.

Within the context of Mexican political culture and history, recommendations and rules for secret balloting and proportional representation in assemblies are only likely to facilitate recruitment and provide

---

[45] For discussion of factions, see especially Johnson, pp. 73–75.

new incentives if the impact of the change seems reassuringly clear to the higher echelons of the party. That the political reform could only very indirectly affect major decisions is clearly indicated by the consistently reaffirmed authority of the CEN. In fact, the changes in procedure continue to depend for their substance, as was always the case, on the discretion of the inner circle of party leaders at the national level.

## Opposition Organizations

Opposition groups in the Mexican political system have been perceived in different ways. They have been viewed both as functioning political parties or, by Brandenburg, as "publics." Using this concept, he placed all the different parts of the Mexican political system in their position on the left, center, or right. This way of referring to the opposition, of course, would make it unnecessary to focus on specific opposition groups.[46] Johnson has pointed out most of the known organized opposition groups. He speaks of the PRI and its related groups as those which are involved in Mexico's "esoteric democracy."[47] Other groups he categorizes as either "satellite" groups or "out-groups." Satellite groups are those most likely to participate in public elections and least likely to use violence as a political instrument. Out-groups, on the other hand, speak frequently of violence and show little, if any, disposition to participate in the electoral system.[48] Brandenburg assumed that policy orientation was the critical factor in distinguishing groups because the organized opposition was supported by the government to maintain an impression of pluralism in ideological arguments. Johnson has found that the Party of National Action (PAN) on some occasions operates independently of Revolutionary coalition *sub rosa* support.[49] The author will treat the legally registered opposition groups as essentially independent, voluntary organizations, while accepting the fact that such groups have occasionally received some degree of financial or other aid from government sources.

## Transient Groups

One basic difference between the organized opposition in the last two decades and in the earlier years of dominance by the Revolutionary coalition is the absence of what can be termed "transient

[46] Brandenburg, pp. 119–140.
[47] Johnson, Chapter 3.
[48] Johnson, p. 114.
[49] Johnson, pp. 122–130; Brandenburg, pp. 144–165.

groups." These used to appear several decades ago challenging the PRI's dominance on the occasion of presidential elections. They presented the only serious threat to the presidential succession. The leaders and support of these groups were composed of dissident factions within the Revolutionary coalition itself. The pattern is worth mentioning because the stresses placed on the existing system of rule may once again make this kind of venture inviting to some member of the higher elite in the Revolutionary coalition who wishes to defeat the coalition candidate. Thus, it is important to know that this type of opposition, apart from its lack of permanence, had *personalismo* as its salient characteristic, with all the attention and loyalty of the group focused on the leader. Since the leader was himself a person who had been part of the Revolutionary coalition but had become part of the opposition through the frustration of his desire for the presidency, both the leader and his close followers had no intention of becoming a permanent, loyal opposition. Their objective was to cause division within the Revolutionary coalition itself, challenging the president's decision which deprived the leader of his hoped-for presidential candidacy. An underlying assumption of these groups historically was the use of force if necessary. This was not surprising in light of the fact that the leader and his followers were more often military than civil in their orientation. The pattern of such post-Revolutionary groups began as early as Obregón's rebellion against Carranza. It was manifest in de la Huerta's rebellion against Obregón in 1923 and in the election efforts of Vasconcelos in 1930. It was clearly represented in the elections of 1940, 1946, and 1952. In 1958 the formation of the Authentic Party of the Mexican Revolution (PARM) under the leadership of General Jacinto B. Trevino carried on this tradition, but it was a mere shadow of the threat posed by the earlier groups, and in fact has become an "official" opposition group.

In 1940 a very popular man in the Revolutionary coalition was frustrated in his presidential ambitions and went outside the coalition, divorced himself from the Revolutionary circle, and formed his own Revolutionary National Unification Party (PRUN). General Juan Andreu Almazán represented a real threat to the supremacy of the inner group dominating the Revolutionary coalition and to the carefully erected procedural framework of the party for validating decisions of the inner circle of influential persons; but in spite of his connections with peasants, some labor groups and other factions of the Revolutionary coalition, Almazán was unable to muster enough support to reverse the decision against him and gain the presidency. The Almazán–Ávila Camacho contest of 1940 was a bitter one and sometimes bloody, but it was fought in the area of civilian organizations, meaning that bodies of the military did not struggle against each other — rather it was organized peasants and laborers who played key roles. Military rebellion never materialized. When the moment of supreme trial had passed, the *almazanistas* never were able to regroup, and a few months later both the group and the leader had disappeared as major factors in Mexican politics. Some of the details of the Almazán affair are worth noting as typical of such cases in the past and likely patterns for the future in the event of a split in the Revolutionary coalition.

The organization of vast sectors of Mexican society into functional groups with strong commitments to support the existing control structure was an accomplished fact by the time Almazán campaigned for the presidency against Ávila Camacho. Almazán had had a considerable amount of contact with both peasant and labor organizations through his position in the military. As Zone Commander in the state of Nuevo León he frequently had occasion to side with peasants of the *ejidos* against the local *hacendados*. Although in doing so he merely carried out the policy of President Cárdenas, Almazán saw to it that the peasants remembered his part in aiding their cause. Similarly, with labor, the general did his best to secure the most political advantage for benefits rendered.

When it became clear that he could not obtain enough support among the groups in the effective power pattern, Almazán moved outside controlling political circles and tried to lure their elements of support to his cause. He asked for endorsements from peasant and labor leaders whom he had aided, then had these printed and circulated among the workers and peasants everywhere. A pledge of support from the officers of the *ejido* of Granja Sanitaria, El Alto, in the *municipio* of Montemorelos, Nuevo León, will illustrate this approach and point up the impression which Almazán sought to create among the peasants while he was Zone Commander in the north.

Señor General of Division
Juan Almazán, Monterrey, Nuevo León.

The undersigned [belonged] to the *ejido* of La Granja Sanitaria at the moment of the taking possession of the *hacienda* of El Alto which it pleased you to cede to us. [We are] thankful to your excellency for [the] great favor that we have received from you in . . . the grand extension of land that amounts to 854 hectares, or twenty times that which had been conceded by dotation to us in Monterrey. [We are also grateful for] the draft animals, plows and other instruments of cultivation that you have given us in addition to the allowance of seed corn that is benefiting us and the water that guarantees our crops. [We] wish to offer you at this time a vote of confidence with our gratitude and that of our families for the ever-so-generous way in which you helped us to resolve our problem.

Attentively,
"Land and Liberty"
El Alto, Nuevo León
14 July 1939

*Comisariado Ejidal —*
Julio Flores
*Consejo de Vigilancia —* Vincente Bocanegra, Luciano Sánchez. Antonio Rodrigues, David Castillo, Nicolas Rodrigues, Isabel Contreras, Juan Hernández, Jesús Martínez, Manuel Gonzales [and so on down the list of *ejidatarios*].[50]

Almazán especially tried to woo the labor organizations that had been identified with the "revolutionary" group but had remained outside the CTM. In Puebla he had notable success and won the Revolutionary Federations of Workers and Peasants (FROC) to his side. The Federation had significant strength in Puebla. However, the storm troops of the CTM attacked the FROC headquarters and broke its organization in the process. Thus, Almazán's base for a raid on the labor fold was cut out from under him.[51]

In 1946 Ezequiel Padilla made an effort to break the Revolutionary coalition by forming the Mexican Democratic Party (PDM) to lead interest group leaders in a secessionist movement. As in 1940, however, the effort failed, and the threat to the dominant position of the Revolutionary coalition and its inner circle of decision-makers was less real. In 1952 the frustrated office-seeker who deserted the Revolutionary coalition to challenge its choice of leadership for the presidency was General Miguel Henríquez Guzmán. This effort to split the Revolutionary coalition was better planned, better financed and more intensely emotional than that of Padilla. In these respects

[50] *Excelsior* (September 27, 1939). Almazán was already campaigning in this fashion against Ávila Camacho and his own former colleagues before the election assembly of the PRM. The assembly began on November 1, 1939. By September 23 General Heriberto Jara, president of the CEC of the PRM, had already announced to the Chamber of Deputies that Almazán would not be considered as a PRM candidate.

[51] *Excelsior* (September 12, 1939). It took the FROC a number of years to recover from the loss of this trial of strength.

it was more like the Almazán episode. Both Almazán and Henríquez were Revolutionary generals who had had important commands as well as important political jobs and high political standing in the Revolutionary coalition. Both men had had extensive relationships with the grassroots leaders as well as close personal connections with the inner circle of the Revolutionary coalition. Henríquez' party, the Federation of Mexican Peoples' Parties (FdePPM) made it seem like a real contest in 1952, just as the PRUN of Almazán had done in 1940.

In part, the splits within the Revolutionary coalition that occurred in the previous decades represented by this type of maverick presidential candidate were traceable to the key political positions occupied by the commanders of the various military zones into which Mexico was, and still is, divided. This was particularly important before the Revolutionary coalition had time sufficiently to stabilize both the procedural framework of the official party, with its accompanying legitimizing symbolism, and the positional relationships among its inner leaders. Commanders of the military zones, by siding with one faction or another, strongly affected the processes of deciding upon a new presidential candidate for the Revolutionary coalition. The leaders, or at least the principal figures in the plots and counterplots which divided the rulers of that time, were sure to be among the military zone commanders.

The importance of these earlier military figures should be viewed in the light of the fact that the army and navy never developed the corporate continuity typical of military organizations in some other Latin American countries. It was not that generals abstained from politics, but simply that the corporate continuity of the army was disrupted with the Wars of the Reform, although important military leaders, such as Porfírio Díaz, Victoriano Huerta, and Venustiano Carranza, continued to play significant roles. These and other generals were the personalist focus of political activity. Loyalty of their followers was not to a corporate military organization. The Revolutionary generals of 1910–1917 often possessed a sense of camaraderie, but this did not mean a sense of unity. This is typified by Obregón, Calles, and Cárdenas, as well as many lesser-known figures. None of these men was professionally trained for the military, and like Porfírio Díaz, they sought to diffuse the explosive possibilities of corporate military loyalty by attempting to focus loyalties on themselves and service within government. Should the political situation depart from the established pattern of inner-circle stability it is a real possibility that the military as a corporate structure will emerge as a weighty factor in a manner atypical of recent Mexican history.

This view of the political potential of the military goes against judgments by such scholars as Cline, Lieuwen, and Cumberland.[52] These Anglo authors speak of the "professionalization" of the military, which they take to mean essentially de-politicization. In contrast, the prevalent belief among the politicians of the Revolutionary coalition is that they have been successful in systematically diffusing corporate loyalties of the military officers by providing them opportunities for participation as civilians in governmental and business bureaucracies. Members of the Revolutionary coalition seem to feel that this established policy of systematic rewards, recruitment, and "retraining" will continue to prove effective in helping to maintain the viability of the present system of rule. This view is in part predicated on the generally successful past experience with the old Revolutionary generals and their immediate successors.

Yet these views overlook several things. As Brandenburg pointed out some years ago,

> The stockpile of several thousand younger officers probably constitutes the most concentrated force of highly educated and surely best-disciplined men in the entire nation. For many years they have observed as their senior officers shared in the allocations of contracts let in their respective military zones, or obtained low-interest loans from government banks. And they have noted that accountants, engineers, small businessmen, and even full-time university professors receive higher salaries than theirs. Without this officer corps behind it, the Revolutionary elite cannot continue to direct the destiny of Mexico — and of late, much of the younger officer corps seems noticeably impatient for more authority and higher income.[53]

Even as more political and administrative duties are required of the younger officers, they are increasingly aware of their own importance and relatively disproportionate rewards. Politically the regime has come to rely much more heavily on these young officers to deal with unceasing terrorism and guerrilla activity. As officers trained primarily for military pursuits, they have been forced into the political task of containing extremist dissidence on a growing scale. The conflict between their apolitical training and their increasingly political roles causes contradictions and doubts in the minds of the younger generations of officers. This is made more acute by the fact that terrorist

---

[52] Cline, pp. 174 ff.; Edwin Lieuwen, *Arms and Influence in Latin America* (New York, 1960), pp. 101–121, 168–170; and Charles Cumberland, *Mexico: The Struggle for Modernity* (New York, 1968), pp. 273–274.
[53] Brandenburg, p. 160.

activity has never before been systematically used as a political tool by the regime's opposition. And the suppressive activity of the military is for the most part directed against the same urban middle-class elements and the same generations from which these officers are recruited. These factors, plus the relative inadequacy of the rewards given them, place a great deal of stress on the loyalty of these younger officers to the civilian leaders of the Revolutionary coalition. "Professionalization" is therefore problematical. In 1975 the military was given the opportunity to express itself as a distinct group in the public forum through its new publication *Insignia*. This is one means of increasing the perceived status of the younger generation of officers. It can also reinforce identification as a corporate military.

## Permanent Groups

Since 1952 no political groups have appeared corresponding to the transient groups led by Almazán, Padilla, or Henríquez. Other political groups which have manifested opposition to the dominance of the Revolutionary coalition have had a different style and have, in some cases at least, shown genuine staying power. Staying power or permanence on the Mexican scene, so far as political groups are concerned, must be evaluated in terms other than participation in presidential elections alone. The real test as to whether a group can be considered a permanent opposition group hinges on whether it shows an inclination to involve itself in the contests that arise between the presidential elections every six years. The posts involved might be those in the federal Chamber of Deputies, in state legislatures, or municipal councils.

By the early 1970s, many American writers referred to any legally participating opposition in Mexico as "co-opted." In the case of the Party of National Action (PAN), this may be too simple, as Johnson has pointed out.[54] Other groups, such as the Authentic Party of the Mexican Revolution (PARM), fit the category rather well. The case of the Popular Socialist Party (PPS) is less clear. Vicente Lombardo Toledano, who founded the party in the late 1940s after being displaced as the leader of the CTM, possessed such personal wealth as to make it doubtful he would ever have risked losing it by leading a determined attack against a unified Revolutionary coalition. The PPS, while legally participating in electoral activity until Lombardo's death in 1968, provided a base of operations for some dedicated young politicians of the left. Both the PAN and the PPS were able to get their views into major newspapers.

[54] Johnson, p. 122.

Under the present regime, the oldest institutionalized opposition in Mexico actually has roots that reach back to the beginnings of independence and beyond. The PAN is the legally participating descendant of those who waged civil war on behalf of the Spanish heritage of power, privilege, and racial dominance resting on the symbiotic relationship of clergy, military, and the wealthy families of the great landholding and commercial classes. The PAN emerged as an opposition party at a time when Mexico had been carried far to the left by the policies of President Cárdenas. Originally it was composed of a small but highly influential group of intellectuals and professional men and was led by Manuel Gómez Morín. The group had economic and human resources far beyond what its small numbers would indicate.

It is important to remember that the PAN never has represented all sides of the conservative opposition in Mexico. It began with a definite elitist orientation, thinking only in terms of a small number and refusing to compete for mass support. This meant that the PAN to be effective at election time had to support some group that was appealing for endorsement of the masses. Thus the PAN in 1940 supported Almazán and in 1946 Padilla. However, in 1952 the PAN began to think in terms of larger-scale involvement in electoral activity on its own and nominated Efraín González Luna as its presidential candidate. This set a new pattern, and the PAN again put forward a candidate for the elections in 1958 with Luis H. Álvarez as standard bearer. In 1964 the PAN presidential candidate was José Gonsáles Torres, and in 1970 the PAN candidate, Efraín González Morfín, also attempted to appeal broadly to voters.

Becoming active in presidential politics placed considerable stress upon the cohesion of the innermost circle of the PAN. Clearly, in order to make any headway as a contender for votes it was necessary for the PAN to expand its membership and in so doing to broaden its appeal. Essentially it was a small group with an elitist focus representing church-oriented political views, the views of some of the older and more prosperous businessmen and drawing to it a number of upper- and middle-class professional people.[55] To develop a mass following, however, it was necessary for the PAN to create new associations or find some group that already had something approximating wide popular support. To some extent the PAN did this in 1952 and followed much the same course in 1958, working with the Sinarquista group, which had wide rural worker support in some areas, particularly

---

[55] Johnson has done extensive field observation on the political attitudes of PAN adherents. Particularly helpful have been his "Ideological Correlates of Right-Wing Political Alienation in Mexico" (a paper presented at the annual convention of the Western Political Science Association, March 1965) and *Mexican Democracy*.

in north-central and northwest Mexico. A few labor unions also joined the PAN, as did many lower middle-class white-collar workers. Support was particularly widespread in the states of the North, where many felt that Mexico City under the PRI had forgotten the interests of their area. In 1952 the PAN could only run a poor third against the overwhelming strength of the PRI and the very strong challenge of the *henriquistas* (FdePPM). With the defeat came disillusionment on the part of those organized groups that had joined the PAN. Some of them disbanded, and others found their way into the ranks of the PRI as part of the Revolutionary coalition.

One group of leaders under González Luna argued that PAN should forget its attempt to muster mass support and return to the original idea of an elitist opposition with an orientation against accommodation within the existing legal and political framework. Another group, however, argued that the more the PAN attempted to recruit broad support and function as a more-or-less loyal opposition, the more the party could influence decisions made within the Revolutionary coalition and that this latter course was clearly the most beneficial. The modified conception of a "loyal opposition" won as the election of 1958 approached. For the most part the Sinarquistas dropped away, but many votes were gained through the outspoken and hard-driving campaign launched by the PAN candidate, Luis H. Álvarez. Álvarez did not demand abolition of a revolutionary program. Instead, he demanded reforms to provide more popular benefits. He particularly emphasized social welfare benefits and better administration of existing programs. He denounced corruption and argued for doing away with the existing rulers because of their ineptitude and failure of devotion to the public service.

As in 1952 the PAN was successful in attracting many supporters in the north. But in general throughout the country the showing was poor, and the PAN claimed that it had been defrauded in the electoral count, and the handful of *PANista* deputies did not immediately take their seats by way of protest over the way votes were handled.

The struggle within the party on the question of whether or not to seek mass support continued, and in 1959 a split occurred. The moderates, led by Gómez Morín, were defeated by the more militant elitist group led by González Luna and a young firebrand, Felipe Gómez Mont. The victorious group was in favor of an intransigent policy toward the Revolutionary coalition, a policy to which they referred as "direct action." The results were riots in the states of Chihuahua and Baja California during the state and local elections of 1959. By 1964 the pendulum had once again swung back to the more moderate position with the nomination of José González Torres as presidential candidate.

Although the approach of the PAN in 1964 can be characterized as moderate, it nonetheless launched numerous attacks against sensitive aspects of the system. The PAN charged that there was lack of equitable distribution of political information and urged that there be more concern for impartiality and truth. The PAN argued that the government should cease supporting a political party, and that the colors of that party cease to be the same as those of the Mexican flag. With regard to the vote itself, spokesmen of the PAN demanded a truly impartial body to count and judge the vote so that "the real vote" of the people would be taken into consideration. PAN leadership recognized its disadvantageous position in relation to the government party, but pointed out that the PAN was fulfilling a civic need in struggling for political liberties and electoral reforms.

Leaders of the PAN suggested that a Communist conspiracy was being carried out in Mexico — labor unions were mentioned in this regard. The PAN complained that labor unions had a tendency to exploit workers for political purposes. To make unions more vital and socially useful organizations it was urged that balloting in the unions should be secret in order to avoid pressure by leaders, that leaders should be forced to account fully for their handling of funds, and particularly that union funds should not be used to advance the personal political goals of the leaders.

Unexpectedly for a right-wing group, the PAN argued that a system of cooperatives would be a useful way of reducing the inequitable distribution of wealth in Mexico. The PAN further recognized that cooperatives were very much in existence on the Mexican scene but charged that they had been deformed and obstructed by government, that cooperativism had been "surrounded by a series of bureaucratic obstacles."

The PAN argued that *caciquismo* and the problems of municipal autonomy presented great difficulties. As the presidential candidate, José González Torres, put it: *"Caciques* have continued even though it would be easy to get rid of them because the government is illegitimate in its origin and in its exercise and finds in the *caciques* the point of support for organization of mass demonstrations." [56]

Not only is the *cacique* a problem of municipal government, there is the problem of federal interference itself. The federal government, PAN said, had taken away legitimate and important municipal income and excessively imposed its authority on municipal governments. This had the effect of "converting municipal government into little more than a police force for collecting fines from drunks."

PAN speakers maintained that one of the gravest problems was a

[56] *Excelsior* (April 3, 1964), translated by author.

land-tenure arrangement in which the government demands political submission of the peasant in exchange for the loan of some land. The PAN position called for all Mexicans to be owners of a small portion of land. In any case, said the PAN, neither small property owners nor *ejidatarios* can be successful where there is a lack of accessible and inexpensive credit.

Another difficulty plaguing the life of the farmer, argued the PAN, has been governmental interference as a middleman in the marketing process. It was charged that the National Popular Subsistence Corporation (CONASUPO), the government marketing corporation, was fixing the value of products at a rate below the market and forcing farmers to sell at that rate while other products remained free under the laws of supply and demand. It was also said that livestock raisers had been suffering undue hardship because the government cancelled certificates of inaffectability.

This program of reform instead of revolution prompted a response which well illustrated the lack of confidence the Mexican people have in the ballot. Specifically, there was the charge from Mexicans (and from American observers as well) that the PAN had made a "deal." There was a widespread tendency to dismiss the PAN as co-opted, especially after González Torres came out against hostility and violence directed toward the PRI candidate Díaz Ordaz. But the PAN replied to its critics by saying that the best posture for the party was one that would fulfill the civic need to struggle for political liberations and electoral reforms, that even a few seats in the Chamber of Deputies and continued participation in presidential election campaigns would be beneficial to democracy in Mexico.

An important consideration for the future of the PAN, insofar as legal opposition is concerned, is that it has become progressively less concerned with those types of charges which were once central to its attack upon the PRI. For example, the charge of collusion between the PRI and a Communist conspiracy in Mexico no longer characterizes the pronouncements of PAN spokesmen. The demands for religious participation in public education also have become much more muted. Of increasing importance are the demands for the decentralization of governmental functions, especially in education and public works, so that the collection of taxes and distribution of monies by the federal government may be lessened in favor of state and municipal decision-making. Moreover, the old bromide that "the PAN is a party of women" might still have some substance in terms of the large number of its women supporters, but it is clear that not all women are attending only on the basis of their dedication to church and clergy. Rather, it may be that the PAN offers a more meaningful

THE CULTURE AND THE PARTIES 103

political role for women than the PRI, especially for younger women. The PAN position indicates a definite awareness of the pressing problems among small cultivators — that the *ejidatario,* for example, should simultaneously be supplied with adequate technical and financial services while being prohibited from abandoning his land. PAN has linked the ever-growing problem of inflation to the tendency on the part of the government to print money rather than admit the scarcity of investing capital.[57] Finally, the PAN had begun to make a direct bid for the mass support upon which the Revolutionary coalition had relied, exemplified in González Morfín's cry in 1970 that "neither blue-collar man, nor *campesino,* nor bureaucrat are anyone's property, whether *patron* or government." [58]

The defeats which the PAN has suffered have not kept the party from continuing its activity within the legal limits afforded by the regime. When Lombardo, the titular head of the legally registered leftist opposition (PPS) died in 1968, the PAN remained alone among the legally recognized parties as a group still partially free of co-optation by the Revolutionary coalition. The PPS continued to exist under the leadership of Professor Jorge Cruikshank García, but the official proclamation of support for the PRI which Cruikshank García gave in the name of the PPS just prior to the 1970 election came as a surprise to no one. Neither was it a surprise when the PPS began to experience desertion by intellectual and labor groups who proclaimed that the only true Marxists in Mexico were within their ranks. The PARM, composed as it was of very old Revolutionary generals and their personal cliques, had long since passed the point of mobilizing real opposition to the Revolutionary coalition. General Juan Barragán as presidential candidate, along with a few candidates for the Chamber of Deputies, was unable to persuade most observers of any real independent effort, despite a proclaimed stand in favor of greater opportunities for youth.

The history of ineffectual legal opposition is clear.[59] No party has been able to challenge the supremacy of the PRI on the national level. However, this does not mean that the Revolutionary coalition does not concern itself with the legalities of electoral reform or theories of

[57] Conchello Dávila, *Hispano Americano* (June 18, 1973), p. 15.
[58] *Hispano Americano* (July 6, 1970).
[59] For contemporary Mexican views on the history of political parties see Jose Gabriel Guerra Utrilla, *Los partidos políticos nacionales* (México, D.F., 1970); Daniel Moreno, *Los partidos políticos del México contemporáneo (1926–1970)* (México, D.F., 1970); Manuel Velázquez, *Revolución en la Constitución, perspectiva de la Constitución, la ideología y los groupos de presión en México* (México, D.F., 1969).

democratic government. For example, in late 1972 electoral reforms were introduced by President Echeverría with the stated purpose of bringing greater electoral participation and democracy to the nation:

> The National Congress and all the Legislatures of the States approved reform and additions to Articles 52, 54, 55, and 58 of our Constitution.
>
> These reforms adjust electoral districts in accord with the demographic growth of Mexico and increase the number of Deputies the party can have, improving participation of minorities in legislative activity. Reforms, in addition to [allowing] election of Deputies and Senators of 21 and 30 years of age respectively, improve the opportunity for the new generations to share in public power. The lower house [Chamber of Deputies] will maintain its effectiveness and will from now on be a more representative organ and correspond more closely to the present composition of the national community.
>
> The Electoral Reform seeks to include a greater number of citizens and social forces in the institutional political process. Its purpose is to increase the representativeness of public power by consolidating on the legal level the new tendencies of Mexican democracy and invigorating the participation of minorities and, in general, it intends to provide all political views expression in the representative organs of national will.
>
> These reforms are part of a general revision of the Mexican electoral system. In this session [of the Congress] I will present an initiative for the reform of the Federal Electoral Law. It will guarantee to all parties full representation, with voice and vote in the electoral organs, and substantial modification in the organization and operation of the National Register of Voters will be provided. These measures will make more efficient the application of the principal of uniformity in the function of the organization and operation of the [electoral] process in which the national government is involved.
>
> It is intended also to guarantee political parties more effective communication with people and better diffusion through various ways of their ideological position, statements of principals, and programs of action.
>
> Respectful of ideological dissidence and committed to perfecting our democratic way of life, we wish to assure [political] minorities of their representation in the organs of the State. *We don't see in parties a menace to stability but rather channels for the expression of the will of distinctive political tendencies. On*

*the other hand, we do not accept activity of groups which press to achieve merely personal interests by an illegal means.*

*Renovation of all parties ought to accompany the renovation of electoral mechanisms.* In these movements in which the country is transformed, these institutions also ought to bring themselves up to date to reflect faithfully the opinions of the electorate.

*In the elections of Federal Deputies which will take place in July 1973, the reforms which we have undertaken will be put to the test. We exhort the citizenry to participate more actively in the political process.* The vitality of democracy depends on fulfillment of civic responsibilities. The development of a people includes all its forms of organization. Political development undergirds and gives meaning to economic progress.

*Democracy is not only a system of power; above all, it is a way of living together.* It is a concern for all Mexicans to convert it to a rule of daily conduct. *We will do our part. We will guarantee and nourish all public liberties.* It is for the political parties, the peasant organizations, the unions, the teaching centers, the mass media, and all organiaztions to democratize their internal life and exercise responsibly their rights.[60]

This policy statement contrasts sharply with the statements made by the President of the National Executive Committee (CEN) of the PRI shortly before the elections of July 1973:

The democratic life of Mexico does not depend just on us for betterment, it also depends on the opposition. What view do we see in this respect? The opposition doesn't even fulfill a basic role which belongs to it in any political regime — resist in order to support. It doesn't resist and therefore doesn't support us. The opposition concerns itself more with us than defining its objectives and proposals. Criticisms of what doesn't concern it are its reasons for existence. We're going to take her [*occuparnos de ella*]; touching her as little as possible [*lo menos posible*], I promise it.

*We repeat that the country needs a clean opposition. We need those who think different from us to participate in the national political life.* And now we ask: is verbal violence as a substitute for real force the way to convert yourself in truth into a real opposition? The National Action Party [PAN], so

[60] Luis Echeverría, Second State of the Union Address, *Hispano Americano* (Sept. 11, 1972), p. 21. Translation and italics by the author.

it appears, expert in ideological juggling games through the entirety of its history, intends today to convert its own unsureness, even if by word, into the only security for the country. ...

We gladly admit that in Mexico there is a plurality of ideas and interests, and that it would be desirable if this plurality of ideas and interests could be translated into a multi-partyism. But multi- or bi-partyism presumes alternatives. Is there by any chance an alternative in our country? If the National Action Party [PAN] in place of juggling one line after another had followed just one line it would have in our day the sincere support of the conservatives that still exist. But the original conservative line has been discarded to the rubbish heap, and today the banner is incongruent opportunism.[61]

As President Echeverría had said, the test of the reforms came in the elections of July 1973. Table 2 indicates seats won in the Chamber of Deputies in those elections. Clearly, the doctrine of democratic pluralism outlined by the President was not the result. After this election there were the usual charges of substantial improprieties in the vote counting. There were the usual rumors that the PAN won substantially in Baja California. The major bases of support for the PAN

*Table 2*

**Seats in the Chamber of Deputies**

|         | 1958† seats | 1964† seats | 1970† seats | 1973 seats |
|---------|-------------|-------------|-------------|------------|
| PRI     | 153         | 175         | 178         | 189        |
| PAN     | 6           | 20          | 20          | 4          |
| PPS     | 1           | 10          | 10          | 0          |
| Other** | 2           | 5           | 5           | 1          |
| Total   | 162         | 210         | 213         | 194*       |

* The discrepancy in the 1973 total is related to disputes over seats in the Chamber of Deputies.

** Most regularly has included the PARM.

† Presidential election year.

[61] Jesús Reyes Heroles, *Hispano Americano* (June 18, 1973), p. 17. Reyes Heroles (as the PRI president) was addressing a major party function. Translation and italics by author. It is interesting to note the inherent violence in his address. The *macho* image comes through clearly, especially with the picturing of the opposition as a female who will be violated.

lie in the more highly developed areas. Baja California is an area of notably rapid urbanization, trapped migrants, and other discontents perhaps intensified by close proximity to the U.S.[62] Despite its poor showing, the PAN probably did not lose substantial support; its recent electoral history showed the consistency of the support given it, and indicated the strength of cultural factors which seemed to assure its continuing support by certain groups in the population. The PAN *was* "taken" as Heroles indicated that it would be. The potential for success of a legal opposition in Mexico continued to depend on the attitude of the PRI.

## Fringe Groups

The reports in the early 1970s of terrorists in the cities and guerrillas in the countryside warrant the mentioning of some of the best known groups whose ideology accepts violent methods. One group deserving mention is no newcomer to the Mexican scene. It comes first on the list because of its ideological connection to Hispanic culture and the values with which Mexican conservatives identified in their struggle against the liberalism of the nineteenth century. Today this group is known as the National *Sinarquista* Union (UNS). The word *sinarquista* comes from two Spanish words *sin* and *anarquía*. The two words in combination mean the antithesis of anarchism and signify a regime with order. The movement has always had a conspiratorial tone which reaches as far back as its foundation in 1937. Despite controversy over whether or not European fascists were the prime movers in the group's formation, the group was associated in the minds of most observers in the late 1930s and early 1940s with that type of Mediterranean authoritarianism which produced fascism in Italy and the *falange* in Spain. The beginnings of the movement appear to have been located in León, Guanajuarto in the mid-1930s, but the movement itself began to receive wide attention both in Mexico and abroad only in the mid-1940s. The rank and file has always been composed of peasantry with near-fanatic church orientation. These

---

[62] Barry Ames, "Bases of Support for Mexico's Dominant Party," *American Political Science Review* (March 1970), pp. 153–167. See also Wayne Cornelius Jr., "Urbanization as an Agent in Latin American Instability: The Case of Mexico," *American Political Science Review* (Sept. 1969), pp. 833–857; Orrin E. Klapp and L. Vincent Padgett, "Power Structure and Decision-Making in a Mexican Border City," *American Journal of Sociology* (Jan. 1960), pp. 400–406. The geographical distribution of PAN strength is indicated by Donald J. Mabry in *Mexico's Acción Nacional, A Catholic Alternative to Revolution* (Syracuse, N.Y., 1973), pp. 142–143. PAN strength seems prevalent in historically proclerical states.

were the same kind of people that made possible the War of the *Cristeros* against the Calles government in the 1920s. The rhetoric of the movement's leaders has always been extremely critical of the existing regime and particularly of whichever member of the Revolutionary coalition was President or the presidential candidate. All men on the political left in Mexico were criticized in the same fashion. In fact, the Revolutionary coalition was for decades equated with communism in *sinarquista* literature. When the *sinarquista* leader José Antonio Urquisa was assassinated in 1938, the UNS embarked upon a program of sporadic rioting which caused some loss of life and lasted into the mid-1940s. The *sinarquistas* spoke of it as their war against the Communist-designed, government-abetted plans to liquidate their organization. Early in the 1950s the *sinarquistas* began to rely on peaceful tactics, and even went so far as to consider a liaison with the Mexican splinter party Nationalistic Party of Mexico (PNM) in 1964, after the change in electoral law had opened the possibility of gaining some seats in the Chamber of Deputies. This particular venture into the fringes of the constitutional framework came to nothing when the Minister of the Interior claimed that the PNM did not have the required 75,000 members necessary for legal participation in the elections.

While the *sinarquistas* have always conducted themselves in a highly conspiratorial fashion, it nevertheless has been easy to determine where their headquarters are, and it is doubtful whether there is much about their operations which is not known to the Interior Ministry and the different agencies of the police which might be interested. It is unlikely that the organization is directly involved in the terror which now plagues Mexico, but its ideology certainly provides sufficient stimuli for any alienated young Mexican of the right who might wish to associate himself with terroristic activity. The main tone of *sinarquismo* is hatred — of communists, Jews, Masons, and the Mexican government — but this is mixed with a strident nationalist tone. In their rhetoric the nation is above reproach; only the government is bad. Action, will, the Catholic faith, and the family are the keys to the Mexico sought by the *sinarquistas*.

*Sinarquismo* affects and is affected by various other organizations with extreme rightist tendencies. One of these is the organization known as Opus Dei, which is thought by some Mexicans to be an organization whose strategy is determined by members of the clergy with roots in the Spanish *falange*. This organization no doubt receives funds from various sources, for it is believed to be well-financed. One of its known connections is the Social Union of Mexican Businesses (USEM). Johnson reports that Opus Dei also contributes to the *sinarquista* movement by channeling funds to their publication, *La Hoja de Combate.* Moreover, wherever the *sinarquistas* or even PAN engage in attacks upon the free textbook program begun by López Mateos, they will find support in the official publication of Opus Dei, called *Gente.*[63] In addition, a small number of youths among the *sinarquistas* who come from atypically wealthy homes and attend a university have their own youth section which connects with the notoriously radical and violent right-wing student movement known as MURO. Support for MURO again comes, no doubt, from various sources, but it would appear that Nuevo León and Puebla are important centers. MURO is structured in secret cells, some of which participated in the student violence of 1968.

To be aware of *sinarquismo* and *sinarquista* ideology thus leads to awareness of the principal ideological value structure for the right wing in Mexico. It is essentially Hispanic, and in the event of civil war it would be no more congenial to United States foreign policy and interests than would the views of the left.

Leftist political orientations have had a history of organizational futility for fifty years, though this does not predict their failure in the future. Ideologically the left of the mid-1970s has roots in the anarcho-syndicalism of the late nineteenth and early twentieth centuries. Among the publicists who most bitterly attacked the personalist regime of Porfírio Díaz was the French theorist Georges Sorel; among the best known were Enrique and Ricardo Flores Magón, who were also familiar with the work of Marx and Engels. From exile these and other theorists fed the basic notions of modern revolutionaries into Mexico through underground papers and pamphlets. Mexican youths of that day absorbed the ideas and took them along when they joined revolutionary armies after the *Pax Porfiriana* broke down in 1910.

Luis N. Morones and his associates in the effort to mobilize Mexican blue-collar workers were affected in their early years by anarcho-syndicalism as well as Marxist theory. The shadowy, conspiratorial air characteristic of organizations with perspectives shaped by such ideologies generally results in reports of the group beginnings and internal maneuvers which are markedly varied.[64] However, it does ap-

63 Johnson, p. 130.
64 Enumeration of the most reliable sources on early Communist Party experiences in Mexico would place the work by Victor Alba and Robert Alexander near the top of the list. Johnson's account illustrates the variation, for example, when compared with Alexander's. Victor Alba, *Histórica del Communismo en América Latina* (México, D.F., 1954). Robert Alexander, *Communism in Latin America* (New Brunswick, New Jersey, 1957).

pear that the Mexican Communist Party (PCM) began to take form in Mexico in 1919–1920. It also seems fairly clear that North Americans from the outset were instrumental in the formation and direction of the party.

All reports appear to agree on the receipt of foreign subsidies. This pattern of dependence upon subsidies seems to have even extended to the receipt of funds by the party from the Mexican government itself. The expression so common now among American scholars, "to be co-opted," which would be vulgarly translated as "bought," is thus an old story to the left in Mexico. It well illustrates a statement attributed to the President of the Republic and General of the Army, Álvaro Obregón: "There isn't a man alive who can withstand a cannonade of silver." This covert attachment to the public trough in the decades since its founding has caused numerous difficulties in the Mexican radical left. From time to time splinter groups have developed and have generally been in their early stages more prone to violence in word and deed than the established PCM. The old-line party has then customarily fired the epithet "Trotskyite" at such upstart groups in the radical left.

Many individuals who began by distinguishing themselves as leftist firebrands wound up living the good life in the mansions of such desirable suburbs of Mexico City as San Angel, where the great former Marxist labor leader Vicente Lombardo Toledano for years had an elaborate home. Lombardo, Velázquez, and Yurén all began with strong ties to Marxism and the PCM, as did in later years the once radical peasant leader of the General Union of Mexican Workers and Peasants (UGOCM), Jacinto López. During the 1960s, when discontent was rapidly growing, still other leaders and organizations appeared in militant leftist roles, only to drop out of political radicalism when offered an establishment-related post or financial reward. Thus the notorious leftist party of Lombardo, the PPS, usually came out for peaceful solution of internal problems after the early 1950s. Similarly, the radical Independent Peasants' Confederation (CCI) also showed signs of aging in the latter 1960s.

The effort on the part of a galaxy of separate groups of leftists, collectively known as the National Liberation Movement (MLN) came to nothing in the early 1960s when it became clear that no one possessed the necessary attributes for uniting the left except for the aging Lázaro Cárdenas (now deceased). However, Cárdenas' association with left-wing movements never had indicated a willingness to threaten the national order and destroy the Revolutionary coalition he helped found. It would, however, be erroneous to suggest that the left in recent years has failed to produce leaders who would go to prison rather than be "bought." Demetrio Vallejo took the risk and suffered for it in leading the rail strike of 1959.

David Siquieros, ranked with Diego Rivera as perhaps the greatest Mexican muralist, was imprisoned throughout most of the 1960s before he was released to die of cancer in relative freedom. But even Siquieros did not live his life in deprivation for the leftist cause, as his home in Cuernavaca illustrated.

Nevertheless, evidence of personal sacrifice for leftist causes is indisputable. Some former members of the MLN showed their intentions to continue the struggle against the regime. For example, Raoul Ugalde and Victor Rico Galán were imprisoned on charges of having derailed trains and other violent acts. Ramón Danzós Palomino of the CCI suffered the same fate. Rebel peasant leader Rubén Jaramillo was assassinated. Some splinter groups from Lombardo's PPS were involved in the guerrilla movements of Michoacán, Guerrero, Oaxaca, and other states.

The willing example of these and other individuals to risk imprisonment and even death makes it necessary for all persons interested in the future of Mexican politics to take political protest seriously. Protesting students inspired the incident at Tlatelolco in 1968 and the street violence of June 1971. The continued terrorist attacks reflected the dedication of protest gone underground. The extent of government arrests for subversive political activity was extensive as the ransom demands of terrorist kidnappers indicated. Moreover, those involved in the national strike committee at the time of Tlatelolco and in the so-called *Grupo Miguel Hernández* did not give up the violent orientation which characterized their actions at that time. The Sparta Communist League (LCE) and the National Confederation of Democratic Students (CNED) widely circulated the Maoist publication *China Nueva* with its intransigent revolutionary line.

The terror waged by some of these leaders and groups hit members of the most venerable, high-status families in the business and social community in Monterrey. They were badly shaken by the kidnapping and shooting of the aging Eugenio Garza Sada, owner of banks, factories, radio-television facilities, and extensive other interests. This took place on a busy Monterrey street and capped "an uninterrupted chain of such incidents. It also [provoked] an unprecedented chorus of complaint among wealthy Mexicans" in Guadalajara and Morelia as well as Monterrey. These circles had previously refrained from publicly criticizing the Echeverría government. Sergio F. de la Garza, President of the Monterrey bar association and spokesman for the family, charged "that no effective action . . . had been taken against the terrorists" and challenged the government's repeated assertion (since Díaz Ordaz' State of the Union message of September 1, 1968) that it is dealing "not with politically motivated guerrillas, but with common criminals." De la Garza demanded that the government "treat the terrorists . . . for what they are, guerrillas." Another relative said "that those who killed Don Eugenio will be punished if captured, but those who poisoned their minds and armed them must be punished as well." [65]

Sons of families who aligned themselves with the Garza Sada family joined with rightist terrorist groups to gain revenge, while their elder spokesmen hinted that losses to great families such as the Garza Sada family should be repaid in blood if necessary. These spokesmen called for the Revolutionary coalition to comply with the promises of "order" which were made by Díaz Ordaz at the time of Tlatelolco. The pattern of attacks showed that these leftist groups were not primarily attacking the Revolutionary coalition, but rather the leading families of the right. These and other incidents raised the spectre of reviving an old conflict between opposing leftist and rightist families.

The hatreds engendered by civil strife beginning with the Wars for Independence and lasting throughout the Wars of the Reform, French occupation, and the co-optation of the *Porfiriato* by pro-clerical families did not die with the Revolution of 1910–1917. Both the *Cristero* Rebellion and *sinarquismo* reflect continuations of this rivalry. The irrational, essentially non-ideological feelings that have lasted this long have been muffled by an uneasy alliance between elements of the Revolutionary coalition and the pro-clerical industrialists of the north and west. Because of the government's development goals and success in establishing a national order, which served the interests of both sides, peace was maintained. The resort to terrorist and guerrilla activity on the part of both wings invigorated a potential conflict situation at the national level which the Revolutionary coalition had to reduce in order to maintain the existing system of rule.

The conservative clerical families represent the direct lineal descendants of those who supported the Spanish cause at the time of Independence, the conservative cause at the time of the Reform, the last years of the *Porfiriato,* and the counter-revolution of Huerta in the 1910–1914 period. Because of their long-standing tendencies, they can never be regarded as trustworthy allies by the major elements of the Revolutionary coalition. By contrast, the Revolutionary coalition has resorted to recruitment and support of members of families with a long-standing leftist tradition.

[65] *The Los Angeles Times* (September 22, 1973).

The Revolutionary coalition is unlikely to destroy these traditionally leftist, urban professional families in order to allay the fears of
the right, although leftist members from time to time are likely to be
imprisoned, or even executed if necessary. The importance of the
claim by the Revolutionary coalition that those involved in these
violent activities essentially represented criminal elements was that the
Revolutionary coalition was not ready for an extensive purge of
members of families that had always supported the basic principles
of nationalism and Revolution. As Cárdenas' reliance on these leftist
families shows, they can be useful allies in furthering the pursuit of
reform and the national interest. The future of the regime in the
early 1970s was very much tied to the success of policies calculated
to deal with the old quarrels and the demands of the newer Mexico.
Should these policies fail, then speculation concerning the use of conflict and coercion might be more to the point than discussion of the
use of the ballot and the electoral future of the PAN.

Public electoral activity has never reflected the realities of Mexican
politics very well, whether internal or external to the Revolutionary
coalition and the PRI. For this reason, the continued legal participation of the PAN as well as its expanded ideological base for attracting
mass support should not be taken to mean that there will soon be an
election in which the PAN can use the difficulties plaguing the Revolutionary coalition in order to win the presidency by popular vote. Such a
manifestation of genuine choice by ballots is difficult to imagine,
taking into account the shallow roots which Mexican experience af-
fords in a United States-style "democracy" for such a shift in governing elites. The use of violence as a political instrument has been
always close to the surface, even across the relatively unruffled decades
of rule which the Revolutionary coalition has enjoyed. Even in recent
history, the 1940s and the 1950s had some significant instances of
violence in political situations. Juan Andreu Almazán, in the presidential succession of 1940, and Miguel Henríquez Guzmán in the
1950s both represented threats of widespread civil disturbance. The
1960s brought an increase in protest demonstrations. Especially in
the latter 1960s, university and some secondary students contributed
to higher levels of conflict. An increased use of government force
was paralleled by a growing abandonment of the peaceful solutions
advocated by the legally recognized opposition. In the face of massive suppression by the government, some groups formed by students
and other dissidents resorted to urban terrorism and rural guerrilla
activity. In the early 1970s the Revolutionary coalition was determined to meet violent public demonstrations and terrorism with any
necessary force. Indications for the future are that the Revolutionary

coalition will seek to maintain control by authoritarian and coercive measures when confronted by a sufficiently severe threat. Although the stated emphasis on opening communication channels and distributing benefits remains a major strategy of the Revolutionary coalition, violence will continue to be an important resource of dissident groups in the future. Legal opposition will continue its role as loser, whipping boy, and peaceful articulator of disagreement.

## The Problem of Change
## in the Pyramid of Political Power

If electoral contests were between strongly competitive political parties, the conduct of elections would have been an important concern of this chapter. Similarly, electoral reform within the parties would have been a major issue. However, both the political culture and the historical experience shaping modern Mexican politics have resulted in rule by dominance rather than an open competition among peers. Undisputed dominance has never ceased to be the highest value of Mexican political life. Participation does not mean a vote for a candidate; it means a political tithe. Gradual emergence of institutionalized continuism by the Revolutionary coalition points up the higher value placed upon dominance, just as in the management of elections by Juárez and the subsequent *Porfiriato*. Beginning with the first efforts for Independence and self-government, Mexican political groups have revolved around the charismatic leader (*jefe*), the clique (*camarilla*), and the alliance of cliques. Mexicans have sought the personalism of leaders sufficiently magnetic to hold diverse interests to a single purpose and control whatever values were there to allocate. Subjectively and objectively, when stripped of rhetorical and symbolic meaning, distribution of power in a strictly hierarchal fashion has meant upward "flow" to leaders, and while crossover alliances can be noted, power is always pyramiding. This is because vertical ties are much stronger in experience and perception than horizontal ones. For the outsider this reality of Mexican political culture has not been easy to accept. That is why some foreign observers have spoken hopefully of the organization of political power according to popular participation in a foreign sense. This is the basis for the often-encountered arguments that replacement of the Revolutionary regime by an authentically revolutionary one would open the way for a true peoples' democracy. Goods would be evenly distributed and votes fairly counted while effectively functioning mass parties compete nonviolently for the majority's support, and for its needs and interests. But the difficulty with viewing Mexican political life through lenses modeled for analysis of non-Mexican phenomena is that they over-

THE CULTURE AND THE PARTIES 115

look the universality of the operative hierarchal, personalist, continuist values and norms. Thus all significant political groups, parties, labor, agrarian, or other groups, are structurally the same. They constitute tightly knit hierarchies. Further, this is true not only of the present regime; it is also true of any other political order emergent in Mexican history. This collectively demonstrates that the values and norms of the nation are oriented toward vertically rather than horizontally structured relationships.

The formal prescription for elections in fact can be shown to have no roots in the Mexican experience. Elections appear more as an overlay on the political system, as an import of democratic ideals. Egalitarianism has never been a vital part of the Mexican experience, but authoritarian paternalism has.

Why have Mexicans in politics continued to invoke the egalitarianism symbolized in democracy? Indeed, why emphasize and institutionalize the recurring formality of elections? Such questions are not easily answered, but there may be an important clue in the fact that the titular power of the Spanish Empire was displaced through a devastating series of conflicts which developed all the characteristics of a civil war — region against region, class against class, family against family, brother against brother. The mutually supporting pillars of legitimacy, Crown and Church, were torn apart. The Church alone no longer legitimized succession. The blessing of investiture by the Church was no longer indispensable, but rather was cause for continuing civil strife. Since the need for a legitimate paternalistic authority was sought, the only way was by adoption of the only other major Western ideal at that time — elections — where the people as a whole allocate legitimate authority. This has an important parallel in cultural terms. When a new patriarch must be found because the old one must be deposed or no clear successor exists, consensus among the lieutenants determines who will accede to the patriarchal mantle. But this is not an election; it more closely parallels the caucusing that determines the Revolutionary party's candidates. The presidential candidate selected by the revolutionary "directorate" is presented to the entire nation first through the PRI and then through the formalities of election.

Politicization of the Mexican people in the Western democratic sense has not been extensive, as many studies have pointed out.[66]

---

[66] See for a notable study Gabriel Almond and Sidney Verba, *The Civic Culture: Political Attitudes and Democracy in Five Nations* (Princeton, N.J., 1963), p. 82. Also see Joseph A. Kahl, *The Measurement of Modernism* (Austin, Texas, 1968), and Robert E. Scott, "Mexico: The Established Revolution," in Lucian Pye and Sidney Verba, eds., *Political Culture and Political Development* (Princeton, N.J.).

Political awareness, where found, generally stops at the level of the nation as a whole, the idea of being Mexican. Moreover, participation for most Mexicans is limited. Only two major alternatives exist for the individual, either to give support and seek personal advancement through the existing dominant hierarchy or to opt out and passively accept the hierarchical dominance. To oppose means in this cultural context merely joining an opposing hierarchy. Since the PRI's candidate continually receives very wide margins of support, this reconfirms the titular role of the Revolutionary coalition. One astute Mexican has observed how continuism is related to Mexico's "democratic backwardness," but implicit in his analysis are the above-mentioned factors:

> Continuism is congenital [in the culture], [it is the] indicator and cause of our democratic backwardness.
>
> Consequently, the governments of Mexico are sectarian [i.e., elitist and with limited constituency], and with the lone exception of the enthusiastic popular election of Mr. Madero after he had managed the feat of stopping the indefinite continual re-elections of President Díaz, there has been in every sense a Grand Elector who supplants the people or the Congress in the designation of the President.[67]

Reform in the Mexican context is essentially a response to doubt. No position of power is inherently invulnerable. Power must be maintained by preventing the formation of dissident coalitions. Reforms mainly distribute rewards — fiefs — to select potential dissidents, thus discouraging coalitions. Reforms also are mainly symbolic, and may weaken resentment for benefits not received. If nothing else, reforms redistribute deference to those short of material rewards. But the actual significance of reforms should not be overestimated, for usually the results are more subjective than concrete. Even changes in rules or formal procedures often mean little change. The nature of the political culture makes it likely that only violence can break the ties of one paternalistic authoritarian regime in order to make way for another.

The authoritarian nature of political control eventually works against the legitimacy of the regime by threatening the regime's self-avowed goals, as this Mexican author's conclusion shows:

> The existence of political control explains such important situations as the recent presidential successions in Mexico where there exists a situation of co-optation [cooptación] in the re-

[67] Daniel Moreno, p. 287. Translation by the author.

placement of him who has title to the executive power, and the greater part of the population of the country votes for the candidate which the PRI selects.

*The political control causes the most beautiful conceptions of political ideals and constitutional regulations to fall down in pieces.*[68]

The following chapters will examine control and conflict in the context of maintaining the regime within the limits of the Mexican political culture. Like the Revolutionary party, the Revolutionary Labor Sector, the Agrarian Sector, and Popular Sector are all integral components of the pyramid of power erected by the Revolutionary coalition. So also are certain middle-sector organizations not directly affiliated with the party. These various hierarchies are discussed in the following three chapters.

[68] Manuel Velázquez, p. 62. Translation and italics by the author.

# ❖ 3 ❖

# The Politics of Organized Labor

The basic, formal organization of the Revolutionary party followed the principle of grouping by functional and class lines after it was adopted by Cárdenas in the 1930s. This at times misleads the observer as to the complexity of the power resources manipulated by Mexico's rulers for the support of the regime. The group loosely categorized in the terminology of the Revolutionary party as the Labor Sector was essentially composed of unions of urban, industrial workers.

Organized labor itself has a long history and many well-organized groupings with extensive memberships. The major confederation which brings together federations of state and local union chapters, as well as the leadership of the major national unions, is the Confederation of Mexican Workers (CTM).

Labor confederations have been organized according to a vertical-horizontal pattern which in some respects resembles the arrangement of the party executive committees. The confederations are really central group governments with formalized rules of procedure. These central governing groups preside in turn over an association of groupings that have some functional interest in common. Federations are the state-level counterparts of the national confederations; these federations and their formalized leadership direct the activities of organized groups at the state, regional, and local levels.

The operation of each confederation from the national level to that of the *municipio* or its subdivision, as well as the style of politics which has developed over the years among leadership at all levels in these organizational frameworks, brings the confederations into contact with the committees or groups operating the PRI mechanism as well as with those holding public office. Men may hold a public office, a party office, and an office in the executive committee of their functional organization at national, state, or local levels.

### Historical Antecedents of Organized Labor

Historical antecedents of labor organizations reach far back in Mexican history, but it serves present purposes to begin with the years of the Díaz era when gradually there grew among the more aware artisans and small businessmen a determination to organize in some way in order to reduce the risk of sudden economic ruin. Mutual aid groups were formed to provide some minimal insurance against natural disasters such as death and accidents, as well as a pool of funds for small loans to constitute a cushion against bad business years and the ever-present threat of business failure.

Eventually, some artisans and elements among the industrial workers began to talk among themselves about the "right to strike." Cooperative societies with a more militant orientation than the mutual-aid associations began to appear. Agitational papers sprang up in which the right to strike was frequently mentioned. Anarchism, syndicalism, and Marxism all contributed to the beginning of a new ferment. Because of the militants' cooperative efforts there emerged in the last decades of the nineteenth century the First Congress of Workers, Mexico's first labor confederation, and the Grand Circle of Workers. Rural workers remained generally unaware of the new ideas.

The growing awareness of Mexican workers as well as miserable working conditions brought violent demonstrations by miners at Cananea in Sonora and by textile workers at Rio Blanco–Orizaba in Veracruz during the 1890s. Strikes occurred with greater intensity during the period 1900–1910. Troops were habitually used to crush the demonstrations and prevent the strikes from spreading. In Cananea not only Mexican soldiers but also armed men from the United States took part in breaking the strike.

The aspirations and determination of Mexican workers in the more prosperous and established industries were reinforced at seeing the living conditions of the foreigners beside whom they worked. These imported workers, not to speak of the higher-level technicians and managers, lived so well that Mexicans began to ask why higher wages, better housing, medical care, and other benefits should go only to foreigners. When the foreigners struck for even better conditions, as the railroad workers did, the message that poverty and misery were not necessarily inevitable facts of life became clear for the first time to many Mexican laborers.

Mexicans used the concept of American railroad brotherhoods in organizing themselves as early as 1888. By the latter 1890s Mexican railroad workers were pushing hard for better hours and increased wages. Finally in 1904 ties were developed with railroad workers in the United States.

When revolution on a large scale finally resulted in the fall of Díaz and the inauguration of Francisco I. Madero as President of the Republic, the new strength of organized labor was reflected in the establishment of a labor office in the government. Through repeated strikes workers demanded shorter hours and higher wages from the Madero government. In response to these labor conflicts, the new labor office formulated projects for the benefit of labor. At the same time a large labor organization known as the *Casa del Obrero Mundial* was formed. However, the Madero government fell before most of labor's goals could be written into law.

One of the most important things to remember about the *Casa,* aside from the fact that most of organized labor was affiliated, is the extent to which future labor leaders were recruited from the men who formed this organization. The *Casa* was not dispersed during the period of Victoriano Huerta's dominance. When Huerta fell, the *Casa* was still very much a force. In recognition of its importance, General Álvaro Obregón, chief lieutenant of Venustiano Carranza in the three-sided revolutionary conflict, succeeded in building a close working relationship with leaders of the *Casa.* Obregón gained six battalions of workers in return for a decree from Carranza in support of unionization and government recognition of the right to strike in labor disputes. Carranza signed a pact with the leaders of the *Casa* in February 1915. The first major labor leaders, those who were to be very important in the 1920s and 1930s and even later, came from the *Casa.* The doctrine of these people was at first anarcho-syndicalist. Later, some of them became Communists. Most of them were anticlerical. Many participated in the organization of the red battalions which aided Obregón and Carranza.

Carranza clashed with the labor leadership again and again throughout 1916, although he was not willing to go all out to suppress such an important organized force. After all, the labor battalions' commitment to Obregón had been an important factor in the defeat of Villa and Zapata. Even so, Carranza acted under the old laws drawn up by the generation of the Reform as early as July 1916 on the occasion of a strike in the Federal District. Several leaders were imprisoned. Later Carranza ordered the doors of the *Casa* in Mexico City closed after a major clash between workers and various antilabor groups in Avenida Madero. Finally, he reconsidered and allowed the *Casa* to operate in Mexico City while he suppressed the leadership of the organization in the states.[1]

When the constitutional convention arranged by Carranza met in November 1916, there were not many delegates who supported the labor position. However, Álvaro Obregón had not forgotten the contribution of labor battalions to his own and others' victories. Also, the energetic and dedicated General Mújica pressed hard to make sure that the demands of labor were not overlooked in framing the new constitution. It was a bitter fight in which Mújica stood almost alone among those who had assembled to frame the constitution. What saved Mújica's position was support from Obregón and a few lesser generals. Quality of leadership and the presence of the organized labor battalions which had served under Obregón carried the day for the labor partisans.

## Earlier Groups and Group Alignments

The new Constitution of February 1917 encouraged various labor leaders to call a meeting of all concerned. In Tampico in October 1917 it was decided to set up a central committee in Torreón, Coahuila. The governor of Coahuila at that time was somewhat more favorable to labor leaders than most other governors. It was felt that a central committee could safely count on the state as a base from which to work for expansion of labor influence. In Saltillo, Coahuila in the early part of 1918 a great congress of labor leaders was held. From this congress emerged the first great Mexican labor confederation of the post-revolutionary period: the *Confederación Regional de Obreros Mexicanos* (CROM) founded on March 22, 1918. The CROM began by claiming a membership of 7,000; by 1920 it claimed 50,000; by 1922 400,000, and by 1926 2,000,000 or more.[2] It was from the circle of CROM leaders that the impetus arose for the organization of the Mexican Labor Party with the aim of either taking complete power, or at least of exercising power within the existing political framework. The group formed during the presidency of Obregón and flourished under Calles.

In addition to the CROM another confederation emerged, the General Labor Confederation (CGT), whose leaders for the most part identified with the international Communist movement and criti-

---

[1] Roberto de la Cerda Silva, *El movimiento obrero en méxico* (México, D.F., 1961), pp. 121–122.
[2] de la Cerda, p. 140.

cized the administration of Obregón on the grounds that it was essentially bourgeois. Although the CGT never had a membership much greater than 80,000 it did at least raise an important issue — whether the labor movement should affiliate with the Communist movement. Some leaders of the CGT attended an international convention (*Convención Radical Roja*) in Moscow in July 1921. However the primary orientation of the CGT was anarcho-syndicalist. Its Central Executive Committee made this clear in a letter to President Obregón, dated November 30, 1922: "For us it is a fundamental truth that there are not, nor can there ever be, good governments. The very word 'government' connotes abuse.... The CGT is not a political organization; it is rebellious, anti-state, and anarchist. It does not preach peace and harmony between wolves and sheep." [3]

In response to the activities of the CGT, Catholic labor groups emerged with the papal encyclical *Rerum Novarum* as their ideological foundation. These Catholic groups were like the old-time labor organizations of Mexico in that they had a strong mutual-aid orientation and emphasized such issues as the eight-hour day and limitations on child labor. They also published several newspapers and organized several regional confederations. By 1925 the national grouping called the National Catholic Workers' Confederation had about 22,000 members and close to 400 unions. However, most organized workers, though considering themselves Catholic, were affiliated with the CROM and the CGT rather than with the Catholic organization.

Emilio Portes Gil became interim President after the assassination of Obregón in 1928. His major emphasis was upon agrarian reform, but he did not entirely overlook the power of organized labor. It was in part through his efforts that the first statutory labor code of national standing was enacted in 1931, although Ortiz Rubio had become President by this time. Neither Ortiz Rubio, who left office without finishing his term, nor General Abelardo Rodríguez did much for the labor movement during their presidencies. By the end of 1933 labor was weakened and divided. The once-proud CROM was but a shadow of its former self, reflecting the loss of presidential patronage since 1928. [4]

Over the next three years organized labor was unable to present anything resembling a unified front. By the time Cárdenas became President in 1934, there were many splinter groups throughout the country with no major unifying organizational cover. Altogether

[3] Quoted in Víctor Alba, *Politics and the Labor Movement in Latin America* (Stanford, Calif., 1968), p. 308.
[4] Marjorie R. Clark, *Organized Labor in Mexico* (Chapel Hill, N.C., 1934), pp. 86–96; 135–144.

there were 13 confederations, 51 federations, and 2,781 unions registered in the nation.[5] A major reason for the chaotic condition of the labor movement had to do with the decline of the CROM. In the years following the assassination of Obregón in 1928, leaders of the CROM were associated by many with an effort to stimulate that assassination, and the unpopularity of the group stemmed in part from this as well as from abuses of the leadership. The CGT was unable to fill the gap as a nationwide organization because it could not get government support from the presidents who succeeded Calles. It had become clear that no existing labor confederation was in a position to obtain sufficient support from the government for expansion into a really large national confederation. The proliferation of splinter groups continued at a rapid pace as different leaders split away from the CROM and the CGT. New groups were formed, such as the General Confederations of Workers and Peasants (CGOC), the Unitary Confederation of Mexico, the National Chamber of Labor, the Union of Railroad Workers, the Union of Electricians, and the Miners' Alliance.

President Cárdenas was determined that the many labor groups should have some kind of overall organization. Thus, with Cárdenas' manifest encouragement, most of the outstanding labor leaders of the country, with the exception of those in the CGT and the CROM, gathered early in 1936 to establish a new organization known as the Mexican Workers' Confederation (CTM). The CTM was a product of the Workers' Coalition and the Committee for Proletarian Defense, both of which were organized through the encouragement of Cárdenas. Due to the backing of the Cárdenas government, the CTM was able to claim 500,000 members shortly after its organization early in 1936. Leaders of the CTM immediately began to reach out for international contacts. Representatives were sent to the World Labor Congress held in London in 1936. In 1938 CTM leaders promoted the establishment of an organization designed to provide leadership for the Latin American labor movement. This organization was known as the Confederation of Latin American Workers (CTAL). The CTAL came into being with Vicente Lombardo Toledano, the general secretary of the CTM, also acting as leader of the new international group. The orientation of the group was essentially anticapitalist and antiimperialist. The CTAL, like the CTM, had a class-struggle orientation. (The original motto of the CTM was "For a society without classes.") This class-struggle bias tended to create a different relationship between the Mexican and United States labor

5 de la Cerda, p. 141.

movements from that during the CROM's superiority in the 1920s. Although Cárdenas supported the CTM unequivocally, conditions never ripened to the point that it was convenient to crush the CROM and the CGT as well as some other unions and state federations which remained outside the CTM.

Following Cárdenas' departure from office, the presidential term of Manuel Ávila Camacho saw a number of labor jurisdictional disputes. The dispute between the CTM and the Confederation of Workers and Peasants of Mexico (COCM) was one of the most bitter labor struggles of the period. There was also conflict between the CTM and the National Proletarian Confederation (CNP). Although Ávila Camacho was able to bring about a settlement of these quarrels, he, like Cárdenas, fell short of the goal of bringing all of labor under one organization. Thus with the CTM as with the CROM earlier, the ideal of a single confederation acting as spokesman for all labor was not realized in spite of overt government support.

Although the CTM never succeeded in stamping out the CGT, the CROM, and many autonomous state-level labor organizations, the story of labor in the late 1930s is essentially about the expansion of the CTM. Its organizational success was based in part on government support throughout the country. However, when Cárdenas left office, the CTM lost much of its stimulus and ideological militancy. The new CTM orientation could best be summed up as an abandonment of the Marxist class-struggle position and a determination to function within the framework of the nationalist Revolution collaborating with government and industry in economic development. Its motto reflected the change in outlook: "For the economic independence of Mexico." The change helped to bring about a split in the CTM, the formation of new rival confederations, and a drop in the number of its members.

During the presidencies of Miguel Alemán, Adolfo Ruiz Cortines, and Adolfo López Mateos, the policy of supporting the CTM over other labor groups continued. It is commonly recognized that leaders of the great worker confederations such as Luis N. Morones, Lombardo Toledano, and others have always been dependent upon government to help them carry out their organizational feats. Labor organizations went on seeking new alliances, always working without success toward the goal of unification of the labor movement. In spite of the splintering tendency of labor, it seemed evident by the mid-1940s, if not earlier, that the movement had definitely arrived as a permanent fixture on the Mexican scene with more than two thousand unions in the rolls of the Ministry of Labor.

In 1949 Vicente Lombardo Toledano, who had been pushed out

of his leading position in the CTM some years before, attempted to create a new confederation which he called the General Union of Workers and Peasants of Mexico (UGOCM). The UGOCM had a Marxist ideology in line with the position usually taken by Lombardo, but seemed to operate more in terms of an effort to exploit discontent for pragmatic goals rather than ideological purposes. After the organization participated or conspired to participate in several large strikes, the government of Miguel Alemán finally ran out of patience. The registry of the UGOCM was refused approval by the Ministry of Labor in 1950, only to spring up again several years later.[6]

In the 1940s mining and electrical workers' unions ignored presidential efforts to stimulate labor unity. A national labor congress was held to try to bring these divergent interests together along with still others, such as the CROM and the CGT, but this effort met with only limited success in reconciling labor-management interests. Moreover the Industrial Labor Pact signed in 1945 by the CTM and the National Chamber of Manufacturing Industries (CNIT) did not change the fact that many labor leaders and rank-and-file were unwilling to accept the CTM's conciliatory policy toward management. In spite of the pact of 1945 — or perhaps because of it — the Single Workers' Confederation (CUT) emerged with leaders who felt that too close a relationship was growing between the CTM and the government and that there was *continuismo* in the union leadership. Luis Gómez separated from Fernando Amilpa and took a group of railroad workers with him to form the CUT, with some other small unions and their leader, Valentín Campo. The confederation used a very aggressive statement of principles reminiscent of the earliest railroad workers' associations, stressing particularly the defense of labor against foreign interests.

At least one authority has spoken of the "decadence of the CTM which began in 1947. . . . Once again a group of confederations and independent unions were criticizing the situation created by too close a relationship between the CTM and the government. . . ."[7] In addition to the CUT and other confederations organized from discontented workers splitting off from more established unions in the years after 1945, there was the effort by Vidal Díaz Muñoz, who organized the Workers' and Peasants' Alliance of Mexico (AOCM). This confederation had as its purpose the intellectual and organizational unity of the Mexican working class. It was neither successful nor long-lived.

In the early 1950s, when there was uneasiness in some Mexican

[6] Guadalupe Rivera Marín, "El movimiento obrero," in *México: cincuenta años de revolución* (Mexico, 1961), II, p. 264.

[7] Rivera Marín, p. 264.

political circles with regard to the presidential succession, another labor confederation emerged, the Revolutionary Confederation of Workers and Peasants (CROC). Its original declaration of principles made a very clear-cut distinction between two classes of people in a society, the exploited and the exploiters, thus giving a kind of class-war orientation to its organizational program.[8] For a short time it enjoyed high favor in government, though it never was able to challenge the CTM. Adolfo Ruiz Cortines, upon taking over the presidency from Miguel Alemán, seemed to find it expedient to offer various opportunities for growth to the CROC. This, of course, did not help the strength of the CTM. As Professor Scott has pointed out: "During his administration, President Ruiz Cortines seemed to be playing the CROC off against the CTM, permitting the former to organize in direct competition with already existing CTM unions and even allowing its leaders to make public attacks charging the CTM hierarchy with having betrayed labor's interests and with having lined their own pockets at the expense of the working man." [9]

In an effort to maintain its supremacy in the later 1950s the CTM banded together with a number of other confederations and large national industrial unions to form a front known as the Workers' Unity Bloc (BUO), which included the CROM, the CGT, the Railroad Workers' Union, the Telephone Workers' Union, and the Motion Picture Workers' Union, along with a number of lesser unions.

Those who were unwilling to accept CTM supremacy began working toward their own national labor front. These groups were first called the Revolutionary Workers' Coalition, later went through reorganization, emerging as the National Confederation of Mexican Workers (CNTM). This anti-BUO coalition included the Mexican Electrical Workers' Union (SME), the Union of Electricians of the Republic of Mexico (STERM), the Revolutionary Confederation of Workers and Peasants (CROC), the Revolutionary Confederation of Workers (CRP), the Federation of Revolutionary Textile Workers (FROT), the Workers' Revolutionary Federation (FOR), and the National Federation of Sugar Cane Workers (FNC). The organization was born on December 4, 1960 under the motto "Unity and class struggle." Old hands in the anti-BUO coalition were much in evidence in the CNTM as Rafael Galván of the electricians was named president while Manuel Rivera of the FROC of Puebla, Enrique Rangel and Rafael Ortega were named to the central committee.

[8] CROC, *Declaración de principios, program de acción y estatutos* (Mexico, 1952), p. 11.
[9] See Robert E. Scott, *Mexican Government in Transition* (Urbana, Ill., 1959), p. 164. Scott's interpretation is supported by Rivera Marín, p. 276.

The CNTM, generally known as the CNT in Mexico, had its first regular national assembly June 21–24, 1963, in Mexico City. It was important enough for the President of the Republic to attend, along with the president of the PRI, Alfonso Corona del Rosal, and the head of the labor ministry, Salomón Gonzales Blanco. The new organization had the following message for its competitors:

We have sent a cordial greeting to all labor organizations and even though it is true that we have differences with some confederations, and in certain cases very deep ones, it is also true, fortunately, that all of us are agreed on the importance of working for the country within the postulates of the great revolution. Therefore we proclaim ... that we are determined to put forth our best effort in any activity involved in the battle for the well-being of the proletariat and the progress of the Mexican nation.[10]

This pattern of organized labor was significantly changed in the mid-1960s with the grouping of all the organizations of labor into one central structure, the Congress of Labor. This was probably initiated by the government to improve the detection of "difficulties" among the Congress' constituent executive committees. In a sense, the principles of hierarchy and order were once again confirmed.

## One Confederation v. Several

This record of maneuvering for position among Mexican labor confederations centers on the question of one versus several confederations within the Revolutionary coalition.[11] The solution turns implicitly on the question of which arrangement is best suited to maintain the dominance of the Revolutionary coalition, but the debate is couched explicitly in terms of improving the lot of the working class. Briefly, a good statement of the most prevalent view which favors unification is that "the atomization of the labor movement represented by the federations and confederations is a fact contrary to labor unity; there ought to exist only one great *central* to seek the achievement of

10 *Excelsior* (May 24, 1964), translated by author.
11 One of the concepts the author used in the early 1960s to explain union politics was "pluralism." But pluralism in the Anglo sense does not provide an accurate description in the Mexican context. It certainly is not an ideological concern of Mexicans. The fact remains that regardless of political slogans, basic alignments exist because of political situations and leaders' desires. Long-term reasons are based on the values and norms inherent in the political culture.

the goals of the proletariat." [12] Unification of all union leadership, given the conditions of the Mexican political system, might well exaggerate some of the most important existing difficulties. One should consider at this point the position of labor organization and the pattern of leadership within the framework of the Revolutionary coalition. The unification scheme would result in stepped-up frustration in the rank-and-file and among aspirants for leadership. This could result in a greater threat to political stability than is the case with the conflicts stemming from a number of confederations.

The case for several confederations can also be argued in terms of utility. Even when the government has provided great support for a single *central,* as it did for the CROM in the 1920s and for the CTM in the 1930s, it has not been possible for these leading confederations to dominate all worker organizations throughout the country. The CROM never absorbed the CGT, and the CTM never absorbed either the CROM or the CGT. President Calles in the 1920s and President Cárdenas in the 1930s saw themselves as catalytic agents in the formation of a giant labor confederation. Their efforts to resolve the internal conflicts of organized labor and to unify the labor movement into a single instrument with one directorate, and thus forge a personal political tool, were inadequate.

The monolithic ideal was never hammered into the operating institutional form of a single great all-encompassing confederation because men like Calles and Cárdenas were unwilling fully to suppress dissident groups. The goals of the doctrine of unification were thus tempered by pragmatic considerations. It was deemed necessary to take into account the personal ambition of leaders, the discontent and highly volatile temperament of Mexican workers, and the diverse and conflicting convictions concerning labor's role and tactics held among the membership and the competitive leaderships of the labor movement. In view of these latter considerations, the political leaders decided it would be a lesser good to crush all obstacles to labor unification if this required total intervention by the government. The special characteristics of the Mexican political environment thus militated against the creation of the single all-powerful confederation of unions.[13]

The federal labor law provided that "both workers and owners [have the right] to form a union . . . without previous authorization. . . .

[12] de la Cerda, p. 150. The Spanish word *central* may be used as a substitute for "confederation."

[13] L. Vincent Padgett, *Popular Participation in the Mexican "One-Party" System* (unpublished dissertation, Northwestern University, 1955), pp. 224–225.

[Moreover,] no one can be compelled to form part of a union or not to form part of a union." [14] Several other provisions of the labor law provide us with a framework for understanding the legal basis of the labor movement. First of all, the public character of unions is recognized in the provision that unions must be registered with the particular council of conciliation and arbitration having jurisdiction in the union area. If the union is within the scope of federal control, it must also be registered with the Ministry of Labor. Secondly, the authorities with whom the unions are registered may rule acts of union officials null and void when such acts conflict with labor law provisions. Particularly important for the range of choice open to the Mexican worker is the provision of Mexican law which recognizes the existence of a "coalition." A "coalition" is essentially an agreement among a group of workers that they are going to band together to defend their common interests. The "coalition" is related to the right to strike in the sense that the right to strike is defined in at least one statute as the "legal and temporary suspension of work as the result of a coalition of workers." In support of the concept of "coalition" the law also says that "any affiliated union shall be able to retire from a federation or confederation at any time, even though a pact to the contrary may exist." [15]

Study of worker alternatives from the standpoint of labor legislation involves many other provisions. The important point for our purposes is that the *Ley Federal del Trabajo* gives the workers freedom to choose whether or not they will continue their affiliation with a given

[14] *Ley Federal del Trabajo* (México, D.F., 1951 as amended), Art. 236.
[15] *Ley Federal del Trabajo*, Arts. 242, 245, 256, 258, 269. The federal Constitution of 1917, Art. 123, XX, is the basis for the system of councils of conciliation and arbitration that have come into being in accord with provisions of the *Ley Federal del Trabajo*. There are councils having only local jurisdiction and there are those having federal jurisdiction. In either case they are composed of an equal number of representatives from labor and industry and are presided over by a representative of the executive branch. Federal councils at the state level may be either permanent or temporary. An inspector from the Secretariat of Labor and Social Protection presides over their sessions. In the Federal District the Federal Council of Conciliation and Arbitration functions on a permanent basis. The councils — local or federal — make judgments in labor disputes, although the role of the council may be merely that of arranging a compromise. The judgments are considered binding unless, as in various cases, they are appealable to the courts. The councils help greatly in speeding solution of disputes and in reducing the burden on the Mexican judiciary. Rafael de Pina, professor of law at the UNAM, discusses the role of these councils in a study of Mexican labor law, *Curso de derecho procesal del trabajo* (México, D.F., 1952), pp. 56, 209–237.

union. Individual unions in a similar way have been afforded the opportunity of deciding whether or not they should maintain connections with a federation or confederation.

The provisions of the federal labor law which guarantee certain rights of choice in labor organization and affiliation have no doubt been abused from time to time by those with authority to administer and execute the law. We do not need to discuss the CROM in this connection because its period of great strength took place before the development of a full-scale labor code. But in the case of the CTM, unquestionably there were times during its great period of expansion in the 1930s when it received government preference over other confederations in the struggle to achieve power through the organization of Mexican workers. It became very difficult for unions to shift away from the CTM to some smaller confederation whenever they wanted to. However, even when workers' unions and smaller confederations refused to affiliate with a government-supported confederation such as the CTM, and were sometimes crushed on that account, there nevertheless were others among the weaker groups which successfully resisted all efforts at incorporation. The combination of confederations forming the BUO (headed by the CTM) and the CNTM (headed by the CROC) appear to have reduced the previously limited range of choice that had existed for working-class, blue-collar groups.

As we have indicated, the restraint which the government has shown in pursuing the realization of one giant confederation is related to some extent to the norms of the labor code and, of course, Article 123 of the Constitution which is the basis of that code. Perhaps it is even more important that there has been, until recent years, a grudging but realistic respect among Mexican politicians for the character and attitudes of their countrymen. Politicians, in other words, seem to understand that the workers' attitudes and aspirations for good administration of union funds and democratic union procedures are centered on the individual union, the basic unit of labor organization. In the overall picture workers have tolerated the fact that promises of better living standards have often surpassed actual benefits. Although over the years there have been many glowing promises, workers have learned not to expect very much in the way of sudden improvements, although they do expect some gradual change for the better. Great promises followed only by very gradual improvement have been accepted as a part of the game and therefore legitimate. What has never been accepted as legitimate is tyranny and mismanagement by union committees. They may often be facts of life, but to the workers they are always just cause for rebellion. In local unions the rank-and-file have demanded a degree of participation, and their loyalty to the system depends to a great extent on the satisfaction of this demand. These considerations are related to the old question of the one great confederation versus rival groups. Because of the way Mexican confederations are organized and function, the confederation committees (and below them at the state level the federation committees) have a tendency to dictate the selection of leaders in affiliated unions. Workers do not object to the practice of selection of their leadership from above if the leadership so selected does an acceptable job of running the union. Often it does. The crisis situation develops only when the top echelons persist in supporting a union committee named by themselves which has abused authority and power to the detriment of the workers under its jurisdiction. Two types of situations have frequently occurred. First of all, there is the alliance of union officials with management for the purpose of increasing productivity by demanding more work and then quelling protests when the guarantees and security provisions of the collective bargaining contract have been ignored. Secondly, union leadership may abuse workers by establishing unwarranted quotas or membership dues in order to benefit the leaders personally. Usually these abuses go on for a considerable length of time before the workers take action.

When federation or confederation executive committees have persisted in supporting the discredited committee of a local union, workers have some opportunity under labor law to mobilize and demand a genuine voice in the selection of their leadership. Although it may be necessary to defy the hazards of *pistoleros* and hired bullies, there is opportunity under the law for the worker to separate himself from one set of leaders and join with another set which promises something better, though the real opportunity depends on the exigencies of the time.

## Political Culture and "Union Democracy"

One of the principal criteria by which workers evaluate the political system is their own experience with the leadership of their local union. Since poor leadership is often closely tied to higher echelons at the federation, state federation, or national confederation levels, it is sometimes very difficult to get rid of the poor leaders within the confederation. Expectations conditioned by the political culture with its assumptions of corruption, cruelty, paternalistic domination, and grudging admiration of the "real bastard" (*grán chingón*) create an impression of patience when viewed through Anglo eyes. In fact, all people have limits of tolerance. It is of great importance that leaders who head the wave of discontent in the local union affiliate with another confederation and seek a new registry for the union within the framework of another organization. The author observed the moves and countermoves involved to achieve a new and more satisfactory leadership for one local union.

In the textile factory of La Covadonga members of a long-established union, including most of the workers, found themselves involved with a corrupt leadership named by the federation officials and approved by the confederation leaders of the CROM. The union had been affiliated with the CROM in the days of CROM supremacy during the 1920s and had stayed on with that confederation during the years of CTM supremacy. Due to the loyalty of groups like that at La Covadonga, the CROM was able to maintain considerable strength in the Puebla–Tlaxcala region. The CROM and its affiliated state federation apparently overestimated the affective ties felt by the rank-and-file at La Covadonga. Neither the CROM central committee nor the federation committee respected the expectations of workers with regard to the conduct of union officers. Pressure was brought to bear upon union assemblies in order that the persons selected by the federation and central committees might be elected union officers, as is often the case, but sometimes these officers were outsiders who had never held jobs at La Covadonga. The union leaders failed to insist that management respect the wage scales assigned to different classes of workers in the collective bargaining contract. Labor leaders surrounded themselves with spies who searched out any malcontents for punishment. When the tension did not diminish, some workers lost their jobs because their attitudes made them unacceptable to union leaders. Discontent with existing abuses heightened when the leadership ordered a seemingly unreasonable increase in the rate of union dues. A number of workers were beaten up as unrest increased.

Finally, opposition to the leadership coalesced, and the dissenters held their own union meeting as permitted under labor law, selecting a new leadership. The records of the meeting were sent to the Department of Registrations of the Labor Ministry in Mexico City, which registers unions and union leadership and presides over evaluation of union elections in conjunction with regional and national labor arbitration and conciliation councils.

Of course the other leadership also sent its report of the events at La Covadonga. In this report the existing leadership said it would be willing to cooperate with the rebels if the latter made "reasonable" demands. Leaders of the revolt, however, realized they either had to leave La Covadonga or stand in jeopardy of life and limb should the old group stay on in power. Thus the leaders' offer of a compromise, while it won over some people in the factory, did not resolve enough problems to quiet the unrest. In this opening round of battle the Ministry of Labor refused to recognize the dissident group as having legal standing. The group then appealed to the leadership of the CTM in Puebla, realizing some "friend in court" was needed if the federal authorities were to accept a proposed change in leadership and registration. The CTM, however, refused to take in the new group (under a different name) as an affiliate of the CTM.

Meanwhile the old CROM committee held a meeting to provide for election of new leadership. Some members of the committee were replaced, and a number of promises were made. Particularly revealing was the pledge that leaders would no longer be selected from persons who had not worked in La Covadonga. It was also promised that many of the workers which the old committee had excluded from the factory would be reinstated. A list of persons who could not be reinstated was also submitted, and these were the leaders of the intransigent group. The old committee promised that it would procure jobs in other plants in Puebla and Tlaxcala for the expelled persons. A quorum of workers was present for the meeting, as was a representative of the state governor, and several other high officials. Some of the labor disputants who were to be ousted refused to accept the decision of the assembly, but in general the union group seemed favorable to the compromise arrangement and voted accordingly. The Ministry of Labor promptly recognized the new compromise committee. The settlement was only superficially satisfactory, however, and peace did not last at La Covadonga. The discontented group again gathered more and more support, and another move was made to enlist the help of the CTM in order to achieve a change of registry and recognition of the dissident group in the Ministry of Labor. This plea was again turned down.

In desperation the rebels turned to the state organization of the CROC in Puebla. At CROC headquarters there was a warm reception. The CROC made available its meeting hall in the city of Puebla, and the workers met there to vote unanimously to separate from the CROM and affiliate with the CROC. Interestingly enough, the charges were the same as had been made against the original CROM committee. Signatures of all those attending the meeting were collected and organized in the form of a petition. This documentation, along with a letter stating the case, was sent to the Ministry of Labor. The ministry then sent out two inspectors to review the situation and conduct a poll of all workers. The formal voting was conducted with both the CROC group and the CROM group having equal representation as observers to make sure that the count was valid. When the tally indicated the group favoring the CROC had the most votes, the way was open for the Ministry of Labor to change the registration of the union at La Covadonga and recognize as legitimate the changes in leadership at that factory. The case became so well known that a final victory celebration was held in one of the largest theaters in Puebla attended by the military commander, the governor of the state, and the federal Minister of Labor. In addition, the entire central committee of the CROC came in from Mexico City.

Unions sometimes change their confederation affiliations. The existence of various confederations keeps open the possibilty of ousting an unsatisfactory local committee or of breaking free from a continuism enforced from above. Thus possibilities do exist for establishing new, more satisfactory conditions of leadership, union administration, and relations with employers. But such transfers occur rarely and when they do they are related to rivalries at the highest levels of the Revolutionary coalition or during extraordinary crises in the political system. Between the time of the Obregón assassination and the formation of the CTM under Cárdenas, there was a period of extensive union realignment. Alemán later gave support to the CROC to offset the influence of the CTM for the presidential succession of 1952. Situations at the national level have had a profound effect on the success of workers in changing their affiliation, as in the incident at La Covadonga. The message seems clear enough: opportunities for choice at low levels in the hierarchy of the political system depend for activation largely upon presidential politics and the policies of the Revolutionary coalition. Rivalries between the confederations do exist, but they are subordinate to presidential politics, an ongoing struggle to control the hierarchy under the President and to maintain control against threats from outside the Revolutionary coalition.

## Recent Labor Alignments

When dissatisfaction with the old leadership reaches a high point and few opportunities exist for changing leadership, forming new unions, or joining new confederations, ample reasons for discontent, and even violence are present. Another important consideration is the spiraling cost of living, because it has usually stayed ahead of wage increases. It was a combination of such factors which created the outbreak of unrest among organized workers, other wage and salary groups, and students in 1958–1959. There were too many old faces in high positions, and these faces had not produced sufficient results. In many cases, labor continuism had produced nothing but suppression of worker demands and personal gain for the leaders. Even if official accounts were correct that Soviet money and influence were involved in support of the rail strike led by Demetri Vallejo, the widespread support he received from railroad workers for his demands suggests that prevailing conditions had resulted in a high degree of resentment and alienation.

Once the labor disturbances of 1958–1959 quieted down, leaders in the CTM joined together in the Workers Unity Bloc (the BUO) along with a large number of autonomous unions and some federations not affiliated with any confederation. In response, other federations and confederations joined together in a bloc generally opposing the BUO, and this opposition was formalized in 1960 with the organization of the CNTM. By 1960, then, anticipating the tendency of subsequent years, a pattern of alliances of confederations existed, each encompassing a number of formerly powerful or still powerful *centrales*.

In the BUO bloc the strongest numerical element was the CTM, followed in importance by the railroad workers' union, the mining and metal workers' union, the petroleum workers' union, the CROM, the CGT, the telephone workers, the motion picture workers, and several smaller and lesser known unions. Most important in the CNT (as the CNTM was known) was the CROC, with the organization of greatest numerical potential being the newly organized National Federation of Sugar Cane Workers (FNC). Both the Union of Mexican Electrical Workers (SME) and the Union of Electrical Workers of the Mexican Republic (STERM) had some importance, not so much because of their numbers, but because of their position in the economy. Speculations were made concerning this division of organized labor into two great alliances of confederations. One prognosis made was of a waste of energy through fighting between the two great alignments. This, essentially, was Scott's prediction:

> So far, the struggle between the right and left wings of Mexican labor has tended to weaken the Labor sector's relative position in the national structure of power, but because of the preponderant strength of the CTM behind the BUO, coupled with the government's crackdown on leftist unions after the 1959 strikes, the battle has been too onesided to threaten disintegration of the sector itself. If, however, the revolutionary government continues allowing the CROC and its allies to build their relative power, a crisis could occur. . . . If these organizing attempts should prove successful, the anti-BUO labor group could surpass the BUO in total membership. Even though the farm laborers may not be so politically effective as their numbers seem to indicate, because of their less sophisticated background and rural

location, the Labor sector of the PRI might split wide open. At any rate, more labor energy and influence may be wasted on internecine battles than applied to the broader function of influencing the national policy-making process.[16]

But it would be erroneous to regard these blocs as monolithic. Schism in the great alignments was seen in the 1958–1959 period when the railroad workers and petroleum workers pulled away from the BUO, although nominally remaining within it. At the same time the electrical workers' unions tended to divorce themselves from the anti-BUO faction which was lending some cooperation to Vallejo and other pro-strike leaders among the railroad workers' committees. Weakness in the BUO camp had also been shown in the ambiguous stance sometimes assumed by the CGT. Another confusing aspect of the BUO stems from the fact that much of its support had come from a group that is not even regarded as a portion of it; namely, the Federation of Unions of Workers in the Service of the State (FSTSE) or federal bureaucrats' union which normally belongs in the so-called "popular sector" of the PRI. In the same way the CROC, which generally tended to be the most important single group in the CNT, always got along with the electrical workers. Moreover, support for the CNT by the CRT, the FOR, and the sugar cane workers had not been fully tested. So the appearance of two great alignments of confederations was somewhat misleading.

The divisiveness of organized labor was under attack as the Díaz Ordaz presidency got underway. All labor organizations were persuaded by the new president to agree to the idea of unity in principle. A national assembly of labor organizations was planned, but the talks preceding it indicated differences among principal leaders that would be hard to overcome. The major question was how to divide the power. In a unified labor movement, what would be the role of such leaders as Fidel Velázquez and Jesús Yurén of the CTM or Enrique Rangel and Rafael Ortega of the CROC, not to mention numerous other important but less prominent figures? Because of their stronger political position the leaders of the BUO took the position that the most desirable step would be immediate creation of a single national labor confederation fusing all pre-existing labor groups. The CNT, including the CROC and many relatively independent unions, had a counterproposal. They wanted to set up a coordinating body, a National Labor Council with representation from all major labor groups, which would leave existing organizations intact. Major questions on which there were divisions of opinion aside from the assignment of positions to the leaders included

16 Scott, p. 168.

such matters as labor housing, minimum wage legislation, setting salary levels for various industries, the problem of company unions, intra-labor organizational conflicts and corruption among leaders. The CNT was not able to persuade the government to its position, and a unified Congress of Labor was established in 1966.

## Relative Strength of Labor Groups

One of the most difficult tasks in analyzing the condition of the Mexican labor movement and the factions within it involves the effort to assess the numerical proportions assigned to the types of unions, federations and confederations. The first thing to note is that leaders have a tendency to inflate estimates of the numbers of members in their unions. It is a natural inclination, since the man who speaks for several million as opposed to several hundred thousand may expect to receive somewhat more attention.

A major factor in making the estimate of membership strength so difficult has to do with changes in types of union affiliation. Information of this type also points up the changing character of labor organization in general. In 1939 there were about 5,886 unions registered in the country with the General Statistical Office; 7,564 in 1950, and 8,607 or a little over by 1960. A little over 54 percent of these were craft unions in 1939, and close to 60 percent were craft unions in 1960. About 15 percent of the unions were organized on the basis of a particular enterprise in 1939 and about 17 percent in 1960. Industry-wide unions were a little over 17 percent in 1939, and close to 18 percent in 1960, while the unions based on various types of activity difficult to classify were nearly 14 percent of the total in 1939 and only about 6½ percent of the total in 1960. (The small increase in industrial unions and the larger increase in craft unions would seem unexpected in light of Mexico's gains in industrial development.) In the last years of the 1950s the number of unions based upon individual enterprises, such as a textile mill, or upon an industry-wide organization, seemed to be increasing after relative declines early in the decade.[17] For the two major confederations, it can be noted that the CTM suffered a decline in the number of unions affiliated with it during the 1950s, going from 58.5 percent of all registered unions in 1950 to 44.3 percent at the end of the decade. In contrast, the CROC began with 25.7 percent of all registered unions in the early 1950s and reached 35.5 percent. The changing pattern of Mexican economy and accompanying changes in types of union alignments and

[17] Rivera Marín, p. 272.

types of activity in which unionized men are to be found, is clearly visible in terms of the increases of union workers in certain kinds of activities, and decreases in others. Thus, unionized workers in manufacturing increased nearly 90 percent during the decade of the 1950s, while those in commerce increased well over 100 percent.[18]

Another example of the difficulty involved in setting numerical strengths for the various union and confederation memberships may be illustrated by the following contrast in estimates. Scott limits the Labor Sector of the PRI to 2,113,000 organized workers in both BUO and anti-BUO or CNT groups. On the other hand, the total number of workers organized in Mexico is estimated by Rivera Marín on the basis of official releases from the General Statistics Office as including only 1,202,917 persons.[19] Still another line of estimates indicates the doubtfulness of any firm statement about numerical strength. One of the commentaries on Mexican labor placed the membership of the CTM in 1936 at the time of its founding at about 500,000.[20] Another source credited CTM membership with a 100 percent increase in membership to approximately 1,000,000 in 1940.[21] A report published in 1954 emphasized the difference between estimates of CTM leaders during the course of interviews in which different spokesmen quoted 1,300,000 and 1,400,000 respectively while the investigator in that case estimated less than 700,000 in the CTM rank-and-file.[22] The author was told by a member of the CTM national committee in 1953 that there were 1,200,000 in the rank-and-file. An amazing contrast to all these estimates comes from a report for 1948 showing the CTM membership as low as 91,436 while the short-lived CUT was credited with 98,218, and the total for all unions throughout the country was set at 771,646.[23] With regard to other organizations besides the CTM in the BUO, Scott's estimate of the latter 1950s set the membership of the CROM at 35,000 while Davis gave as a maximum figure 71,244.[24] López Aparicio placed the number of the CROM membership at 50,000.[25] On the anti-BUO side Davis placed the maximum

[18] Rivera Marín, pp. 276–277.
[19] Scott, p. 166, and Rivera Marín, p. 277.
[20] de la Cerda, p. 149.
[21] Alfonso López Aparicio, *El movimiento obrero en México* (México, D.F., 1952), p. 219.
[22] Horace B. Davis, "Numerical Strength of Mexican Unions," *The Southwestern Social Science Quarterly* (June 1954), p. 48.
[23] José E. Iturriaga, *La estructura social y cultural de México* (México, D.F., 1951), pp. 43–57.
[24] Scott, p. 166, and Davis, p. 49.
[25] Aparicio, p. 181.

figure for CROC membership at 436,015; Scott placed it at 150,000.[26]

The author obtained information on the relative strength of labor organizations from the Ministry of Labor. The values are reported in Table 3. Despite the authoritive source, the data still presents some ambiguities and inadequacies, primarily because union record-keeping is still far from perfect. Thus, even though the figures may be the best available, they may still be essentially inadequate.

Perhaps more to the point than union membership is the relative power of the labor organizations in the Congress of Labor. This is determinable by examining the control of the committees of the Congress. Tables 4 and 5 examine who holds the two highest positions in the committee structure. What is notable is the high proportion of confederation secretaries-general and other high ranking officials, and the high proportion of these committee posts going to the largest confederations (which by implication are the most powerful).

These facts point to the further concentration of control within the organized labor movement itself since the early 1960s. One crucial committee, the Work and Legislation Committee, is headed by Fidel Velázquez. In fact, most significant committees are headed by someone from either the CTM, the FSTSE, or the FTDF. The political importance of the FSTSE is based on its including all federal bureaucrats; the FTDF is important because it is the major federation of workers in the Federal District; the CTM is the only one of these powerful organizations to be nationwide and not clearly connected with the federal government. However, superficial appearances can be deceiving, for the CTM has had a long history of association with the government. The reason for the duration of this association, and the continued success of the CTM, lies in the secretary-general, Fidel Velázquez. The data clearly show the prevalent concentration of control which is closely tied to the leaders of the confederations, and some of these leaders are classic cases of continuism at work.

The Confederation of Mexican Workers (CTM) is at present, as it always has been, the greatest union confederation in Mexico. This confederation in the mid-1970s numbered more than three million affiliated members. The exact number of members is variable from time to time, but the CTM is the center and nucleus for organized labor in Mexico. The CROM, CROC, and CGT are now facades with very little rank-and-file membership. Each continues to have a framework of officials, and in formal terms maintain some membership. The actual affiliated members were fewer in the mid-1970s than

[26] Davis, p. 49, and Scott, p. 166.

## Table 3

### Membership in the Congress of Labor

| Membership as of fall 1974 | Date of inception | Date of registration | Membership |
|---|---|---|---|
| Confederation of Mexican Workers (CTM) | February 24, 1936 | July 20, 1936 | 3,000,000 + est. |
| Revolutionary Confederation of Workers and Peasants (CROC) | May 7, 1951 | July 7, 1952 | 1,000,000 approx. |
| Federation of Syndicates of Workers in Service to the State (FSTSE) | December 5, 1938 | | 900,000 approx. |
| Regional Mexican Worker Confederation (CROM) | May 12, 1918 | April 7, 1932 | 100,000 approx. |
| Revolutionary Worker Confederation (COR) | December 18, 1967 | February 7, 1968 | |
| Syndicate of Railroad Workers of the Mexican Republic (STFRM) | January 13, 1933 | February 8, 1933 | 105,000 approx. |
| Industrial Syndicate of Miners, Metallurgical and Related Workers | May 23, 1934 | July 11, 1934 | 147,500 approx. |
| Federation of Workers of the Federal District (FTDF) | March 30; 1949 | | 500,000 approx. |
| Syndicate of Mexican Electricians (SME) | December 14, 1914 | November 1, 1933 | 23,000 |
| Syndicate of Petroleum Workers of the Mexican Republic (STPRM) | August 15, 1935 | 1936 | 45,665 |
| General Confederation of Workers (CGT) | February 1921 | | 90,000 approx. |
| Syndicate of Telephone Workers of the Mexican Republic (STRM) | August 1, 1950 | August 2, 1950 | 147,000 approx. |
| National Syndicate of Educational Workers (SNTE) | 1943 | | 362,000 approx. |
| Federation of Grouped Workers (FAO) | November 20, 1957 | July 30, 1963 | |
| National Association of Actors (ANDA) | November 6, 1934 | | 20,000 approx. |

Syndicate of Cinematographic Workers of the

| | | | 6,000 approx. |
|---|---|---|---|
| | | October 11, 1922 | |
| Syndicate of Technical and Manual and Other Workers of the Studios and Laboratories for Cinemagraphic Production | April 26, 1968 | May 16, 1968 | 930 approx. |
| National Federation of Textile and Other Related Industries (FNRTOI) | April 24, 1939 | June 2, 1939 | |
| Syndical Association of Aviation Pilots (ASPA) | August 4, 1958 | December 29, 1958 | |
| Revolutionary Confederation of Workers (CRT) | April 1, 1954 | May 21, 1954 | |
| Revolutionary Federation of Textile Workers (FROT) | November 1, 1953 | December 2, 1953 | 1,000 approx. |
| Syndical Association of Aviation Stewards (esses) (ASSA) | April 8, 1960 | May 13, 1960 | |
| National Federation of Cane Workers (FNC) | September 7, 1948 | | 5,000 approx. |
| Confederation of Workers and Peasants of the State of Mexico (COCEM) | November 24, 1944 | November 24, 1944 | |
| Union of Linotypists of the Mexican Republic (ULRM) | March 21, 1909 | August 7, 1931 | 350 approx. |
| Alliance of Transportation Workers of Mexico (ATM) | October 27, 1927 | | 3,000 approx. |
| Industrial Syndicate of Wool and Related Workers | August 14, 1934 | July 28, 1934 | 2,400 approx. |
| League of Autonomous Maritime and Related Port of Veracruz Workers | August 28, 1944 | August 30, 1944 | |
| Alliance of Unions and Syndicates of the Graphic Arts | February 27, 1932 | May 2, 1932 | |
| Syndicate of Press Workers | November 19, 1954 | | 800 approx. |
| Syndicate of Flight Engineers (ASIV) | April 18, 1960 | June 6, 1960 | 53 |
| Congress of Labor | February 16, 1966 | not applicable | all unionized workers |

SOURCE: Author's government sources.

*Table 4*

Committee Leadership in the Congress of Labor
(July 5, 1973–January 5, 1974)

| Committee | Relative Importance of Comm. (H = High; L = Low) | President [Rank* (Organization)] | Vice-President | Other characteristics |
|---|---|---|---|---|
| Office of Official Mayor | L | SG(CGT) | S$^1$ (CTM) | |
| Organization and Inter-Union Problems | H | SG(FSTSE) | SG(SME) | |
| Work and Legislation | H | SG(CTM) | SG(STRM) | |
| Work, Social, and Professional Education | L | SG(SNTE) | SG(Tech. & Man.) | |
| Economic and Social Affairs | H | SG(FTDF) | SG(ASPA) | |
| Social Security and Cooperative Development | L | relative of SG(CROC) | SG(STPRM) | |
| Political Affairs | H | S$^2$ (CTM) | SG(FNU-TEP) | 3 Deputies, 1 Senator (who is President). |
| Social, Syndical, National and International Affairs | L | SG(CROM) | SG(CRT) | |
| Finance | L | X(FSTSE) | S$^3$ (FAO) | |
| Press and Propaganda | H | SG(ANDA) | SG(ASSA) | |
| Sports Development | L | S$^4$ (FTDF) | X(CROC) | |
| Women | L | X(FTDF) | X(ANDA) | President is a Deputy; only women on committee. |
| Juvenile | L | S$^5$ (CTM) | X(FSTSF) | |

* S$^1$ = Secretary of Promotion and Organization; S$^2$ = Secretary of Political Action; S$^3$ = Secretary of Organization; S$^4$ = Secretary of Sports; S$^5$ = Secretary of Press and Propaganda; SG = Secretary-General; X = no identified high rank.

SOURCE: Author's governmental sources.

*Table 5*

Concentration of Control in Committee Posts in the Congress of Labor
(July 5, 1973–January 5, 1974)

| Labor organizations | Congress of Labor Committee posts held | |
| --- | --- | --- |
| | President | Vice-President |
| CTM | 3 | 1 |
| FSTSE | 2 | 1 |
| FTDF | 3 | 0 |
| CROC | 1 | 1 |
| CROM | 1 | 0 |
| SNTE | 1 | 0 |
| ANDA | 1 | 1 |
| CGT | 1 | 0 |
| Other | 0 | 9 |
| | Total 13 | 13 |

| Rank in his union grouping | Congress of Labor Committee posts held |
| --- | --- |
| Secretary-General | 58% |
| Committee Secretary | 19% |
| Other* | 4% |
| No high post | 19% |
| | Total 100% |

\* Related to Secretary-General
SOURCE: Author's government sources.

previously. What used to be considered the BUO (*Bloque Unido Obrero*) has now become the Labor Congress (*Congreso del Trabajo*), and nearly all unions of any significance are in it; groups outside the Congress have comparatively few members. Realignment of unions continues. Approval for realignment still depends upon decisions within the Registration Department of the Ministry of Labor. During the 1970s the tendency toward increase of CTM membership was pointed up by a number of cases, among them a labor dispute at the textile factory of Ochotrán which resulted in a review by the Ministry of Labor and eventual loss of 2,400 members who transferred their affiliation from the CROC to the CTM. There was also a labor conflict in the restaurant industry in which some 1,300 workers established their own union and became an affiliate of the CTM. These are small-scale cases, but they indicate a trend that has continued for quite some time.

In the mid-1970s the continuing supremacy of the CTM at the national level was primarily maintained through the status and the connections which the labor leader Fidel Velázquez established in the Revolutionary coalition and among secondary leaders and bureaucrats in industrial unions. CTM supremacy was also maintained through the services and support which Velázquez and his immediate entourage secured for themselves in large measure through their long contacts in the labor field. The pattern of continuism so evident in this case is traditional and fits the tendency in Mexico to continue leaders in positions of authority and to hear their counsel when this seems to provide greater security and support for those of higher status, in this case the President and his immediate advisors. Velázquez is an excellent example of a leader who filled the specifications required of him by the President better and longer than others have done. He regularly delivered support in critical industrial areas and in strategically located CTM affiliates. Through the years he manifested a striking intuitive capability in assessing and neutralizing possible personal opposition within his circle, while anticipating currents of change and opinion developing within the Revolutionary coalition. Thus he sided with Cárdenas and worked with other leaders, such as the heads of the CNC, when Ruiz Cortines succeeded Alemán in the presidency. Earlier Velázquez participated in the removal of Vicente Lombardo Toledano during the more right-wing Ávila Camacho presidency. The supremacy of the CTM was maintained and Velázquez remained dominant for years.

## The Dynamics of Labor Organization

As indicated above the multiplicity of labor's organization structures poses the question of centralization versus decentralization. But it appears that weaker organizations exist even in times of great labor centralization and that this takes place for a number of reasons.

Presidents in the past have never been willing entirely to destroy rival labor organizations while supporting a major one. This was true when the CROM was the major confederation and when the CTM was dominant. Causes for this are deeply rooted in a culture that values maintaining possibilities for relationships. Removal of some leaders can scarcely fail to destabilize the power relationships among the remaining leaders and deplete their power resources. The removal of an organization and its bureaucracy jeopardizes the most careful political stratagem.

The facade structures in the labor movement, even when weaker or moribund, are quite often possible alternatives to the existing dominant association if it is seen as a liability. When the CTM refused to go along with Alemán in choosing a successor, he placed greater emphasis on the CROC, which then became a vital labor force under Ruiz Cortines. The CROC subsequently continued in its status as a national confederation, though it had a small membership. The dynamics of this phenomenon relate in some respects to the importance the Mexican people have always placed upon the family as a social institution. Tradition, lineage, and the strong attachment to regional roots all endure despite the effects of modern influences. All of these traditional emphases have been summed up by Charles F. Andrain as being "primordial." [27]

Primordial values discourage attack upon a group such as the CROM or CROC which no longer has much effective power and appears to be a liability. Such fundamental conservatism reinforces the tendency of the Revolutionary coalition to maintain the membership and skeletal committee frameworks of essentially moribund organizations, whose existence provides continuity and protects vital family connections with organizational structures and membership in or alliance with the Revolutionary coalition. The culture thus provides a counter-balance to conflict. The maintenance of the many intricate relationships of the extended family and related social and political structures, such as Masonic Lodges and union committees, partially moderates the emphasis on violent competition associated with *machismo*. The attachments to family and continuism are sufficiently strong to resist leaders' pursuit of complete dominance. This means a loss of power within the psycho-cultural complex of *machismo,* where giving away any personal power is a loss of potency and ability to control events and one's destiny. However, the psychological compensation in foregoing dominance is the ruler's sense of himself as a paternal figure watching over those in his care. He is in effect the head of the whole national family, and he is giving power to his sons. In this way his sense of personal loss is compensated for, because he diffuses rewards and privileges to a very large extended family: the nation as a whole, and more particularly to those he considers to be in the hierarchical system over which he presides. Conversely, he has the right to take back some of the power he distributes from those in subject roles. For example, under Alemán, Lombardo Toledano was removed from the direction of the CTM and replaced by Fidel Velázquez. Lombardo was compensated by being allowed to form his own opposition political party. At the same

[27] Charles F. Andrain, *Political Life and Social Change,* 2nd ed. (Menlo Park, Calif., 1974).

time though, Alemán was reducing the dominance of the CTM over organized labor while increasing that of the CROC. Yet the CROC was probably never intended to replace the CTM as the dominant labor confederation. It is true, however, that during difficult times it has often been necessary to reconcentrate power in the major labor confederation, the CTM.

The stronger a paternal figure feels the less he needs to close his accessibility and reconcentrate power in his own person, when he feels threatened. (The fact of an increased concentration of power by a President such as Cárdenas should not necessarily be taken to mean that a government is threatened: his goals appeared to pose clear policy reasons for the reconcentration.) But there is also usually a genuine cause based on the objective necessity to maintain potential reserves of political strength and additional sources of information which may be tapped as needed by those who make authoritative decisions. Thus a cadre may be activated if the machinery and loyalties are there. The facade structure can also be activated if its support is needed. The skeletal framework provides feedback with which to measure perceptions of events and situations. It is hard to overlook the survival capacity of multiple information channels in a society where rivalry and conflict are aggravated by the values of *machismo* and the *grán chingón*. In a climate where the survivor in politics is the man with more information than his opponent, the right communications channel at the right moment is invaluable. Facade structures are vital resources where conflict has no limits beyond the traditional values of family and continuity, where the price for failure may mean ruin, violence, death, or the fall of the regime.

The position of facade structures as well as the continued supremacy of Velázquez both fit well in the context of Mexican political culture and related strategies. First, in spite of the fact that Velázquez is maintained as the greatest labor chief, he is never allowed the power that complete hegemony over organized labor would bring him. Second, reliance upon him as the *main* labor leader goes with the tendency to continue him so long as he is able to demonstrate to his peers and the immediate presidential circle that the support he brings can outweigh liabilities his continuism creates. Third, the leaders of the Revolutionary coalition tend to continue groups or individuals potentially useful to the Revolutionary coalition. Fourth, the minimum rank-and-file as well as union committee members who occupy the positions at various levels of these facade hierarchies provide reserve power potential, and are cadres in a sense. They are there for the stormy day when the President needs to establish new alignments in order to maintain his supremacy or that of the Revolutionary coalition. Fifth, *machismo* politics necessitates a never ending search for sources of support in the hierarchy and for sources of information that will distinguish supporters from enemies. In sum, maintenance of skeleton union confederations among organized labor groups serves many needs at minimal cost. Facade organizations provide continuity and deference to families that have dropped in the hierarchy, thus minimizing the need to coerce, suppress, or eliminate family members and so averting conflicts with the family and its branches, friends, and godfather ties. Facade organizations also provide listening posts, bench marks, and a possible retreat for losers in the high stakes of a political game of constant flux and conflict.

The coalition's Labor Sector depends upon good will from above. "Radicalism" results in alienation from the center of power. Policy concerning organized labor is discussed at the highest government levels with organized labor: although it is involved, it cannot stray from the government's policy. Whatever ideological commitment exists within the high levels of the Labor Sector (especially those labor unions which are most closely tied by rewards) generally goes along with the dominant views in the coalition.[28]

The stoppage of the channels of advancement by continuism can be circumvented by young dissidents splintering off and attempting to form their own unions or confederations. However, since it is often difficult to obtain the approval of the Department of Registrations, this means of circumvention, though sometimes successfully used, is not a very viable way of achieving success. The difficulty of success is further compounded when these dissident organizers attempt to entice workers to join their new organizations. This attempt usually involves winning them away from an existing affiliation, which they usually believe will be able to do more for them than any new splinter group, barring some sign of presidential favor for the new group.

The system of organized labor is heavily weighted in favor of the existing relationships. Both benefits and control from above and the inherent conservatism of the workers below tend to continue the leadership of local unions. Unions' affiliations with confederations fluctuate according to presidential predilections and political exigencies, but the supremacy of the CTM has not been effectively challenged since its inception in the 1930s with Cárdenas' blessing. This reflects a recognition that benefits to leaders and workers alike have been most easily obtained through the CTM, though other labor confederations (facade structures) continue to exist with minimal support and small, though sometimes devoted, memberships.

[28] Robert J. Alexander, *Organized Labor in Latin America* (New York, 1968), pp. 197–198.

# ❖ 4 ❖

# The Politics of
# Agrarian Organizations

Prior to 1910 the Mexican countryside consisted of a relatively few large farms (*haciendas*) concentrating approximately 50 percent of the total area of the country.[1] Scattered here and there were the owners of smaller extensions of land. Throughout Mexico, those who lived on communal lands or owned their own small farms were a tiny minority compared to the great number of *peones acasillados* who lived in a condition of quasi-slavery through the practice known as "debt-peonage."[2] On the *haciendas* where they were born and worked, these persons, who numbered 90 percent or more of the rural population, lived their lives at the economic mercy of the owners, the *hacendados*.

In the central part of the Republic there were still many Indian villages which had possessed their communal lands under Spanish grants since the Conquest. The fact that the Díaz government had begun ending the communal holdings provided a major impetus for peasant involvement in the Revolution of 1910–1917. It was mainly from among the people of this central region that the *zapatista* movement recruited in its struggle against the Díaz government. The promises held out to the rural population during the Wars of Independence, the mid-nineteenth-century Reform, and the resistance to the French intervention had resulted in a regime that served only to

[1] An excellent source (although unpublished) is Brian Loveman's study, *Land Reform and Political Change in the Countryside: the Mexican and Cuban Cases.* He uses with great discrimination the work of such leading authorities as González Roa, George McBride, and Eyler Simpson.

[2] Loveman.

reinforce the worst of the oppressive practices known in the country-side for centuries. Not surprisingly, therefore, both the Revolution of 1910-1917 and post-Revolutionary Mexican history have been intimately tied to the legacy of struggle by Mexican peasants to liberate themselves from the semifeudal economic and social conditions prevalent under colonial rule.

## Development of Peasant Organization

The attempts to organize peasantry who were integral elements of the Revolutionary forces continued as the fighting ended and leaders confronted the need to establish a post-revolutionary equilibrium. (The term *peasant* has been traditionally applied to poorer farmers and rural workers. From the time of Cárdenas the term has been officially applied to rural workers in the organizational base of the Revolutionary party.) The militant armed followers of the assassinated Emiliano Zapata had to be mollified. The labor organizers who were expanding their activities to include the rural population had to be accommodated. It was in this context that there emerged in 1920 an agrarian group, led by *zapatistas* for the most part, called the National Agrarian Party (PNA).

Local peasant movements in the early 1920s were particularly in evidence in Yucatán, Tamaulipas, and Michoacán. Of importance in these grass-roots organizations which took the form of peasant leagues were Ursulo Galván and Graciano Sánchez. These men and other leaders finally brought together the peasant leagues of fifteen different states and the Federal District in an organization known as the National Peasant League (LNC) in 1926. Later many members of the LNC banded together to oppose conservative tendencies in Calles' government, and some even joined the Communists. Some of these refused to give up Communist membership to join the National Revolutionary Party (PNR) when it was formed, but in 1930 a majority of the LNC leaders voted to join the new PNR.

Graciano Sánchez was one of the LNC leaders who joined the PNR and it was his leadership, along with the efforts of Emilio Portes Gil, which made it possible to hold a peasant convention in the spring of 1933. This convention developed a strong agrarian reform plank that was written into the program of the PNR at the time of the presidential nomination of Lázaro Cárdenas. In place of the LNC the peasant meeting of 1933 formed a new group known as the Mexican Peasant Confederation (CCM). But the CCM did not succeed in uniting even a majority of the potentially organizable peasants in the country. Some labor unions had peasant groups affiliated with them; other peasant groups refused to join any national organization. Labor groups, particularly the CROM and the CGT, struggled to expand influence into the countryside by organizing the peasantry. Moreover, remnants of the older LNC continued to function. Most leadership cadres of the first nationally organized peasant groups were not composed predominantly of peasants. Graciano Sánchez carried the title of *profesor,* and Emilio Portes Gil was a *licenciado.* These initial efforts to institutionalize the peasants' participation in the Revolutionary coalition derived from the desire of urban professionals to build their own base of support within the Revolutionary apparatus.

### Cárdenas and the CNC

Lázaro Cárdenas decided to build an agrarian group which would have as its core the *campesinos* included within the agrarian reform program. His ideal involved a national association organized as a single confederation which would bring together all of the rural people related in some way to the agrarian reform program. In a decree in July 1935 Cárdenas put the strength of the government of Mexico and of the Revolutionary coalition behind the effort to create such an organization. On the basis of the decree, work went forward immediately to organize local groups in the many *ejido* communities throughout the country and then bring these together in state organizations. In each state there was to be a League of Agrarian Communities and Peasant Unions *(liga).* It was out of the formation and unification of these *ligas* that there developed the National Peasants' Confederation (CNC). The impetus for organization of the CNC and the procedures for carrying out the task originated from decisions taken in the presidency. Under organizational changes which Cárdenas arranged, the CNC was incorporated into the official party as the Agrarian Sector. The move was designed to keep labor and peasant organizations separate while at the same time strengthening each in its own field.[3] The CNC claimed as its special area of organization the peasantry living in *ejido* communities. In addition, the scope of the CNC was recognized as encompassing rural wage laborers and people farming their own small plots.

A pattern of hierarchical rule is evident in the organization of the CNC, which is best seen as an executive committee heading a

[3] Daniel James has a good discussion of the background of the formation of the CNC in *Mexico and the Americans* (New York, 1963), pp. 265–267.

series of other executive committees organized in a vertical-horizontal pattern reaching from the national to the state levels and so on down to the local *ejido* communities. The highest members are lawyers, with the exception of a few old Revolutionary peasants. The top organizational unit at the state level is the executive committee, which constitutes the working machinery of the state *liga*. Under each *liga* there are several regional committees, which bind together different locally organized units. The CNC has essentially the same structure as the other "political" organizations of the PRI — the Labor Sector (the confederations) and the Popular Sector (CNOP).

There are at least six types of locally organized units which form the basis of the CNC with its claim for acting as the special organized representative of the agrarian aspect of Mexico's Revolution. Among the local groupings there are, first of all, the "executive agrarian committees" which are formed to help peasants petitioning for grants of land under the land distribution programs. There are then commissariats of *ejido* communities elected as the community government of the *ejido* by the *ejidatarios*. Local organized units may also include members of "agricultural colonies." The members of the agricultural colonies are people who have solicited expropriated land from the government and received it under an arrangement by which each member of the group pays the government for the plot he receives rather than receiving it free of charge without proprietary rights, as in the case of the *ejido*. Members of the agricultural colonies have private plots that range anywhere from one or two hectares up to fifty. Another type of group is the "urban colony." Urban colonies are frequently found within *ejido* communities where the younger generation of the community has demonstrated need of land to build houses in order to form homes of their own. The land for these houses within the *ejido* community is received as a government grant. In addition, local groups affiliated with the *liga* and the CNC may include small property owners who have formed themselves into a union. Their land seldom exceeds fifty hectares. Finally, there are unions of workers formed in connection with industries related to agriculture such as sugar, coffee, cotton, bananas, and other crops that require an accompanying processing industry.

Each local group has its own executive committee, and where the boundaries of a regional organization of the *liga* do not coincide with those of a *municipio* there will be a municipal delegate who acts as a kind of coordinator for these groups. Representation of the rank-and-file in the highest councils is indirect. There are local organization meetings which send delegates to municipal or regional meetings. From the regional level the delegates chosen, usually members of the regional committee, will gather together to choose the members of the *liga* committee. It is well known that members of the *liga* committee are usually, but not always, chosen according to the wishes of the governor of the state. It seems doubtful that this method of recruitment, so closely connected to the cultural norm of hierarchical rule, will be altered in the near future.

### Patterns of Conflict and Articulation of Demands

For the Revolutionary coalition and the *campesinos* the new organization was supposed to serve three major functions: to mobilize support among the peasantry to guarantee the peaceful succession to public office of candidates named by the leadership of the Revolutionary coalition; to defend the interests of the peasantry in dealing with government officialdom; and to find solutions for internal problems which had created divisions and discontent among the peasantry detrimental to their support of the regime.

The CNC commonly confronts several types of conflict. First, there is the situation in which a large landholder wishes to gain control of the organizational machinery of the CNC, usually at the level of a regional committee, for the purpose of securing his own holdings against petitioners for land. He might also want a resurvey of the land adjoining his property in the hope of finding some difficulty with the boundary which would result in the expansion of his holdings at the expense of an adjoining *ejido* or small private-property plot. These situations occur less frequently as the land tenure system becomes more set in the wake of agrarian reform, but problems like these still face those farming small parcels.

A second conflict centers around the effort of a municipal president to control local interest groups, particularly where the jurisdiction of a CNC regional committee coincides with the jurisdiction of the *municipio*. Control of the regional machinery of the CNC in conjunction with the governmental machinery of the *municipio* provides influence and financial rewards difficult to overlook. In a rural *municipio* the CNC organization may well be the only organized hierarchy other than the Revolutionary party. Control of the CNC organization is an important step in the formation of a local machine through which a man can become the boss (*cacique*) of the *municipio* for a long time. By controlling the regional committee of the CNC it is possible to become a factor in the selection of the *liga* at the state level. Thus, though a position as municipal president may slip away as the term of office ends and "no immediate re-election" bars the way to an extension in office, continued prominence in the CNC and acceptance in the high circles of decision-making at the state level is possible through the president's "machine."

Still a third conflict within the framework of the CNC involves domination of a local *ejido* community through continuism in the office of president of the *ejidal* commissariat. Not only the CNC is involved in such cases, because the Department of Agrarian Affairs and Colonization, the Department of Agriculture and Livestock Husbandry, and the Ejido Bank all have, in addition to the CNC, some formal status in *ejido* administration under the Agrarian Code. When one man perpetuates himself at the head of the administration of the *ejido* community to the detriment of its members through fraud or arbitrary action of some sort, the organizations most concerned are the CNC and the Department of Agrarian Affairs and Colonization (DAAC).

The prestige and influence which a local resident has among his neighbors are significant considerations for becoming president of an *ejido* commissariat, but so also is his standing with the chief-of-zone of the federal DAAC and the officials of the regional CNC committee. It is important, of course, that the man is willing to give up a certain amount of his time to take on the responsibility of occupying the top office of the *ejido* community. Many are unwilling to devote time to this type of activity, and for that reason alone continuism itself is not ordinarily a cause for disturbance within the *ejido* community. However, continuism coupled with use of authority which deprives others of their rights can lead to a crisis.

The government of the *ejido* is conducted through three formal organs: the assembly, the commissariat, and the committee of vigilance. The assembly, composed of members of the *ejido,* elects the other organs. The commissariat actually manages the *ejido.* It is composed of three members: the president, secretary, and treasurer. The committee of vigilance is also composed of three members who are supposed to watch the performance of the other officers and report them to the assembly. The president cannot be immediately re-elected. The term of office of these posts is three years. A two-thirds vote re-elects the other officers or removes them (including the president). The *cacique* is usually always on the commissariat, though not always as president.[4]

The author found that one *ejido* president not only had been re-elected a number of times but had built support for himself through cultivating factions within the community. With this support in hand and the community divided, it was possible for him to deprive a

---

[4] *Ley Federal de Reforma Agraria,* 1972 (México, D.F.), Chapter 2.

number of *ejidatarios* of portions of their rightful plots of land and also to embezzle the tax money which he as president was supposed to collect from the *ejidatarios* to pay to the state and federal governments. The experience of the *ejido*, Ignacio Romero Vargas, provides a useful case study in the problems of abusive continuism at the *ejido* level and some insight as to how the CNC and other organizations intertwine in dealing with such problems.

## A Case Example: Continuism at Work

The *ejido* of Ignacio Romero Vargas in the *municipio* of Cuatlancingo is located about ten miles from Puebla. The original grant of land for the *ejido* was 355 hectares. The people began their efforts to get the land in 1922. In 1924 the land was granted on a provisional basis, and on April 22, 1925 the *ejido* was granted with finality (*en definitivo*) by presidential decree.

This *ejido* had been distinguished by the quiet, orderly character of its community life until Donato Bello became president of the commissariat. His election marked the beginning of troubles for the *ejidatarios*.

On being elected, Bello began to build political support that would enable him to maintain control of the *ejido* when and if he might relinquish office. Bello's support came chiefly from the *colonos,* sons of the original *ejidatarios* and others, who had been granted parcels of land for the construction of houses on untillable ground within the circumference of the *ejido*. The *colonos* voted in *ejido* assemblies like other members of the community, but lacking plots of their own they formed a kind of underprivileged group. Backed by the *colonos,* Bello controlled *ejido* elections and, upon relinquishing the presidency, was able to name one of his group, Fidencio López Pérez, president of the commissariat. Through López Pérez, Bello continued to manage *ejido* affairs from behind the scenes.

There were two principal abuses of power and authority by the Bello faction. In the first place they illegally revised a number of the agrarian certificates by which the government guarantees to each *ejidatario* the use of an assigned plot of land so long as the *ejidatario* lives and conforms with relevant stipulations of the Agrarian Code. Thirteen *ejidatarios* lost portions of their plots to the Bello group. Second, the *ejido* commissariat was entrusted with the collection and payment of the *ejidatarios'* state taxes, but too often when the *ejidatarios* paid their tax money it never reached the state officials. Six years after Bello first became *ejido* president, the Office of State Tax Collections advised the community that the *ejido* had consistently failed to meet its obligations, and that its debt to the state amounted to 3,598 pesos. Further, the Office of State Tax Collections announced its determination to attach *ejido* property with value equal to the debt.

A number of *ejidatarios* had become aware of the alterations in the agrarian certificates and were indignant about them. However, the abuses had been at the expense of a few, and most of the *ejidatarios* had their own problems. They did not care to become involved in the complicated and sometimes dangerous area of politics into which steps against Bello would take them. But when the news reached the *ejidatarios* that their tax money had not been paid by the commissariat and that their goods, houses, and equipment might be attached by the state government, there arose a threat of hardship sufficient to alarm even the most apathetic among them. A group was quickly formed that began to work for the downfall of the Bello faction.

A principal difficulty in replacing Bello, who had by this time again assumed the *ejido* presidency, involved the positions taken by the zone chief and the *delegado* of the DAAC. When it became clear that these two officials would stand against any effort to displace the Bello faction, the group of discontented *ejidatarios* went to the committee of the *liga,* pointed out what was happening, and asked the secretary general of the *liga* committee to help them. The secretary general agreed to lend his aid on the basis of the long list of petitioners put before him and the proof of fraud in the way the Bello administration had mishandled the tax money. Enough people had saved the receipts verifying their payments for it to be shown that at least 1,450 pesos had been paid by the *ejidatarios* without any ever having been received by the state officials.

The secretary general of the *liga* went to see the governor. The situation at the *ejido* of Ignacio Romero Vargas was explained, and the difficulty of resolving the matter in the face of the position taken by the delegate of the federal agrarian office was pointed out. The governor then resolved to act on behalf of the dissident *ejidatarios.* He brought about the replacement of the *delegado,* and early in October a new delegate arrived to take over.

With the stage so set, the dissident group came out in the open and held its first assembly in the federal school in the *pueblo* Ignacio Romero Vargas. The auxiliary municipal president presided. A copy of the assembly record signed by all who attended went to the *liga* committee. To the record was attached a letter from the committee of *ejidatarios* who were leaders in organizing the resistance to the Bello group. The *ejidatarios* who spoke in the assembly reflected the indignation and wrath of all in attendance. The words of Everardo Vera López recorded by the secretary were much like those of his fellow *ejidatarios:*

> He in particular has not been affected [by the abuses of Donato Bello] but in no way does he agree with the disorder that the *ejido* representatives are carrying out agitating in this way a village which has always given signs of order and tranquility. . . . He condemns the conduct of Donato Bello . . . who continues despoiling [*ejidatarios* of their land rights], and he disagrees with the way money has been demanded of the *ejido* people without ever calling an assembly to explain to what use the money is put. [He says] this ought not to be, because the Agrarian Code does not authorize such vile tricks [*chanchullos*].

In their letter attached to the record of the proceedings, the committee for the protesting *ejidatarios* said:

> The existing system of oppression and tyranny [in our *ejido* community] is denounced. May this system imposed by Donato Bello be terminated forever because never has been known in the past a time like the one which now embarrasses us.
>
> We hope that once the investigation is terminated competent persons of recognized integrity in this *pueblo* will be substituted for the present commissariat of the *ejido* — and that those who have lent themselves to the tactics of Donato Bello may be excluded from all representation.
>
> Finally, we ask that there be a measure of order, that the tranquility of this *pueblo* continue as always, that justice be done our comrades and that the due guarantees be given to everyone without distinction between those who are and those who are not *colonos*. With this will follow the peace we desire for our humble *pueblo* of Romero Vargas.

The effort to normalize the situation in the *ejido* community of Ignacio Romero Vargas was an extended one. An assembly was held in the presence of the delegate of the federal agrarian office in which the charges were repeated from the assembly of the previous day. Then, three days later, there was another assembly in the salon of the same official, José T. Balderrama. Also present was Miguel Mendieta, financial secretary for the *liga* committee, who had been given the Romero Vargas problem as a special assignment. The question at hand was that of the tax money owed to the state. The evidence of fraud was reviewed, as was the state's position on the debt. As a result of this meeting the *delegado* ordered the Bello faction to appear before him within a week for the inspection of the *ejido* accounts. Instead, the Bello group went to the *liga* committee to complain of the tactics of the dissident group and to enlist the sympathy of the secretary general. The beleaguered *ejido* officers were only partially successful, and the secretary general secured for them an extension of time. However, it was not an indefinite extension, and further, the Bello group were ordered to present the accounts without fail at the end of the time extension. At this point three weeks had elapsed.

When the appointed date came, the *ejido* officials again did not appear with their records. Instead, they went to the office of the federal *delegado* and asked for another extension. The official intervened to secure it for them.

Meanwhile an investigation of the manner in which Bello and his group had used their authority to alter the agrarian rights certificates of the *ejidatarios* was under way. Charged with carrying out the investigation was Joaquín González Rosas, agrarian organizer attached to the DAAC. Miguel Mendieta, representative of the *liga* committee, also participated. The investigation was completed in a short time, and there was evidence that Bello and his following had endeavored to enrich themselves by illegally revising the certificates of thirteen *ejidatarios*.

Two months later the judgment of *ejido* accounts was carried out in the offices of the director of state tax collections. The *ejido* officials refused to come and bring their books, but the state gave the *ejidatarios* credit for the money they had paid on the basis of the receipts in their possession.

In view of the continued lack of cooperation on the part of the *ejido* officers, both the *delegado* and the *liga* committee asked the federal district prosecutor to take the case "because of the infractions of the law committed by the *ejido* officers."

Six months after the first assembly denouncing Bello there came a federal order which brought the expulsion of the members of the *ejido* commissariat for violations of the Agrarian Code and stipulated that their alternates (*suplentes*) take office.

The deposed *ejido* officials twice appealed to the second federal district court of Cholula for a writ of *amparo* to stay the federal order. The *amparo* is a federal writ which stays government officials from action that the courts feel is not in keeping with the federal laws and Constitution.[5] In both cases the writ was denied on the grounds that

[5] See Chapter 6 for a more detailed description.

removal of the plaintiffs from their positions on the commissariat was in keeping with relevant legal provisions.

Still later, the *ejidatarios* of Ignacio Romero Vargas were convoked by the delegate of the federal agrarian office in order that they might elect a new commissariat and council of vigilance. The governor's representative and federal officers and the leaders of the *liga* were present. However, in spite of the important people who attended the assembly, the situation with regard to *ejido* officers remained fluid and was not settled until fully a year after the initial assembly had been held. At such time another commissariat was elected, and one José del Razo Espinosa became president of the *ejido* organization.

José del Razo Espinosa was a leader of the original group that solicited land from the government in 1922. As president of the executive committee that represented the group he had received the first certificate of agrarian rights when the grant of 355 hectares was definitely approved in 1925. He had served as president of the *ejido* commissariat for one regular three-year term. He did not play an active part in the political life of the *ejido* again until the Bello episode. At that time, as he expressed it,

> there . . . came a political situation that was insupportable to me because twelve widows and two blind people as well as the whole community were being abused and despoiled. And this is how I came to return again to face the difficulties of responsibility.[6]

The *ejido* of Ignacio Romero Vargas returned to the tranquility that had characterized it before the Bello era, and as a consequence of their struggle, the *ejidatarios* were pleased to find that other benefits accrued to them above and beyond their chief goal, the destruction of the Bello machine. Indeed, the internal conflict in the *ejido* in a sense put it on the map. Officials began to take the *ejidatarios* into account in a way they had not done previously. Within a year of the episode's close the long-desired aid from the National Bank of Ejido Credit was received. There was a 13,000 peso loan, and the community formed a "society of *ejido* credit." As a result of the loan the members were able to purchase the tractor they had wanted for so long. (When the author visited Ignacio Romero Vargas to interview various *ejidatarios,* the tractor was resting proudly in its shed at the head of the main street of the village.) The community also received a new, modern school. Financial aid from the state government made the project possible, although the *ejidatarios* also contributed their

---

[6] Interview with José del Razo Espinosa at his home in Romero Vargas.

money and labor as well. The governor came to the school's inauguration ceremony.

Three centers of authority and power at the state level had been involved: (1) the federal *delegado;* (2) the governor of the state; (3) the committee of the *liga.* An alignment of the latter two had produced a just arrangement according to the relevant provisions of the Agrarian Code. It is possible that a still different alignment would have served the Bello faction. Although the *ejidatarios* of Ignacio Romero Vargas succeeded in deposing their delinquent officials, this does not mean that like situations can always be resolved according to the formal rule of law and the wishes of the majority. Abuses by *caciques* have traditionally been part of rural life, and other incidents can be found. The *Ejido Plan Libertad* in Baja California included similar abuses, observed in the early 1970s. Eyler Simpson in *The Ejido: Mexico's Way Out* reported the same type of behavior in his research conducted during the 1920s and early 1930s, so it seems unlikely that the policy of continuing local *caciques* will soon cease to be part of the Mexican rural scene.[7]

In this conflict there are several important factors which should be noted. First, the cultural characteristics of Mexican politics are operative at the lowest social levels in the rural areas. Protest and "democratic government" are not normal parts of the political processes of rural communities:

> Protests are few, and those that do occur generally find little support and die out as disruptive attempts of the moment on the part of some individual troublemaker (a community definition). This collective collusion goes a long way toward explaining the election and re-election of corrupt office holders who are well-known for crimes against the very office to which they are reelected, as well as the election and re-election of weak, irresponsible, but controllable and nondisruptive candidates. In litigation, it is reflected in the general absence of witnesses against the accused and in the absence of vengeance, even against murderers of kin.
>
> It is a puzzling phenomenon, this mass collusion in the maintenance of a system. *It imitates the outward appearances, but not the actuality, of responsible democratic government, for the individual who takes private advantage of a public trust rational-*

7 Jim Mohr, "Observations of *Ejido Plan Libertad,* B.C., Mexico" (unpublished student paper, San Diego State University, 1974). Also see David Ronfeldt, *Atencingo: The Politics of Agrarian Struggle in a Mexican Ejido* (Stanford, Calif., 1973), pp. 121–215.

*izes that everyone does what he does, which is true.* This is not his defense, however; his defense is denial, and his security lies in the knowledge that the village will not pursue inquiry or public accusation very far. One would think that a system as corrupt as this, which is nevertheless maintained somehow and whose forms are still approved and seemingly valued, would require a great deal of rationalization to reconcile the discrepancies between real and ideal behavior. Yet this is not the case. To a certain extent, individual responsibility is submerged in the notion that everyone will steal given the opportunity. An individual most often regards this as true even of himself.

Behavior thus rationalized is not, however, rationalized away. It is neither denied nor treated with indifference. It is a matter of common discussion and protest in the village, but it rarely "goes public"; rather, it is discussed in small groups outside public meetings and on occasions when people are called upon for further action. *It may be said, in fact, to rationalize nonparticipation and withdrawal from responsibility.*[8]

Thus, a local *cacique* is traditionally accepted by the local populace. For those in control, several factors are of importance in continuing a *cacique.* The Revolutionary leadership has always made efforts to integrate local leadership into the national hierarchy of control, and looks unfavorably on expressions of regionalism and independence.[9] Another important consideration is the level of support maintained among the rural populace for the Revolutionary regime. Since the regime regularly seeks support in some form (through elections, if nothing else) it will act to build support when the need becomes apparent. Only when a *cacique* seriously threatens regime support will he be removed. Keeping him on maintains a proven power relationship. However, these considerations still take place within the context of hierarchies, *camarillas,* alliances, and the individual's support system. The effort to remove Donato Bello was protracted because of his connections in the hierarchy. He was known to deputies, members of the *liga,* and federal bureaucrats. If the *ejidatarios* had been unable to find a spokesman with equally good

[8] Reprinted from pages 120–121 of *Conflict, Violence, and Morality in a Mexican Village* by Lola Romanucci-Ross by permission of Mayfield Publishing Company, formerly National Press Books. © 1973 by Lola Romanucci-Ross.

[9] Jesús Reyes Heroles, PRI National Executive Committee president, noted that the PRI has attempted to counter the influence of many of these independent *caciques* in Guerrero in a speech reported in *Excelsior* (Dec. 7, 1972), p. 1.

connections, it is quite possible that the issue might not have been resolved as easily as it was. The *ejidatarios,* it is evident, fit some of the characteristics Romanucci-Ross noted. But the difficulties in the *ejido* so eroded support that the government was willing to pay the cost of regaining support.

Local *caciques* must maintain a supporting faction and the acquiescence of the other *ejidatarios* in order to remain in favor in higher circles. This can be done rather easily unless abuse of power is severe beyond popular expectation, as in Bello's case. After all, the assembly of all *ejidatarios* is supposed to elect the *ejido's* executive officers, and there are ways of dealing with assemblies: (1) the *ejido* executive can call them at awkward times when most *ejidatarios* will not attend; (2) few people have any interest in attending; (3) the assemblies are conducted so that no dissident views or leaders are given representation. In addition, once a *cacique* has emerged, the longer his tenure the clearer is his title to the office according to the norms of the political culture.

It is significant that the intricacies of control are being altered by Mexico's changing situation. In the case of Ignacio Romero Vargas the *colonos* (a second generation) contributed significantly to Bello's dominance. Since that time, the original *ejidatarios* who struggled for land have not only been dwindling in numbers, but are being overwhelmed by the newer generation of the countryside.[10] These individuals have different perspectives, higher expectations, and graver problems. The problems facing *ejidatarios* across the nation are in many respects similar. These include population pressures, boundary disputes, struggle for *ejidal* rights, illegal use of *ejido* lands, continuism of *ejido* leaders, factional struggles within *ejidos,* corruption and prevalent personalism, outside agitation and demagoguery, political intrigues with interests outside the *ejido,* tendencies to violence and assassination, crop diversification, collectivization, and local problems facing each *ejido.* The complexity of these problems does not promote unity within the *ejido* except on the relatively rare occasions when a distinct threat to personal dignity and family is perceived.

Although internal power struggles and personality clashes can absorb much of the interest and energy of the *ejidatarios,* often an external enemy is perceived. Historically, this is the nearby *hacendado.* But with the changing character of the economy and the more advanced political integration of the rural areas into the national power

[10] Rural population growth has been great. For instance, *Ejido Plan Libertad* when initially established in the 1940s had about twenty *ejidatarios*; in the early 1970s there were over seventy with a total population of about 500 residing on the *ejido.* Mohr, p. 2.

structure, the enemy is now identified as one of a variety of figures: nearby commercial interests, a local cooperative, a government ministry, the state governor, a municipal president, nearby *ejidos* or villages, or anyone who seems to oppose the *ejido*. But the *ejidatarios* face difficulties in resisting these threats. As Ronfeldt comments on the case of Atencingo, "It is clear that the *ejidatarios* had very little political or economic power. Rather, they were highly dependent and subordinate partners in the larger political and economic system." [11] The task facing the *ejidatarios* is first to gain power, access to a channel where their voice will be heard. Ronfeldt identifies three alternative political strategies which have been employed by *ejidos*: defiant isolationism, revolutionary struggle, and reformist struggle.[12] Isolationism, the traditional peasant attitude, is less viable nationally due to the integration of the local areas into the context of the nation as a whole. Revolutionary struggle, due to the values of rural culture, is difficult to mobilize nationally. Reformist struggle with its narrower goals fits into the regional context and existing power structure. However, the relative success of any of these strategies varies from locality to locality, depending upon the available power resources — political connections, economic assets, and the perceptions of the actors involved. Success is often related to the correct interpretation of the interactive situation. And Ronfeldt has noted that success in gaining power and reform has ultimately depended on the accommodation of the government's political and economic interests.[13] When reformist struggle has succeeded, the government-sponsored CNC has been the key route (except for the President or the state governor on occasion).

By the time López Mateos took office in 1958, it had become clear that the CNC was not maintaining the desired level of support for the Revolutionary coalition among peasants, agricultural workers, and others within its organizational sphere. Many rural inhabitants were not sharing in the prosperity related to industrialization. Moreover, the militancy and determination of the CNC as a channel for effectively transmitting the desires of the peasants upwards seemed to be gradually decreasing. In these circumstances, demonstrations in the rural areas, and even violence on occasion, were followed by the efforts of minor agrarian leaders to create new militant organizations which would articulate the demands of the rural people. Giving added impetus to the efforts of these men were certain general conditions

11 Ronfeldt, p. 219.
12 Ronfeldt, pp. 226 ff.
13 Ronfeldt, pp. 222–223.

throughout the country as well as a few notable instances of local deprivation. Among these conditions were the environmental factors of climate and soil fertility. Regional droughts alternate with violent windstorms and cloudbursts; rocky, infertile soil is commonplace; waves of crop and animal pestilence still sweep the countryside. Such an environment, in company with the precarious economic conditions that small-scale rural cultivators must confront in a modernizing economy, often result in continued impoverishment beyond the endurance of many human beings. In addition, the facilities promised by leaders throughout the years of the Revolutionary regime have too often failed to materialize. Severe difficulties in resolving problems of credit and related capital needs, along with the declining purchasing power of *campesinos,* made the profits of middlemen in the food chain extremely high. In fact it was often impossible for peasants to realize a profit even in an excellent crop year. Meanwhile, until 1969–1970 the governments of the Revolutionary coalition continued to hold out hope that the distribution of land would continue indefinitely, regardless of population growth. Moreover, government spokesmen continued to stress the theme of an overall agrarian reform dedicated to the renovation, social as well as economic, of the rural way of life.

The CNC remained the government's sole organ for representing the *ejidatarios* and other workers living in the countryside in 1958. This had remained the same since the days of Cárdenas. Moreover, the CNC at that time was headed by a professional, Graciano Sánchez. And since small farmers and rural laborers are almost by definition "unavailable" for the administrative tasks of a bureaucracy, the CNC leadership was always taken from the ranks of the middle-sector professionals, particularly lawyers and city-type agricultural engineers. It became common among Mexicans at all levels to refer to the CNC as "an organization run *for* the peasantry *by* lawyers." The implication was clear: jobs for professionals in the CNC committee hierarchy were more important than representation of peasant interests. The Revolutionary coalition and the CNC were able to coast on the rural workers' political support built by Cárdenas in the vast land expropriations of the 1930s. The CNC continued to provide a show of deference and some material rewards for as long as the older men, such as Vicente Salgado Paez, the Magaña brothers, and others with memories of the Revolution were alive. The new generation of CNC bureaucrats had never really experienced the "peasantry-in-arms." The leadership of the CNC could not communicate a sense of responsiveness to the peasantry, especially when it did not supply material rewards. Deference as a value was seldom well distributed through the peasants' organization.

Rural unemployment, which rose rapidly in the 1950s, in company with increasing stagnation in the CNC bureaucracy, made this channel of accessibility to higher levels of the hierarchy increasingly unsatisfactory to the ordinary rural citizen. It became uncommon for the CNC to meet nationally more than once a decade. Statutes were not amended to give even a formal appearance of responsiveness to the changes occurring in Mexico. From this and other evidence, the CNC was clearly out of step with these changes.

By contrast, even where land was distributed or where government services were improved, the rate of population growth of around 3.5 percent a year (placing Mexico among the top five countries in the world) could not help but obscure the relatively small improvement in services for or benefits from *ejido* plots. The pressure growing from such conditions during the late 1950s and early 1960s stimulated conflict and much open discussion within the CNC. The outcome favored the status quo and simply served to encourage dissident elements in the countryside to go ahead and try to form their own organizations. The impact of the Cuban Revolution on the Mexican left, the formation of the National Liberation Front (MLN), and the reappearance, with great political fanfare, of Cárdenas and his son Cuauhtémoc, all stimulated aspiring rural protest leaders to form their own organizations outside the CNC.

## The "Independent" Peasant Movement

A meeting was held in Mexico City on January 6–8, 1963, to which twelve independent peasant organizations sent delegates for the purpose of forming a new peasant confederation. They called the organization they agreed to form the Independent Peasants' Confederation (CCI). (Subsequently, in 1964, the CCI went through a typical process of internal splintering. Two blocs emerged, the smaller one taking a definite communist stance.)

It was at first not easy to assess the sources of strength or dynamics of these twelve organizations newly federated. Clearly the CCI was not a movement of the right wing of the Mexican political spectrum. In its association with the MLN the personal image used most frequently by the CCI to legitimize its aims was that of Cárdenas. The dynamics of the member groups seemed to stem largely from general conditions in the countryside, as well as from specific local conditions such as a regional drought, or (as in Baja California) the issue of soil salinization brought about by the Welton-Mohawk irrigation project. The state organizations of the CCI were called agrarian leagues, in contrast to the state-level CNC organizations called *ligas de communidades agrarias*.

The state agrarian league of the CCI in Baja California provides a useful illustration for examining the organization's history. The state organization in Baja California began on September 5, 1958 when a group of dissident CNC local leaders asked for an opportunity to use the assembly hall of the *liga* of the CNC and was refused. The group then went to the office of the Regional Confederation of Workers and Peasants (CROC) and held its assembly. At that time a new organization was formed, though there appeared to be little thought of organization on a national scale. In due course, presidents of various *ejido* commissariats in the Mexicali area began to join the new state agrarian league and leave the old CNC *liga*. Where presidents of *ejidos* did not join the new organization, unofficial commissariats within the *ejidos* affiliated with it independently. Rallies held by the state agrarian league of Baja California were extremely successful and often had as many as 20,000 peasants and salaried rural workers in attendance. The bitterness over the salinization of the soil from the polluted Colorado River water (which had been a continuing issue over the years) as well as countless other lesser irritants, including the decreasing ratio of *ejidatarios* to *colonos*, helped produce overflowing crowds at the frequent rallies. The league never lost an opportunity to maintain that it was carrying on the true agrarian tradition in the Baja area which had been abandoned by the CNC. Finally in January 1961 the league was large enough to purchase its own building and a lot for 125,000 pesos. It continued to appeal to small farmers, *ejidatarios*, and landless persons living on the *ejidos* through attacks on the role of middlemen in agricultural sales, credit practices of private lenders, and administration of the Ejido Bank. The Baja state agrarian league squarely headed the attack and articulated the resentment about the salinity of the Colorado River.[14]

Mexican officialdom adopted a tolerant but nonsupportive stance in dealing with the new agrarian leagues. Representatives of the government and, on occasion, a representative of the President of the Republic would come to the large gatherings to hear the criticisms which the members of the state agrarian leagues had to make of both federal and local government in connection with official handling of agrarian

---

[14] *Brecha: México es primero,* Organo de la Liga Agraria Estatal de Baja California, CCI, No. 4 (Mexicali, B.C., January 27, 1964).

problems. Some government sources made the point publicly that the state agrarian leagues were doing the country a service in articulating discontent which had for too long been suppressed or glossed over. The federal government's position clearly was that it could get along with the CCI despite its ties with the CNC, which were officially established under the Agrarian Code.

In the case of Baja California, however, there was evidence by 1965 that negotiations between the Mexican government and the United States regarding the salinity of the water had progressed sufficiently to relieve some of the worst tension, thus weakening support for the CCI. In addition, the peasants' attitudes were less favorable for the CCI in many parts of Mexico, as Ronfeldt noted.[15] Also, incoming President Díaz Ordaz was taking a tougher line with dissident groups than had been the case under López Mateos. And Castroism had lost much of its early magic. Some of the irreconcilable leaders, such as Ramón Danzos Palomino, had been removed from the ranks of the CCI through arrest by the government. Danzos had sided with some of the more determined groups in the MLN in order to form a new party, the Popular Electoral Front (FEP). His open advocacy of violence had incurred the wrath of the government and he was imprisoned, leaving the CCI without its most determined leader. The strength of the CCI was also undermined by Alfonso Garzón's move to Mexico City. By the summer of 1965, Garzón occupied a government position relating to the distribution of grain import licensing sought by milling concerns in Baja California. Moreover, the new organization in 1965 had to deal with stiffer opposition from the Revolutionary coalition. Still more difficult to overcome was the traditional lack of funds suffered by organizational efforts among the population of the countryside. And there was an obvious desire on the part of the aging (though still charismatic) Cárdenas to avoid the kind of activist, revolutionary stance which might have made up for the lack of concrete benefits needed to recruit and maintain the rank-and-file of the organization. Out of these difficulties, there emerged an organization less revolutionary in orientation but with a rank-and-file sufficiently large to warrant a seat in the Chamber of Deputies for Alfonso Garzón. This latter event appeared to be part of a developing pattern of policies designed to give some substance to the publicly avowed intent of President Echeverría to improve the situation of *ejidatarios* and allow organized dissent by members of the rural work force.

---

[15] The variation in the agrarian political situation from region to region is pointed up by Ronfeldt; he found the CCI quite unsuccessful around Atencingo. Ronfeldt, p. 231.

The experience of the CCI, however, was not novel for the Mexican scene. It provided a lesson repeated with persuasive frequency over the decades of rule by the Revolutionary regime: without positive support from the government — something different from mere toleration — the organization and success of such groups within the parameters of non-revolutionary political activity was most unlikely. The emergence of the CCI and the impact of Castro upon the Mexican left (which brought about the formation of the MLN) did result in public discussion of the shortcomings of the CNC. But without some national leader whose charisma resembled that of Cárdenas in the 1930s there could be no real restructuring of the CNC to deal with the needs of the growing rural population.

Thus, the institutionalized agrarian themes of the Mexican Revolution, articulated by the bloody sacrifice of Emiliano Zapata and reiterated by every national political figure since Calles, plus the decades of continuous land reform, did not lay to rest the agrarian question nor the problem of maintaining support among the masses of the rural people. Despite the vast amount of land distributed since 1910, the cumulative character of land reform produced problems which the existing institutional-political structure did not solve satisfactorily from the standpoint of either policy-makers or the expanding numbers of the rural labor force.

Expectations among both the peasantry and government officials are geared to an age-old pattern of dominance. In this there is a mutually reinforcing tendency that leads to acceptance of the existing political order. For this reason a government seems stable when juxtaposed to the mass of inert peasantry. But there is also a traditional familiarity with the idea of violence as an alternative. Thus it was possible for the Díaz government to appear as one of the most stable in the world until the moment of ultimate decision, when political apathy exploded into political violence. Frustrated rural political activism has often been analogous to the lit fuse on the bomb of political violence and rebellion.

Yet, as Ronfeldt notes, direct confrontation and violence can be effective tools in helping to achieve reform:

Certainly no major breakthroughs were ever achieved by an *ejidatario* opposition faction without resort to direct action. . . . Yet direct actions were never in themselves sufficient for success, either on major or minor issues. . . . By contrast, when a large popular following and influential government allies already supported a peasant opposition struggle, and when high-level government officials were already preparing some major resolution of the conflict, then direct-action tactics served as a final dramatic pressure that forced the government to act.[16]

But even if the violence of the *ejidatarios* is countered by the government, the threat of escalating violence is there. The tradition of rural violence is reinforced in the newer rural generations of have-nots. It thus propagates a continuing challenge to the continuity of the Revolutionary regime.

[16] Ronfeldt, p. 234.

# ✤ 5 ✤

# The Politics of Emergent Aristocracy: The Popular Sector

The Mexican Revolution was carried out in the name of land and liberty. It was ostensibly a rural revolution, but its beneficiaries became increasingly urban, with middle and higher incomes. Some of these, when organized, were incorporated into the Revolutionary party in a new organization called the Popular Sector. This was done during the reorganization of the Revolutionary party by President Cárdenas. Although the structural provision for a Popular Sector appeared alongside the older and more traditional Labor and Agrarian Sectors, it was not until several years later during the presidency of Ávila Camacho that a systematic effort was begun to give real political meaning to the Popular Sector.

The National Confederation of Popular Organizations (CNOP) was founded on February 7, 1943 in Guadalajara, Jalisco. Mexican politicians traditionally have spoken of the CNOP as "the organized middle class on the march." The formation of the CNOP marked the beginning of the ascending political fortunes and official representation of interests that were previously on the periphery of the Revolutionary coalition, as well as newly emergent groups.

Unlike the peasant and labor organizations, the organized groups of the CNOP were not based on those ideological areas originally tied to the key moral and legal pillars of the Revolutionary regime. Moreover, neither constitutional, statutory, nor decree law have defined the position of the CNOP in the formal government structure. It has no responsible ministry or department as do labor and agriculture. However, certain organizations in the CNOP are closely connected to governmental agencies — some even staff those agencies. Other organizations in the CNOP, rather than depending upon formally defined public offices, agencies, and legal procedures to provide strategic advantages in the political process, rely on superior education, technical training, and personal connections with highly placed individuals within the Revolutionary coalition. Increasingly, the material and personal resources of certain CNOP elements have placed this confederation as well as leading affiliated associations in a position of political leadership. Individuals from these elements have been closely connected with the regime's concern with economic growth. From this vantage point, the Revolutionary coalition's Popular Sector has come to overshadow the large mass of peasants and the many labor groups with their long-established ties with the Revolution and the Constitution of 1917.

## The CNOP

The National Confederation of Popular Organizations (CNOP) is the full title for the extensive, varied series of groupings forming the third and final sector of the Revolutionary party organization. The party statutes term it the Popular Sector. The CNOP, like the other sectors, has a hierarchy of committees, national, state and municipal. Its rank-and-file members are largely contained in several major independent organizations. Most notable are the Federation of Unions of Employees in Service to the State (FSTSE), the National Union of Workers in Education (SNTE), the National Association of Co-operatives, the Unified Center for Small Commerce, the Owners of Small Agricultural, Livestock, and Forestry Property (CNPP), and the Confederation of State and Municipal Workers. Some of the smallest affiliates of the CNOP claim only a few hundred members.[1] Two of its major organizations, the FSTSE and SNTE, have extensive memberships obviously and directly dependent upon the government because of their lack of an independent merit system. Another major group, the CNPP, has a small but dominant section whose members, small property owners in the rural areas, are the major beneficiaries of government agricultural policy. Many other people organized within the CNOP are dependent upon the government for licensing (small tradesmen and commercial people, as well as very lowly commercial operators such as street vendors, strolling musicians, and

[1] David Shears, *The Popular Sector of the Mexican PRI* (unpublished dissertation, University of New Mexico, Aug., 1972).

bootblacks). In this way the arm of the government touches even the smallest private entrepreneur, which enables the CNOP to have a certain amount of leverage to use with these groups according to political exigencies. In fact, the independently organized but centrally controlled hierarchies of the CNOP (at all levels) illustrate the ancient strategy of building alternate channels of access and communication, formal and informal, within a political corporativist system.

Each organization of the CNOP is defined according to its own function and is structured to fit the formal levels of regional jurisdiction stipulated in the Constitution. Each, regardless of size, has its own internal, hierarchical power structure, and those at the top of that structure are primarily concerned with maintaining access to even higher levels for purposes of rewards, both in material goods and in opportunities for upward mobility. To be successful in these goals, the higher ranks must control those below them.

These structural features of the CNOP reflect the Mexican system. The system fits fairly well Linz' model "authoritarianism." [2] "Authoritarianism" is considered an "ideal type" (a conceptual category with an indefinite number of variations), and the Mexican case with its many hierarchies, formal and informal, is a variation of the general category. The practice of allowing various institutional bases, such as the Church, the family, the variety of hierarchies, and the mixed economy, creates a situation where there is an interwoven, ascending-by-level system of control, a variation distinct both from the historical pattern of dictatorship and from Linz' typology of authoritarian government by military *junta*. In Mexico the CNOP reflects this condition of many hierarchies within a hierarchy by its position as the Popular Sector of the Revolutionary party, an organization with quasi-governmental status, and a branch of the informal system of control.

Much has been said about the all-inclusive nature of the CNOP, because everyone not in the Agrarian or Labor Sectors is in the Popular Sector. In fact, the CNOP has an internal political life in its skeletal network of committees which provide status for many but advancement for few. But the all-inclusive appearance of the CNOP does not mean that it is different from other organizations of the system because it includes so many more types, classes, or conditions of people. It is true that the CNOP includes many professional groups as well as both urban and rural poor, and even a number of politically privileged individuals in both city and country. But to a lesser extent the CTM and the CNC have also included diverse groups. Even if the

[2] Juan J. Linz, "An Authoritarian Regime: Spain," in Erik Allardt and Stein Rokkan, eds., *Mass Politics: Studies in Political Sociology* (New York, 1970), pp. 251–283.

theoretical inclusiveness of the CNOP is not unique, and is without material rewards for many people, an important political value is served by incorporating everyone into the system, giving everyone a chance to be part of a political hierarchy if he wishes.

The Revolutionary coalition through the CNOP thus distributes something of value to all petitioners, no matter how humble. This is more like a "limited" corporativist political system than a "limited" pluralist system. What is allocated first of all in Mexico is deference, and finding ways to allocate deference is fundamental to successful control in the political culture. This is because in the Hispanic tradition *dignidad* (the dignity of one's person) is often more important than material reward. The value of *dignidad* is much increased in Mexico because of the emphasis on *machismo*. Organizations such as the CNOP which describe themselves as all-inclusive contribute to the popular feeling that one has a place, a status, which gives one a right to be heard.

A man's dignity is thus to some extent assured. The intermediary function of a low official in a CNOP committee requires him to listen, haggle, angrily argue, and often refuse demands for immediate rewards. It is sufficient to many Mexicans that that official be accessible, and that he not refuse to listen or interact. His role is indispensable to the dignity of the petitioner, for in the hierarchical society one petitions an intermediary and believes that he will somehow take information to higher levels where it will eventually bring about the desired result. One can meanwhile have patience because one has been heard; one's dignity has been observed. Mexicans speak favorably of individuals in political positions who are "accessible;" they talk very little about what is "delivered" — not that they are unconscious of it, but rather it is not their top priority. *The unpardonable political sin in Mexico would be the development of a system with no way of feeding one's demands into the hierarchy, regardless of results.* This bewilders the Anglo mind.

The CNOP provides a place for those who do not fit easily into other hierarchical slots in the political system; it provides jobs and a chance to move vertically for the politically motivated; it provides channels of communication upwards. The intermediaries in the committees not only pass information downward to the masses but also horizontally into other hierarchies. The CNOP provides hope and deference for the masses, a convenient training-ground for aspiring young politicians, and a legitimate political identity with the Revolution for men whose professional training or wealth makes them eligible for high posts though they lack a background of service in political life.

All these groups tend to fall into territorial categories, and are grouped as municipal and state leagues of the CNOP. There are also nationally organized affiliates in Mexico City with their own directive committees and some degree of autonomy. Leaders of these groups are among the most influential in the CNOP, the government, and the Revolutionary coalition generally. For example, Adolfo López Mateos, later President of Mexico, headed the FSTSE during the early 1950s.

Affiliated individuals and groups are theoretically supposed to work through the central executive committee of the CNOP, which in turn is represented in the central executive committee of the Revolutionary party. In fact, the secretary-general of the CNOP is usually the same person as the Secretary of Popular Action on the party's Central Executive Committee. In practice, representation of CNOP affiliates, especially for those most economically significant, occurs directly with the President of the Republic and his closest advisors. Military officers who are members of the CNOP have especially strategic points of access in the Secretariat of Defense.

The CNOP has included many Mexicans in lower income brackets, but its orientation has increasingly turned toward those who play a productive role in the economy, those from the growing urban population who have participated in the decisions of the Revolutionary coalition. Through their organized business and professional associations, and their political base in the CNOP, the Mexican middle class has achieved great success in maintaining the Revolutionary myth while at the same time obtaining the necessary material support for urban modernization.

The CNOP's political momentum derives largely from the advantages possessed by its most prominent groups and leaders. Taken together with the Revolutionary coalition's emphasis upon modernizing the economy and the development of an urban-industrialization complex, the educational advantage and the urban economic advantage of these individuals have been of great importance. Many of the leaders came from families that were already upwardly mobile at the time of the Revolution. Those are the same families which have increasingly produced the managers of the organized labor and peasant bureaucracies. These families have often had a close identification with the European rather than the Mexican heritage. Unique social and cultural characteristics, as well as certain economic attributes, have come to characterize these upper echelons of the ruling sector. The prestige and influence of the CNOP in Revolutionary circles has constantly expanded. Part of the reason for this success has been a high quality of leadership. There is a higher percentage of people holding professional degrees in the popular sector than in any other. Those with professional degrees not only have the great prestige which such degrees are assigned in Mexico but also emerge from the universities with political contacts already well developed because of the great emphasis on political action in Latin American universities — a matter in which Mexico is no exception. Confederation leaders have been tireless and competent organizers who have endeavored to bring into the fold any cluster of individuals having an interest in common. After 1947 two groups now forming the backbone of the confederation, the FSTSE, or bureaucrats' union, and the teachers' union left the CTM and moved in with the CNOP. Finally, support from President Miguel Alemán helped a great deal. By 1953 the CNOP claimed a total membership through its affiliated organizations of approximately one million persons. By the latter 1950s its membership in Congress and other elective posts roughly doubled the highest figure from any other organized sector of the Revolutionary coalition. Along with their increased formal dominance, the frequent representation of labor and peasant groups by professionals magnified the control of the regime by the middle-class element.

The CNOP was created for the purpose of bringing into the circle of Revolutionary groupings people with interests not readily susceptible of inclusion within the organizational pattern of the CNC and the labor confederations. This has meant great diversity in composition. The professional man, the wealthy businessman, the small shopkeeper, the artisan, and the very poor day-laborer have all been included by the CNOP leaders.[3] In order to accommodate such contrasting groups and keep them as enthusiastic supporters of the Revolutionary coalition, CNOP leaders give the membership some tangible benefits and much time.

The popular sector is described by leaders as "eminently political" in its orientation. A report by the secretary-general of the CNOP in Veracruz offered some insight as to how large groups of people, heterogeneous in their cultural background and interests, have been drawn into the CNOP, providing a useful base to the leaders in their bids for increasingly higher positions in the available bureaucratic and electoral offices:

> We petitioned and [the governor] granted us a special audience Wednesday of every week. In this *audiencia* the popular groups from all over the state advised by the federation [*de Organizaciones Populares del Estado de Veracruz*] presented

---

[3] The ensuing discussion applies only indirectly, if at all, insofar as two of the important affiliated groupings of the CNOP are concerned. The National Teachers' Union and the FSTSE have certain legally formalized connections with government not common to other groupings affiliated with the confederation.

fully their petitions and problems to the governor. To [the governor's] consideration have been submitted 751 memorandums requesting among other things: teachers for schools, lands for the creation of *colonias urbanas* and sports [or recreation] fields, scholarships for poor students, pensioning off of public employees, introduction of potable drinking water, sanitation works, cooperation for festival ceremonies of a cultural-civic nature, etc.

We recognize that thanks to the generosity of [the] governor ... and his closest co-workers ... the majority of the petitions were favorably received. With the aid of [these officials] and through the efforts of our federation, four hundred humble families of the city of Veracruz, grouped in the *colonia*, Ing. Miguel Angel de Quevedo, were favored in their just desire to construct their own homes because we arranged an agreement ... [by which] they could acquire the necessary lots at the very low price of 1.35 pesos per meter ... [and the families] were given up to twelve months with the easiest possible installments in order to make the corresponding payment.

In an interview the secretary-general gave other illustrations of "eminently political" activity. However, it is important to keep in mind some of the conclusions which Fagen and Tuohy drew from their observations in Veracruz:

Authoritarian practices have been leavened with sufficiently large doses of flexibility and responsiveness to create a stabilizing mix. . . . participation in the design and implementation of public policies normally occurs — if at all — on terms set by the authorities themselves. Even when uncontrolled participation occurs ... the attendant uncertainty is usually transitory. . . . The same authorities that manage participatory institutions in an attempt to ensure that all runs smoothly, have substantial reserves. . . . The governor has great latitude in deploying these reserves. Thus ... opportunities for the unrestricted expression of conflict-generating demands are minimized.[4]

The above petition is representative of the demands of CNOP leaders throughout the country on the behalf of members who do not possess the social status and economic standing enjoyed by the middle class. But it is necessary to keep in mind that the CNOP is dominated by professionals who are often propertied people with interests in urban and rural business ventures. Thus the CNOP stands

[4] Richard R. Fagen and William S. Tuohy, *Politics and Privileges in a Mexican City* (Stanford, Calif., 1972), pp. 133–135.

against any raise in property and income taxes. It also promotes the rural property owner against the demands for expropriation by landless peasants, and it stands for emphasis upon urban improvements and public investment for industrialization rather than larger budgets for credit programs for the *ejidos.*

There has also been created and expanded a network of informal understandings among highly influential persons as a basis for preferred access to government officials. The activist leaders are found among people in small businesses who begin their affiliation with the CNOP as propertyless semiliterates. While working as apprentices at some craft or as minor employees in a business establishment, they begin to participate in the CNOP's manifestations of support for the regime. Later their perseverance is rewarded when they are given key roles in the organization of such demonstrations. During this period their contacts with more established members of the CNOP provides business insight, credit, and access to licenses which they need to begin their own small-scale ventures. A baker may want to open his own business. To do so, he must have a license, credit, and advice on products and how to steer safely around official obstacles. He values the deference that comes to him from his contacts in the CNOP, but there must be some material benefits as well.

Top CNOP leadership is recruited almost entirely from economically aspiring persons at middle or higher levels in the economy. They are more highly motivated than the leaders of the older established sectors, who tend to be either aging remnants of another era or the sons of established middle-class families trying to live in the style of the *hidalgo.* The fact that the CNOP leadership has had goals connected with its class and interests has led to political success. Thus the devotion to the CNOP leadership has come from various sources, and the rewards of success are in evidence. Nearly everyone of ministerial rank claims political connections with the CNOP, as do most members of the Chamber of Deputies and the Senate. These are the people who have the greatest access to the President and who most clearly influence the policy of the government. Even the Presidents of Mexico, ever since civilians began to hold the office in 1946, have been clearly identifiable as people of middle-class status, and have been identified with the CNOP in their prior political activities.

## The Federation of Civil Servants' Unions

The single most powerful organization within the CNOP is the Federation of Unions of Workers in the Service of the State (FSTSE). The FSTSE developed from an earlier organization, the FNTE (National Federation of Workers of the State) which was one of the founding organizations of the Confederation of Workers of Mexico (CTM) in 1936. President Cárdenas later obtained passage of a law entitled Statute of the Workers in the Service of the State which spelled out the legal position of the organized bureaucracy and enabled bureaucrats to reform their union and make it into the present-day FSTSE with autonomous status. Later, during the government of Alemán, the FSTSE affiliated with the CNOP.

The FSTSE encompasses over thirty unions throughout the major departments of the executive, legislative, and judicial branches of government, as well as governments of the territories, the federal tourism department, and the national university (UNAM). In all, the persons affiliated with the FSTSE through its member unions number approximately 900,000. They have their own social security establishment which makes a wide range of benefits available through the Institute of Security and Social Services for Workers in the Service of the State (ISSSTSE). The ISSSTSE, with over one billion pesos in reserves, provides an extensive program of medical, hospitalization, and pharmaceutical aid as well as pension plans, numerous low-rental housing projects, low-cost housing for purchase and short-term loan arrangements to free members from usurious interest rates.

The FSTSE has a loyal, well-disciplined, and well-informed membership. The enthusiasm of the group, which is clearly manifest in the large numbers that turn out for political demonstrations, stems in part from the high level of political activism expected in the membership and also from extensive benefits received through the programs of the FSTSE in conjunction with the ISSSTSE. The result of loyalty based upon benefits received is cohesion and activism in the rank-and-file which makes the leaders' pronouncements authoritative in the CNOP or any other group or alliance with which the FSTSE has close ties.[5] Bureaucratic leaders speak for the best organized group in the Popular Sector which, as indicated above, has become the most influential of the sectors. Bureaucratic leaders often hold top positions in the legislature. When there is a division of opinion in the Popular Sector these are the deciding voices. It is their organizational strength which makes the case.

Another organization of considerable importance with a membership similar to the FSTSE in extent, though little has been written about its activities, is the National Syndicate of Employees in Service to State and Municipal Governments. Through the regional groups

5 Rómulo Sánchez Mireles, "El movimiento burocrático," in *México: Cincuenta años de revolución* (México, D.F., 1960), II, pp. 289–305.

and hierarchy of control, this organization transmits demands to the appropriate centers of power in Mexico City. While the rank-and-file of this organization does not enjoy the privileges and status accorded the organization of federal bureaucrats, it would be a mistake to overlook its importance in local politics, the CNOP, and the national government. Many members play key roles in support of the regime, and their needs and loyalty cannot be dismissed by those who rule Mexico.

The primacy of the FSTSE in the CNOP, and more generally in the national councils of the Revolutionary coalition, has various manifestations. One of these is a separate social security organization from the one set up for the Mexican populace. Another is the tendency for top leadership of the FSTSE to move into some of the most coveted government positions. Adolfo López Mateos first became visible as a major contender for the presidency during the 1940s when he rose to prominence first within the FSTSE and then nationally within the CNOP. Another aspirant has been Rómulo Sánchez Mireles, who became secretary-general of the FSTSE and then moved to the key post of majority leader in the Chamber of Deputies. This post has easy access to the President of the Republic and is a respected and sensitive post in all sectors of the PRI. Sánchez Mireles was overshadowed by Alfonso Martínez Domínguez, who first attracted attention when López Mateos was heading the FSTSE. When López Mateos was Secretary of Labor during the Ruiz Cortines presidency, Martínez was becoming increasingly prominent. And when López Mateos became President, Martínez moved to be secretary-general of the CNOP. This position in formal and hierarchical terms ranks as the top FSTSE post. After this Martínez became president of the PRI, Governor of the Federal District, then fell victim to political maneuvering when the new President, Luis Echeverría, sought to renovate the image of the regime and the Revolutionary coalition in 1971.[6] The history of these individuals has most significance when viewed collectively as a sign of the growth of middle class dominance in the hierarchy of the Revolutionary regime.

## Organized Groups in Industry and Commerce

Two legally defined groups which do not fall within the organized sectors of the Revolutionary coalition but which must be taken into account by the government are the Confederation of Chambers of Industry of Mexico (CONCAMIN) and the Confederation of National

[6] Mexican politicians explain Martínez' extended tour abroad in the early 1970s with a shrug of the shoulders and a laconic *"se cayó,"* that is, "he fell."

Chambers of Commerce (CONCANACO). (Individual businessmen are members of the CNOP, but business organizations are not.) Other organizations for Mexican businesses also exist, such as the Bankers' Association (ABM), the Mexican Association of Insurance Institutions (AMIS), and the Mexican Employers' Confederation (COPARMEX). All but COPARMEX are national in scope. They are to some extent cooperative and are exclusively for private enterprise.[7] Although not within the organizational framework of the party nor formally affiliated with it, the two major groups do have a semiofficial status because their membership and organization are provided for in public law.[8] All but the very smallest commercial and manufacturing enterprises are legally required to affiliate with some member chamber of one of the parent organizations.

The idea of grouping commercial and industrial enterprises into chambers which in turn could be confederated with a national directive committee to speak for them stems from early Mexican experience. Merchant organizations received a major stimulus from the formation of the first Chamber of Commerce of Mexico City in 1874. Ten or more chambers were organized in other cities of Mexico from 1874 to 1911. An effort to combine representation of industry with that of commerce was made in the Mercantile and Industrial Confederation of the Mexican Republic, spanning the late 1880s and early 1890s. After the Constitution of 1917 was promulgated, the new Revolutionary government sanctioned the development of confederations of chambers of commerce and industry. Eventually, these became CONCANACO and CONCAMIN. Their definitive structure dates from the public law provisions of 1936, with the separation into chambers of commerce and chambers of business and industry coming in 1941. The ABM came into existence in 1928, COPARMEX was founded in 1929, and was followed shortly by AMIS. Although the original intent of the government was to classify enterprises under public law so that businesses of a like nature could be grouped into one overall classification with an executive committee to act as the sole bargaining agent for that classification, the growing complexity of the Mexican economy made this extremely difficult to maintain. For the CONCANACO, CONCAMIN, and COPARMEX, the effort has been to make membership compulsory under law so that government ministries can deal with types or categories of businesses rather than of individuals.

[7] Robert Jones Shafer, *Mexican Business Organizations: History and Analysis* (Syracuse, New York, 1973), p. 65.

[8] The Minister of Industry and Commerce has supervisory capacity over these organizations. See William P. Glade, Jr. and Charles W. Anderson, *The Political Economy of Mexico* (Madison, Wis., 1963), p. 94.

This arrangement has not resolved many of the often harmful conflicts of interest among private businessmen, but it has afforded government officials important channels of communication for learning needs and demands of specific types of businesses before announcing policy decisions. Though by no means foolproof, this arrangement has prevented much embarrassment and disappointment on both sides, because each chamber can best present the views of its members to the government, and those of the government to the businessmen. The pattern of hierarchical bodies characteristic of the political system is again reflected in the structuring of businesses into these organizations.

Frequently the demands of these groups are phrased in the form of proposed laws which are given to the government. Most *cámaras* (chambers) keep a staff of specialized lawyers to draft legal proposals, either as initiatives or as counterproposals to government initiatives. The strategy is to emphasize that the proposal of the *cámara* or the confederation fits not only special interests but also general interest. Thus even though personal contacts and advantage have continued to be vital in policy successes, spokesmen for business interests must also justify them in light of the public interest.[9] Blatant self-serving can damage chances for a successful outcome. The effort to de-emphasize preferred treatment to individual businesses, at least in the overt sense, has been reflected in the tendency of government to consult primarily with the confederation representatives. (However, strong personal ties with government officials still bring businessmen benefits.) Consultation procedure has become more or less institutionalized. This has enabled the government to manage policy direction more effectively, since specific economic interests are discussed involving many areas of industry or commerce. Although spokesmen for the CONCAMIN or the CONCANACO participate with representatives of the member's individual *cámaras,* negotiations conducted on the basis of the collective *cámara* have become a general pattern.

The CONCAMIN and the CONCANACO have become increasingly important in Mexico since 1950. Of particular significance also is the sector of the CONCAMIN called the National Chamber of Manufacturing Industries (CNIT). The CONCAMIN and the CNIT are not the same. The CONCAMIN includes the CNIT, but the CNIT has a distinctive orientation and constituency. The CNIT was the major instrument of a new group of industrialists that arose in the latter 1930s and early 1940s who were allied with the Revolutionary coalition. Formed in April 1942, its membership was necessarily

---

[9] Brandenburg, Anderson and Glade, and especially Shafer are basic to an understanding of how the chambers work and of their parts in the governments of the Revolutionary coalition. Frank Brandenburg, *The Making of Modern Mexico* (Englewood Cliffs, New Jersey, 1964).

limited because some of the most important manufacturing industries
which had been longer on the Mexican scene already had their own
associations.
The CNIT threatened the older industrial groups of the north and
west. It initially made a bid to capture control of the CONCAMIN
via its extensive smaller-enterprise membership, but failed to do so.
It was threatening in the more important respect of having close ties
with and access to the Revolutionary coalition. Within a few years
after its creation in 1941, the CNIT was regarded as ostentatiously
nationalistic, strongly supportive of the government's business policies
against more traditional business attitudes, and incessantly pushing the
need for rapid industrialization. After the initial period of rapid
organizational growth and while the economy continued to develop
in the early 1950s, different groups of industries started to withdraw
from the CNIT, signaling its decline. The CNIT, despite its connections with the Revolutionary coalition, never provided significant gains
or influence in policy-making for its members other than its constant
propaganda. The government refused to allow the further decline
of the organization from the latter 1950s on by refusing to allow
branches of industry to leave the CNIT.[10] The other larger and
tradition-oriented businesses suffer from long-standing socio-economic
status and political commitments which make it impossible for them
to have a relationship with the Revolutionary regime which is anything more than a *modus vivendi,* a matter of temporary convenience
for both sides. The major discontent with the government's keeping
industries trapped in the CNIT was lessened in the 1960s when they
were allowed to create their own industry-wide chambers separate from
the CNIT, although withdrawal from the CNIT was still formally prohibited. The outcome suited no one completely, but allowed the
continuation of the CNIT while substantially satisfying the demands
of the dissidents.[11] Despite relatively close ties with the government,
the CNIT has never been dominant in Mexican industry.[12] It has
remained a part of the CONCAMIN, although it operates as an
independent fief, and in fact is still somewhat isolated from the main
body of the CONCAMIN. One of the important characteristics of
the new group of industrialists was that they tended to use Mexican
rather than foreign capital, especially that made available through
*Nacional Financiera,* the major government development bank.[13] This
set them apart in financial and political outlook from older industrial

[10] Shafer, pp. 54–58.
[11] Shafer, p. 68.
[12] Shafer, p. 99.
[13] Sanford A. Mosk, *Industrial Revolution in Mexico* (Berkeley, Calif.,
1950), pp. 21–52.

firms with Mexican ownership as well as from the other manufacturing firms funded with foreign capital. In spite of the demand created by the scarcity of goods during World War II, these proliferating young industries were unable to establish a sound borrowing basis with Mexico's principal financiers and lending institutions, thus the connection with government and the Revolutionary coalition was cemented by their financial dependency. These ties with government were further strengthened when the war ended. The industries of the CNIT needed tariff protection to prevent competition between their products and those of the older industrial countries. The development program of the government provided protection for these and other Mexican industries.

Unlike the CNIT, the COPARMEX has long been considered by Mexicans, particularly those in the government, as an arm of the Monterrey and Jalisco industrialists. The COPARMEX was created in 1929 as an agency for employers. Its members operate under federal law through their affiliation in the CONCAMIN. The leadership continues to come from Monterrey.[14] This fact, along with the strong Roman Catholic orientation of the COPARMEX propaganda, has highlighted the regionalism and potentially anti-Revolutionary political stance of the old industrialists of the north and west. The COPARMEX, however, is rather unique in that it is a completely voluntary association which attempts to provide such important services as information or personnel management, executive training, worker safety and hygiene, social security, and profit-sharing. The organization focused on upgrading its own expertise with some success, but its overall appeal is hindered by its air of paternalism and political Catholicism. Despite this, in 1966 the COPARMEX had 32 centers nationwide, with many nationwide businesses supporting it.[15] It also gained a reputation as the most independent spokesman of the private sector.

Mexico's civil associations (organizations with "A.C." after the title) have been useful to most middle-sector business groups. These civil associations are private, non-profit bodies under Mexican public law and must be registered in the *municipio* where they have headquarters. The purpose of such an organization may be furthering business techniques, but it is also legitimate to have "educational" or "charitable" purposes. Civil associations are politically significant for several reasons. One, they generally support the drive of the middle class toward increasing political and economic advantage. Also, staff work in the civil associations provides suitable employment for educated sons of

14 Shafer, p. 59.
15 Shafer, p. 72.

middle-class families. Three, the use of the civil association may provide a way of escaping from some institutionalized arrangement which a particular branch of business considers unfavorable to its interests. The formation of the National Chemical Industry Association (ANIQ) in 1960 was a notable example of the way a civil association was used to realize goals barred by the existing institutional structure.[16] And four, the staff members of many civil associations play a part in local chambers of commerce as well as in political activity of the CNOP, thus providing an important connection of businesses to the Revolutionary regime.

The CNOP and the other organizations of the "new aristocracy," despite their differences, all have essentially the same outlook. In Mexico this bias has meant concern for urban growth, urbanized industrialization, and preferred positions for professional people and government employees. The result has been that the importance of rural problems and the older Revolutionary goals have been reduced in the eyes of Mexican policy-makers. The members of these organizations are the people who have benefited most from the overall development policy that has characterized Mexican presidencies since the time of Alemán.

## The Great Pyramid

The record of the preceding pages reflects the position of the Revolutionary coalition as Mexico's governing group. The Revolutionary coalition is not to be found in any single, discrete political body or social organization. Rather it is composed of individuals who are in most segments of the political system. The more important a policy, or the greater its potential for conflict, the more the Revolutionary coalition relies on its internal, interconnected, personalistic, hierarchical structure for policy-making. This system of informal interconnections constitutes the Great Pyramid of political power in Mexico. Major policies are derived (primarily informally) from among different discrete political hierarchies through the strategic interconnections of members at all levels of the Revolutionary coalition. Since the discrete hierarchies are not of equal importance, because some have greater impact than others upon the operation of the political system, this in turn has a bearing on the status of a member in his role in the Great Pyramid. Significantly, the most important discrete hierarchy

16 Shafer, pp. 69–71. This group of firms sought to break away from its affiliation to the CNIT, but because it was one of the few major industrial groupings left in the CNIT it was not allowed to do so.

controls more resources than any other, and these resources are increasingly found in governmental executive bureaucracies and public enterprises.

Figure 6 represents how the Mexican political system is composed of these interconnected hierarchical structures.[17] The interconnections and routes used for political advancement in the Revolutionary coalition are, with a few exceptions, not formal in nature; generally they

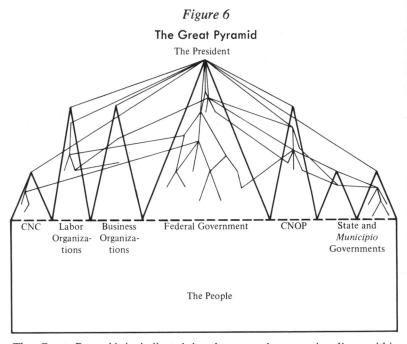

*Figure 6*

**The Great Pyramid**

The President

CNC    Labor    Business    Federal Government    CNOP    State and
       Organiza-  Organiza-                                *Municipio*
       tions      tions                                    Governments

The People

The Great Pyramid is indicated by the upward converging lines within and across the formal hierarchical bodies (which are indicated by the bold-line pyramids). The people at different times are in the base of different pyramids, thus the dashed line at the bottom of each pyramid showing how they incorporate the people. The Great Pyramid culminates with the President.

[17] David Ronfeldt has astutely noted this pattern in his in-depth field study of Atencingo: "The executive organization was far from monolithic or even strictly hierachical. Rather, it could be described as a set of parallel hierarchies, one headed by the state governor and several others headed by the federal ministers and presidential appointees, with the president himself presiding over all." David Ronfeldt, *Atencingo: The Politics of Agrarian Struggle in a Mexican Ejido* (Stanford, Calif., 1973), p. 224.

occur through the existence of *camarillas,* alliances, and an individual's personal security system. At the same time, the many discrete lower hierarchies do have formal relationships with the discrete higher ones. A formal pattern of control does exist. It is critical to realize that this formal control is not obviated by the existence of the Great Pyramid, but rather is often utilized as the means of enforcing political decisions reached through the Great Pyramid. Formal government is thus often dependent on the informal Great Pyramid for policy-making, while the Great Pyramid is usually dependent on the formal hierarchies for policy implementation.

In effect, there are two legitimacies, that of the formal structures of government and that of the Revolutionary coalitions. At the highest levels these are joined as one. The viability of this interdependence is based on two basic factors and a corollary. One is the formal structural existence of governmental extensiveness and control over the national life. The other is the official ideology and existing rule of the coalition. The dynamics of the political culture stress the hierarchical nature of authority relationships in both the formal government and the informal Revolutionary coalition. The corollary states that because of the simultaneous legitimacy of both the Revolutionary coalition and government there is one leadership which *must* occupy the peak of both pyramidal hierarchies. This leadership thus possesses a legitimacy which stresses the values of order and continuity, as well as the legitimacy of the Revolution, which exalts the values of Indianism (*indigenismo*), nationalism, and social justice. Both of these sets of basic factors — "State and Revolution" — constitute an historical, pragmatic dualism which fosters an inherent tension in the system that has not been resolved. The fact that they are to some extent contradictory suggests that the present melding of the legitimacy of the two at the highest levels — within the person of the President, some of his predecessors, and his circle of advisors — is the only viable way of maintaining legitimate control.

The most essential characteristic of the most successful members of the Great Pyramid is their relatively large numbers of important ties, strategic interconnections and contacts, with other members in other discrete hierarchies. Since the time of Alemán's presidency the most powerful individuals increasingly have been those with more strategic channels. These members have usually identified themselves with the CNOP. It is this fact that has been the basis of the rise to prominence of the Popular Sector of the PRI. The ascendancy of the CNOP reflects the urban, developmental foci of its members. And this orientation was carried into the highest councils of government, and has since dominated the national priorities of those who rule Mexico.

# ⁕ 6 ⁕

# At the Peak of Power: The Presidency

Just as the Revolutionary coalition claims its legitimacy as lineal descendants of the peoples' will expressed through the Revolution, the President of the Republic claims legitimacy as the lineal descendant of supreme secular authority, and in effect is the crowned head of the Revolutionary coalition. In Hispanic culture the supreme secular authority occupied a position halfway between God and man. The holder of the Crown was a semidivine figure, a mythical reincarnation of Santiago Matamoros, who was the supreme transcendental figure in the Spanish cosmos, patron saint of all the Spanish, the mystical blood-brother of Christ, and the greatest of all the intercessors. During the centuries of intermittent warfare that accompanied the reconquest of the Iberian peninsula from the Moors, all legitimacy became focused on the Crown of Castile and Aragon. From here it was passed to the Viceroy who ruled in the great Spanish colonial empire of the Western Hemisphere. The Viceroy of New Spain, later Mexico, was the supreme head and a great nationalistic, paternalistic figure for millions of colonial subjects. The President of Mexico is a surrogate for the Viceroy, a role made necessary by the political break with Spain and the continuation of the political culture that was part of the Spanish colonial legacy.

Each occupant of the Mexican presidency thus becomes while in office the lineal descendant of a centuries-old tradition. Benefits received from the government come from him, while poor government is due to evil or inept men under him. Even a President deposed by an armed popular rebellion, as in the case of Díaz, may be forgiven many of his mistakes by blaming the *científicos, gringos,* opportunists, and other malevolent figures surrounding him. As the peasant told his son when the President passed by them on the road, "There goes the government." The President is a semidivine father-figure to the people, inherently good in caring for his children. He is never directly challenged, as for example in the press, because that would shake the very basis of secular government. He is the *jefe* of *jefes*, who makes all final decisions. Each new public work is still his gift to the people, who (especially in the rural areas) petition him for the things they need in the same way that the Viceroy was petitioned centuries ago. The passage of time has changed much, but these deep-rooted practices with their supporting norms and symbols have not died — they live on in the aura of the President of Mexico in the closing years of the twentieth century.

### Presidential Nominations and Elections

Both the part the elections play and the way they are carried out differ markedly from two-party or multi-party systems. Rather than having an aggregating function involving interplay between two parties or among several parties, the interplay of interests and the accommodation of competing demands that might normally mark the campaigning of candidates representing various parties takes place largely within the Revolutionary coalition, the institutional manifestation and electoral symbol of which is the Institutional Revolutionary Party (PRI). The focus within the Revolutionary coalition is upon nominations for posts in the executive, with the competition somewhat less keen for legislative positions.

The many campaign trips to all corners of the country made by the president-designate — the presidential candidate of the official party — are in large part a device for reaching people to create a favorable impression that will increase support for the regime. Such journeys also permit the candidate to study the most pressing problems and demands in all sections of the Republic. On these trips conferences of national leaders, community leaders, businessmen, politicians, and technicians are held in the principal cities and even in some of the outlying towns to discuss the problems of a given region. The conference device probably does a great deal, not only to improve the candidate's knowledge of a given regional situation, but also to broaden his understanding of the personalities involved in the various regions and localities of the country. In addition there is an opportunity to evaluate the capabilities of the staff chosen to arrange the meetings.

The effort to reach the Mexican people at campaign time extends to the most isolated villages. Though the candidate himself cannot possibly visit every population nucleus in Mexico, his representatives go out to all villages. The campaign teams bear posters with the candidate's picture and carry audio-visual equipment to show the candidate and project excerpts from his campaign speeches. An effort is made to bring the personality of the candidate home to Mexicans everywhere so that support will be strengthened as people are given the sense of "knowing" their next President. At election time the newspapers carry many accounts of these election teams of young PRI supporters barnstorming in the remote villages of Mexico. Such efforts were first made during the time of Lázaro Cárdenas and have continued. They are designed to bridge the gap between the still-extensive sections of isolated rural Mexico and those other parts now linked with the communications and transportation networks. The problem of the urban politician in his attempt to carry on a dialogue with rural people is familiar to every student of developing countries. The Mexicans make an outstanding effort to solve this problem.

The campaign trips also afford the president-designate an opportunity to test the sentiment throughout the country, and change the emphasis on one or another program in accord with that sentiment. The candidate, sensing discontent, can shift his stance on relevant issues. For example, the problem may well be the balance between benefits for countryside against cities, or the needs of a particular area. It is not so much that the president-designate shifts positions from one section of the country to another, a tactic used in many countries; it is rather that the president-designate attempts to promote a dialogue with influential persons in all sections to evaluate the political feasibility of his policy line. This is facilitated by the government's advantageous position in radio and television.

The person who is usually considered for the presidency (*presidenciable*) has been a cabinet officer. Cárdenas and Ávila Camacho were respectively Minister of War and Minister of Navy before their nominations. Alemán, Ruiz Cortines, Díaz Ordaz, and Echeverría were Ministers of the Interior. López Mateos was Minister of Labor. In recent years the critical steppingstone to the presidency has been the Ministry of the Interior, although the Ministers of the Treasury and ministers attached to the presidency are also in the forefront.

There is a constitutional provision commanding a cabinet officer to separate himself from office six months ahead of the election date, but this does not restrict presidential aspirations of cabinet officials in any significant way. A further constitutional requirement which has eliminated potential candidates is that the candidate have parents who are both Mexican.

The important consideration for a candidate is the degree of his acceptability to the presidential incumbent. Acceptability operates both at the level of consideration of personal relations and on the level of political convictions of the potential candidate, i.e., his probable choice of policy alternatives. Physical appearance and health make a difference; neither should be clearly negative. A man must have a reputation for an energetic approach to his tasks. It is helpful if the aspirant's wife has a moderate interest in public affairs. No presidential nominee in the past two decades or more has leaned strongly toward or away from religion. Most presidents have come from a middle-class background. In such circumstances there is not too much wealth nor too little to provide some education, and from such a social stratum can come a man who has some feeling for the masses as well as some understanding of the expectations of the affluent.

Presidents tend to be chosen from large and economically prosperous states. Since the time of Cárdenas these states have been on or near the central *mesa* of Mexico. Another consideration is training in practical politics and government. Since the time of Cárdenas, presidents have always had experience as governors or senators, although not immediately before nomination. Those chosen for the Revolutionary coalition's nomination have always served at the head of some ministry.

It is important that the successful candidate for the nomination be well known nationally and acceptable to all of the major groups which in one respect or another have a voice in the highest circle of decision-makers around the incumbent President. A successful player in this most strenuous of all Mexican political contests must not be too closely identified with any single major interest association and must avoid extremes. It pays to be moderate enough so that neither of the major wings of the party will oppose the nomination on the grounds of too close alignment with the other wing.[1] For example, Mario Moya Palencia, the Minister of Interior and a key contender for Echeverría's succession, lost some important support by being too closely identified with the Population Control Law of 1973.

Daniel Cosío Villegas, one of Mexico's most noted commentators and historians, said in 1974 that foreign observers too often fail to accept the fact that the succession of Presidents can be dependent entirely upon arbitrary choice, even the "caprice" or "whim" of the outgoing President. He explained that the Mexican political system could realistically be viewed as built around a "sexennial absolute monarchy" and the "monarch" might very well choose "a prince who seems like

[1] See Frank Brandenburg on wings of the party in *The Making of Modern Mexico* (Englewood Cliffs, N.J., 1964), pp. 131–136.

himself." [2] Thus, although other factors may be present (such as the aspirant's "masculinity," health, vitality, revolutionary antecedents, middle- or lower-class origin, distinction in profession or political activity, administrative skill, right geographical base, or the pendulum effect between the left and the right of the political spectrum), they must all take second place in the end to the President's preference.

All the above factors play a part, certainly, but the distinctive contribution of Cosío Villegas is his insistence on the extremely limited, if not unilateral, basis for the succession decision. The Anglo tendency to view such a decision from a pluralist perspective may easily hinder understanding of the selection process. Because of Cosío Villegas' unique status in Mexican society, his evidence, although anecdotal, must be considered of major importance. He described two episodes drawn from conversations with intimates familiar with relationships within the presidential inner circle. In the case of the selection of Adolfo Ruiz Cortines in 1952, Cosío narrated the situation in which the President of the PRI, Rodolfo Sánchez Taboada, had a group of close friends for dinner with the intent to begin work on the presidential campaign as soon as the candidate's name was revealed. After dining, coffee and liqueurs were served, and then still more coffee and liqueurs, but it was two hours or more before some word reached the assembled guests. However, even this news was indefinite, and further telephone calls came over succeeding hours. In the words of Cosío Villegas,

> After the third call, Sánchez Taboada came back to the table in a bad humor — not only for the long wait, but because the situation was confused. He described the situation to his guests, exclaiming, "Now it turns out that even little old Ruiz Cortines wants to be President!" And scarcely a half hour later the message was received that Don Adolfo (Ruiz Cortines) had been revealed as the candidate. Sánchez Taboada communicated this news to his dinner companions without any other comment than, "Get to work, boys." [3]

The same author also recounts conversations between General Olachea, the president of the PRI, and Ruiz Cortines in trying to choose

---

[2] Daniel Cosío Villegas, "Tapado a la Vista," *Excelsior* (November 26, 1974). Translated by author. Cosío Villegas' article is an excerpt from a forthcoming book, the third in a series. The first two are *El sistema político mexicano* (México, D.F., 1973) and *El estilo personal de gobernar* (México, D.F., 1974).

[3] Cosío Villegas.

a successor in 1958. Olachea went down the list of possible candidates to get Ruiz Cortines' reaction on each.

Angel Carvajal . . . "We love this countryman of ours a great deal, we know him well. We're not going to analyze why we know him well!" Flores Muñoz . . . "A very hard choice! A very good friend, a very good worker." Doctor Morones Prieto . . . "Ah! Honest like Juárez, austere like Juárez, patriotic like Juárez. Just like Juárez! Yes, sir!" Ernesto Uruchurtu . . . "What a good President he would be for the first eighteen years!" And Olachea didn't mention anyone else. Without pausing, the President then asked him if anyone had spoken of López Mateos, and Olachea answered, "That one is very young, Mr. President." But Ruiz Cortines said to Olachea that he should investigate anyway whether or not López Mateos was — how do you say — interested." [4]

According to our raconteur, General Olachea was left with the impression that the President in likening Morones Prieto to such a great national hero as Juárez meant surely to name Morones Prieto as candidate of the Revolutionary coalition and, in effect, President-elect of Mexico. However, the turn of events was most surprising and supported the basic proposition of Cosío Villegas that choices may be most unexpected even by the President's closest associates. Thus, when Olachea again visited the presidential chambers to report on the seemingly routine investigation of López Mateos' possible desire to be a candidate, the first mention of the man's name elicited an exclamation from the President, "Now, you don't have to go on, General. That's the one!" [5]

The results of a poll taken in the fall of 1974 by *Acción Comunitária*, A.C. also emphasized the President's preference. This cross-sectional survey of the Mexican elites brought to light the opinion that the single most important factor generally considered in an aspirant being chosen was his personal relation to the President. However, the results also indicated that other factors were seen as important to the presidential decision. [6]

One of the most difficult jobs facing the president-designate is the responsibility of making sure that there are people in the Congress and the administration on whom he can rely. While the power of

[4] Cosío Villegas.
[5] Cosío Villegas.
[6] Acción Comunitária, A.C., *Punto Clave* (November–December, 1974).

Congress is limited, incumbent Presidents want to avoid public signs of dissension within the coalition. Nominations to the Congress are sought by many, and there are not nearly enough positions to go around. There is added influence, access to the President, prestige, and some income connected with these positions, and they need to be parceled out carefully as coveted prizes. These choices are generally subject to the approval of the president-designate. There are at least three types of persons from whom the president-designate takes suggestions for nominations to the Congress. The first type are those who form the inner circle (usually ministers) around him; the second are the leaders of the major interest groupings, including high-ranking military officers; the third is made up of the governors of the states. When the choice of a pre-candidate involves a conflict, the ability of the president-designate to avoid offending members of these three groups provides a major pre-election test of his political capacity.

## Internal Rivalries

The presidency is the most important political and constitutional office in the country; consequently the major scramble for nomination to office within the Revolutionary coalition centers around it. The organizations of the PRI's three sectors as well as many non-sector organizations related in some way to the party become involved in rivalries which reach the highest peak of intensity. Because rivalries are so intense, the man in the presidency, as election time rolls around, usually seeks to put off the time when actual electioneering (*futurismo*) by presidential hopefuls in the cabinet begins. Once electioneering does begin, the incumbent seeks to postpone the announcement of the selection of a president-designate, since everyone will turn to that man in an effort to win his favor. The difficulty for the President is that the announcement of his successor encourages men in politics to neglect their immediate administrative responsibilities to seek the establishment of a close relationship with the future President. Thus the President seeks to avoid giving the final nod of approval necessary for the naming of his successor until the last possible moment.[7]

The role of the presidential incumbent during the pre-nomination period is difficult. There is a pressing necessity to balance achievements of his administration against the difficulties created by the intrafamily struggle for the presidential nomination. Each person who

[7] Robert E. Scott, *Mexican Government in Transition* (Urbana, Ill., 1959), pp. 197–199.

fancies himself a candidate for the nomination puts in action a whispering campaign calculated to undermine his closest competitors. Such rumor-mongering does not have the best effect on public regard for the incumbent President's administration, since many of the unfavorable rumors run against its members. The rumors frequently question the economic condition of the country in regard to its balance of payments, store of foreign currency, and other vital matters.

In the campaign for the presidential nomination as Revolutionary coalition candidate, pre-candidates seek to establish the impression of great popular support by stimulating and welcoming the formation of supporting organizations and committees. These seek to have their choice nominated by focusing attention on that part of the incumbent's program with which their man has been especially associated. Although in some ways critical of the outgoing President's performance, no pre-candidate nor his supporters publicly castigates the incumbent.

A high point in the pre-nomination activity occurs on the occasion of the President's State of the Union message on September 1 of the year preceding the general election. All categories of politicians — governors, senators, deputies, commanders of military zones, regionally prominent leaders — come to Mexico City ostensibly to hear the President; they are, however, more concerned in looking up their best sources of information in order to find out who is on the inside track for the presidential candidacy. Each politician seeks to visit as many as possible of the potential winners in the nomination race. Government offices, the central offices of the PRI, favorite restaurants, and hotel lobbies hum busily reflecting the stepped-up interaction in the Revolutionary coalition.

After the State of the Union message it becomes more difficult than ever for the President to avoid the final act of approving a successor. By late fall of the year prior to the general election businesses begin to slow down, and soon interest is at a peak as people manifest their excitement in a growing willingness to place bets concerning the outcome of the nomination race. The necessity of bringing the successor into the open is increased because of the threat of economic slowdown as businessmen delay decisions on inventory and investment. In the most recent decision, López Mateos was able to withstand the pressure only two months following his State of the Union message. The first declaration of a major interest organization in favor of Díaz Ordaz came from the CTM federation of the state of Nuevo León on November 1, 1963. By November 3 the opening salvo had become a barrage of high-powered endorsements from the Labor Sector, and the issue was no longer in doubt.[8]

Brandenburg provides a detailed description of the decision-making process, and discerns nine stages. The first three encompass the designation of a president-elect and the ensuing scramble to climb on his bandwagon. The process is initiated by inquiries from the presidential incumbent as to the relative acceptability of several individuals, usually cabinet ministers. The President consults the few individuals who advise him most closely on policy and a slightly wider circle including cabinet officers, leaders of major interest groups in the Revolutionary coalition and spokesmen of powerful economic interests outside the revolutionary circle.

When a consensus has been reached, and the time appears propitious to the presidential incumbent, the Minister of Interior is informed of the choice, if he has not been included in the decision-making circle, and the president of the PRI is also told at this point. The public announcement comes from one of the major interest groups of the Revolutionary coalition. The privilege of making the announcement is awarded by the president-designate himself (*el verdadero tapado*).

The announcement of the choice is the second stage of the process which is followed immediately by a third stage (*irse a la cargada*) in which every power-seeker and politically articulate person affiliated with the Revolutionary coalition strives to outdo the others in praising the future President. Shortly, thereafter a fourth step provides the official nomination of the new man at a giant rally of the PRI in Mexico City. After many speeches, the one and only real candidate is accepted unanimously by the nominating convention.

The fifth, sixth, and seventh stages are respectively the campaign, which serves many purposes other than vote getting, the general election, which the PRI candidate always wins by a wide margin, and official acceptance of the vote which is conducted through formal agencies dominated by the Revolutionary coalition. Eighth and ninth steps include the choosing of a new presidential administrative team for the future President with all the patronage belonging to each office and the final step of weighing carefully the timing for the announcement of these appointments in order to obtain the best political effect.[9]

With the exception of the PAN, the party which tries harder than

[8] Florencio Zamarripa M., *Díaz Ordaz: Ideología y perfil de un revolucionario* (México, D.F., 1964), pp. 14–15.

[9] Brandenburg, pp. 145–150.

any other to give the PRI competition, other parties seem to interest themselves in jockeying for position from which to attempt to influence the choice of the PRI nominee. Parties such as the PPS and the very small PARM attempt to achieve specific goals through supporting the pre-candidate of the Revolutionary coalition whose views come closest to theirs. This kind of activity appears to be regarded by the Revolutionary coalition and the officials of the PRI as perfectly compatible with the interests of the dominant party, since the minor parties, in working to affect the nomination, seldom exert much influence but do derive psychological benefits from participation in the system.

Since 1952 attention among top decision-makers has focused primarily upon nominating a man capable of balancing the right and left wings of the Revolutionary coalition, the *alemanistas* and the *cardenistas*. In addition to the general division between right and left there are also many interest groups with specific narrower goals which must be considered and to some extent satisfied. The problem is to select the candidate who will be, as President, moderate and flexible enough to adjust his program to the nation's major needs while at the same time accommodating the most important conflicts between left and right and satisfying the outstanding demands of the most significant interest groups. The success of the revolutionary tradition in assimilating a wide variety of interests and many shades of political opinion has now raised the problem of acquiring a skilled compromiser to lead the nation.

The diverse wings of the Revolutionary coalition are strong, in part because each represents a main current in the stream of revolutionary thought. Those closely identified with the memory of Cárdenas favor benefits for small farmers and other mass interests and are often critical of capitalism as an economic system. For the *alemanistas,* the push for industrialization is most important, with a strong emphasis upon government-assisted private enterprise. The whole approach of the *alemanistas* to Mexico's problems is somewhat reminiscent of the Calles formula of an earlier day. However, neither the *alemanistas* nor the *cardenistas* have ideological positions so clearly defined that they exclude the other group. Furthermore, the lines between the two are often blurred because of personal ties which have little to do with socio-political goals. Neither wing far outweighs the other, for the *cardenistas,* while they have a larger popular membership, are not so well organized or financed as the *alemanistas*. One thing is certain, the existence of the two conflicting interpretations of Revolutionary goals accompanied by major coalitions on right and left have made it necessary as well as feasible for Presidents to assume a middle-of-the-road position in order to maintain the broader coalition which encompasses the two wings.

One reason that a President can take a middle position with regard to the two wings of the revolutionary group is that even for people on the extremes there exists a core consensus of Revolutionary values. There is the common memory of participation in a common movement and the common interest in a stronger Mexico to be developed on the basis of a tradition encompassing positions both of right and left. Particularly, there is a recognition of the value of compromise in order to keep the Revolutionary coalition intact. At the top, giving way on certain points in order to gain others is a prized strategic end. It is this attitude toward accommodation, the high value placed upon conciliation rather than force, which makes it possible for a right, a left, and a center to coalesce in support of a hierarchical control structure.

## The President's Role

### Institutionalization

The problem of transferring power from one leader to another in Mexico's highly charismatic pattern appears to have been relatively well worked out by changing the outward symbols of charisma from the individual leader to the office he holds. It is the office which commands the respect, clothes the leader with dignity, and endows him with charismatic qualities. Thus over the years there has evolved a situation which is less personal and more mechanical and procedural. Personalism and caesarism are limited although some personal identification carries over for some Mexicans. The key difference is that the recipient of such loyalty tends to be himself a product of the system rather than its major originator and supporter. In this arrangement a new person takes office every six years. He is clothed with viceregal dignity and power, and at the end of his term is replaced by another individual who by reason of the office receives the same attributes. Thus are the powers of the office institutionalized.

The President is chief of government and nearly always head of the Revolutionary coalition. In these roles recent Presidents have been highly successful in balancing competing interests in a situation featuring the rapid proliferation of organized groups. This success would not have been possible had the President alone had to gather the information and make the decisions necessary to the balancing process. Fortunately for the Revolutionary coalition, their choices for President have seen the necessity of increasing staff and delegating responsibility, a development which has culminated in the establishment of an Office of the Presidency to provide the staff assistance necessary for effective action in all areas of political activity. The situation today presents a marked contrast to the lack of administrative and political talent backing up the presidency in the 1920s and early 1930s.

The institutionalization of the presidency has created a situation in which the office automatically provides great authority and power while at the same time puts a premium upon a degree of moderation and mildness in the political style of the President in order to balance successfully contending pressures. The office itself, however, gives its holder such strength that even a relatively mild man seems to be able to stand independently of his predecessor, even a dynamic predecessor. The normal condition seems to have become one of an ex-President's leaving his successor alone to carry out the duties of his office as best he is able, and in support of this rule there is the understanding that no ex-President is to be punished or harried. Whatever differences may exist between the outgoing President and his successor are worked out privately, a fact which in turn tends to maintain the legitimacy of the presidency in the eyes of Mexican citizens.

From 1940 until 1970 it appeared that the presidential incumbent, with an institutionalized office to clothe him with charisma, did not need in himself the dynamic characteristics necessary in the first years of the Revolutionary regime. Mexican Presidents during this period (1940–1970) demonstrated their independence but at the same time were different personally from the old *caudillo* type. The presidential political style during these years was characterized by a bland approach which seemed useful in maintaining equilibrium among many diverse interests within the Revolutionary coalition.

The comparison of the type of politician who held the presidency in earlier decades with Presidents of more recent times is striking. There have been fourteen Presidents since 1920, five of whom were generals, two leaders of armed forces without a corresponding military rank, and seven civilians, but five of those seven civilians have held office consecutively in most recent times. When Alemán left office in 1952 he was the first civilian executive to have completed a full presidential term since Benito Juárez. Alemán, Ruiz Cortines, López Mateos, Díaz Ordaz, and Echeverría (all civilians like Alemán) have all used the political and constitutional powers at their disposal to balance contending interests, provide greater stability, and achieve a higher level of productivity for the nation than such strong-man Presidents as Obregón, Calles, and Cárdenas could do under the conditions existing at the time of their leadership.[10]

The civilian Presidents since 1946 have had a number of characteristics in common, but outstanding among these is the determination to deal with serious trouble before it can get out of hand. Thus in Alemán's case a major oil refinery strike tested his will, and the strike was broken, demonstrating the strength of the man who governed. Ruiz Cortines, when he first took over, proceeded to attack corruption on a grand scale, even though it hurt many friends of the former President. He also successfully avoided a threatened general strike in July 1954. López Mateos had to face a major wildcat strike among railroaders in March 1959, after taking office in December 1958. Swift and efficient action proved he could control the situation. A number of major leaders were imprisoned, and the strike was effectively broken. Díaz Ordaz carried this tendency to deal forcefully with civil disturbances to an extreme at the Plaza of Tlatelolco in 1968. While constraints exist on Presidential decision-making, including the maintenance of the Revolutionary coalition and of the Revolutionary myth, the President exercises the final directing hand. Still, the presidency needs a decision-making apparatus which can adjust to the ever-expanding needs of the country in order to provide effective administration. The expanding Ministry of the Presidency, heads of the executive departments, the heads of the major interest groups, both in and out of the Revolutionary coalition, heads of some nongovernmental bureaucracies and the high officials of the PRI all help.

## Formal Elements of the Presidency

The strength of the Mexican presidency is based in part upon constitutional powers. Included in this field are a broad power of appointment and removal, fiscal powers, the capacity to initiate and veto legislation, and control of the military.

Election is by direct popular vote. In order to be chosen, an individual must be male, 35 years old by election day, and a native-born citizen who is the son of Mexicans, themselves citizens by birth, and must have resided in the country a full year (official missions excepted). A presidential candidate cannot be a minister of a reli-

---

[10] "The presidential function does not now make the same demands upon personalistic leadership to evoke singular and immediate emotional response by followers in the heat of battle that it once did." Scott, p. 148.

gious sect nor have any ecclesiastical status. Anyone who wants to be President and who is in the military, in the national cabinet, or holds the governorship of a state or territory must retire at least six months prior to election day. Mexican Presidents may never be re-elected. Should a President become too ill to carry on, or if he should die in office, an interim President is appointed by the Congress.

The President has a wide variety of ceremonial activities connected with his office. Scarcely a day goes by that he is not involved in the dedication of some new public building or public work, whether it be a highway or a new sewage plant. Often such dedications are occasions for fiestas in the countryside at which the President, surrounded by a large group of his co-workers, appears before the people in a kind of holiday atmosphere in order to speak to them of the ongoing Revolution and its accomplishments. Conventions of farmers, workers, or professional people all provide occasions for the appearance of the President, as do gatherings on patriotic days. Finally, there are the visiting dignitaries to be met, educators and scientists and public benefactors of all kinds to be congratulated.

Presidential authority in relation to the military is extensive. Not only are there powers of appointment but there is also the authority to order troop movements relating to internal security and external defense. The power over internal troop movements in a country such as Mexico, which has had little necessity to defend its borders, looms much larger than does the defense function insofar as the armed forces are concerned; and in it is reflected one of the central facts of domestic politics. The specific role of the military in Mexico over recent decades has given rise to the impression that the military is no longer as important a mainstay of the presidency as it once was.[11] While we still lack empirical studies, the supposed "non-political" character of the Mexican military remains to be carefully examined.

With regard to legislative functions, initiation of legislation is carried on almost entirely by the President. Though legislators have the right to initiate bills, they seldom do. In addition to the President's vast field of action with regard to the initiation of legislation and his work to secure its passage there is also a presidential veto power which never comes into play in practice because the legislature does not amend bills without prior consultation with the executive, thus eliminating the necessity of employing a veto. The veto remains, however, as a legal means at his disposal.

Following passage of legislation, there remain under Mexican law

[11] See Martin C. Needler, "The Political Development of Mexico," *American Political Science Review* (June 1961), p. 311.

a number of important functions for the President to carry out. He must promulgate the law, which is an act recognizing the authenticity and regularity of the legislation. Publication of the law in the official gazette of Mexico, the *Diario Oficial,* is also a presidential act carried out in company with other administrative officers. After promulgation and publication a *reglamento* must be issued. The *reglamento* is a form of sub-legislation by which a number of basic rules giving effect to the more general provisions of a statute are laid down. The *reglamento* is a traditional step in governmental procedure which continues despite the fact that it is not provided for in the Constitution. A valid *reglamento* has the same force of law as has the statute to which it refers. Presidents have also acted to legislate through decree power, but this is an emergency power which has not been relied upon since World War II.[12]

Congress is subordinate to the President. Those who arrive in the legislature fit into the hierarchy of power and influence at a step just below the cabinet ministers and governors. At the highest step of the pyramid, of course, is the President of the Republic and his closest advisors as well as a few other individuals who lead the wings of the coalition and together with the presidential group form the inner circle of the most powerful. It is indispensable to think in terms of degree in distinguishing the powerful from the power seekers and others of even less significance in the system. In making distinctions concerning the degree of power and influence one must take into account also the degree of support which different individuals and groups are able to offer or the dependence which the most powerful have upon these lesser groups and figures for a rendering of support. It is at this point that an overly simple view of presidential power may result in a distorted impression. For it is possible to assume so much power in the President and the inner circle of the Revolutionary coalition that no significance attaches to people at other levels, such as legislators, who through their political militancy or activism provide the dynamic, the input of active support necessary for the system to function.[13] As long as the official party carries out its functions of liaison and political communication effectively, and as long as the President successfully balances interest conflicts with regard to special goals of the various organizations, there is every reason to expect that legal approval for the acts of the President can be obtained from the Congress without question. There have been periods in earlier

[12] William P. Tucker, *The Mexican Government Today* (Minneapolis, Minn., 1957), p. 108.
[13] For an interesting schematic suggestion of power structure see Robert A. Dahl, *Modern Political Analysis* (Englewood Cliffs, N.J., 1963), p. 56.

days, notably during the presidency of Ortiz Rubio, when these "if" conditions were not satisfied, but recent decades seem to indicate a high and fairly stable level of performance in taking care of such requisites. The presidential capacity to keep Congress in line holds true both for legislation and for appointments. In fact, the legislature as an immediate and effective check upon the presidency lacks significance.[14] There are aspects of the legislators' role, however, which do merit more attention than is customarily given. For one thing, there is a significant amount of open discussion in the Congress in which the small number of opposition members are allowed to take part, and the merits of bills are discussed in these sessions. It also is true that the legislators of the PRI seldom attain their posts without long service in government, interest-group bureaucracy, or both. Their function as political communicators and mobilizers of support would seem significant in light of their career records.

With regard to the powers of a judicial type the President has authority to appoint judges and seek their removal by Congress. The President may also intervene directly in this area of activity through his capacity to grant pardons. The courts are in a large part dependent upon the presidency, but there are areas in which the judicial rule corresponds in some measure to the constitutional and legal provisions. For example, Pablo González Casanova has shown that the Supreme Court has come into conflict with the President in a number of cases and ruled against him. There are recorded 3,700 conflicts of this type from 1917 through 1960. In these conflicts, most of them involving the *juicio de amparo* (a writ calling for a stay of government action), just over 1,000 were decided against the President in behalf of those requesting suspension of action ordered by the Chief Executive. However, González also shows that favorable action usually has resulted in the case of economically powerful persons or groups.[15]

Generally, Mexican courts do not pass upon the constitutionality of the law itself. Rather, they act in terms of decisions on specific questions of law in a given case. The most important appeal is the *amparo*, available only through national courts.

*Amparo* has some elements of the writ of injunction and some of habeas corpus as known in Anglo-American law. Cases in *amparo* rise from acts of government agencies at any level which are claimed

---

[14] Scott has provided a good example of legislative dependency. See Robert E. Scott, "Budget Making in Mexico," *Inter-American Economic Affairs* (Autumn 1955), pp. 3–20.

[15] Pablo González Casanova, *La democracia en México* (México, D.F., 1965), pp. 19–21.

to infringe constitutionally guaranteed rights. *Amparo* can also arise from the claim that a national law has invaded the sovereignty of a state, or that state laws have invaded national jurisdiction. Perhaps most important with regard to *amparo* are the personal procedural rights which it is designed to protect, although these do not reach to political matters, as the courts define political matters. This is because the Supreme Court has ruled that political rights, since they are not part of the first 29 Articles of the Constitution (the guarantees of individual rights), do not come under *amparo* protection.

There is, in addition, a specific form of *amparo* known as *amparo contra leyes*, in which the only judicial question is that of the constitutionality of the law in question. The constitutionality question also is sometimes part of the legal argument in an ordinary *amparo* proceeding. When the court thinks it necessary, it will decide this question. However executive and legislative officials are required to comply with the judicial decision in the specific suit in question, and no other, even when a clear precedent has been established.

To a certain extent precedent operates in the case of *amparo*, since five similar decisions on a point of law by the Supreme Court create a fixed application in *amparo* proceedings. The primary concern of the judiciary, however, is with the specific case of the petitioner, and not a class of universally applied precedents, although precedent, decrees, and writings of highly respected jurists are often cited in support. This is different from the binding character in Anglo usage of precedent, in which the petitioner seeks to support his legal argument by reference to a group of historical decisions which will cause a favorable decision to be granted in his case. Thus the law outranks the ruler in the Anglo case, whereas in Mexico, the law is temporally based and connected to the paternalistic nature of the ruler.[16]

*Amparo* is applicable only against acts of government authorities, but in spite of this fact the number of writs of *amparo* has increased rapidly. This increase seems to indicate there are many types of cases in which people can expect satisfaction through the courts in dealing with the government. In fact it is on the point of the constantly increasing number of *amparo* cases before the courts that the case for the courts as a limiting device with regard to agencies of government seems to turn.

Since the role of the judiciary vis-à-vis the executive — especially the President — is relatively weak, if a petition seeks relief from a current major policy of the President or one of his close official col-

---

[16] A fundamental exposition of *amparo* is by Ignacio Burgoa, *El juicio de amparo,* 3rd ed. (México, D.F., 1950).

laborators, it is unlikely that a decision will emerge granting the writ. Early in the administration of President Ruiz Cortines a commercial motor carrier operating in Jalisco and other western states asked for *amparo* against a decision of the Ministry of Communications and Public Works. The minister became involved in a controversy with the judge hearing the case. The judicial decision was for *amparo,* but the minister maintained that he was not going to abide by it. After several days of discussion prominently covered in the newspapers, a solution was found: the judge resigned.[17]

## Central Control

Mexico is nominally a federal system, but the Constitution in this respect is observed more in the breach than in practice. Presidential control of state governments is based upon a wide variety of legal-constitutional instruments, which in turn are backed by sources of power, political, traditional, and economic in character. Major constitutional powers would include Article 89, Section 4, and Article 76, Sections 5 and 6 of the Constitution of 1917. The former has to do with the legality of state elections, the latter with the capacity to intervene and declare null and void the powers of a state government. Since 1952 these powers have not been much used. Instead, less explicit considerations such as availability of grants-in-aid, control of police, support from the military, and cooperation from interest groups controlled from the national level all place a kind of pressure on a governor which demands his resignation in the event that he becomes unacceptable to Mexico City. Despite this dependence upon the national chief executive, however, governors and state politicians in general seldom feel the direct threat of intervention. Unless a President is unusually aggressive, and this was not characteristic either of Ruiz Cortines or López Mateos, the governors are likely to be allowed a free hand in spending state funds and selection of personnel for state elective and appointive offices. Only if decisions in matters of this kind begin to result in manifest political unrest on the part of major interest groups will a governor begin to experience close observation from Mexico City and know the threat of intervention. State administrations usually act in close collaboration with the national government in matters of joint interest and receive national government support and a relatively free hand in the administration of state affairs.

---

[17] The judge involved was an esteemed writer on Mexican jurisprudence, Ignacio Burgoa.

The fact remains, however, that the President is the ultimate power in state politics. He has authority to intervene to replace personnel of state governments with those who promise greater service in satisfying his policy needs. Under Article 76 of the Constitution, the President, acting through the Senate and the Ministry of Interior, is able to declare that the constitutional powers of a state have disappeared and appoint a provisional governor pending new state elections.

The power of the President as head of the central government is clear in relation to state governments in the area of public finance. For example, in the early 1960s, the federal government received about 75 percent of all government income, while the share of the state governments did not exceed 10 percent.[18] Moreover, in some cases, over 30 percent of the small income available to the states came from subsidies or loans through some federal agency in the period 1950–1960. Federal sums may fluctuate as much as 100 percent in the case of a given state. Obviously the states depend enormously on the President in carrying out state development plans. The amount seems to go up particularly in accord with the strategic position of a governor during a presidential succession year, or whether it is the first year in office for a governor with whose success the President feels especially identified. Governors will usually receive more support for their state governments if they have been selected by the President in office rather than carried over from a previous presidential term.

At the level of the basic local unit of government in Mexico, the *municipio,* the pattern of centralization is even more pronounced. Each state has a municipal law which holds true for all *municipios* in that state. In thirteen states the governors can depose municipal authorities at will under the states' municipal laws, and in the other states the facts of political life make for a similar decision. Thus the governor, who takes office on the basis of presidential choice in the one-party system, in turn commands the municipal authorities.

The facts of municipal dependence are based, as in the case of state governments, largely upon financial considerations. The federal government pre-empts most of the tax sources with the state governments taking almost all that is left over so that for all *municipios* the percentage of public funds available runs below 5 percent. This means that annual average income of *municipios* throughout Mexico

[18] Roger D. Hansen, *The Politics of Mexican Development* (Baltimore, 1971), p. 47, Table 3–8. See James W. Wilkie. *The Mexican Revolution: Federal Expenditure and Social Change Since 1910* (Berkeley, 1967) for the most comprehensive analysis.

stands at about $22,000 (U.S.). Some *municipios* have to run on a budget as low as $40 a year. Clearly the condition of municipal services suffer under such circumstances. As the author found in a study of Tijuana, Baja California, any public-works improvements must be made through intercession with the state government and, more often, the federal authorities. Basic services, such as police protection, are often provided through aid of the state if they are provided at all.

At the state level, transfer of power from one governor to the next is primarily a matter of presidential control. Occasionally the President defers to the judgment of regional strongmen, such as the late Lázaro Cárdenas in the state of Michoacán or the leaders of the Ávila Camacho family in the state of Puebla, but this is not the rule. The normal consultative procedure prior to a decision on the gubernatorial succession involves of course the President's most intimate advisors but probably also includes prominent interest-group leaders, the incumbent governor, spokesmen for major economic interests outside the Revolutionary coalition, military zone commanders, and at times representatives of opposition parties. The men they will be discussing are persons who have accomplished enough politically to be eligible for a governorship by having become a senator, a military zone commander, a cabinet minister, or a federal deputy. A survey of governors over the period 1946–1960 indicated that more governors had held a federal deputyship previously than any other kind of post.

Governors dominate state politics in an immediate sense, although the President ultimately controls. Limitations on a governor's discretionary powers with regard to decision-making stem not only from his relationship to the President but also from the necessity of dealing with the bureaucracy of the PRI and the leadership of many interest groups which help to make up the Revolutionary coalition. The interest groups (CTM, etc.) are in close contact with the leadership at the national level, and the national leaders depend for their success upon the good will of the President. In this relationship the President is able to use interest groups in case there is lack of cooperation on the part of government officials at the state level. Interest organizations may find a state official preferred by the presidency over their own leadership in case of a conflict of goals, so that only in particular cases can interest groups actively pursue specific goals independently or in spite of the state or local executive bureaucracy and its leadership.

The capacity of the President to intervene in both state and national affairs places the leadership of all major interest groups at his mercy in the short run, although ultimately the regime needs their loyalty and that of their membership. Success or failure in achieving a satisfactory response to the demands of members depend upon relations with the chief executive. For labor, the key is the executive power to declare a strike legal or illegal. For groups in the Agrarian Sector it is the executive power with regard to roads, irrigation projects, control of *ejido* events, and control of credit. For business groups, it is the executive power over state and municipal indebtedness and taxation. The capacity to distribute patronage is particularly important in terms of the President's control of the Popular-Sector organizations whose members frequently depend upon government employment. In all of these dealings with organized interests the President need not provide optimum satisfaction for mass membership; there need only be some vestige of improvement on major issues to which the leaders can point as an achievement; the leaders themselves expect rewards in the form of more remunerative government jobs.

With the multiplicity of demands for the President's personal supervision, it was only a matter of time until he would need an extensive personal staff. This has been provided for in a recent reorganization establishing a Ministry of the Presidency. The head of this cabinet-level post has become a key figure in the President's entourage.

## Foreign Affairs

In no area is the leadership of the President more clearly assured than in that of foreign policy. The Constitution and other laws of the land as well as the expectations of the Mexican people assure his prerogatives in this field, as does also his key position in the Revolutionary coalition. Thus it is the President who sets recognition policy and who ultimately decides to approve or disapprove treaties. Along with the Congress he is empowered to make a formal declaration of war, and he commands the armed forces. Political refugees must look to the President for asylum, and it is his order which brings expulsion of undesirable foreigners.

The whole area of economic foreign policy — devaluation of the currency, trade agreements, tariff schedules, and many similar policy questions must be decided in the end by the President. More recently, the growth of Mexico's industrial sector and the need to ease balance-of-payments problems have forced him to make the acquisition of foreign markets a major concern. Along with this there has been an expansion of Mexican diplomacy. The older priorities were generally centered on the United States, the hemispheric organizations, Central America, South America, and the United Nations. Although these priorities remain essentially unchanged, solutions to problems and friendly relations are being sought elsewhere in the world. President Echeverría travelled widely in the early years of his presidency, more than any preceding Mexican president. In particular his visit to the Peoples' Republic of China indicated his willingness to seek new markets wherever they might be. Also, by visiting China he indicated his awareness of the changing world order, and committed the nation to a course of action unfettered by diplomatic and ideological limitations demanded by the United States-led bloc. His second State of the Union message makes his perception and commitment clear:

> The post-war saw two antagonistic blocs of countries born. Their confrontation produced an unstable balance of power based on reciprocal fear. A definition of closed zones of influence limited the international alternatives of nations. . . .
>
> Today, the alliances are dissolved, renewing forces are appearing. Nevertheless, the great powers have not renounced their aspirations for hegemony. . . .
>
> . . . We are actively grouping ourselves with the Third World, and especially . . . with Latin America. . . .
>
> *We are practicing an independent foreign policy and we shall continue doing so.*[19]

In carrying out his policy decisions, and to some extent in making them, the President relies upon several groups for help. There is, first of all, his professional diplomatic service headed by either an outstanding career man or an outstanding Mexican intellectual. Advice also comes from the Ministry of Interior in affairs having to do with extradition and asylum. The Bank of Mexico, *Nacional Financiera*, and the *Banco Nacional de Comercio Exterior* (the National Bank of Foreign Commerce) all are used as sources of information and opinion on the basis of which to make foreign economic policy.

There are certain basic principles which have long been the cornerstones of Mexican foreign policy to which the President must adhere in choosing from the alternatives available. The first of these is the doctrine of national sovereignty which in practice means that states other than Mexico have no authority over Mexican residents: the Mexican state is the supreme authority in Mexican territory. Other principles are corollaries of the first. There is, for example, the principle of sovereign equality which the President must uphold. From

---

[19] Luis Echeverría, Second State of the Union Address, *Hispano Americano* (September 11, 1972), p. 30. Translation and italics by author.

this principle there follows naturally the concept of self-determination. Particular emphasis is placed upon the right of each country to develop the forms of government and economic activity which seem best to fit the needs of its people. The people of a particular nation are the only ones who have a right to decide the nature of their society. Finally, a fourth and related cornerstone is the principle of non-intervention. Several decades ago, when Mexico was in the throes of revolution, one of the leaders, Venustiano Carranza, denounced any kind of intervention or occupation of foreign territory for any reason no matter how elevated the motivation. This has been Mexico's position ever since. However, with the passage of time and Mexico's struggle for economic growth, concern has gradually shifted to problems of economic imperialism on a world scale. This was particularly important in the area of international financing for continued development.

No President is politically free to overlook the history of intervention, especially as this has affected the relations of the United States and Mexico. In both military and economic realms, the impact of United States policy has at times jeopardized Mexico's desire for self-determination. This, more than anything else, explains why Mexico has a consistent record of voting in regional and world organizations in favor of an absolute hands-off policy concerning the internal political affairs of any state. Closely related in this connection is Mexico's Estrada Doctrine which calls for automatic and immediate recognition of any new government. Other principles playing a part in presidential decisions concerning foreign policy include peaceful settlement of disputes, collective security, membership in regional and world organizations, and pledges to promote human rights.

The manner of application of these principles is not always clear to the President and his advisors. Choices have to be made of policy alternatives concerning problem areas such as Cuba and the Dominican Republic. In both of these crises of the 1960s the President, with the support of the Revolutionary coalition and the nation as a whole, condemned United States actions, although not to the point of jeopardizing Mexico's sources of capital. Until 1968 such sources were mainly private investors, but later the sources were tied to government funds.

Other questions which have confronted the Presidents of recent years have concerned the reduction of saline waters which have been dumped by the United States into the Colorado River, damaging Mexican irrigation systems, treatment of Mexican migrant workers, and the limit of territorial waters affecting the activity of United States fishermen off Mexican coasts. Credit for a solution favorable to Mexico as well as the blame for unsolved problems is laid at the door of the President. In the end it is he who determines, within the limits of the historically possible, the practical details of relations with the United States as well as the success of Mexico's bid to lead fellow Latin American countries on many issues.[20]

## The Nexus of Interest Aggregation

The presidency is the single most important agency in the Mexican political system, and its characteristic must be strong political leadership. In fact the need for leadership is so great that no President is free to take actions which would reduce his own paramount position. For example, it would be a violation of the role to treat a legislative body as equal. In this sense it is impossible for a President to free himself from the necessity to act in accord with the values that condition the working of the system. This does not mean that personal tendencies, preferences, and attitudes of each individual incumbent do not influence the tone of a given administration. But the preferences and attitudes of one man with his vast personal power no longer suffice to describe the nerve center of Mexican politics. While the President's rule is personal, it is the office with its institutionalized forms and institutionalized rule which constitutes the nub of the political environment.

As the central aggregating factor in Mexican politics, he forms the nexus of a network of interest associations and other types of political organization. His capacity to work through the presidency in order to direct the system and aggregate demands successfully and in sufficient degree depends upon two major considerations. The first is acceptance of the legitimacy of the Revolution and its political machinery by the majority of Mexico's politically articulate. Secondly, the President has a wide variety of resources which can be called up and brought to bear should opposition arise. Such resources are of many types: legal, political, popular, traditional, economic, and military.[21]

Mexican interest groups and associations are often interconnected and tend to be arranged in hierarchical order. The leaders of these groups and associations interrelate with each other, and their loyalties intertwine, but always in ascending order culminating in the President.

[20] For more comprehensive treatment see Brandenburg, pp. 318–340. A discussion of the basic tenets of Mexican foreign policy is to be found also in Jorge Castañeda, "México y el exterior," in *México: cincuenta años de revolución* (México, D.F., 1961), III, pp. 267–287.

[21] Brandenburg spells out these devices in considerable detail, pp. 163–164.

Standing at the top of the hierarchical arrangement, he is able to maneuver one group or one leader against another in order to achieve the balance of forces necessary for political stability. In this situation no regional leader or high-ranking political figure at the national level can hope to remain influential for any length of time in his sphere of activity if he allows himself to stand in opposition to the majority of interests in the coalition, and the majority usually is with the President. One's position is likely to deteriorate rapidly if he allows himself to fall into a posture of conflict with the presidency. Ultimately, for any elected official, and particularly for governors and national legislators, the good will and support of the presidency is essential if the demands of special interest organizations are to be balanced in relation to the needs of the general public in such a manner as to allow sub leaders an opportunity to appear successful in their respective roles as interest articulators.

Although the presidency stands at the central and highest point of the pyramid of power, there are secondary control centers which are also important and which are related to each other both horizontally and vertically. The organization of the official party and of all major interest groups has this horizontal as well as vertical aspect. "Horizontal" refers to the fact that the loyalties are not entirely monopolized by the presidency. There are also loyalties to state organizations and local organizations which tend to provide the major difference between a monolithic model and the more diverse and diffuse power arrangement characteristic of the Mexican political system. Another division of loyalty may occur between the interest organization and the governmental agency. Sometimes a division occurs between an interest group and a government organ on the one hand and the party on the other. While the paramount loyalty to the President remains, these sub-loyalties and divisions of loyalties offset the monolithic picture which a focus on the domination of the presidency may too easily provide.

### Decision-making and Consultation

Presidential government in Mexico, while emphasizing the authoritative character of the President's decisions and the power of his position, is nevertheless, as Scott has pointed out, "government by consultation." [22] The political system has become too complex for the President to have personal contact with all upon whom he must rely for support and whose lives and political careers he affects by his

[22] Scott, p. 279.

decisions. Little by little, procedures and methods have sprung up by which people are able to consult at lower levels, preparing the way for a kind of consensus which only the President can articulate authoritatively.

Vital to his success is his choice of ministers. These men compose his administrative team and are major factors in carrying out interest aggregation and rule-making functions. The presidency rests in the end on a ministerial base which must be of high calibre if the various aspects of governmental policy are to be implemented. The kind of men whose capacities are vital to Mexico and the nature of their previous experience is somewhat clearer in terms of Table 6 based on research on recruitment patterns.

After discussions have provided a consensual basis, those ministers directly concerned with a policy proposal, some of the top interest

*Table 6*

**Selected Categories of Previous Experience of Cabinet Personnel in Five Recent Administrations**

|      | NDES | Other high | Inter-mediate | Deputy | Senator | Governor |
|------|------|------|------|------|------|------|
|      | (%) | (%) | (%) | (%) | (%) | (%) |
| 1946 | 15.5 | 43.7 | 50.0 | 25.0 | 15.5 | 18.7 |
| 1952 | 23.5 | 64.7 | 82.4 | 17.6 | 11.7 | 30.4 |
| 1958 | 28.0 | 52.0 | 84.0 | 0.8 | 16.0 | 0.8 |
| 1964 | 21.7 | 52.2 | 69.5 | 30.4 | 21.7 | 21.7 |
| 1970 | 13.2 | 65.8 | 92.1 | 18.9 | 15.8 | 7.9 |

NDES — Ministers of Interior, Foreign Affairs, National Defense, Treasury, Agriculture, Education, Labor, Public Health, Public Works, Industry and Commerce, Water Resources, National Patrimony, Navy, Department of Agrarian and Colonization Affairs, Communication and Transportation, Department of the Federal District, Pemex, Social Security Institute, National Railways, Central Purchasing and Distributing (CONASUPO), Tourism Department, President of the PRI, and other positions of similar rank.

Other high — Assistant Ministers, Chief Justice of the Supreme Court, Ambassadors, General Secretary of the PRI, Rector, UNAM, Chairmen of some special and most permanent commissions, Managers of federal banks and other positions of similar rank.

Intermediate — Bureau chiefs and officers of similar rank. Prosecuting officers, Federal District attorneys, Federal judges, Assistant managers of federal banks and other positions of similar rank.

group leaders, and interested members of the coalition's inner circle sit down with the President to work out the final policy statement. The enforcement of the policy in detail in turn is worked out (except for questions involving a major conflict) at levels lower than that of the presidency itself. The task of securing maximum cooperation and enthusiastic implementation falls to persons forming the President's staff in charge of conducting relations with the legislature, the bureaucracy of the PRI, and the leadership of major interest groups.

Policy demands which the President must consider are presented by various means of communication. Messages come through whispers and conferences in guarded tones at lunch or in hallways or offices. They come through the press and other mass media, pronouncements of interest groups, speeches by the leadership of the PRI, statements by legislators, and sometimes a public airing of views by opposition party members. Perhaps most important of all are the policy demands stemming from the major executive agencies of government which have their own vested interests in promoting their own programs.

The President and the institutionalized Office of the President must balance the competing demands coming from these various sources and develop overall policies generally acceptable to the articulate elements of the system. These articulate elements include both official and semi-official government agencies, political bodies such as the committees of the party, and the leadership both for regionally based groups and economic groups. It is also necessary to consider many organized commercial and manufacturing interests which are not identified in any formal way with the Revolutionary coalition. Since it is not the function either of the dominant party or of the legislature in the Mexican system to aggregate authoritatively, the only other consultative organ which can perform this indispensable function is the presidency. The cabinet, as such, is not an implementing mechanism; the heads of major executive departments do not meet regularly and collectively with the President. He meets with specialized committees for specific questions or with his ministers individually on problems pertaining to their own special area of affairs. The extent to which ministers or special committees are given latitude in making recommendations or even making decisions depends upon the individual President. There are narrow committees for narrow problems, and broad committees involving the membership of several ministers as well as interest group leaders to deal with broader problems cutting across a number of areas of concern. Generally, in these groups, the debate that takes place is not made public. Decisions are reached, and legislative initiatives are hammered out before Congress is consulted in any formal way as a body, although legislative committees do hold hearings and collect evidence. In this respect they carry on useful work in gathering information for the executive and in sounding reactions to possible proposals. This is an aspect of the legislator's role which is all too frequently overlooked in light of the fact that Congress does not exercise an effective veto on presidential initiatives.

The important things to remember about presidential committees are that they are ad hoc, they serve a specific purpose, they die a sudden death, and their formation is seldom given any significant publicity. The important thing to know is that they exist, they are constantly changing, and their impact on the President's final decision is probably known only to himself. Certainly they do not publish their findings, though they may have more effect than if they published a long report to be filed away for use at some indeterminate future date. In view of the Mexican *modus operandi* it is likely few of these committees ever produce a written document. They produce instead points of view and possibly a consensus.

It is imperative to keep in mind that the President selects the members of committees which he desires to form in connection with some problem, such as a drive against illiteracy. He may choose several ministers whose particular efforts he wants devoted to the problem, some government economists, and some leaders from the business world. The usual technique is to announce the drive against illiteracy without specifically naming a committee or committee personnel. The President may only call them together once to ask their support and get their opinions. After that, the committee is forgotten. Other committees last longer, but the structure and temporary character are always the same so that no researcher, Mexican or of other nationality, discusses these committees in detail; he simply knows that they exist and that they appear and disappear with great ease and no fanfare.

Policy news releases do not come out without careful advance preparation in the press. Usually this entails publication of some feature stories on the general subject, pronouncements by prominent government officials and a widespread discussion at all levels, national, regional and local, sponsored by the PRI and various of the most vitally concerned organized interests.

## Summary

The President of Mexico is not *elected* in any sense meaningful to Anglo-American readers. Rather he is *chosen* by a relatively few individuals who make their decision in terms of what they consider to be politically advantageous for themselves and politically acceptable to the articulate groups in Mexican society. The nomination of the official party candidate, the president-designate, differs in procedure and manner from the expectations of people on the United States side of the border; it is a much more closed arrangement with fewer effective participants. In the same way the presidential campaign also differs from United States experience in the functions it performs. These differences in turn are related to the pattern of perennial electoral victory on the part of the official Revolutionary party (PRI).

The role of the presidency is to some extent conditioned by the nomination and election pattern. This holds true in the sense that the nature of the Mexican presidential nomination and election places the nominee in the position of carrying out some presidential functions prior to assuming office. Thus it is usually the president-designate who must bear responsibility for confirming nominations for lesser elective posts which have been arranged in the first place by the party, its affiliated interest groups, or the inner-circle members of the coalition. Also the primary responsibility for the image of the regime which the Revolutionary coalition wishes to convey to the public shifts at election time from the incumbent President to the president-designate. The playing of the presidential role thus begins before a man ever becomes President.

Once he has taken office the man who is to govern Mexico for six years must never lose the father-image which he first began to build for himself as president-designate. He must remember that his attributes as President, while institutionalized in large part, still carry with them personality characteristics which he must at least pretend to have. He is supposed to be a benevolent father. Whatever he does for the masses, he does for them personally — he endows them or gives them public structures, sanitation plants, schools, and roads. By the same token, if he fails to provide these things, he has failed in his vital fatherly role. It is paternal government, but it is only legitimate if it is benevolent paternal government. Thus there are great pressures to produce material and psychic rewards which are the penalty that a President must pay for standing at the heart of the political system.

In his role as the central factor in interest aggregation the President in the 1970s is confronted with an increasingly difficult problem. It is the problem of bearing responsibility for a growing multitude of actions on the part of government in a situation where personal capacity to check on these acts is limited. The paramount chief must delegate an increasing amount of responsibility. It is tempting to regard each expansion of governmental function as an expansion in presidential power: to perceive presidential power as *cumulative*.

Thus one can generalize about the ever-increasing power of the President. It is possible, however, to view the growth of governmental activity as *distributive* insofar as the President vis-à-vis other government officers is concerned. In this sense, then, he experiences a relative decline in power to control events around him despite the great scope of his authority. This is the paradox of the presidency in Mexico, for it is demanded that he accept responsibility for all governmental acts even though he cannot possibly be personally well informed on all facets of these activities. As he becomes in one sense more powerful, therefore, he becomes simultaneously more dependent. It is the case of the leader and his staff described by Max Weber as "routinization of charisma." The culturally determined character of the presidency has not been greatly altered by the economic modernization and increased sophistication of the nation as a whole. The President must cope with all the traditionally determined characteristics of his role, while at the same time he is surrounded by an increasingly more complex environment.

# ⁜ 7 ⁜

# Labor Policy

## The Historical Backdrop of Major Labor Policy Areas

In placing the labor movement in the revolutionary tradition as well as in the present regime, Mexican writers sometimes go back in time to the position of the lower classes in the Maya and Aztec societies of pre-Conquest days. Their point is that the Revolution of 1910–1917 was a revolution to satisfy an ancient need for change not only in the area of individual and political rights, but also for the renovation of the economic and social order. Mexican labor organization and Mexican labor law, in accord with this historical view, have evolved from communal beginnings in the sense that the major laboring units in Aztec or Maya society (*calpulli*) are viewed as essentially cooperative in character.

After the Conquest, the medieval European concept of guild organization was introduced by the Spanish and became a factor in the development of modern Mexican values concerning the role of labor. Guild organization protected workers by setting standards, providing access to government officials, providing security in case of trouble, and training new generations of skilled workers. Guilds were not set up to sharpen competition but rather to dull its sometimes painful edge. Guilds were based on skills, and often the law awarded monopoly privileges to one guild for the entire area of work involved.

Aside from the guilds, Spanish legislation recognized and attempted to protect more humble day workers and Indians of town and countryside. One decree provided for a weekend of rest amounting to at least forty-eight hours. There were other decrees setting minimum wages and maximum hours for labor at all levels, but legal stipulations of this type were not often successfully enforced except for skilled artisans.

As the colonial period wore on, the situation of the masses doing

216

common labor came to be structured in terms of such institutions as the company or *hacienda* store. In the company store people received, rather than money, goods for which they were customarily overcharged. Other characteristic features of life for the common laborer were twelve- to fourteen-hour work days, abuse by foremen, debt slavery enforced by government officials, and a general misery and low level of living that is difficult for modern unionized workers to comprehend. Difficult conditions even among more highly skilled urban laborers sometimes led to disturbances. Something resembling a strike was reported in Mexico as early as 1788. As colonial days ended, there were rudimentary strike attempts and slowdowns in the factories as well as attempted rebellions in the countryside, though such occurrences still were not frequent.

When independence was won the situation turned out to be very little different from what it had been under the Spanish colonial rulers. The old oppressive institutions — the company store, the tiny wage, the bare subsistence level of living, and the incredibly long hours of labor — continued to dominate the situation of the lower classes. Roberto de la Cerda says that the situation was "worse than during colonial times." [1]

When the generation of the Reform met to frame the Constitution of 1857, one of the leading men of that period, Ponciano Arriaga, called attention to the fact that nothing had been done since independence to better in any material way the situation of artisans and workers in the cities or rural areas; but the men of the Reform generation made it clear in the Constitution of 1857 that their concern was reform primarily of a political-legal character rather than economic or social.

After the liberals of the generation of the Reform had fought a civil war and beaten the French intervention effort, they set about reconstructing the country. Throughout the late nineteenth century, railroad building and new industries sprang up alongside older activities such as mining and textile manufacturing, but little of the new prosperity touched the workers of the fields, factories, mines, and railroads. The urban day laborers and the peons and Indians of the countryside continued in the same miserable circumstances. Stratification was made more rigid by use of foreigners as skilled workers, technicians, and managers. Foreign entrepreneurs were in the forefront of the expansion of industry, railroads, and modern communications in Mexico.

[1] Roberto de la Cerda Silva, *El movimiento obrero en México* (México, D.F., 1961), p. 62.

New demands were articulated in early organizational and strike efforts of workers, and treatment of unions emerged as an issue. After the Revolution against Díaz came the recognition of the new demands in fundamental law. Article 123 of the Constitution of 1917 crystallized basic policy goals for labor as central to the purpose of the new regime and the renovated political system. Foremost among these provisions were rules providing for better working hours and conditions.

Reactions to perennial abuses in many aspects of employer-employee relationships were evidenced in Article 123. In the sphere of compensation there were provisions against contractual obligations for employee purchases at company stores, infrequent wage payments that might cause workers to borrow from employers against future wages, requirements for the payment of wages in legal tender, minimum wage levels (set up at the state level), and double pay for overtime. Conditions of work for women and children were regulated; for them there was to be no more work under unhealthy conditions or in specified types of enterprises. The number of hours was set for all workers. There was to be an eight-hour day with shorter periods for night work. Overtime was limited in general and prohibited entirely for women and children.

Large-scale employers were assigned a number of specific obligations in addition to those included in the above provisions. Among the most important were requirements for construction of housing and provision of schools and hospitals when these were lacking within a reasonable range of the factory or mine. Also indicative of efforts to remedy past abuses were the provisions that the employer provide safe and hygienic conditions of work. Employers were bound to pay compensation in case of industrial accidents. Employees were given the right to organize, strike, and bring cases before arbitration boards for the settlement of disputes. Machinery for enforcement and settlement of disputes was to center around local, state, and national boards, called boards of conciliation and arbitration.

For some years after the promulgation of Article 123 little was done to implement the forward-looking provisions of 1917. The conciliation and arbitration boards, major labor decision-making machinery envisaged by the Constitution, did not receive their recognition as true courts by the Supreme Court until the mid-1920s. By 1930 two-thirds of the states had passed comprehensive labor laws which were at great variance with one another. The Federal Labor Law, badly needed to bring order to the situation, did not emerge until 1931 after an amendment to Article 123 placed all legislative authority for labor matters in the federal government.

The labor law of 1931 (as amended) is still the code in force.

Under it, organized Mexican workers have been awarded privileges and benefits their forefathers never would have believed possible. In order to protect Mexicans against foreign technicians, employment preferences go to Mexicans up to 90 percent in all skilled categories. Union members, as well as capable former employees, also have preference. Wage payment cannot be postponed merely on the owner's wish; it must come no less frequently than once a week. Collective contracts can and usually do include a closed shop clause: that the employer must hire only union members. Compensation, first-aid services, and in some cases hospitalization are provided in case of injury. Employers can rescind a work contract only in the most unusual cases. Employers must continue to pay wages while the worker is on strike when the strike is ruled "legal" by the board of conciliation and arbitration having jurisdiction. (Benefits in practice are more likely to correspond with legal provisions in the larger firms, and smaller firms usually receive less attention from enforcing officials.) Since 1931 these benefits, as well as many others, have been placed in operation under federal labor law. In 1933 labor affairs were located in an autonomous agency, the Department of Labor; in 1940 labor administration began to operate at the ministerial level.

## Major Policy Areas

### Social Security

A working social security program is a basic element in any general policy oriented toward the improvement of conditions for wage earners. In 1942, during the presidency of Manuel Ávila Camacho, conferences were organized to discuss and propose ways and means of establishing a social security program. In January 1943 came the legislation which provided the basis for a system of social security which has been expanding in coverage and benefits ever since. The law of 1943 created the administrative machinery for carrying out a social security program. The new agency was called the Mexican Institute of Social Security (IMSS) and a director-general was appointed by the President. The IMSS was given the status of a "decentralized agency," as distinct from a "state-participation enterprise," regular line department, or regulatory commission. The IMSS was treated from the outset as an agency performing a public or social-service function with autonomous status designed to protect it to some extent from political maneuvers of a purely political type, such as interpersonal or intergroup conflicts which might obstruct its intended mission.

By 1944 coverage began in the Federal District and by the first part of January 1947 a number of important cities such as Monterrey, Puebla, Guadalajara, and Orizaba had social security coverage available with 631,099 persons participating in the program.[2] In 1946, two years after the IMSS began its operations, there were only 246,-547 persons participating as pensioners with an annual cost of a little over $110,000.

During this initial two-year period there was a great effort to select talented and skilled people to form the core of the IMSS staff. The goal was to form a pool of talent which would acquire a high proficiency over the years in handling social security problems. IMSS staff salaries went up 90.88 percent from 1943 to 1946 in an effort to attract the best people. Courses in social security began to be taught in the National University (UNAM) in 1950. The efforts to attract capable people were successful. The IMSS is generally respected as one of the best-administered agencies of the government. A wage dispute involving doctors working for IMSS in 1965 did not alter the favorable picture.

During the presidential term of Miguel Alemán, 1946–1952, the IMSS greatly expanded its functions. Its program included not only construction of hospitals, clinics, aid stations, and factory first aid, but also varied responsibilities to pensioners. Those covered under the IMSS program and their beneficiaries grew to number 1,140,883 persons. A network of modern hospitals and clinics sprang from drawing boards and became reality. Every type of medical assistance doubled or trebled. Mexicans for the first time had access in large numbers to the benefits of antibiotics. Amounts granted in pensions rose from a little over 200,000 pesos in 1947 to above 4,500,000 in 1952. In addition to coverage in Nuevo León, Puebla, Jalisco, Veracruz, and the Federal District, the IMSS began operations in Tlaxcala, Tamaulipas, the state of Mexico, and Oaxaca. The Fourth Inter-American Conference on Social Security was held in Mexico City in 1952, and Mexico was assigned the chairmanship of the Permanent Inter-American Committee on Social Security. It was a period of great strides forward for the social welfare represented by IMSS, but it was also extremely costly. Contributions of those in the program had to be raised from 6 to 8 percent of wages and salaries. Employers had to match employee contributions.

In December 1952 Antonio Ortiz Mena took over the reins of the IMSS, and Adolfo Ruiz Cortines began his six-year presidential term. The new director stressed rigid observance of budgets, constant re-

[2] Miguel García Cruz, "La seguridad social," in *México: cincuenta años de revolución* (México, D.F., 1961), II, p. 524.

organization of services to achieve greater effective uses, continued expansion of coverage into more states and into the countryside, and further expansion of the number of IMSS installations, hospitals, clinics, administrative buildings, and so forth. Operations of the IMSS greatly expanded over the following six years. Expenditures were 841,211,049 pesos in 1958 while they had been only 260,479,041 pesos in 1952. Income was 1,110,676,898 pesos in 1958 and had been only 298,672,254 pesos in 1952. With sound management, reserves which stood at 383,250,568 in 1952 rose above 1,257,963,997.[3] Expenditures for medicine increased 40 percent, from 73,481,315 pesos in 1953 to 102,558,075 pesos in 1958.

Operations were extended so that there was some form of IMSS program in twenty-nine states. The number of clinics was increased from 42 to 226, 139 urban and 87 rural. From 19 hospital units with 1,698 beds in 1952, the system expanded to include 105 hospitals with 7,410 beds in 1958. The number of pensions went up 80 percent while the amount of money outlay increased 40 percent. In an effort to improve rural housing patterns, 6,168 small model dwellings were built in the countryside. On the negative side there were in 1958 only 99,542 rural persons with social security coverage — about 7.5 percent of all persons covered.[4] Clubs, or so-called Houses of the Insured (Casas de las aseguradas) were organized throughout the country to provide women with elementary instruction in hygiene and family administration. Throughout the IMSS system the policy of keeping highly effective, highly paid staff members was reflected in the fact that the number of personnel in the system went up 50 percent from 1952 until 1958, while salary levels climbed 250 percent. The number of doctors in the system grew to approximately 4,000, while the nurses numbered over 5,000.[5]

When the presidency of Ruiz Cortines ended in 1958, Benito Coquet was chosen to head the IMSS during the presidency of Adolfo López Mateos. Coquet promised a continued effort to improve technical and administrative organization especially with regard to medical services. In addition, a major aim was the expansion of the social security program in the countryside. There was further expansion of the building program for hospitals, clinics, and other basic installations, and there was a renewed effort to improve liaison among em-

[3] Instituto Mexicano del Seguro Social, Subdirección General Técnica, Población Amparada por El Seguro Social: Cifras Estadísticas, 1944–62.
[4] García Cruz, p. 540.
[5] García Cruz, pp. 543 and 552–553. A strike of doctors in Mexico early in 1965 indicated that IMSS had been unable to meet salary standards in this area despite all efforts to do so.

ployers, labor, and government to extend the progress of the social security program.

During the Ruiz Cortines administration the average annual increase in the number of persons covered under the social security program was 628,000. By 1964 the program was functioning in 510 *municipios,* an increase of more than 100 percent in two presidential administrations. The Ruiz Cortines administration also marked the beginning of hospital construction in the countryside, as well as the addition of more services through the construction of administrative centers, clubhouses, classrooms, and meeting rooms. The rate of increase in social security staff and services has continued through the succeeding Presidents' emphasis on providing coverage to rural workers. Continuing problems are the further coverage of the rural population and the increasing difficulty of maintaining high-quality personnel as the system grows.

As the IMSS increased its reserve funds and expanded its system, it also became a significant investor in both private and quasi-public enterprises. In this way, it became a major factor in the debate over the desirable proportions of the private and public sectors of the economy.[6] At the same time social security remained, as Coquet described it in 1958, a "goal unreached." The evidence did indicate, however, that through the IMSS millions of Mexicans were experiencing some concrete returns from the promises of the Revolutionary regime. Until the 1960s the IMSS program benefited the urban working force almost to the exclusion of the rural workers. It remained to be seen whether the millions in the countryside, as well as the masses of unorganized urban labor, could be benefited by the promises of the recent administrations. Despite the legal extensiveness of these programs, the IMSS and the ISSSTE (bureaucrats) are just 24 percent of the population.[7]

## Profit-Sharing

In 1962 a decision was made calculated to resolve, at least temporarily, one of the issues which had grown from increasing labor demands over the 1950s. This issue had to do with the role which labor might play in business enterprise. Some had suggested that labor leaders or labor councils might participate in governing an enterprise. It had also been suggested that labor might participate

[6] Raymond Vernon's *The Dilemma of Mexico's Economic Growth* is a careful statement of some key factors in this debate.

[7] Thomas G. Sanders, "Mexico 1974: Demographic Patterns and Population Policy," *Fieldstaff Reports* (July 1974), p. 9.

somehow in the gains to which it contributed. This latter demand was expressed in the labor law of 1962 which enabled workers to participate in the profits of the enterprise in which they were employed.[8]

Under the *reparto de utilidades* (profit-sharing) the workers collectively receive a portion of the earnings of the firm. Under the law as amended, the Ministry of Labor and the Ministry of Industry and Commerce, together with the Ministry of the Treasury and Public Credit, set the major outlines for distribution. The tool of these ministries for making investigations and studies concerning the proportion of profits to be shared in particular industries and enterprises is the National Committee for Participation of Workers in Profit-Sharing (CNRU). The existing practice is to establish a minimum of 20 percent of the income of the enterprise as taxable under federal law.[9] This is the base sum assigned to the collectivity of unionized workers of the enterprise. The sum is reviewed not only by the Ministry of the Treasury (as the major tax-collecting agency), but also by the Ministry of Labor and the Ministry of Industry and Commerce. The amount available for division among the workers may on occasion be expanded through individual contract, collective contract, or collective bargaining, backed up by a strike declared legal by the Ministry of Labor. In any case, the key guideline is that capital should receive sufficient interest or return on its investment. The findings by the CNRU are always subject to review relative to this guideline.

The income on which profit-sharing is to be computed should be the same as that reported to the Ministry of the Treasury. Workers or their representatives must make their objections to the estimate of the income by the firm to that ministry. Under the provisions of law the ownership or management of the firm must inform the workers or their organization what the firm's statement of earnings is within ten days after it is submitted to the ministry. Within thirty days

[8] *Diario Oficial*, December 31, 1962.

[9] This figure is derived after certain deductions are made. The first deduction totals 30 percent of the taxable profits and represents "interest of invested capital" and "reinvestment incentive." From this remainder, a deduction based on the capital to labor ratio is made which may range from 10 percent to 80 percent. It is from this last remainder that 20 percent is given to the workers. Consequently the share of the profits which must be shared can range from 12.6 percent to 2.8 percent. Susan Purcell, *Public Policy and Private Profits: A Mexican Case Study* (study scheduled for publication, Berkeley, Calif., 1975), pp. 46–47. This is an intensive study of the profit-sharing decision and its consequences, and provides much useful insight.

of that time the heads of the union who speak for the workers in the factory, or the majority of the workers themselves constituted as an *ad hoc* group, must send their statement of approval or disapproval to the ministry. The ministry makes the final decision on the question of whether or not the firm has submitted the correct returns, and this cannot be appealed by the workers. Distribution of the profits to be shared among the workers is supposed to take place within sixty days after the deadline for payment of taxes on the submitted estimate of earnings by the firm.

The pool of money to be divided is separated into two kinds of funds. One type of fund is divided equally among all workers on the basis of the number of days they worked in a year. Another kind of fund is divided on the basis of proportion of gain; that is, on the basis of the highness or lowness of their salaries over the year. The salary of the worker in connection with the last type of division of profits is determined strictly on the basis of his daily wage; special benefits are not included, and the daily salary is actually an average of all daily wages earned throughout the year. The division of profits are limited by the legal criteria of "reasonable return on investment" and confinement of profit-sharing to taxable income. There is also the common-sense fact that administrative salaries count in all countries as "costs," so that the more generous the administrator's salaries, the less profits there are to divide among the workers.

An initial determination as to the money going to particular workers in a given factory is made by a commission organized at the factory level composed of an equal number of workers' representatives and management. If this commission cannot reach an agreement, then an inspector from the Ministry of Labor makes the decision, and the workers, in turn, if they are dissatisfied with this, can submit their own opinion to the Ministry of the Treasury and the Ministry of Labor. If there is a year of loss, this year of loss in which the workers get no return from the division of profits cannot be made up from the profits of a good year. Moreover, salaries cannot be figured on the basis of various indemnities which might come to workers because of injuries or some other kind of peripheral benefit payment. Finally, the law explicitly states that the right of workers to share in profits does not imply in any way capacity on their part to participate in the direction or administration of the enterprise.

Certain enterprises are excluded from the profit-sharing plan. Any enterprise that is in its first two years of operation or any enterprise with an entirely new product in its first four years of operation is excluded. The novelty of the product will be determined by criteria already entered in Mexican law. A period of exploration for materials in an extractive industry will not be subject to the profit-sharing plan. Neither private foundation operations which exist for humanitarian purposes rather than profits, nor the IMSS are subject to profit-sharing. Certain enterprises capitalized at a very small amount are not included. Within the enterprise the top management people are excluded from the profit-sharing plan, as also are apprentices. Part-time laborers participate only if they have worked at least sixty days for the enterprise during the year.

Unquestionably a piece of legal machinery can be improved from time to time from the standpoint of various groups. However, no legal machinery works well without the element of good faith. The establishment of such a psychological climate must be accomplished. A second major problem is that of administration. There have been difficulties in both areas. In the initial years of profit-sharing, it was difficult to get workers to agree among themselves on a formula for dividing the profits. A representative of the CTM, Juan Moises Calleja, pointed this out. Calleja said that workers seem to think the sum to be divided among them should be 20 percent of the *gross* income of the enterprise. Calleja stressed that the law only called for distribution of a minimum of 20 percent of the *net* income.[10] He then illustrated his point by saying that a great majority of firms in Mexico (in 1964) grossed less than 300,000 pesos before taxes, and a typical firm would be one with a gross of 200,000 pesos per year. In such a case, the initial basis for calculation would be a probable net income of 17 percent of the gross income before taxes, or 34,000. Specified types of taxes are collected from this amount. The sum left might typically be 30,700. An additional 30 percent, or 9,200 of this, would go for interest and reinvestment of capital. The net profit as a basis for distribution would be 21,490 pesos. Out of this, 20 percent, 4,298 pesos, would be distributable to the workers. Thus, while workers might assume that of the original 200,000 pesos there would be 40,000 pesos available for distribution, there would be, in fact, only a little over one-tenth of that amount. This illustration seemed to provide some insight for observers of the Mexican scene as well as information for the workers concerning the benefits of profit sharing.[11]

[10] *Excelsior* (June 27, 1964).
[11] Purcell cites an interview with a COPMAREX economist who made a pilot study of 83 firms. His conclusions were that the profit-share of an average worker between 1966 and 1970 increased from 1191 to 1717 pesos. Taking the increase in the cost of living into account, the average profit-share increased approximately 350 pesos (calculation derived from data in footnote 95, Chapter 5), Purcell, p. 56.

Another question has involved the inclusion in the profit-sharing plan of enterprises among government-operated decentralized firms. For example, Fidel Velázquez, leader of the CTM, proposed that all of the decentralized public enterprises of any size such as the electrical enterprises and firms such as Altos Hornos (steel) should be included. Velázquez took the position that nearly all enterprises, public or private, should be included in profit-sharing, and that when firms attempted to avoid their obligation it would "be necessary for the unions to act energetically." [12] Velázquez' demand was satisfied concerning Altos Hornos, but difficult questions continue to be raised in both the public and private sectors.

The additional amount of money distributed among the consumer/worker population was supposed to have a major effect on retail sales. By 1969, however, this was still difficult to perceive. The good faith that was supposed to have been established between workers and employers was frequently lacking. In fact, many worker representatives even charged management with fraud. In addition, the spokesmen for the workers claimed that the firms were paying the shares at Christmas, thus eliminating the traditional (and voluntary) Christmas bonus. The late secretary-general of the Federation of Workers of the Federal District (FTDF), Jesús Yurén, had pointed out that while some employers followed the formula of the CNRU to the letter, others were doing their best to avoid their proper obligations under the profit-sharing law. Yurén was especially concerned with the unwillingness of a number of enterprises to make known the amount of their profits. This he declared to be a definite violation of the provision of the original law that the statement of profits should be available to the workers shortly after it was sent to the Ministry of the Treasury.

Another problem had to do with fiscal arrangements. The accounting of some of the enterprises for the fiscal year made it difficult to determine at a particular moment the profits from which the shares should be drawn. The clear implication was that there were firms keeping duplicate sets of books which were used to obscure the difference between the billion pesos previously estimated to be available for profit-sharing by 1969, and the less than half-billion which both public and private sources calculated was available for distribution. This is why it is sometimes argued by labor leaders that even if employers claim there are no profits, they ought to submit a statement of their accounts to the unions for examination. The desire to have a closer look at the employer's records was based on the

12 *Excelsior* (June 27, 1964).

position that labor would know the amount of material going into the firm and could therefore estimate from this the cost of manufacturing, sales price, and the number of units sold. These estimates would give a rough idea of the profit or loss position of the management and could provide a more realistic basis for hearings conducted by the Ministry of the Treasury. Such demands, however, still had not been satisfied in the mid-1970s. Charges continue to be made that the Ministry of the Treasury does a very uneven job in its supervision of the law: some reports indicate that as much as 80 to 90 percent of the factories in major manufacturing areas are successfully dodging the law.[13]

Another labor complaint has to do with the size of profit shares in small factories, where it is said that profit shares given to laborers in some cases are ridiculously small. Bottling plants are given as an example: labor leaders claim that shares in some of these plants drop to as low as twenty pesos. Leaders have been presenting these cases and others to the President of the Republic and the Ministries of Labor and Treasury.

Labor-management differences in estimates on profit-sharing are sometimes dramatically highlighted by individual cases. In one major case involving an electricians' union (SME) and the publicly owned Companía de Luz y Fuerza del Centro, S.A., the estimate of the management and of the union leaders as to the amount to be distributed among workers differed nearly 100 percent. The company was willing to distribute 2,500,000 pesos, whereas the union felt that a proper accounting would indicate at least an additional 2,500,000 pesos. Fidel Velázquez, head of the CTM, pointed out that about 4,000 enterprises must operate under the profit-sharing law, and he felt that only about 3,000 were really attempting to carry out their responsibilities. Velázquez demanded that the government initiate proceedings against those companies which were acting in such a way as to attempt to avoid their obligations. There have been examples of success, however, and perhaps one of the most successful of the efforts to distribute the profits has taken place in connection with the Mexican oil monopoly, Pemex.[14]

Even though management in some smaller enterprises apparently has attempted to avoid obligations entirely with regard to distribution of profits, and even though management in some of the larger enterprises has presented calculations of profits which have not met with labor support or labor approval, management in general has not ap-

[13] Shafer, p. 352.
[14] *Excelsior* (June 6, 1964).

peared desirous of overtly obstructing the new legislation. Certainly leading business organs have not manifested great alarm with regard to the implications of the profit-sharing legislation from the standpoint of their own operations. Because of the capital-labor force ratio, the most highly capitalized industries pay relatively smaller shares. Thus the smaller businesses (ranging from 120,000 to 300,-000 pesos gross income) usually pay relatively higher rates.[15]

The National Chamber of Manufacturers (CNIT) has taken the position that there are four critical points in the administration of the law. These involve the incentive which a law may give to productivity of labor, the problem of accounting in connection with the new income which workers should receive in relation to increased productivity, the determination of the percentage of profits susceptible of distribution in relation to the capital of the enterprise, and the establishment of the reasonable return recognized by the law as an important factor in stimulating investment.

The CNIT has held many round-table discussions throughout the country, has kept its members informed, and has hired a team of specialists in fiscal and statistical matters to evaluate proposals coming from the membership. In general the CNIT would propose that an establishment which showed extraordinary profits should take the worker into account in this respect as an element in the success of the enterprise and give him something beyond what ordinarily would be the case under the existing arrangements for profit sharing. The chamber believes that the amount of money available should vary according to the success of the enterprise and the type of enterprise. But workers should not feel they have some voice in management because they are sharing in profits, and the CNIT is adamant about this. At the same time the chamber believes it is very important for management not to feel that a profit-sharing plan eliminates the need to adjust base salaries in accord with the standard of living. From the chamber's point of view, these are the most important points related to the law itself.

Aside from the views of the CNIT, other widely articulated points among spokesmen for Mexican business touch on several areas that are of vital importance in connection with the further administration and elaboration of the law. There is the question of the attitude of foreign investors in connection with this law; here again it appears that while some groups are rather alarmed at the prospects, in general this is not regarded as a plan that will upset the usual relationships

[15] Purcell, p. 47.

in the Mexican capitalistic system, or perhaps one should say social-istic-capitalistic system. One Mexican official was quoted as saying that on the average he estimated profit-sharing would amount to less than two weeks' pay for employees the year around, while W. S. Jones, a hotel operator, said that "this will be another needle in our side, but it won't put anyone out of business."

The important fact to remember from the standpoints both of foreign and domestic firms is that the law makes allowances for taxes which the company must pay and also for opportunities for reinvest-ment on the part of the company. The Mexican businessmen stress that one of the major reasons why such plans have failed or have not done well in Venezuela, Peru, Colombia, Chile, and Argentina is that the importance of reinvestment needs has not been recognized in the legislation in those countries. Mexican policy-makers expect to take some of the pressure off themselves through this law, feeling that it is just one less thing which the radical left can offer in the way of redistribution of wealth. Mexican industrialists themselves, such as José Riojas, Jr., manager of Industrias Riojas, S.A., manufacturer and distributor of Wurlitzer products in Mexico, have said that even though they originally resented the profit-sharing plan, they now recognize that the government has a point in providing workers with some additional income. They recognize that at least the whole thing has a certain psychological appeal for the wage-earner. At the same time management is protected through the reinvestment and tax-quota provisions. In general, profit-sharing appears to have benefited some groups of urban workers, and since employers have been given no cause to feel threatened, there is some basis for arguing that in gen-eral both employer and employee groups have received a measure of satisfaction through the legislation. On the other hand, it must also be said that the transcendental effects of better understanding between employers and workers and the "maintenance of social peace" in the country, which accompanied the first years of the experiment, have fallen short of the mark in the mid-1970s.

A major problem with regard to profit-sharing goes to the heart of the whole series of other problems recognized by most Mexican leaders. In Mexico's drive toward industrialization and modernization there is a growing discrepancy between the benefits received by those in urban areas and those who remain in the countryside, particularly those who work for wages. Over half the Mexican population is classified as rural, and yet available records and census data are ex-tremely inadequate. The practice of census-takers, for example, is to record only those workers in the rural occupations that can be immediately related to agriculture and forestry. Customarily, this has amounted to less than seven percent of the male labor force. If one considers that by 1980 the male labor force in agriculture may still amount to about 38 percent of the total work force, then it is not difficult to understand the problem of discussing the impact of profit-sharing on rural workers.[16] Then there are many others who are part-time workers, or who for some other reason do not fall into the occupational categories customarily used.

Other problems with the census bear on the application of profit-sharing legislation to the countryside. For example, many *ejidatarios* employ rural workers either on a permanent or part-time basis, as do cattle ranchers and people engaged in the exploitation of forestry reserves, and those in the fishing industry. The accounting of such employers is often very skimpy. It is very difficult to come to any conclusions as to just what their profits are, and what share of the profits should go to their workers. As the former Minister of the SAG, Julián Rodríguez Adame, said: "Agriculture is really a way of life more than it is a business, and the whole accounting problem is much different." Added to these considerations is the fact that there is no census of agricultural cattle or sheep-raising entrepreneurs, nor is there a census of persons exploiting forest resources. Under such circumstances it is next to impossible to find out who are the entrepreneurs and how many people they hire. Thus, as one official commented, "in its complexity, it would be real work for Romans," to apply the law of profit-sharing to the countryside.

The implications of this situation were spelled out in a report by Federico Sánchez Fogarty of the CONCAMIN, which was sent to the President of the CNRU, Hugo B. Margáin. The core of the message was that the gap between the purchasing power of the organized working groups in the urban situation and of those who are laborers in the country grows greater all the time. Fogarty argued that the profit distribution plan would work to increase this gap. He also pointed out that the growing discrepancy means a decreasing internal market. Thus, regardless of the manner in which difficulties are ironed out in the administration of the profit-sharing law, and regardless of the conflicts between labor and management in the industrial, commercial and transport sectors, the problem of bringing the law to the countryside continues to be one of the most pressing in connection with this legislation as well as other types of legislation designed to improve the lot of the less affluent in the Mexican society.

[16] Jorge Balán, Harley L. Browning, and Elizabeth Jelin, *Men in a Developing Society: Geographic and Social Mobility in Monterrey, Mexico* (Austin, Texas, 1973), p. 24.

**Strikes and Labor Training**

The Mexican Labor Code provides an extensive conciliation system for the resolution of strikes. The Constitution of 1917 recognizes the right of every worker to strike, including government employees. But through the Labor Code a means is provided for the control of strikes: the Ministry of Labor determines whether a strike is in effect or not — whether it is "existent" or "non-existent." In 1965 it was estimated that about 50 percent of the reported strikes were "non-existent." [17] In other words, the labor disputes involved were not legitimate according to the criteria of the Mexican Labor Code, and not within the "right to strike" provisions of Article 123.

A strike not legally accepted by the government under the Constitution of 1917 is quickly doomed to failure because it becomes "civil disobedience" and can have economic and legal sanctions "legitimately" applied. Hence this is a powerful means of controlling organized labor, and indicates that the prudent labor leader will attempt to determine the government's position before calling a strike. For a strike to be "existent" it must first be classed as "legal." Legal standing is granted by the appropriate government authority when it is decided that "the proper procedures" have been followed.[18]

Once a strike is begun, a complex set of laws comes into play. If agreement between employer and employees is not reached within a certain time, then the action proceeds to boards of conciliation, and after failure there, to boards of conciliation and arbitration. These boards exist at both the local and federal levels. Yet despite the complex arbitration system, "It must be recognized that in general conciliation by the boards has been a failure; consequently it has been necessary to set up administrative services which step in and suggest lines of settlement to the parties . . ." [19] One commentator has estimated that at least 90 percent of collective disputes are settled by administrative procedures.[20] This would clearly indicate how important a role the government plays in deciding the actual terms of most labor contracts in the nation.

Government, in dealing with the organized bureaucrats and with other unions in the public sector, finds itself in the role of manage-

---

[17] Baltazar Cavazos Flores, as referenced in Geraldo von Potobsky and Efrén Cordova, *et al.,* "The Settlement of Labour Disputes in Mexico," *International Labour Review* (May 1971), p. 494.

[18] Purcell emphasizes the difficulty of securing legal standing for a strike, pp. 14–16.

[19] Euquiero Guerro, *Manual de derecho de trabajo* (México, D.F., 1962), II, p. 269.

[20] Attributed to Baltazar Cavazos Flores in von Potobsky, *et al.,* p. 487.

ment while labor finds itself affected with the public interest. Under these circumstances difficult problems can arise. This is particularly true in that area where benefits involving costs of the enterprise or costs of government are concerned. Medical benefits, housing opportunities, working conditions and, obviously, wage levels are all involved here. These are the principal subjects when workers start negotiating with management of public enterprises. The problem is doubly difficult because the managers themselves are placed there by those who are the controlling policy-makers of Mexican government. In the end, all owe their jobs to the President of the Republic. Thus management must never be defied openly because to do so is to defy, in fact, those who are the governors of the Mexican people, which can be construed as an act of defiance toward the system. So a stand against management takes on overtones of subversion, and can become an act of high treason, against the Revolution itself or against the Revolutionary regime.

A number of modes of praise are invoked in connection with any request or public statement by leaders concerned with employee demands. These modes of praise are highly formalized to indicate the greatest possible respect and admiration for those who are in the top policy-making positions. As a matter of fact, these signs of respect are designed to legitimize top decision-makers as trustees of the Revolutionary tradition who are doing the best possible job within the framework of the norms and the goals set forth by the regime.

For example, when workers in the Ministry of Water Resources (SRH) wanted to add new categories of employees to pension and vacation plans, they encountered great opposition from the Assistant Minister of the Treasury. In spite of their claims of support by their own Minister of Water Resources, it was necessary in presenting this situation to the higher authorities to proceed through a number of formalities. Thus the President of the Republic was extolled for all of the things that he had done for the workers in the various government agencies, including Water Resources. So also was the Minister of Water Resources praised for his support of these demands by the workers. In addition there was praise for the constructive role of the head of the bureaucrats' union (FSTSE), Jesús Robles Martínez. The demands or the requests that were being made were then stated, and the nature of the problem with the official of the Ministry of the Treasury was clearly described. The final stage in this appeal, as in the case of any other appeal of the same nature, included a statement of complete loyalty, confidence, and admiration for the President of the Republic and for his collaborator with whom the SRH workers were so closely connected: namely, the Minister of Water Resources.

In another case, the Pemex workers, in the process of renegotiating their contract with management, invoked Revolutionary tradition and the act of expropriation which had taken the oil from foreign hands and placed it in the hands of the Mexican government. Former President Cárdenas was also praised as the man who carried out the expropriation. Succeeding Presidents, particularly then-President López Mateos, were praised, so was Gutiérrez Roldán, whom López Mateos appointed to run Pemex. These people were lauded as persons acting in accord with the tradition of the Revolution and of Cárdenas and other heroes of the *petroleros*. Particularly, the workers' pronouncements stressed the helpful attitude of the President in renegotiating collective bargaining contracts throughout his years in office and mentioned the various improvements that had been made in relation to the standard of living of the workers during this period. Especially mentioned were the small industries and retail outlets which had been sponsored with government capital in order to provide certain necessities for the workers at lower cost. On the other hand, the difficulties which the workers had had in finding an adequate and understandable procedure in financing houses for themselves and their families were also mentioned, as were the actions of some contractors in using deficient materials in the houses under construction for the workers. The overall orientation, however, was toward labor-management cooperation within the framework of the norms and heroes of the Revolutionary regime, with petitions for change and redress well cloaked in ceremonial style.

In this case, as in others, it is interesting to note that "cases of open dispute between the government and its employees do not arise," thus again stressing the decisive authoritative role played by the government in most labor situations.[21]

Yet control is not assured all the time. In 1959 Demetrio Vallejo led a massive railroad workers' strike. Although it was not sanctioned, the extent of the discontent was probably unsettling to the Revolutionary coalition, because violence was so intense.[22] Subsequently, more attention was paid to increasing the benefits of the military forces.

The needs of the nation vis-à-vis the organized laborer extend beyond those of social security and strike procedures. One important area as yet untouched concerns job-training. This area received little emphasis in Mexico until the early 1960s. In 1963 Mexico applied

[21] von Potobsky, *et al.*, p. 496.

[22] Philip B. Taylor has written about events at this time in considerable detail in "The Mexican Elections of 1958: Affirmation of Authoritarianism?" *The Western Political Quarterly* (September 1960), pp. 722–744.

to the International Labor Organization Special Fund for assistance in developing the first national job-training institute, the National Vocational Training Service for Industry (ARMO).[23] The ARMO, however, does not directly assist workers, but rather assists businesses in establishing their own training programs. The need for this is clear when one considers the highly technical nature of much of modern industry. Mexican vocational schools are too few to fill the needs of industry, and the jobs often require more training than can be given. Of the estimated 180,000 new workers entering Mexican industry in 1969, 100,000 needed special training, and 20,000 workers changing jobs needed retraining.[24] In addition to the ARMO, there were 30 training centers in 19 states to train workers, and there were plans to open another 72 centers in rural areas, reflecting the rural weakness of the nation.[25] However, the burgeoning needs of the nation cannot be adequately handled through these measures; the rapid growth of population in recent decades has produced greater needs than the present capabilities of controlling labor dissent and training new workers.[26] Greater productivity (and this also means more training per worker) is essential for maintaining the present standard of living. The number of dependents per 1000 workers increased from 1410.5 in 1950 to 1859.1 in 1970.[27] Just maintaining the present level of productivity through worker training is in jeopardy.

### The Labor Force and "Progress"

The emergence of technologically advanced industries, although the most dynamic part of the economic system in productivity, does not automatically absorb or reduce the size of the more traditional, preindustrial parts of the economy. Even in the cities many aspects of the economic system are still traditional in nature, although the largest industry in Mexico is still agriculture. Significantly, the labor forces

[23] Xavier Caballero Tamayo, "The ILO and Development in the Americas," *International Labor Review* (December 1969), p. 529.

[24] Caballero Tamayo, p. 529. These figures are the estimated annual values for these categories.

[25] Caballero Tamayo, p. 529.

[26] A recent computer simulation has indicated that the number of unskilled agricultural workers can be held constant while the number of skilled workers increased sufficiently to absorb most new entrants to the labor market. See Louis M. Goreaux and Alan S. Marre, *Multi-level Planning: Case Studies in Mexico* (Amsterdam, 1973), pp. 55–84.

[27] Thomas G. Sanders, "Mexico 1974: Demographic Patterns and Population Policy," *Fieldstaff Reports* (July 1974), p. 4.

associated with these have not changed in proportion with the changes in productivity.[28] The problem of creating new approaches to new problems in a society undergoing rapid change was stressed in the findings of Joseph A. Kahl, who found that lower-level workers in large factories, often recruited from rural areas, were generally content with their lot. He saw the problem of discontent as arising from the middle-level employees who had a predominantly urban background and secondary-school training. It was these individuals who felt their aspirations stifled because the upper-level employees were generally recruited from families which occupationally had already reached managerial status.[29] This is related to the problem of middle-class expansion, as John J. Johnson has emphasized.[30]

Balán, however, found that "Most working-class men have relatives who have crossed class lines, from marginal to integrated [i.e., unionized] or from working- to middle-class.... Kinship ties are such that a move up or down does not mean a severing of contacts. The upwardly mobile men are not expected to pull their immediate kin up with them, but they are expected to maintain social contacts and to help out if possible." [31] In contrast to this is the fear of the middle and upper-middle classes of downward social mobility, a grievous blow to family honor and the dignity of the individuals involved.[32] Yet Balán notes that despite these possible pressures for conflict, there is little class conflict in Monterrey.

Although Balán's study was conducted in one of the most economically dynamic areas of Mexico, his findings are indicative of the general impact of the growth of industrialization in the nation. Migrants to Monterrey, and indeed the inhabitants of the surrounding rural areas, report that upward-looking young men should migrate to

[28] Jorge Balán, et al., p. 305. This is a significant study examining the complex effects of economic development on different economic groupings both within and around Monterrey.

[29] Joseph A. Kahl, "Three Types of Mexican Industrial Workers," Economic Development and Culture Change (January, 1960), pp. 164–169; The Measurement of Modernism: A Study of Values in Brazil and Mexico (Austin, Texas, 1968); Comparative Perspectives on Stratification: Mexico, Great Britain, Japan (New York, 1968); and (with Pablo González Casanova and Raul Benítez Zenteño) La industrialización en América Latina (México, D. F., 1965).

[30] John J. Johnson, Political Change in Latin America: The Emergence of the Middle Sectors (Stanford, Calif., 1958).

[31] Balán, et al., p. 307.

[32] Richard R. Fagen and William S. Touhy, Politics and Privilege in a Mexican City (Stanford, Calif., 1972), chapter 4.

the big city. The migrants to Monterrey in Balán's survey report that 68 percent believe that their work is better than their fathers', while only 22 percent believe it worse.[33] But expectations of all Monterrey inhabitants for their sons are quite optimistic: 65 percent of the natives aspire to university education for their sons, while 49 percent of the migrants do so; 61 percent of the natives aspire to a professional or top executive career for their sons, while 44 percent of the migrants do so; 80 percent of the natives expect that their sons will have non-manual occupations, while 66 percent of the migrants do so.[34] When asked how their eldest son would live, both migrants and natives responded virtually the same: 28 percent said "much better," 60 percent said "better," ten percent said "the same," and one percent said "worse." The 88 percent who responded in the "better" categories were further questioned. Sixty-four percent gave as reasons for their optimism increased education or superior occupational training, while 11 percent responded that the general progress of Mexican society and economic development would be the reasons.[35] Significantly, Balán poses the question of how much longer can the pattern of general optimism continue?

The process of development as described by Balán has two major components: a reliance on an increasingly more complex technology coupled with a greater bureaucratization of the system. From these he deduces two related consequences. First, there will be an increasing emphasis on education and training within the population. Second, there will be a greater stress placed on education in the placement of individuals in the occupational structure. Although this latter point may well be tempered by cultural emphasis on family and individual ties, especially in government bureaucracies and family-dominated businesses, these are not immune to the effects of generally rising standards of education and ability.

As a result of growth, the future of laborers in urban settings is less clear than the present pattern of control and stability. Balán notes several reasons why the generally favorable attitudes may change. First, the ratio of favorable comparisons of sons' livelihoods and life-styles to their fathers' will decrease, because more of them will not have lived through the rural-urban transition. Second, the system will appear more closed because of greater emphasis on education, which the higher classes can better afford. And third, the over-emphasis on

[33] Balán, *et al.,* p. 314.
[34] Balán, *et al.,* p. 316.
[35] Balán, *et al.,* p. 327.

education as a sure route to status advancement will be shown to be unrealistic.[36] He concludes:

> In one form or another, we anticipate a greater activism among the once nearly quiescent marginal groups. It seems clear to us that, for virtually all the groups we have reviewed, what made for acceptance of authority and a smooth transition in the past will be much less effective in the future. Thus, we arrive at the somewhat paradoxical conclusion that the very success of Monterrey's development over the past several decades, far from ensuring a continuation of the "formula" that has worked so well in the past, has created the conditions for a rise in discontent and an increase in group and class conflict.[37]

[36] Balán, *et al.*, p. 330.
[37] Balán, *et al.*, pp. 330–331.

# ⁘ 8 ⁘

# Agrarian Policy

## Historical Background of Agrarian Reform

A basic factor in the Mexican Revolution of 1910 was the desire for agrarian reform. In fact, Mexican agrarian reform can be regarded as a direct consequence of the role of the peasant movement in the armed struggle: a consequence of revolution and not of evolutionary planning. Its postulates and its form emerged as a response to the predominant usages and abuses evident during the first decade of the twentieth century and for some time prior to that.

Nearly all authors who discuss the agrarian movement and agrarian politics point to the high concentration of land ownership in the rural areas of Mexico and the poor distribution of wealth as a backdrop for the Revolution of 1910 and the agrarian reform. It should be noted, however, that this pattern of high concentration of rural property characterized the Mexican countryside since early colonial times. It developed as a direct consequence of the Conquest and domination of the Indians by the Spaniards in a situation in which the conqueror established himself in organized Indian villages and carried out the first of many land grabs that were to follow. Thus the roots of the agrarian reform are to be found in the deterioration of the land tenancy system through the efforts of those who undertook the Conquest, though this deterioration was noticeably intensified in the decades prior to the Revolution of 1910.

Initial grants by the crown to the conquerors on a large scale were later followed by an institution called the *encomienda,* a device by which the King of Spain assigned a given number of Indians for a stipulated period to a white landowner in order that the landowner might protect them and instruct them in the ways of Spanish culture and religion. In return for this help, the Indians were to pay tribute, either in labor or in kind.

The general picture of land distribution which characterized the colonial arrangement was one of large private holdings for Spaniards and *criollos,* large Church holdings, and some communal property assigned to Indian villages. It is possible to view the poor distribution of land under this arrangement as one of the causes, if not a principal cause, of the War of Independence. Father Hidalgo issued an agrarian decree as early as December 1810 which commanded some distribution of land among the poor people. Attention to the concentration of land was also given by José María Morelos who succeeded Hidalgo as the leader of the movement against the Spanish.

These early considerations of the land problem were not given a place in the final settlement guaranteeing the independence of Mexico. Instead, following independence, if there was any pattern at all, it was change toward even further concentration of rural property in fewer hands. The Reform, and the Wars of the Reform, were fought in part over the land problem, specifically over the question of the amassing of land by agents of the Church.

The great clerical properties were broken up by the leaders of the Reform era. But their efforts did not break up the concentration of rural lands. Instead, some of the great *latifundia* changed hands. In other cases men were able to create new large holdings. The pattern of unequal distribution — a few rich and a great many poor — continued to be the dominant feature of the Mexican countryside.

The concentration of great amounts of land in the hands of a few was particularly evident during the decades reaching from the triumph of the Reform to the Revolution of 1910. By 1910, the geographer McBride calculated, the rural inhabitants of Mexico holding property were fewer than they had been at any time in Mexican history.[1] "In all but five states of Mexico, 95 percent or more of the rural population was landless, and the highest proportion of rural heads of families holding land in any state was 11.8 percent." [2] Simpson estimated that there were at least eleven *haciendas* that possessed as much as 100,000 hectares each.[3] And it seems to be the consensus among writers who studied the period that no more than 1,000 families held over 90 percent of the arable land of the country.

There were four basic dimensions in the amassing of land during this period between the time of the Reform and the Revolution of

[1] George McBride, *Land Systems of Mexico* (Washington, D.C., 1923), p. 155.

[2] Brian Loveman, "Land Reform and Political Change in the Countryside: The Mexican and Cuban Cases" (Unpublished paper, 1969), p. 92.

[3] Eyler N. Simpson, *The Ejido: Mexico's Way Out* (Chapel Hill, N.C., 1937), p. 32.

1910. Probably the most notorious activities centered around the boundary surveying and colonizing companies.[4] Almost as bad was the maneuvering to take the communal property of Indian villages.[5] There were also payments of land by the state to private individuals as compensation for some types of debts or reward for services. Finally, an important factor in land concentration was the absence of legislation setting a maximum limit to property holding.

Among the great farms were the classic cases of the Hacienda San Blas in the state of Coahuila and the holdings of the Terrazas in Chihuahua. But whether a *hacienda* had 10,000 hectares or several hundred thousand (such as the two mentioned above) the common characteristic of a *hacienda* was that it was an essentially self-sufficient economic unit encompassing rich agricultural lands, lands for grazing, forests for providing wood, and water resources. On these lands there would sometimes be many villages, the inhabitants of which worked for the *hacendado*.

There were two types of peons, workers by the job (*peones de tarea*) and workers by the year (*peones acasillados*). Both received wages, though the job workers received only about half the usual thirty-one centavos daily earned by the *peones acasillados*. A major factor in keeping workers on the *hacienda* was the *tienda de raya*, a kind of company store that sold goods to the peon and his family. These stores also made special loans for occasions such as the Holy Week celebration. Accounting was done by the *hacendado*'s clerical help and the debt was deducted from wages. Often the peon mortgaged not only himself but his children to pay for goods sold him by the *hacendado*'s storekeeper. If peons fled from the *hacienda*, the federal rural police (*rurales*) would hunt them down.

The *haciendas* thus employed quasi-feudal modes of production including debt-peonage. But unlike their feudal predecessors, the Mexican *hacendados* relied on governmental support to maintain their dominance in the countryside. Small property owners had the worst of the situation in competition with the great land holdings. *Latifundia* were frequently exempt from payment of taxes, workers were kept in a state of semi-slavery, and expenditures in salaries were recovered by the owner through the company stores. Historians are not in agree-

---

[4] Victor Manzanilla Schaffer, "La reforma agraria," in *México: cincuenta años de revolución* (México, D.F., 1961), III, p. 232.

[5] From one such case emerged the great peasant leader of the Revolution, Emiliano Zapata. A good study of Zapata's early involvement is by Robert A. White, S.J., "Mexico: The Zapata Movement and the Revolution" in Henry A. Landsberger, *Latin American Peasant Movements* (New York, 1969), pp. 101–169.

ment about the effectiveness of the *hacienda* as a productive unit for surplus produce going to the cities, but the general picture seems to have been lack of efficiency in utilization of land.

The regime of Porfirio Díaz remained aloof from the hardships of the masses of the people and considered only policies for resolution of problems pertaining to the favored classes and the friends of the regime. When the Revolution of 1910 did break out, its first great leader, Francisco I. Madero, lost the support of many devoted revolutionaries, such as Emiliano Zapata, because of his unwillingness to promise large-scale reform of the land-tenure conditions in Mexico. After Madero lost power, those who wished to take his place at the head of the Revolution — Zapata, Villa, and Carranza — all issued pronouncements favoring the dissolution of the great properties. The Agrarian Reform decree issued by Carranza on January 6, 1915 is generally taken as the beginning point of Mexico's practical agrarian reform experiences. That decree formed the basis for Article 27 of the Constitution of 1917, which in turn provides the legal basis for agrarian reform legislation of today.

## The Beginnings of Agrarian Reform

In his decree of January 6, 1915, Venustiano Carranza as "First Chief of the Revolution" siphoned off much of Zapata's political support. The decree proclaimed that land which had been illegally taken from a large number of villages of various political categories, *pueblos, congregaciones, rancherías,* should be returned to them. This was to be accomplished either through "restitution" of lands on the basis of demonstrated evidence of title or through grant or "dotation" if for some reason the village was unable to show documentation of its claims. The decree referred specifically to legislation of the Reform which it pointed out had been misapplied under the *Porfiriato*.

The legal machinery for putting the decree into effect was to be found in the provision for a National Agrarian Commission, as well as agrarian commissions at the state and local levels. Provisionally, land redistribution took place through action of the state governors, state agrarian commissions and local executive committees. Decisions made at the state level were then reviewed by the National Agrarian Commission, and final title to the land was granted by a decision of the President of the Republic upon the recommendation of the commission.

The decree placed principal emphasis upon restitution of land to villages and reflected little serious consideration of the use of outright grants (dotation) on any considerable scale. Only villages having what was called political status (*categoría política*) were eligible under the decree. This meant that a multitude of small communities resident on the *haciendas* known as *acasillado* communities had no status in the reform situation. The decree was drawn up so as to put the initiative for action on the villages themselves, not on state and national officials. Relief from land distribution proceedings was available through the ordinary courts to the landholders so that proceedings could be held up for a great length of time under the existing court situation of the day through the writ of *amparo*.[6]

Carranza was in power a little less than five years after the promulgation of his decree. During that time only 190 villages received definitive possession of land. The total amount of land distributed amounted to about 180,000 hectares benefiting some 48,000 *ejidatarios*.[7]

When Álvaro Obregón took power in 1920, his original legislative efforts had little effect other than to indicate enthusiasm for revitalizing the reform, but in April 1922 a more thorough law was passed spelling out more clearly what kinds of villages would be eligible to receive land and the amounts they could receive. This legislation formed a more solid basis on which further legislation could be enacted over the ensuing years. A tendency was begun to extend the rights of villages and to narrow the rights of landlords. In this legislation the procedural rules for action by the National Agrarian Commission, governors, state agrarian commissions, and village executive committees were more clearly spelled out.

The legislative and administrative action of the Obregón government quickened the reform. From 1921 to 1924, 624 villages and 139,320 heads of families received about 1.2 million hectares of land. This more than tripled the number of villages receiving land under Carranza. By the end of 1924 about 814 villages and 187,702 heads of families altogether had been beneficiaries receiving 1.4 million hectares of land.[8]

Following Obregón, the administration of Plutarco E. Calles enacted the law of April 23, 1927. This legislation dealt with several key problems. First, it adjusted the legal position of villages relating to the classification of "political category." [9] The courts had become filled with cases in which villages were petitioning to have their "political category" changed so that they could ask for land. The 1927 law

---

[6] *Amparo* is sought against federal officials who can be shown in the courts to have exceeded their authority. See chapter 6 above.

[7] Simpson, p. 79.

[8] Simpson, p. 87.

[9] Frank Tannenbaum, *Peace by Revolution* (New York, 1933), p. 204.

greatly simplified the different classifications making it possible for nearly all types of rural communities to apply for land. In addition, the law attempted to clarify further the procedural rules of the various committees in the program. Procedure for initiating a petition was simplified, thereby landholders were prevented from selling off part of their land to avoid expropriation. On the other hand, the position of the landowners was strengthened and clarified by providing a 150-hectare limit below which land was not affected by the reform.

Calles was in a better position to see the agrarian reform experience in perspective than his predecessors had been; he realized that it was necessary to provide new institutions for financing the reform programs in order for productivity and the rural standard of living to be raised. Thus, under Calles there were a number of decrees which provided for agrarian bonds and a National Bank of Agricultural Credit.

Other Calles legislation touched on the problem of irrigation and the colonization of new lands. Not only did Calles improve the legal situation with regard to the agrarian reform, he also provided concrete evidence of the commitment of Revolutionary governments to implementation of the reform by distributing 3.2 million hectares over the period January 1925–December 1929, to the benefit of 1,576 villages and 307,607 *ejidatarios,* better than a twofold improvement over the whole period of the reform from the date of the 1915 decree to the time that Calles took office.[10]

Emilio Portes Gil became interim president of Mexico in December 1928, and the year 1929 under his leadership marked a high point in the distribution of land for a one-year period. During that year 693 villages and 108,846 *ejidatarios* received more than a million hectares of land. Gil also sponsored legislation further restricting the area of maneuver remaining to large landowners, and a new water law definitely gave the nation inalienable control of all factors pertaining to the water supply.

When Portes Gil was succeeded by Pascual Ortiz Rubio, the major trends that had developed in agrarian reform, facilitating petitions for land and restricting landowners in their capacity to resist, were interrupted and for the moment reversed. In May 1930 Ortiz signed an official resolution addressed to the president of the National Agrarian Commission which set a period of sixty days for all communities planning to petition for land to present their case, after which there would be no further appeal. This so-called "stop law" was to apply to the state of Aguascalientes to begin with, but in the next year and a half similar presidential orders affected twelve other states. The results

---

[10] Simpson, pp. 94–97.

were sudden and concrete: land distributed in 1930 dropped from over 1,000,000 in 1929 to 744,091 hectares, and in 1931 to 610,304 hectares. In 1932, only 384,401 hectares were distributed. However, a positive step in favor of agrarian reform was taken while Ortiz was President in that the capacity of the landowners to use *amparo* to obstruct land reform petitions was ended by legislation in December 1931.[11]

Opposition from various sources within the circle of revolutionary leadership led Ortiz Rubio to resign in September 1932, and he was succeeded on the designation of Congress by General Abelardo L. Rodríguez. In July 1933, after he had been in office about ten months, President Rodríguez issued a decree which quietly put an end to the so-called "stop laws" of Ortiz by abolishing all time limits set on village petitions for land. State agrarian commissions which had been dissolved were then quietly reconstituted. Thus the agrarian reform was put back on the track in accord with the tendencies developed through the governments of Obregón, Calles, and Portes Gil.

In December 1933 the first complete agrarian code was put into effect by President Rodríguez. A new Agrarian Department was provided to handle petitions for land at the national level. The state agrarian commissions became "mixed" agrarian commissions, and their functions were spelled out more clearly. Governors of states continued to play a major part at the state level, and there were in addition agrarian executive committees and commissariats of *ejidos*. Though the procedural roles which these bodies were to play were still not clarified so as to end all difficulties, the provisions were more clear as to which lands were to be distributed and which were not. Moreover, rights of individuals and *ejidos* with regard to water and other resources of the countryside were more clearly defined. Dotation as a way of distributing land was for the first time treated as the larger part of the agrarian reform. The code was in fact the most important statement of goals and procedures outside of Article 27 itself.

In addition to the refinements in the code there was a related yet distinct area of concern treated by the Rodríguez government: credit. The Calles government had pioneered in this area by setting up the National Bank of Agricultural Credit. Under Rodríguez there was a Law of Agricultural Credit issued on January 24, 1934. This law provided at long last some operating funds for loans through the National Bank of Agricultural Credit to go to the *ejidatarios* meeting criteria of worthiness.[12] At the same time opportunities for loans to

[11] Simpson, pp. 111–120.

[12] Lucio Mendieta y Nuñez, *El problema agrario de México* (México, D.F., 1937), p. 300.

individual agriculturalists of certain classes were provided with preference being given in competitive cases to *ejidatarios*. Moreover, the rights of resident peons (*peones acasillados*) were clarified.[13]

In spite of the new legislation, however, a very substantial segment of opinion led by Calles himself believed that the basis of agrarian reform should be small, privately owned property rather than the *ejido*. Much of the discussion over the six-year plan that was proposed in the December convention of the Revolutionary party in 1933 as well as the maneuvering with regard to naming a candidate centered around the question of whether or not the basis of the agrarian program should be founded on small property purchased by the peasantry, or upon the idea of the *ejido*. There were other issues, but certainly this was one of the most crucial.

## Agrarian Reform Under Cárdenas and Subsequent Developments

Out of the convention of December 1933 came the candidacy of General Lázaro Cárdenas. Cárdenas made several changes in the Agrarian Code of 1934. One of the most important affected the resident peons in their capacity to petition for land. Although this code was the first to give them any right to share in the redistribution of lands, it nevertheless limited the right considerably. The limitations were removed by a decree of Cárdenas in August 1937, making it possible for these resident peons to exercise the same agrarian rights as other segments of the rural population. The act greatly increased the number of *haciendas* subject to subdivision. Perhaps the resident-peon provision, more than any other, was basic to the great expansion of agrarian land distribution under the Cárdenas government.

During the first year of Cárdenas' presidency, 2,900,226 hectares were distributed, better than twice the amount for any one year up to that time. The amount was increased in the second year of his presidency, 1936. In no year were less than 1,700,000 hectares distributed, and in one year (1937) the number surpassed 5,000,000. Altogether in the six years of his presidency, 1934–1940, there were 17,890,577 hectares distributed among the people.[14]

With the coming of Manuel Ávila Camacho to office in December 1940, the pace of land distribution slowed somewhat, although there was by no means a radical withdrawal from the program. In 1941 the land distributed by Ávila Camacho was less than a million hectares,

[13] Nathan L. Whetten, *Rural Mexico* (Chicago, 1948), p. 132.
[14] Whetten, p. 125.

but it went considerably over that in 1942 and stayed around a million hectares per year until the last year of his administration. Altogether Ávila Camacho distributed 6.6 million hectares, not the same pace set by Cárdenas, yet more than any of Cárdenas' predecessors.[15] (See Table 7.)

The rate of land distribution declined still more after Ávila Camacho, although it did not come to a standstill. President Alemán from 1946 to 1952 distributed over four million hectares.

Legislation of the Alemán presidency has formed an important basis as well as a limiting framework for subsequent agrarian policy. Of particular importance are two measures. First of all, there is the amendment to Article 27 of the Constitution which went into effect on February 12, 1947 shortly after Alemán became president. This amendment revived in part the *amparo* proceedings eliminated during the presidency of Ortiz Rubio. Under the amendment any owner or possessor of an agricultural or livestock holding who had been granted a certificate of inaffectability, or might be granted one in the future,

*Table 7*

**Land Distributed under the Presidents (in hectares)***

| | |
|---|---|
| Carranza and de la Huerta | 381,949 |
| Obregón | 1,730,684 |
| Calles | 3,173,343 |
| Portes Gil | 851,282 |
| Ortiz Rubio | 1,495,182 |
| Rodríguez | 2,056,268 |
| Cárdenas | 20,107,044 |
| Ávila Camacho | 5,306,922 |
| Alemán | 4,210,478 |
| Ruiz Cortines | 3,563,847 |
| López Mateos | 7,935,476** |
| Díaz Ordaz | 24,491,000** |
| 1915–1970 total | 75,303,475 |

* Note: 1 hectare equals approximately 2.47 acres.
** Official figures for the last two Presidents vary. See text discussion.
SOURCE: Rosa Tirado de Ruiz, "Desarrollo histórico de la política agraria sobre tenencia de la tierra, 1910–1970" in Ifigenia de Navarrete, *Bienestar campesino y desarrollo económico* (México, D.F., 1971), p. 53 (from data from the Departamento de Asuntos Agrarios y Colonización).

[15] Howard F. Cline, *Mexico, Revolution to Evolution, 1940–1960* (London, 1962), p. 213.

was given the capacity to initiate injunction proceedings to prevent the taking of his lands and waters for expropriation under the land-reform program. The reopening of the resort to *amparo* was designed to prevent attacks upon smaller-scale property holders by landless rural labor groups such as that led by Ruben Jaramillo.[16] Large landholders not eligible for certificates of inaffectability remained excluded from recourse to the *amparo*.

In December 1949 a series of alterations appeared in the Agrarian Code which again acted to slow up land distribution or put limitations upon those seeking land, though they did provide better organization for overall distribution. Under the provisions added to the code in this year of Alemán's presidency, the minimum *ejido* grant was raised to 10 hectares of irrigated land or 20 of seasonal land. The result intended was reduction of the incidence of small uneconomic plots, sometimes referred to as *minifundia*. The importance of the private smallholdings, often large in comparison with *minifundia*, was restated by continuing the grants of inaffectability. The recourse to *amparo* was written into the code as an additional insurance against squatter raids.

Some large holdings involving badly needed crops such as bananas, coffee, and sugar cane were covered under the inaffectability procedures, and the code provided that in the case of cattle-raising, lands could be extensive enough to graze up to 500 head or their equivalent in other livestock. Special cases were recognized in which as many as 50,000 acres of pasturage could be made inaffectable for 25 years. No change was made in the prohibition against foreigners owning real estate within 100 kilometers of the nation's borders or 50 from the seacoast.

Thus many more restrictions were placed upon land distribution, and there were corresponding advantages evident for landholders. Yet the amount of land distributed during the Alemán government was by no means negligible. The new procedures, while protecting private holdings in some respects and giving perhaps greater order to the agrarian distribution program, did not by any means end it. But the procedures made clear that the government's agrarian program was evolving toward a heavier dependence on private commercial agriculture, with land being concentrated increasingly in the hands of the private sector.

The importance of the smallholdings was increasing in the pro-

[16] Local leadership predominated in these groups, but comparative outsiders were sometimes involved. Politicians within the Revolutionary coalition occasionally encouraged the squatter groups (*paracaidistas*) for personal advantage, as in the raids during the governorship of Braulio Maldonado in Baja California in the late 1950s.

gram and was planned to be the instrument feeding new millions of urbanized Mexicans. The Alemán presidency also set the course for future governments toward the opening of virgin tropical lowlands as an escape-valve for frustrated land hunger among the rapidly increasing population of the countryside. Thus two projects were begun and others were planned during the Alemán administration. The most ambitious of these was the Papaloapan Project. Under the Commission of the Papaloapan, created in 1947, this ambitious project was an enlargement of the Tennessee Valley Authority concept in the United States. Four great dams were to create the energy for electrification and manufacture of huge amounts of artificial fertilizers to avoid the soil depletion associated with agriculture in the tropics. The annual flooding of this huge basin, which stretched across the states of Oaxaca, Puebla, and Veracruz, would be prevented, along with associated tropical diseases, and irrigation and drainage could be provided. A smaller-scale project of the same type got underway with the formation of the Tepalcatepec Commission under the leadership of ex-President Cárdenas. Through these projects and others being planned, the fruits of modernization were to provide resettlement space, food, and industrial products for the expansion of the population.

Alemán's successor, Adolfo Ruiz Cortines, distributed 3.5 million hectares. In his last year as president, 1958, Ruiz Cortines informed the Congress in his State of the Union Address that land for redistribution was becoming scarce.[17] He emphasized yet again the continuing importance of the smallholdings. The two pillars of Mexican agriculture, the *ejido* and the smallholding, had to be considered in any future programs to improve social and economic conditions in the countryside. The government's attention should be focused on creation of new resources rather than further division of land under cultivation, which simply aggravated an existing evil, the expanding number of inefficient *minifundios*.

To deal with the land hunger of the rural masses, Ruiz Cortines emphasized expansion of the fledgling colonization program, and the creation of new *ejidos* on previously uncultivated land. The government was to provide persons unable to obtain land in their own areas with an opportunity to settle on the new lands opened up through irrigation or reclamation projects. As of 1958, Ruiz Cortines reported that there were about 924 colonies occupying some 6.2 million hectares of land. Ruiz Cortines had probably cleared with his successor the substance of his last message to Congress, so the message set expectations for future action.

17 Cline, pp. 213–214.

Ruiz Cortines' solutions were essentially a continuation of the ideas and policies pursued by Alemán. Since the Alemán years the smallholding had become ever more important in the thinking of government planners. The difficulties with the *minifundios* had also been discussed. What was new was the scale of unrest in the countryside from the early 1940s into the first years of Ruiz Cortines' government. It raised once again the question of whether the regime, within its policy constraints, could continue to manage land tenure and rural labor.

The regime's pronouncements and the hopes of well-wishers at home and abroad seemed overoptimistic. Even if there were improved agricultural production and modernization in the form of dams, irrigation works, roads, electrification, and telecommunications much in evidence, and even if private commercial agriculture had proved economically feasible, the facts of rural poverty and land hunger persisted. Many of the *ejidos,* especially in central Mexico, remained at the edge of subsistence, and their extraordinarily high birth-rate expanded a rural laboring class that was not only landless but devoid of primordial roots. Overcrowding on the *ejidos* and throughout the rural areas caused young men to be driven from their families, communities, and native regions by hunger and unemployment. Their wandering existences told of the great difficulty of finding a steady, remunerative job on the land.

The problems raised by the presence of these *golondrinas* were increased by two tendencies under Ruiz Cortines. One was that public works were substantially reduced in both rural and urban settings in comparison with the Alemán years.[18] The other was that the government of the United States was placing limitations upon the number of Mexicans who could come into the United States for temporary employment. It was especially the *bracero* program that was suffering from 1960 on. Still a third factor contributed a great deal to reducing any employment benefits for the unemployed rural masses: the increase in agricultural productivity. The newer technologically advanced smallholdings had so rationalized their procedures that they had less need for manual labor. Opportunities for employment were diminishing at exactly the time that production was increasing in the countryside — not an unknown phenomenon in other countries of the world.[19] But as Tirado points out, "prosperity in a sector, 'commercialized and efficient,' does not mean that the country

[18] For a concise overview of the rural situation see Tirado de Ruiz, pp. 36–50.

[19] See, for example, Solon Barraclough, "Employment Problems Affecting Latin American Agricultural Development," *The Monthly Bulletin of Agricultural Economics and Statistics* (July–August 1969).

has arrived — that is, reached the goal of an economic development which would include general prosperity of the rural labor population."[20] Finally, the tendency to move slowly through the process of dotation to create new farms for the landless was significant. The victim of these factors was the expanding population which did not benefit from the fruits of technology and industrialization.

The growing demands of rural labor for lands and their frustration over the complicated procedures were connected with these factors. Demands were evident in the state of Morelos, just south of Mexico City, and in Chihuahua and Baja California in the north, where the difficulties were reflected in squatter raids, in which the landless would invade a large farm and sow their own crops before anyone even knew they were there. The demands of Jaramillo in Morelos were similar to those of other radical leaders in Guerrero.

Ruiz Cortines' successor, López Mateos, showed no disposition to depart from the policy of his predecessors, though he responded to the growing signs of rural unrest. In his first two years in office he often repeated that distribution of land to the landless would continue to be a major concern of his government. He also ordered a re-examination of existing grants of inaffectability, promising that his government would view as affectable for distribution any land falling into relevant legal categories. Many large farms and pastoral operations enjoying certificates of inaffectability saw their certificates revoked during the ensuing years. In his first two years in office, López Mateos distributed 3.2 million hectares of land.[21]

López Mateos claimed he distributed more land than any President since Cárdenas. But accounts of land distributed were beginning to vary from one official source to the next. (See Table 7.) The growing scarcity of land and the continuation of rural unrest were clear. The variations suggested that different sets of books were being kept, any one of which might be cited according to the convenience of the President or his spokesman. López Mateos told Congress and the nation in his final State of the Union message, "It had been affirmed for years that lands susceptible of distribution in accordance with law no longer existed or were on the point of disappearing. My government, in six years, has distributed . . . *more than a third of the lands distributed during the 44 years that the Agrarian Code has been enforced* . . ."[22] According to López Mateos, between January 6, 1915, when Carranza issued his decree, and December 1958, when

[20] Tirado de Ruiz, p. 49. Translated by author.
[21] Cline, p. 214.
[22] López Mateos, Sixth State of the Union Address, *Hispano Americano* (Sept. 7, 1964), p. 15. Translation and italics by author.

López Mateos took office, the land distributed amounted to 43.5 million hectares, to which he claimed to have added roughly 16 million hectares. By this count, the total distributed by all the revolutionary governments would have been very close to 59.5 million hectares. However, the difficulty with López Mateos' total of 16 million hectares was that six years later, the next outgoing president claimed that he had distributed 25 million hectares, which would have brought the grand total to some 84 million hectares, nearly 9 million hectares more than the 75,303,475 the Díaz Ordaz government claimed had been distributed by the end of 1970.[23]

Despite these inconsistencies, the López Mateos presidency was characterized by an explicit recognition of the shortcomings in the older agrarian reform institutions. There were overt commitments to corrective measures for dealing with difficulties in the existing *ejidal* system, as well as new approaches to the place of the *ejido* in the overall picture of land tenure and production in rural Mexico. Along with the determined support for colonization and resettlement programs, it was hoped that these changes within the existing arrangement would prove adequate to deal with the discontent and population pressure in the countryside.

Within the existing *ejidal* system, the government continued to support compartmentalization of *ejidos* to provide urban zones, which were in turn subdivided to permit the members of new generations of offspring from the original *ejidatarios* to possess small plots of their own on which to house their own families. These urban zones or *zonas urbanas* began to be created within existing *ejidos* in the 1940s. They reflected the population expansion and consequent overcrowding on the existing *ejidal* lands. The difficulty of feeding these new generations, the sons and grandsons of the original *ejidatarios,* was further reflected in an innovation of the López Mateos government known as the *solar urbano,* a garden plot added to the urban zone plot which permitted the *ejidatario* and his extended family to raise some food to further what was often a slim margin of subsistence. Ordinarily the plots were used for vegetables, poultry raising, and the like.

Another difficulty of the existing *ejidal* arrangement was illustrated in the effort of the López Mateos government to deal with the abandonment of *ejido* plots and their illegal use by large, private agricultural interests. Not infrequently, the plots were rented out by *ejidatarios* who found it impossible to make a living on them. Many then moved to urban areas. On the basis of findings from a govern-

[23] Díaz Ordaz, Sixth State of the Union Address, *Hispano Americano* (September 1970).

ment study, some 75,000 judgments were rendered by the DAAC which deprived people of *ejidal* rights, either for abandonment, illegal renting, or some other abuse of *ejidal* holdings.[24] These judgments showed the inadequacy of *ejidal* land and malpractice by the agrarian leadership, who were found in a number of cases to have made private rental contracts with large interests in the private sector. Such contracts, placing *ejido* land temporarily under private control, were cancelled as a result of the efforts of the López Mateos administration. New administrative devices were worked out to assure that only authentic *campesinos*, as distinct from land speculators masquerading as peasants, would receive benefits under the existing irrigation and construction programs.

Indications of difficulties were also to be found in pronouncements by government officials and in essays by specialists associated with the regime, particularly in the much-endorsed concept of "integral" improvement of *ejidos*.[25] There was also support for the concept of the model *ejidos* (*ejidos tipo*), which the government hoped would influence *ejidatarios* in the surrounding areas of the countryside and by its example create more effective patterns of living and farming among the rural population. Over the six-year period of López Mateos' presidency seventy model *ejidos* were established. The law was redrawn to permit members of existing *ejidos* to develop a model *ejido*. The government showed a new interest in the problems of social solidarity among the *ejidatarios*, and the internal organization of many *ejidos* came under close scrutiny. There was a renewed effort to assure respect for the deliberations and resolutions passed by the general assemblies of *ejidatarios*. The government's proclaimed goal at this point was to do away with *caciquismo* at the *ejido* level by removing and replacing all *ejido* authorities who had finished their stipulated terms.

The government also announced measures to make more efficient the older procedures under the agrarian reform laws: dotation, restitution, and amplification (expanding the size of *ejidos*). This was done by placing emphasis on the *ejido* as an economic unit of production. This recognized the fact that because of dotation many *ejidos* were too small for efficient production, and there would have to be

[24] López Mateos, pp. 15–16.
[25] See Marco Antonio Durán, "Agrarismo y desarrollo agrícola," *Investigación Económica* (Cuarto trimestre de 1963), pp. 677–708; Marco Antonio Durán, "Las funciones de la propiedad de la tierra en la reforma agraria mexicana," *El Trimestre Económico* (Abril–Junio de 1964), pp. 228–242; Ramón y Ricardo Acosta, Fernández y Fernández, *Política agrícola* (México, D.F., 1961); and Victor Manzanilla Schaffer, pp. 227–263.

a greatly expanded use of fertilizers and technology if they were ever to be made productive. This was a change from dependence on rudimentary means of cultivation, an assumption that the government could and would provide both the material and human resources to carry out these changes. The DAAC announced plans to expand the number of skilled agricultural advisers and technicians by means of new training facilities. The manner of instruction was also altered, with greater emphasis on skills the technicians needed to give basic help to those in the countryside. These skills included an understanding of machinery, fertilizers, basic agricultural practices, rudiments of good financial practice, and social skills calculated to produce co-operative relationships in the *ejido* communities. The government thus hoped to encourage *ejido* members to take risks and make efforts to learn so that crop diversification could proceed where it was badly needed. The model *ejido* was a small-family farm where people would not only cultivate the soil but would also take an interest in bee-keeping and poultry-raising.

Through such diversification people on the *ejidos* were to become more closely linked with the national economy than ever before. This was the hope of López Mateos' government. The old concept of the *ejido* as a self-sufficient unit that consumed whatever it might produce was seriously questioned by government officials and social theorists alike: they believed that this concept was merely a version of the *hacienda porfiriana* in microcosm. The resulting closed economy would seriously inhibit the integration of the *ejido* system into the general economy of the country. The problem of the *ejidatario* was now diagnosed as that of a person too long in tutelage, and its correction lay in an emphasis upon the *ejidatario* as a small-farm proprietor who could make an integrated contribution to the social and economic life of the country.

The new roles of *ejido* and *ejidatario* and their incorporation into the economic system were based on more than agriculture. The *ejidatario* was to begin to participate in the processes of simple manufacture. Part of the technical aid that would go to him would develop skills and acquire equipment to enable him to begin processing *ejidal products*. Thus along with the concept of the small-family farm there was also the concept of the small-family industry, able to perform the initial stages of manufacture and operating as a resource-pool for skilled workers. The gap would be narrowed between the manufacturing activity of the cities and the agricultural activity of the countryside. As theorists and government spokesmen presented this picture, it seemed a solution to *ejido* and agrarian problems and a complement to other facets of the economy.

Along with the concept of the small-family industry and small-family diversified agricultural unit was a third conception for the future development of *ejidos*. This was the concept of the livestock-raising *ejido*, 86 of which were established during the administration of López Mateos. In a number of cases, a type of communal effort in the handling of the livestock was established. Stock was held in common, and all members of the *ejido* acted jointly as herdsmen or drovers to care for the herds that belonged to all of them. In addition to the livestock *ejidos*, a large number of communal forestry *ejidos* were created. The basis of both the livestock and forestry *ejidos* was a decree of April 23, 1959, in which new regulations were promulgated concerning planning, control, and supervision of investments on communal *ejido* farms. This permitted a much more careful examination of the *ejidal* credits and debits. There was also to be governmental tutelage of *ejido* management to encourage cooperation among the heads of families and better conservation and accounting practices.

Modern knowledge was to be made available for soil conservation and to fight erosion, particularly important on many Indian communal lands which were often on hillsides where there had been much slash-and-burn cultivation: the land was worn out as well as strained by overpopulation. To protect the Indians and the inhabitants of areas where settlement was planned, and to protect the claims of old, established *ejidos*, boundary surveys were pushed toward completion. The results of Indian claims on communal lands and other unsettled boundary claims were clearer by the time the Díaz Ordaz government finished its six-year term.

Where private property was involved, the López Mateos government was either very lenient or very strict. The major sources of land for distribution to the peasants were the remaining *latifundios* and the various land monopolies, along with the certificates of inaffectability granted to many cattle ranches. With respect to the inaffectability of livestock-raising properties, the stringency of government policies could be seen in the fact that 46 certificates of inaffectability were rescinded while none were issued during the six-year period. The lenient side of the López Mateos approach to private property were the 40,260 certificates of inaffectability issued to small agricultural properties. Creating affectable smallholdings was not regarded any longer as being at odds with the agrarian reform, since reform was now part of "integral development." Since there was still much unoccupied or relatively unused land in the public domain which could be colonized by technology and social engineering, it was possible for government policy-makers to envisage a total transformation of the countryside into the habitat of middle-class producers and consumers. All the conflicts between smallholders, the landless, and the large prosperous landowners could be reconciled. Moreover, with this new prosperity, harmony, and modernization in the countryside, there could also be for the first time a rational distribution of social security coverage in rural areas.

## The Extensive Tropical Development Plans

With the expropriation of *latifundios*, the cancellation of fraudulent certificates of inaffectability, and the elimination of the old *caciques* of the *ejidos*, the government hoped that at last it was in a position to view the future with equanimity. There would be plenty for all, and prosperous small farmers could continue to expand and develop their holdings. López Mateos summed up the vision of plenty which he felt his agrarian program would promote:

Action has been focused upon compliance with the juridical principles sustained by Mexican agrarianism and the maintenance of peasant unity. We consider that, if we act according to law and protect within constitutional norms both the *ejido* and the smallholding, we will have order and tranquility. The latter are the bases of productive work which will permit achieving the standard of living needed to accomplish the great tasks confronting the country.[26]

López Mateos' successors would be vital to the success of this dream. But it could only be achieved through the Revolutionary coalition's continued ability to siphon off resurgent demands for land through expanding efforts toward colonization and population resettlement in the humid tropical lowlands. López Mateos continued his predecessors' colonization and resettlement programs but also reflected changing emphases. Over his six-year presidency, 119,801 certificates of agrarian rights relating to this dimension of public policy were issued. Twenty-eight new population centers were constructed in the Panuco region, seven in the Alto Candelaria in Campeche, 12 in Quintana Roo, 45 in the south zone of Veracruz, and 60 in Oaxaca. In the fall of 1964 there were thousands of persons, according to López Mateos, moving into the new population centers with surrounding lands prepared under the government projects. It would appear that the creation of these new settlements had some bearing on the

[26] Departmento de Asuntos Agrarios y Colonización, *Seis años de politica agraria del Presidente Adolfo López Mateos, 1958–1964* (México, D.F., 1964), p. 79. Translated by the author.

## Figure 7

### Climatological Regions of Mexico

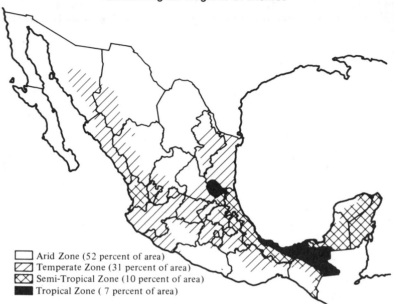

☐ Arid Zone (52 percent of area)
▨ Temperate Zone (31 percent of area)
▨ Semi-Tropical Zone (10 percent of area)
■ Tropical Zone ( 7 percent of area)

SOURCE: Adolfo Orive Alba, "La irrigación como factor del bienestar campesino," in de Navarrete, p. 93.

distribution of approximately 2.9 million hectares of public land by the government during 1958–1964. The new settlers were being evacuated from overworked and overcrowded lands in the states of Zacatecas, Jalisco, Guanajuato, México, and from the multi-state Laguna region. Some were moved from still other areas where poor land and/or excessively small plots had made farming unprofitable. In this way, López Mateos added a total of 152 colonization or resettlement projects to the 924 projects on 6.2 million hectares claimed by official sources in 1958.[27]

These policy decisions brought still more clearly into focus the Revolutionary coalition's determination to put to the test the dream of agricultural abundance waiting to spring from the soil of the world's tropical lowlands. Will, imagination, and technology were to make

[27] López Mateos, pp. 15 ff.

*Figure 8*

Ranking Agricultural Productivity in the States (1960)

☒ High Productivity
☒ Medium Productivity
☐ Low Productivity

SOURCE: Ifigenia M. de Navarrete and Arturo Cardenas Ortega, "Un modelo de desarrollo agropecuario y bienestar campesino 1970–1980," in de Navarrete, p. 153.

unusable tropical lands into a vast source of food and raw materials. Although sufficient economic and scientific information was lacking for the careful assessment of early results of tropical development, decision-makers had given the green light to the planners. "Modernization" as a process was replaced by "modernization" as dogma. The numerous economic and technical issues of economic and environmental feasibility were shunted aside as the vast investments were made and the colonization gathered momentum.

The temptation to bypass the technical questions was great, for if planning could make possible rapid regional development, it could surely provide a cure for rural discontent: accelerated, humane colonization and resettlement. This social goal was a basic aspect of regional development efforts. The accelerated population growth could then be regarded as a blessing instead of a problem, and the growing generations of Mexicans could benefit from the fulfillment of the regime's welfare goals. The country's population and modernization could support each other as the wastelands turned fruitful. In recent years this dream has been questioned. The established policy of directed colonization on new lands no longer appears to be the rapid solution it once appeared to be. In fact, in a crucial recent study, Michael Nelson argues that the experience with directed colonization in tropical, humid lowlands was not successful, despite massive government investment.[28] Nor does directed colonization appear to have made a significant contribution to solving the unemployment problems that continue to plague rural areas. In a study of 24 tropical colonization projects throughout Latin America, Nelson found that the instrument most relied upon by the policy-makers to achieve a favorable cost-benefit ratio for resettlement and colonization may very well be unsuited to the needs of the countries' environments and economies. This method of directed colonization for securing results as easily and rapidly as possible under government sponsorship and control seems to have fallen disappointingly short of expectations. In the four Mexican cases included in the study, the results have been uniformly disappointing, although the reasons differ from one project to another. Nelson considers the four projects as encompassed within the category of directed colonization. This involves very intensive planning, support by massive investment for the development of infrastructure, and extensive supervision by the government developing, planning, and investment agencies. One of the Mexican examples could have fallen under the category of "semidirected" settlement because "spontaneous" settlement was involved, but the degree of government supervision led Nelson to include it in the directed category. This project was La Chontalpa, located on the coastal plains of Tabasco and under the control of the Grijalva (River) Commission. The other three are Nuevo Ixcatlán, Cihualtepec in the lower Lalana–La Trinidad Basin, and La Joya, located on 60,000 hectares in the state of México between the Valle Nacional and the Playa Vicente Rivers, both tributaries of the Papaloapan. Some of the reasons Nelson gives for his critical view of directed colonization in Mexico are as follows. Nuevo Ixcatlán and Cihualtepec gave an ambiguous picture on investment

[28] Michael Nelson, *The Development of Tropical Lands: Policy Issues in Latin America* (Baltimore, 1972), © The Johns Hopkins University Press. Published for Resources for the Future by the Johns Hopkins University Press. See especially pp. 20, 73–74, 97 and 108–109. Nelson's concept of directed colonization and semidirected settlement, along with his definitions, are basic to the following discussion.

returns, with negative results from income distribution. La Joya showed negative results from investment, population, abandonment, and production decline. La Chontalpa presented a picture of heavy "impositions on the *campesino* . . . dictated by both economic efficiency and welfare criteria." Nelson says developments of human resources are vital in terms of self-reliance, self-discipline, and willingness to innovate in the *ejido* situation. "Production efficiency requires that qualified technicians make and implement the management decisions . . ." Plans for more intensive cultivation have tended to give way to banana plantation and cattle-ranching operations.[29]

In summing up the results of his survey, Nelson recommends semi-directed settlement rather than directed colonization.

In spite of the evil reputation spontaneous settlement [that is, semidirect settlement] has acquired because of natural resource destruction and shifting subsistence agriculture, it offers the best chance of success in developing new lands where capital and administrative resources are scarce. The key element is highway access, preferably to areas on the periphery of an existing settlement where soil is reasonably good. The pioneer settlers who follow such roads will better match the development task than those who come as the result of elaborate promotional and selection procedures.[30]

Clearly, even in such settlement situations as Nelson recommends there would still have to be a good deal of government support on a systematic basis. There would have to be flexible phases of support, which would involve consolidating and expanding a number of programs relating to marketing capabilities, feeder roads, as well as some project-centers of an urban nature to house essential local services and processing plants. Especially important would be a major urban center to provide an industrial labor market in the region. This in turn might create a sense of identity with the locality and facilitate the administration of municipal government. Dispersion of settlers to all parts of the region would have to be avoided in the beginning stages in order to facilitate the growth of such an urban center.

Another prerequisite would be the formation of some medium- or large-sized development organizations, whether public, quasi-public,

[29] Nelson, pp. 74–84.
[30] Michael Nelson, *The Development of Tropical Lands: Policy Issues in Latin America* (Baltimore, 1972), p. 288. © The Johns Hopkins University Press. Published for Resources for the Future by the Johns Hopkins University Press.

or private, to act as sources of necessary production and industrial services. These organizations and their technicians (people with knowledge of the area's cultivation and management needs) would be located in the major regional center. In later stages this center would mobilize additional capital as well as management talent for the project's further expansion.

As Nelson sees it, success in directed resettlement-colonization efforts depends on the capacity of governments to overcome traditional obstacles in providing support for the above plans. One difficulty was knowing which areas were appropriate to a certain agricultural activity. Another was maintaining control over land-use and land-tenure in the area. Still another was getting the best balance between land-use, land-tenure, and an infant commercial-industrial complex.

If semidirected settlement or colonization has the greatest chance of success, as Nelson argues, then some entrenched expectations, hopes for quick and easy solutions through directed colonization, must be abandoned. It was an accepted doctrine that population overflow and consequent food shortages could be handled with a comparatively small capital outlay. This low cost in relation to the results of development was based on the assumption that there were rich, unexploited natural resources that required little in the way of extraction costs. Just as attractive was the vision of the productive absorption of an extensive unemployed labor force which would demand only minimum remuneration. Herein lay the assumed basis for the creation of new wealth: the new capital would in turn stimulate new industrial and commercial establishments. This scenario, in conjunction with the new food and raw materials supplied, would hasten modernization, progress, and national self-sufficiency. Internal demands, first of a region, then of the whole country, would be manageable and the extent of dependency on external sources of supply would drastically decline. But this doctrine was a dream.

The dilemma facing policy-makers is the conflict between promised benefits and the viable routes to development. Despite the immense investment over three decades in tropical lowland development, productive employment and sufficient food for the burgeoning population could not be obtained with the investments made in the short run. The more prolonged spontaneous development approach requires abandoning the commitments to expanding rural social benefits. This can only alienate those rural workers who already committed themselves to development projects. In the spontaneous approach at least a generation, if not more, of the colonists could expect nothing but a life of deprivation, heart-breaking toil, and the real possibility of failure. This unattractive picture was clearly difficult to accept.

No North American scholar better epitomized the hopes for progress and prosperity through technology and planning than did the great Mexicanist Howard F. Cline. His book, *The United States and Mexico,* published in 1953, legitimized the fondest hopes of both Mexican and American policy-makers.

Under the twin drives of industrialism and technical agrarianism, some of the wide gaps between city and country are slowly being bridged ...

It is more important to measure how far Mexicans have already come than to carp about how far they have yet to go. And they have come far in rural Mexico under President Miguel Alemán.

The major new departure [of Alemán] ... is the idea of rehabilitating vast waste areas by drainage and irrigation. ... it joins agrarianism and industrialism into a harmonious whole.[31]

Cline wrote concerning the Papaloapan project of a "preplanned city, Ciudad Alemán, to act as the social, administrative, and economic hub of the zone." The Papaloapan Commission was only formed in 1947, but Cline prematurely assumed the completion of the new city. His description of the city in 1952 gave the impression that in five short years, 1947–1952, the region had been fully developed.

From [the city] radiates outward a network of roads, canals, and airways to lesser but comparable urban groupings, each in turn surrounded by agricultural and industrial villages, ... all [growing] subsistence and industrial crops — vegetables, maize, sugar cane, cotton, high-grade bananas, pineapples, ... and [supporting] light manufactures. ... An aluminum works and a paper factory got underway in 1952. ... Factories and new inhabitants benefit from the hydroelectric power created by four huge dams ...[32]

Cline was impressed by the magnitude of this project. He saw it as a super-TVA development which would prove once and for all man's capacity to triumph over the forces of nature and the limitations of his intelligence.

More interesting in many ways than the sheer magnitude of the enterprise is its concept of harmonious and balanced de-

[31] Howard F. Cline, *The United States and Mexico,* Revised Edition, Enlarged (Boston, 1953), pp. 382–383. © Harvard University Press.
[32] Cline, *United States and Mexico,* p. 383.

velopment. . . . Equally important has been a large-scale, long-term attempt to interweave the two aspects of the industrial revolution, urban and rural, and to bring them into some definite relation to each other.[33]

Almost three decades after Cline and others had their golden vision of Mexico's future, with the fruits of modernization and the exploitation of tropical lowlands, Nelson argued that "massive support to colonization areas frequently has been largely wasted — benefits have been short-lived, the social infrastructure has fallen into disrepair and become inoperative, colonist turnover has been high, and per-capita production has been low. Consequently, public funds would have been better used in other endeavors to achieve social goals." [34] This does not mean that there is no hope for development of the areas in question. It simply means that quick solutions for the pressing population problems in rural areas must be discounted.

It goes without saying that it is better to have than not to have these resources [the tropical lowlands], but to equate them with Argentina's pampas or Venezuela's oil is indeed wishful thinking. None can deny that with yet-to-be developed technology, enormous wealth might be derived from this [tropical lowland] region. In the meantime, it can be argued that these unexploited areas have some potentially negative features in that euphoria over their development prospects causes nations to divert resources and energy from the really crucial problems to be solved. Employment is undoubtedly one of the primary issues facing developing countries. But the idea that a government can take a preselected, underemployed group, say, 100,000 families, from city X, region Y, or industry Z, transfer them to the jungle and expect economic or social success is patently ridiculous. It can be asserted with some confidence that over the next decade or so, expansion of the agricultural frontier inevitably will result in the destruction of natural resources. Extention services will be inadequate. The majority of colonists will not be capable of effectively using credit and, even if they

[33] Cline, *United States and Mexico*, pp. 384–385. Compare Cline's timeframe with the schedule for development phases suggested by Nelson, p. 73.

Successive stages of development (pioneer, consolidation, or growth) of a tropical land frontier are somewhat arbitrary. . . . Pioneer zones are primarily subsistence economies. . . . The consolidation stage may follow five to ten years after initial pioneer settlement. . . . The growth phase may follow five to ten years after consolidation.

[34] Nelson, pp. 288–289.

were, sufficient credit would not be available. Market and freight rates will constrain the flow of private capital into agricultural, forestry, and industrial enterprises.[35]

## The Remaining Difficulties

In light of the new information which Nelson and others have contributed regarding the colonization of the tropics, and in light of the events subsequent to the López Mateos presidency, it no longer seems surprising that the extensive colonization, resettlement, and *ejidal* reform efforts of that administration and its predecessors since Cárdenas failed to resolve the perennial problems of Mexican agrarianism. In the end there were really no new departures from existing prescriptions for the agrarian problem, except for colonization. Beginning with Alemán, each new government had made heavy psychic and material investments in tropical-basin development with the hope that homesteads, employment, and surplus food production, which had not become available by the mid-1940s, might somehow be brought into being. But there was need for an astounding degree of success if the roughly ten-million increase in population every decade was to be accommodated. By 1964 it was clear these projects were not even close to providing relief for rural employment and land hunger among the masses of the countryside. Moreover, it was not clear that reform within the existing system of *ejidos* and private holdings would generate more jobs even if productivity could be increased.

Like its predecessors, the López Mateos government, in spite of its concern for the agrarian problem, placed urbanization and industrialization at the highest level of priority. These two high-priority goals dictated a third: promotion of the smallholding as the main instrument for increasing agricultural productivity. Other agrarian policies: land redistribution, development of the tropics, innovation, improvement, and reform among *ejidatarios* and institutions of the *ejidal* system, and the integration of the *ejido* as a productive unit within the national economy, would all have to remain secondary to the higher goal of rapid increases in agricultural production.

When Díaz Ordaz became president, his inheritance included a series of well-established policies and programs, and continuing agrarian difficulties. The most pressing problem was the perennial shortage of land relative to demand. A related difficulty was the proliferation of very small land parcels, whether *ejidal* or privately-

---

[35] Nelson, pp. 290–291.

owned. The magnitude of the problem was pointed out by Francisco Hernández y Hernández. Counting *ejidatarios* with private property holders, the smallest holdings of from one to five hectares numbered well over two million plots on approximately ten million hectares. Holdings larger than 51 hectares numbered only a little over 25,000, and accounted for over six and a half million hectares. Holdings of a more medium size, six to fifty hectares, came to something over 160,000 and accounted for a little over three million hectares of land.[36] Clarence Senior found the same pattern of too many people on inadequate holdings in the Laguna region.

The area of irrigated land per capita in 1950 of the two major land-venture systems was: . . . *ejidos,* 4.4 hectares; private properties, 25.7 hectares. The average for the private properties does not show two phenomena of importance: (a) the fact that 5 percent of the owners held 26 percent of the private land and 14 percent owned 55 percent, and (b) that even these data underestimate the amount of concentration because they do not reflect the simulated sales which took place widely on the eve of and immediately following the expropriations.

Furthermore, it should be noted that 66 percent of the land possessed by the private owners was irrigable land while only 37 percent of that of the *ejidos* was so rated.[37]

This problem, instead of being reduced, was actually compounded by governmental policies. Table 8 shows most of the newly created irrigated farmland was going to *minifundistas,* and in addition the more moderately sized holdings were significantly decreasing in extensiveness. The problem of the small, economically inefficient plots, *minifundios,* was visible throughout the rural areas of Mexico. In *ejidos,* the vast majority of *ejidatarios* were holders of small parcels, and the average annual per-capita income for over a million *minifundistas* allowed little beyond subsistence. At the other extreme, only 7 percent of private landowners were able to expect an average annual income of about one million pesos. This tiny group accounted for 35 percent of total agricultural income. A look at the concentration of property in irrigation districts alone provided ample illustration.

[36] Francisco Hernández y Hernández, "El movimiento campesino," in *México: cincuenta años de revolución* (México, D.F., 1960), II, pp. 231–233.

[37] Clarence Senior, *Land Reform and Democracy* (Gainesville, Fla., 1958), pp. 95–96.

*Table 8*

The Concentration of Land Ownership in Irrigation Districts

1958

| Size of property in hectares | No. of users | % of all users | Area (in hectares) | % of irrigated land area |
|---|---|---|---|---|
| 0–20 | 249,929 | 92.2 | 1,033,625 | 52.2 |
| 20.1–50 | 15,711 | 5.8 | 499,939 | 22.7 |
| 50.1 and up | 5,185 | 2.0 | 497,774 | 25.1 |
| Total | 270,825 | 100.0 | 2,031,338 | 100.0 |

SOURCE: Adolfo Orive Alba, "Las obras de irrigación," in *México: cincuenta años de revolución* (México, D.F., 1960), I, p. 367.

1966

| Size of property in hectares | No. of users | % of all users | Area (in hectares) | % of irrigated land area |
|---|---|---|---|---|
| 0–20 | 331,402 | 95.4 | 1,515,808 | 63.3 |
| 20.1–50 | 11,412 | 3.3 | 397,472 | 16.6 |
| 50.1 and up | 4,632 | 1.3 | 482,214 | 20.1 |
| Total | 347,446 | 100.0 | 2,395,494 | 100.0 |

SOURCE: Adolfo Orive Alba, "La irrigación come factor del bienestar campesino," in de Navarrete, p. 107.

When Díaz Ordaz became president in 1964, the rural work force numbered six million in contrast to the 2,500,000 estimated for the year 1915. After fifty years of land reform, the government claimed to have distributed more than 57 million hectares of land to the benefit of 2,500,000 *campesinos*.[38] *Thus, in 1965, there were more landless rural workers theoretically eligible to obtain ejido plots than when the Carranza decree of 1915 was issued.* The continuing pres-

[38] *"Sintesis de la obra de Díaz Ordaz" Hispano Americano* (Nov. 30, 1970), pp. 26–30. Address by the Minister of Agrarian Affairs and Colonization. This was the key summation for the agricultural policy of the Díaz Ordaz government and, as such, must be regarded as carrying the full weight of an official pronouncement. The occasion was the granting of 1,788,643 hectares to *campesinos* of Baja California Norte.

sure of land hunger and the consequent "spontaneous colonization" of squatters was no longer a phenomenon confined to the north country of Baja California or traditional strongholds such as Guerrero and the inaccessible areas of Morelos. Already in the spring of 1965, just subsequent to the inauguration of the Díaz Ordaz government, these same problems appeared throughout the central states where the *ejido* system had first been established. In Tlaxcala, for example, during the spring of 1965 the land invasions brought about a crisis for which the only solution was a decision that was hailed as marking new precedents in agrarian reform. The solution involved a purchase by the state government of 1500 hectares from the landowners whose holdings had been occupied. In addition, the owners themselves contracted to compensate the squatters for the crops they had sown. The nature of the land was indicated by the fact that the National Cattle Confederation acted as go-between to produce the settlement. Simultaneously, the federal government was being asked to depose the governor of the state of Colima because he was "obstructing the expropriation and redistribution of land of a number of large *haciendas* in that state." [39]

At this point, the government sought to develop a more extensive plan for the future of agrarian reform. An ambitious topographical study, including aerial photography, was to be the basis of this plan, which was aimed at classifying the land-use patterns existing throughout Mexico. In November 1970 the head of the DAAC reported that this study took in 82.5 percent of the area of Mexico (165 million hectares). On the basis of the information gathered by the planners in connection with the topographical study and related investigations, the DAAC hoped to define once and for all which land would be considered affectable for distribution under dotation or amplification. As the government studied the extent of the agrarian problem, decisions were made on several occasions to incorporate land from the private sector into the *ejidal* sector by making the extension of irrigation systems subsidized by the government contingent upon the selling of portions of the private farms to the government. One of the most extensive land transfers in this connection took place in the Valle de Carizo in the state of Sinaloa. There the government claimed to have allocated to *ejidatarios* 80 percent of the 40,000 hectares to be placed under irrigation. [40]

The Díaz Ordaz government did not, however, depart in any major way from that of López Mateos and his predecessors, even though

[39] *Excelsior* (June 5, 1965). Translated by author.
[40] Aguirre Palancares, p. 27.

the pressure for land distribution had accumulated with the great population growth from one decade to the next. The tone for the next six years was set in an interview granted by the Minister of the DAAC in June 1965, only two days after the Tlaxcala decision. The main outlines of the policy were: one, the technical improvement of *ejidos*, an idea widely propagated under López Mateos; two, the gradual absorption of *ejidatarios* into semi-manufacturing and service industries such as food processing, cooperative cattle-ranching, and operation of resort hotels; three, the promise to overcome the obstinate resistance to dotation and amplification by certain classes of landowners, a concern of every government since the beginnings of agrarian reform; four, the acceleration of bureaucratic procedures concerning petitions for dotation and amplification; five, the resolution of drawn-out boundary disputes involving both *ejidos* and Indian communal lands; finally, the continuation and expansion of colonization and resettlement in the tropical lowlands developed under river-basin projects. The dream of a solution for land overcrowding was thus a characteristic of the Díaz Ordaz government's agrarian policy package, just as it had been in previous administrations, and the ultimate resolution of agrarian reform was still seen in tropical lowland development. The interview with the Minister of the DAAC contained the following exchange:

Questioner: Does this mean, sir, . . . that when this immediate program has been carried out, the peasants who have not yet received lands will remain without them?

DAAC Minister: To take care of this contingency, we are resorting to the creation of new population centers. [To do this] we will turn to the *possibilities offered by our tropical rain forests with their lands so rich and good, and we shall be able to settle there many of those who have petitioned for land without having received benefit.*[41]

The determination of the government to base future land distribution upon the openings of new land, almost entirely in the humid tropical areas, was the corollary of the continuing policy of reliance

[41] *Excelsior* (June 7, 1965). Author's translation and italics. The problem of boundary disputes involving Indian communal lands — mentioned above — was in some respects related to the plans for developing and resettling lands included in the river basin projects. The final solution announced in 1970 was the definition of some 8,100 Indian families as possessors of property rights. Whether or not this involved all Indians connected with the communal boundary settlements was not made clear by the government. Aguirre Palancares, p. 28.

upon the smallholdings as the chief instrument of agricultural production. Thus the Minister of the DAAC, in his last major public address in 1970, reported a "growing deficit in the confrontation between peasant production and land . . ." at the same time that he was lauding the president for distribution of approximately 25 million hectares benefitting 406,732 *campesinos*.[42] He told the people explicitly that affectable land had almost run out, thus officially recognizing that agrarian reform, as it had been known in Mexico, was approaching an end. Aguirre pointed to the fact that even as early as 1966 the Díaz Ordaz government had been deeply concerned over the backlog in the DAAC of petitions for dotation and amplification which officials felt could never, in the end, be honored. There were at that time, according to Aguirre, as many as ten thousand petitions pending a second review, the first appeal having been denied. He stated explicitly that it would be unjust to continue in this way because it meant "maintaining the hope of the *campesinos* when rejection was the only possible [outcome]." [43] Aguirre then pointed out that in 1966 President Díaz Ordaz had set the course of public policy for the future when he said,

> It is not a pleasant task for the President of the Republic to deny or reject the petition for land by peasants; but it is necessary, useful, and obligatory to tell them the truth. We are going to rule on pending petitions so that *campesinos* who have been waiting for years may receive some definitive response to their petitions. If, in the end, the results are negative, it will be better for them when they find out. But we consider this preferable to uncertain and indefinite waiting.[44]

As the decade of the 1960s drew to a close, the demands for land coincided with increasing agrarian unrest. Once again bands of guerrillas appeared in the countryside. While not an immediate threat to the regime's stability, this unrest seemed to have a continuity which, by its very existence, could not help but affect the pattern of political relationships that had emerged from the Cárdenas era.

As successor to the presidency and inheritor of policies left by former Presidents, Luis Echeverría Álvarez began his term in 1970 by reaffirming the approaching completion of the re-distributive phase of agrarian reform. He told the Mexican people that

> The *ejido,* the property held in common, and the true smallholding are fundamental institutions. To respect them and to

[42] Aguirre Palancares, p. 26.
[43] Aguirre Palancares, p. 28.
[44] Aguirre Palancares, p. 28.

make them productive is to encourage peace and prosperity in the countryside. Agrarian distribution has not concluded. *Legally and physically,* there still exist lands to be distributed . . . *To colonize is to populate* . . . We shall reach out to whatever regions are most promising, overcoming resistant anachronisms and avoiding the errors of past epochs . . . . *We shall transfer to the country a greater flow of financial resources* and administer them with rectitude. *Minifundismo* . . . is contradictory to the nature of the *ejidal* system. We shall strengthen the *ejido,* converting it into an active, truly democratic, and productive unit. Wherever possible, if the peasants want it, we shall group the parcels [of the *ejidos*] and [we shall create] co-operative work, thus making possible *authentic rural enterprise.*[45]

Echeverría then went on to promise more educational opportunity, more training and application of technology, better ways of cultivation to avoid land erosion, better seeds, fertilizers, and insecticides, better methods of distributing the agricultural products to the people, reduction of the unemployment rate in the countryside through the formation of small centers and factories dedicated to processing agricultural products, and the opening of once-arid zones for combined plant and animal raising (*agropecuaria*). In both his inaugural speech and in a special message to the Chamber of Deputies, he insisted that the tradition of cattle-ranching, while continuing, must at the same time be expanded to provide facilities for raising other livestock, and that certificates of inaffectability for cattle ranchers would be dependent upon evidence that the rancher was attempting to improve his land in order to support more animals per hectare.[46]

The end of dotation, amplification, and restitution as central considerations in agrarian policy was underwritten in the Echeverría government's 1972 version of the Agrarian Law. Also in the law from the time of Alemán was a reaffirmed commitment to the smallholding as the mainstay of agricultural production. The new law made the attainment of land even more difficult, but it could not change certain situations which existed in the countryside.

Although the new Federal Agrarian Reform Act prohibits the working of the common land by the system of tenant farming or share-cropping, the situation exists in Mexico in the following forms: an *ejidatario* is a beneficiary of the land reforms who uses part of a land grant to a rural population group to be worked

[45] Luis Echeverría, Inaugural Address, *Hispano Americano* (Dec. 7, 1970), pp. 16–17. Author's translation and italics.
[46] Luis Echeverría, pp. 16–17.

directly by it, subject to the restrictions and conditions provided for in the Act; an *aparcero* is a person who cultivates land rented from a third party against delivery of a pre-determined percentage of the crop in payment; a *mediero* is a person practicing a form of share-cropping in which the crop is shared equally between the landlord and the share-cropper.[47]

The key provisions of the law guaranteed inaffectability, always providing the proper legal procedures had been followed, for 100 hectares of irrigated land, 150 hectares of irrigated land in cotton, 300 hectares of irrigated land in bananas, sugar cane, coffee, henequén, hule, cocotero, grapes, olives, quina, vanilla, cacao, or fruit trees, enough land to maintain 500 head of cattle or the equivalent in smaller livestock (the amount to be determined by the technical reports of the *Delegación Agraria*), 200 hectares of arable land, unirrigated, 400 hectares of good quality pasture or summer graze (*agostadero*), or 800 hectares of mountainous or arid land. Under the law it was possible, as it had been even in Cárdenas' time, for different combinations of these kinds of lands to form one smallholding. Moreover, these combinations clearly can exceed 1,000 hectares in all. In addition, a provision existed which allowed an owner to keep his certificate of inaffectability for all his holdings if he can show that improvement by irrigation has been undertaken on his initiative and expense. This seems to favor maintenance of larger holdings and at the same time to encourage private investment in the improvement of such holdings. Government encouragement to improve and cultivate land rather than to keep it for grazing or to have it lay fallow was seen in the provision that inaffectability will be removed should the land remain without cultivation or equivalent use for two consecutive years. While this encourages productivity, there was also an escape clause which works to maintain inaffectability regardless of productivity. This provision allows the owner to plead "acts of God" (*causas de fuerzas mayor*) as an excuse for violations of this provision.[48]

The significance of such provisions for land concentration and for land hunger among the growing rural population can be thought of in various ways. The writer has found it helpful in this connection to return to Nathan L. Whetten's *Rural Mexico,* a study published in 1948 based upon 1940 census data. Whetten pointed out that *ejidatarios* and private *minifundistas* (five hectares or less) accounted for

[47] Lucila Leal de Araujo, "Extension of Social Security to Rural Workers in Mexico," *International Labor Review* (Oct. 1973), p. 300.

[48] Articles 249–251. *Nueva Ley Federal de Reforma Agraria* (México, D.F., 1972), pp. 113–115.

almost 90 percent of agricultural landholders in Mexico. From such a perspective, it appears that the Mexican countryside is populated by small, yeoman-type farmers. However, looked at from the standpoint of land censused in 1940, *ejidatarios* and private *minifundistas* accounted for 23.2 percent of the land while .3 percent of the landholders each owning a thousand hectares or more accounted for 61.9 percent of the land.[49] This tendency toward land concentration has, if anything, become more pronounced, as Tirado de Ruiz pointed out in 1971.

Finally, it is important to observe that Gini index coefficients have increased in regard to land concentration since 1940 . . . .464 in 1940 to .508 in 1950 to .523 in 1960. . . . This means that [concentration of land] has been growing over this period in a degree similar to that of family income, where the index on [income] concentration showed .50, .53, and .55 for 1950, 1958, and 1963, respectively.[50]

She shows that between the years 1950 and 1960, the tenth decile of land owners increased their ownership of land from 51.4 percent to 55.4 percent of the total farmland.

As the Revolutionary aspect of land distribution subsided, other rural commitments assumed greater importance. Rural social security coverage was first made explicit in the Social Insurance Act of 1943, when coverage of the nation as a whole was made a public policy goal. It was not until 1954, however, that the first rural programs were operational. At first only *ejidatarios* and the beneficiaries of other land reforms were given benefits. Other groups of rural workers were gradually given coverage based on their growing certain crops in irrigated areas, as in the sugar cane groups in 1956, the henequén group in 1972, and the tobacco group in 1973. The Social Insurance Act of 1954 also provided coverage to those who were members of local production cooperatives. In 1956 benefits were extended to provide coverage for members of credit societies. Rural credit societies were included to aid some producers who were neither in the *ejido* category or organized in production cooperatives. Thus in absolute terms there was a steady increase in the number of workers receiving the benefit of the IMSS services.

A number of innovative ideas were implemented. In 1963 it was decided that cooperatives and credit societies could be considered as "employers" for social security purposes. Also, tenant farmers

[49] Whetten, pp. 176–177.
[50] Tirado de Ruiz, pp. 58–59.

(*aparceros*) and sharecroppers (*medieros*) were included because they were vital to the diversity of needs in the rural areas. In 1969 rural workers who received any regular remuneration, in cash, in kind, or in service, were considered covered.[51] Many self-employed workers (both urban and rural) were covered by this criterion.

In recognition of the difficulty of financing these expanding goals, the governmental share of support for urban social security was reduced from 25 to 12.5 percent, so that the remaining 12.5 percent could be applied to rural social security.[52] Financing by law is derived from two sources, the employer and the government. However, differing needs caused the creation of three groups of beneficiaries.

First, there were those rural workers who were truly wage earners in a conventional sense or those who were in local producers' cooperatives. They were handled much the same as urban workers in terms of coverage and social security financing. Second, rural workers' credit societies were given special conditions of financing and coverage. Types of benefits included were sickness, maternity, disability, unemployment, old age, and death. Half of the premium was paid for by the employer and half by the government. *Ejidatarios* and the *minifundistas* (owning not more than ten hectares of irrigated land) not belonging to some type of credit society were provided with insurance against employment accidents and disease, with half of the premium being paid by the federal government. The new benefits were financed by the 12.5 percent of the government contribution being subsidized by urban sources, thus providing a greater equality of welfare distribution, and shifting part of the burden of costs to the urban areas. Third, coverage had existed since 1960 for casual and temporary workers.[53] Requirements for their social security eligibility were employment with the same employer for twelve consecutive working days or thirty days in a two-month period. The goal desired was financing and coverage comparable to those cited above. Finally, in addition to these there were special programs in industries which were particularly vital, for example, sugar cane. Insurance for these workers was shared by the sugar manufacturers (50 percent), the cane producers (25 percent), and the government (25 percent).

It was recognized that the new measures were proven inadequate in solving the financial problems involved for complete social security coverage in rural areas. The government explicitly anticipated that the contributions of employers would be gradually increased so that

---

[51] This refers to the Federal Labor Act of December 2, 1969. Leal de Araujo, pp. 307–308.
[52] Act passed December 31, 1965. Leal de Araujo, p. 307.
[53] Regulation of June 24, 1960. Leal de Araujo, p. 310.

as new rural groups were brought under coverage no severe financial strains would be felt. And this "horizontal" expansion of coverage to untouched groups or those groups theoretically protected but not in fact supported became an established policy goal.

In summary, not only the pronouncements of President Echeverría, but the tendencies observable in the available data seemed to support the conclusion that the smallholding was continuing to be the mainstay of Mexican agriculture and livestock production, with a legal status that permitted existence of relatively large private agricultural enterprises. This situation lent itself to an ongoing concentration of most good land in relatively few hands and, with the continuing emphasis on productivity and the expansion of mechanization to agriculture, it offered less employment opportunity while the need for employment in the countryside continued to increase. This was an obvious target for critics of the government as well as encouraging *paracaidistas* and "spontaneous colonization," if not the rise of guerrilla bands harassing owners of the great commercial farms.

The ideal of rural social security remained essentially an ideal as far as most rural Mexicans were concerned, and relatively little support was given to those who most needed it. The dilemma of Mexico has been the need for a more productive agricultural sector that would provide both expanding employment opportunities and feed the people of the mushrooming cities. But while production has increased, the *ejido* and the *minifundio* classifications continued to produce excess labor that urban enterprise could not absorb. The escape hatch for three decades or more has been the hope that tropical lowlands would provide food, employment, and a surplus for unlimited population growth. This escape hatch has proved illusory. The evidence in the mid-1970s seems to be that the time lag and the population boom involved in the overall agrarian situation produced a climate of frustration and anger, and embryonic political violence. Since the time of Emiliano Zapata, the countryside has been the key to the political stability of Mexico. In the mid-1970s it remained the biggest headache of the regime.

# ✤ 9 ✤

# National
# Development Policies

The focal issues of the Revolution have continued to be of major importance. They have definite symbols such as "effective suffrage — no re-election," the right to organize and strike, "land and liberty," separation of church and state, literacy, and, most important, national autonomy. Under twentieth-century conditions, success in fulfilling these goals as well as finding solutions for traditional points of conflict were perceived by the Revolutionary victors as dependent to some extent upon industrialization. But economic development itself has never been explicitly placed on a level equal with national autonomy by Revolutionary leaders. From the *Grito de Delores* to Tlatelolco the predominant theme of the Revolutionary tradition in Mexico has been independence from foreign control. For this goal Mexican intellectuals, activist leaders, and the masses suffered through successive infernos of foreign intervention and civil strife. In 1810, 1846, 1857, 1862, 1910, and again moving into the latter quarter of this century, the issue of governmental legitimacy has continued to be tested by criteria of national autonomy. National autonomy was to be achieved by national self-sufficiency through economic development.

## The Issue of "Development"

The Revolution of 1910 and the fall of the Porfiriato taught that for industrialization and economic development more Mexicans had to have some share in the benefits from "progress." Welfare values were thus added to the Revolutionary tradition, which later found expression in Articles 3, 27, and 123 of the Constitution of 1917. Education for all, land for rural workers, national right to subsoil wealth, and extensive social and economic commitments for all Mex-

274

icans were made explicit. The dilemmas of governments from 1917 to the 1970s have centered on the adjustment of policy to promote both economic development and adequate social welfare. Though conceptually interdependent, both social welfare and economic development have received primary emphases from different and often antithetical groups. The formation of national identity and realization of national autonomy for Mexico has always assisted the success of the Revolutionary coalition in attempting to maintain a balance between both welfare and development orientations which otherwise might have dissolved into political violence. And yet the perennial threat posed by potentially contradictory aspirations among different groups of Mexicans has not been banished.

Mexicans have had much to do to maintain the course chosen. Evaluating the country's performance in all phases would be impossible. Earlier chapters have discussed some critical areas of Revolutionary ideology, political competition, and public policies associated with agrarianism and organized workers. The achievements and shortcomings of these policies have been in part based on the changes wrought through the development of basic industries and their supporting infrastructure: fuel and energy, transportation, and communications. More extensive public education, a basic commitment of the Revolution, was fundamental to the success of these other endeavors. Government involvement in both economic development and welfare services has brought inputs to the public sector that have been steadily increasing to meet the demands of change. Certainly industrialization is a leading component of meeting these demands.

Hopes for the industrialization of Mexico arose long before the Revolution. In spite of the mercantilist policies of Spain during the colonial period there were a handful of persons who argued even then for diversification of the economy and industrialization. However, Spanish policy-makers never took these arguments seriously.

After independence, those who looked appreciatively toward the industrial techniques that were being developed in England found that many political and economic obstacles had to be overcome before Mexico could take a similar road. Even amid the chaos and civil war characteristic of Mexican politics in the early nineteenth century, there appeared an early "developmentalist" economic orientation. Such diverse individuals as Estevan Antuñano, Mariano Otero, and Lucas Alamán all recognized that it was largely industrialization that separated Mexico from equality with Western centers of power. Indeed, early Mexican political economists sound remarkably modern in light of the twentieth-century concern with dependence, neoimperialism, and the international division of labor.

The bastardized application of liberal economic principles and the thoughtless emphasis on foreign trade increases our burdens. . . . For the nation to prosper it is essential that our workers be occupied in all spheres of industry, and particularly that manufactured products be protected by import prohibitions wisely arrived at.[1]

Until the 1850s and the victory of the "reform generation," Mexican policy-makers focused explicitly upon industrialization as the principal way to make Mexico "the richest nation in the world." [2] These policies included operation of a Development Bank and creation of a small textile industry and other manufacturing establishments.[3] But the laws of the Reform and the edicts of its leaders, while they made inroads against the power of the Church, the higher military leaders, and some powerful landowners with commercial interests, failed to bring about the necessary changes. Mexico did not develop a pattern of balanced agricultural and industrial growth similar to that of the United States and Western Europe. By 1876, when Porfírio Díaz became President, the preponderance of economic activity was still centered on the great landholdings. Rudimentary railroad and telegraph systems, a few textile factories, a little milling, and some cottage-type industries were the bases of Mexico's industrial plant.

The positivist motto of the Díaz regime, "Order and Progress" was suited to an authoritarian, developmentalist state. A degree of stability and an encouragement to investment, especially for foreigners, was provided. This enabled the regime to produce substantial beginnings of a national railway network, a national system of communication (telegraph, to some extent telephone, and improved postal services), and the revival of the mining industry with modern technology and large capital investment. Reestablishment of public credit was also accomplished. Generally, there was substantial encouragement of new industries. The Díaz years, in fact, provide a classic example of a stable dictatorship that stimulates economic growth through dependence on foreign capital and repression of the working classes. In this sense, the Díaz regime could be termed "prototypical." [4]

[1] Manifesto del C. Vicente Guerrero, message of the second president to his countrymen (México, D.F., 1829), pp. 16–17, in Brian Loveman, *Economic Ideologies and Policies: Mexico and Argentina in the Nineteenth Century* (unpublished paper, Berkeley, 1965).

[2] Mariano Otero, *Ensayo sobre el verdadero estado de la cuestión social y política que se ageta en la república Mexicana,* 2nd edition (Guadalajara, 1952).

[3] See Robert Potash, *El Banco de Ávio en México: en fomento de la industria, 1821–1846* (México, D.F., 1959).

[4] Brian Loveman, pp. 77–78.

The Revolution of 1910 brought most industrial activity to a standstill. There was widespread destruction of capital equipment. After the fighting ceased and consolidation began under Obregón in 1920–1921, a number of factors combined to favor renewed development. Businessmen prominent in pre-Revolutionary days returned to the country from exile. Younger men emerged to stimulate continued development. These protagonists of the 1920s and 1930s expanded their enterprises not only under Obregón and Calles, but under Cárdenas as well. Many of these men had led forces during the Revolution of 1910–1917. The same energies that had made them successful on the battlefield were applied to commerce and industry. Carlos Fuentes' fictional prototypes, Robles in *Where the Air Is Clear* and Artemio Cruz in *The Death of Artemio Cruz,* as well as real-life actors such as General Arrón Saénz and General Abelardo Rodríguez, are illustrative along with many lesser known individuals.[5]

A particularly notable opportunity for Mexican capital was afforded under Cárdenas, who refused to tolerate foreign businessmen who would not cooperate, as shown by his expropriation of the foreign petroleum interests. On the other hand, Mexican businessmen who were able to show some Revolutionary spirit received encouragement from the government. Both World War II and the Korean War stimulated industrial and commercial growth. Devaluation of the peso gave a competitive advantage, while other changes raised import tariffs, brought about extensive financial aid from government, and important economic controls. Improvement in public services, infrastructure, and basic industries of the economy occurred, especially production of steel, electricity, and petroleum. Indeed, since Miguel Alemán's term, Mexican presidents consistently have seemed to assess progress towards industrialization by reference to these three major elements of the economy.[6]

In the last quarter of the twentieth century the commitment to these aims was still evident. The major emphases of development were in-

[5] Carlos Fuentes, *Where the Air Is Clear* (New York, 1960); *The Death of Artemio Cruz* (New York, 1964). Also helpful is Walter M. Langford, *The Mexican Novel Comes of Age* (Southville, Ind., 1961).

[6] Presidential State of the Union Addresses, especially those at the end of presidential terms, are a particularly useful primary source for information on major government policies. Because of the useful historical perspective they provide and because most of the substantive matter can be treated as reliable, an important perspective on the policies of development is given. The best way to use this source is to keep in mind that over time, the pattern is one of omitting or sliding over areas of low achievement while positive accomplishments tend to be described in great detail, thus providing a continuity of information about the shortcomings and successes of major policies.

dicated in President Echeverría's Fourth State of the Union Address.
Here he said that 17 percent of the public investment went for agricultural and livestock promotion and rural development; 32 percent
went for industrial projects, with emphasis on oil, gas, electricity, and
steel; 27 percent went for highways, railroads, ports, airports, and
communications networks; 22 percent went for social services; and the
remaining 2 percent went for administration and defense expenditures.
The sum total of these was over 66 billion pesos, and represented a
15 percent increase from the prior year.[7]

## Developing the Bases of an Industrial Society

### Steel

Mexico has moved with relative ease toward the goal of industrialization in part because of large deposits of coal and iron ore.
The first major mill, *La Fundidora de Fierro y Acero de Monterrey,*
was founded in 1903. Later another mill, *La Consolidada,* was also
founded with private capital in northern Mexico. In 1944 the great
integrated steel mill, *Altos Hornos de México* (AHMSA) began operations. Located at Monclova, Coahuila, this mill was financed
largely with government capital.[8] The plant received extensive government support under the presidency of Miguel Alemán, and by 1952
Mexico produced more than 600,000 tons of iron and steel products.[9]
The official position was that basic steel would provide the nucleus for
heavy industry that would assure Mexico's economic growth in the
future.

The concern for steel development continued through Ruiz Cortines'
presidency, and he claimed in 1958 that iron and steel production had
been increased by 80 percent.[10] The *La Consolidada* plant was subsequently absorbed into *Altos Hornos* under López Mateos' term in
1962.[11] Steel clearly became a major industry of the public sector,

[7] Luis Echeverría, Fourth State of the Union Address, *Mexican Newsletter Separata* (Sept. 1, 1974), p. 12.

[8] Frank Brandenburg, *The Making of Modern Mexico* (Englewood Cliffs,
1964), p. 277. Mexico and Brazil were leaders of all the Latin American
countries in this area of economic development. They were the only
countries to have integrated mills prior to 1950, i.e., mills that produce
at one site pig or sponge iron used for refinement into steel in another part
of the plant.

[9] Miguel Alemán, Sixth State of the Union Address, *Hispano Americano*
(Sept. 5, 1952), p. 6.

[10] Ruiz Cortines, Sixth State of the Union Address, *Hispano Americano*
(Sept. 8, 1958), p. 17.

[11] Banco Nacional de Comercio Exterior.

and in his midterm State of the Union address in 1973, Echeverría announced to the country that the *Altos Hornos* complex alone would produce 2,500,000 tons yearly in 1975.[12] The extent of progress has been rapid, for in 1974 Echeverría announced that expansions were underway which would double the capacity of the governmental steel plants.[13]

In 1973 there were over ten companies in Mexico which produced 15,000 or more metric tons of steel ingot per year. The big four were AHMSA, *Fundidora de Monterrey, Hojalata y Lamina, S.A.* (HYLSA), and *Tubos de Acero de México, S.A.* (TAMSA). AHMSA falls under control of the public sector through majority holdings by *Nacional Financiera.* In TAMSA, the government is a minority holder through *Nacional Financiera.* HYLSA is privately owned and *Fundidora* is the largest privately owned steel plant in Latin America.[14]

## Petrochemicals and Petroleum

Petroleum was, at an early date, a major factor in the economic growth of Mexico. Production began as early as 1901 when an American, Edward L. Doheny, brought in his first well near Tampico in the state of Tamaulipas. Subsequently the British began operations in the Tehuantepec region. From 1901 to 1921 total production in Mexico increased every year until the country became the number two oil producer in the world. This phase ended about 1921, and oil production declined a little every year from 1922 through 1932. Government policy toward the oil companies, development of saline deposits in some major fields, and of course, world depression all brought reduced production.

As the years of the 1920s and 1930s passed there were repeated crises between the government and the oil companies. Conflict centered around interpretations of Article 27 of the Mexican Constitution which vests sub-soil rights in the state, and the difficulties finally reached a point which prohibited reconciliation. First came a labor-management dispute which the government was unable to resolve, then there was a dispute between the government and the companies themselves which resulted in an impasse when they refused to obey a government directive. When the companies questioned the word of President Cárdenas the expropriation order went out on March 18, 1938.[15] Following the expropriation, the government formed a new agency entitled

[12] Luis Echeverría, Third State of the Union Address, *Hispano Americano* (Sept. 10, 1973), p. 7.
[13] George B. Blake, ed. *Business/Mexico* (México, D.F., 1968), p. 138.
[14] Luis Echeverría, Fourth State of the Union Address, p. 18.
[15] See Chapter 1.

*Petroleos Mexicanos* (Pemex). The petroleum industry of Mexico has been under the supervision of this autonomous governmental agency ever since. The responsibilities of the new organ were spelled out in a constitutional amendment in 1940. Under that amendment only the state could carry on exploitation in the petroleum fields.[16] The early years were very difficult for Pemex; abroad the industry faced the hostility of the great foreign oil companies with their control of tanker service on the world's seaways, while at home government oil executives confronted excessive demands by labor, expectations of graft on the part of subordinates, and unrealistic pricing policies developed at the presidential level to keep the price of fuel oil and gasoline uniform across the country.

The Mexican oil monopoly was put on an effective operating basis through the services of Antonio Bermúdez under Presidents Alemán and Ruiz Cortines. When Alemán left office in 1952 the production of petroleum and natural gas had practically doubled since 1946.[17] Continuing development was reflected in Ruiz Cortines' report of a 50 percent increase in the consumption of gas, 80 percent in kerosene, and 126 percent in diesel fuel in 1958 over 1952. Exploration indicated known reserves of 3.5 billion barrels. Refinery capacity increased from 190,000 to 330,000 barrels per day. Consumption of refined petroleum products was up significantly and they were exporting some semi-refined petroleum.[18]

By the later 1960s, refining capacity had surpassed 500,000 barrels daily. Sophistication in the manufacture of byproducts was growing steadily, and Díaz Ordaz stressed the continued growth of petroleum and petrochemical production. The value of expanding plants in petrochemicals in 1966 was estimated by United States' business sources at $397.3 million divided between the public and private sectors as follows: $120.8 million in government plants in operation; $21 million in mixed government and private plants in operation; $17.4 million in private plants in operation; $86.8 million in government plants under construction $41.5 million in private plants under construction; $36.5 million in government plants planned but not started; $5.2 million in mixed government plants planned but not started $68.1 million in private plants planned but not started.[19]

[16] The role of the petroleum industry in Mexico's economic development is covered in Padilla Aragón, "La industria y su influencia en el desarrollo industrial," in *La industria petrolera mexicana* (México, D.F., 1958), pp. 45–67.

[17] Miguel Alemán, pp. 6–7.

[18] Ruiz Cortines, p. 17.

[19] Blake, p. 149. (*World Market Encyclopedia* and *International Petroleum Encyclopedia* state that Mexico has the largest petrochemical industry in Latin America.)

Mexico in 1970 had maintained its export level while increasing storage capacity, port facilities, and distributive capabilities to meet national demands. Import substitutes were relieving some of the burden upon the balance of payments. Díaz Ordaz emphasized that the last limited contracts with foreign oil firms in either exploration or exploitation had been concluded by December 1969, and the 23 ships of Mexico's tanker fleet (20 acquired 1964–1970) made Mexico a country of major importance in the world petroleum market. Increase in petroleum and petrochemical exports occurred despite greatly increased national consumption.[20] The new fields discovered in the mid-1970s gave promise of providing a significant impetus to further industry growth, development in less-developed states, and aid in Mexico's balance-of-payments problems. In addition the subsidization of fuel prices throughout the country was ended in 1974. The subsidized prices were reflected in operation deficits in Pemex, but industrial consumers benefited. Reorganization of the financial structure of Pemex was intended to stimulate related users of Pemex products.

## Electricity

Much of the energy for industrialization was to come from electricity, but the generation of electric power in Mexico began with private companies in mining and textiles who needed electricity. Electrical utilities as such emerged as early as 1881, providing street lighting for a small section of Mexico City. With the appearance of European and American firms in the early 1900s, electrical generating capacity expanded rapidly. The major company was dominated by a Belgian group, Mexican Light and Power Company, and known as Mexlight.

From the mid-1920s there was considerable concern in governmental circles concerning foreign ownership of electrical power facilities, and so in the late 1930s the Federal Electricity Commission (CFE) went into operation. Foreign companies became alarmed and investments and generating capacity in Mexico increased very little between 1937 and 1945. Increase in generating capacity grew markedly from that latter date, and the pattern of use of electrical power by industry gradually shifted from use principally for consumer-oriented manu-

[20] Díaz Ordaz, Sixth State of the Union Address, *Hispano Americano* (Sept. 7, 1970), pp. 32–34. Mexico exported only one petrochemical product in 1964, but six by 1973. Over 50 percent of investment in petrochemicals was held by Pemex, and another 10 percent by *Guanos y Fertilizantes*. In all, it appeared that between 60 and 70 percent of the petrochemical industry was controlled by the public sector. Echeverría, Third State of the Union Address, p. 6.

facturers to capital goods manufacturing by 1960. From 1952 onward, it was clear that the Revolutionary coalition had decided to force out foreign capital in nationally important industries. By 1961 the government had bought out all such major foreign holdings, thus 98 percent of all Mexican public electricity service was being handled through the CFE.[21]

Mexico's determination to advance electrical generating capacity through public enterprise was evident in the fact that under Ruiz Cortines, production of electrical energy had reached 2.5 million kilowatts, with 1.1 million of these being produced under direct management of the CFE.[22] López Mateos claimed 5,286,000 kilowatts with 2,309,928 coming from plants managed by the CFE. He also spoke of the importance of "rural electrification" for "integral agrarian reform." [23] By 1970, while production capacity had risen 42 percent to 7,494,738 kilowatt hours annually, the demand had risen 80 percent since 1964.[24] In 1973, two million more people were using electricity than in 1970, with a total existing capacity of 7,532,518 kilowatts, and an additional 5 million kilowatt capacity under construction. A nuclear electrical plant at Laguna Verde would be producing 1.3 million kilowatts annually in 1976.[25]

Growth of the electrical power industry was impressive. However, by the mid-1960s it was already clear that industrialization was making great demands in terms of ever-higher investments for installations, and that Mexico would have to obtain loans from the World Bank, the Export-Import Bank, and other multinational lending agencies to expand production to keep up with growing demand. Extension of electricity to the impoverished and more remote regions became a persistent politico-economic problem. Indicative of the concentration is the fact that 50 percent of Mexico's electric consumption as of 1964 was located in five federal entities: the Federal District, and the states of Puebla, Veracruz, Michoacán and México.[26]

---

[21] For a thorough discussion of the Mexicanization of electric power see Miguel S. Wionczek, "Electric Power," in Raymond Vernon, ed. *Public Policy and Private Enterprise in Mexico* (Cambridge, Mass., 1964), pp. 91–106.

[22] Ruiz Cortines, p. 17.

[23] López Mateos, p. 12.

[24] Díaz Ordaz, pp. 32–34.

[25] Luis Echeverría, p. 6.

[26] Obstacles in this connection were illustrated by the effort to expand electrical facilities in the sparsely populated territory of Baja California del Sur where the government planned to spend over 39,000,000 pesos to bring electricity to over 85 percent of the widely scattered population by the end of the 1960s. *Excelsior* (January 31, 1965).

As of 1974 the total installed capacity reached 9.9 million kilowatts of which 8.3 million were in the governmental sector. Work was also underway on other facilities. The *La Angostura* plant was scheduled for operation in 1975, and it will generate .9 million kilowatts, and work has begun on the *Chicoasén* hydroelectric plant. When completed it will be one of the twenty largest in the world, and its output will equal 25 percent of Mexico's current capacity. Its estimated cost is eight billion pesos.[27]

Expansion of electric power has clearly been a major emphasis, both in production and distribution. As of 1974 electricity was available in approximately 15,000 cities and towns, with a total population of 37 million. In line with the government's policy of attempting to mitigate the costs of development to the country's poor, electric rates remained the same from 1962 to 1974 despite cost increases. But in order to balance the costs and the need to expand the nation's continuing electrification, a rate increase was initiated in 1974. The new rates were to be "progressive." Echeverría announced, "This new system has done away with this [the previously existing] unjust state of affairs and requires each one to pay according to his financial means." [28]

## Transportation

The importance of steel, petroleum, petrochemicals, and electricity in Mexican politics is their essential contribution to the building of a national industrial establishment. To build such an establishment it was necessary for Mexican policy-makers to combine their concern for expanding production with programs to integrate physically diverse regions into a national economy. Rail networks, roads, telephone and telegraph lines, and a system of airlines have helped the Revolutionary regime overcome much of the traditional regional and local barriers to the integration of a national political system. Thus the effort to develop these elements of the infrastructure has been a continuing objective of Mexican policy from the time of the early Revolutionary leaders until the present.

In 1910 some of the existing Mexican rail system had been built with European capital, and thus was narrow-gauge line, but there were also many miles of broad-gauge track which was a consequence of United States investment. The problem of developing a uniform rail system plagued governments of the Revolutionary regime for almost three decades after the Revolution, and much of the early post-Revolution expenditure on rails went to develop a uniform broad-

[27] Luis Echeverría, Fourth State of the Union Address, p. 18.
[28] Luis Echeverría, Fourth State of the Union Address, pp. 17–18.

gauge network. Although there has been only a slight increase in kilometers of track line — from 23,000 kilometers to 25,000 in the post-Revolutionary era — all presidents have included the rail system in their State of the Union Addresses, emphasizing the conversion to broad-gauge track.[29] Alemán, for example, spent over a billion pesos on the railroad system. Since that time, changes from steam to diesel have been made, passenger service has improved, and there have been extensive improvements of the terminals going north from Mexico City to the United States and south from Mexico City to Yucatán. Gradually the main use of the railroad system has shifted from passenger to cargo transportation.[30] Rails, however, were steadily pushed into a secondary role by transportation devices using the internal combustion engine. In 1940 Mexico had about 93,000 automobiles, but by 1950 there were almost double that number in addition to buses, cargo trucks, and the like.[31] The growth of automotive transportation meant more expenditures for paved major arteries and feeder roads. Alemán added roughly 11,000 kilometers to the system. By 1958 usable road (*caminos federales y caminos vecinales*) had increased from 23,000 kilometers to 43,500 kilometers,[32] and by 1970 there were 70,244 kilometers of federal and neighborhood roads, making all regions of the Republic accessible by hard-surface road.[33] Echeverría was then free to allocate more resources to the construction of badly needed feeder roads in the less-accessible rural areas. By 1973 30,000 kilometers of such road had been added.[34]

The Mexican government has developed its own national airline, Aeroméxico (earlier known as Aeronaves de México), in addition to other privately owned airlines. There are over 44,670 kilometers of national air routes covered by the flights of Aeroméxico. Díaz Ordaz reported a continued investment in airport facilities, as did Echeverría. The vital political and economic role of the airlines in promoting communication between Mexico City and the outlying regions has been well emphasized.

Mexico had an operating telegraph service in 1910, but much of the line was destroyed during the Revolution. A major concern of the Revolutionary government was to repair and extend the network.

[29] Jorge L. Tamayo, *Geografía moderna de México* (México, D.F., 1963), p. 355.

[30] In the time of López Mateos alone, cargo transport increased 159 percent. Passenger service increased 45 percent in comparison.

[31] Tamayo, pp. 360–363.

[32] Ruiz Cortines, p. 19.

[33] Díaz Ordaz, p. 36.

[34] Luis Echeverría, pp. 1–6.

By the mid-1960s much of the basic work had been done. There were also over 138,000 kilometers of telegraph line and 1,050,000 kilometers of telephone circuitry. Both systems were wholly owned and controlled within the public sector. In addition to these newer systems, post-Revolutionary governments have expressed continued concern for the expansion of postal routes throughout the Republic. Postal service was increased to cover more than 241,000 kilometers of routes, and air-mail service covered 69,000 kilometers.[35] Radio had also become a fact of life for nearly all Mexicans, and television was rapidly becoming as much of an institution as in the United States. By the mid-1960s it was not uncommon to find television in the homes of rather low-salary workers; among the professional classes, it was nearly universal.

## Education

Fundamental to the welfare goals of Revolutionary leaders from the earliest days has been universal literacy. Meeting the developmental needs of the nation in the latter half of the twentieth century involves a great deal more than achieving universal literacy. All the technical skills for a place in the modern economy must be taught, and at the same time there must be an ever-wider sharing of values in order to permit the degree of cooperation necessary for a complex interdependent society. Clearly, literacy by itself neither guarantees wider participation and greater psychic satisfaction nor does it ensure cooperation for balanced economic growth. On the other hand, social welfare orientations as well as economic considerations have played a part in the announced goals of nearly all twentieth-century revolutions. In Mexico these aspirations were reflected in such slogans of the Revolution as "land and books" or "to educate is to redeem," and the third article of the Constitution of 1917 was concerned with education.

No one knows the extent of illiteracy in Mexico prior to the Revolution of 1910, but it seems fair to estimate that the average for the country was about 80 percent with the rate in some areas running several points higher.[36] Despite some progress through the emphasis assigned to education in the Constitution, in subsequent laws, and in the budgets of many administrations since 1917, progress has not been sufficient to meet Mexico's needs. The obstacles to educational goals have been great. First of all, Mexico has one of the highest birth rates

---

[35] López Mateos, pp. 17–18.
[36] Eighty percent is the minimum figure. Some writers estimate ninety percent or over.

in the world.[37] There has also been a vast amount of indifference in rural areas, especially where there have been complicating linguistic and cultural patterns. There are many communities which still have no schools, and many others where schools offer no more than one or two grades.

As in the usual Latin American pattern, Mexicans who can afford to do so send their children to private schools, but there are few such schools, so the main burden of educating the nation falls to government.[38] While some of the existing private schools are overtly Catholic and demand the learning of catechism and attendance at mass, many private schools overlook these matters. Generally, the Roman Church has lacked the financial and personnel resources necessary to make it an effective educational force on a national scale. Moreover, constitutional provisions and the general trend of government policy have obstructed clerical efforts in the educational field. One of the most notable exceptions is the Jesuit Universidad Ibero-Americana in Mexico City.

Mexican education is composed of different systems of schools. These are the federal schools, the state schools, the "joint" public and private schools, and the purely private schools. Many of the latter category are Church-operated. Each system ranges in grade from pre-primary up to university. The diffusion of support makes it difficult to see the complete picture. Consequently the federal expenditure is the only consistently available indicator of the expansion of education. In addition, the federal expenditures constitute the single greatest facet of the educational budget.

Educational efforts have hardly been an unqualified success, but neither have they failed. With scarce material resources the Mexicans set out to innovate to meet the challenges of their environment. They learned how to establish schools in rural areas, trained personnel to teach in Indian schools, and developed devices known as the "cultural mission" and the "rural normal school." Anti-illiteracy campaigns were inaugurated in the 1920s and 1930s, and in the 1940s a sweeping effort to have "each one teach one" produced observable results.

In general, the percentage of government budgets devoted to education rose during the 1930s and 1940s. In the latter 1940s emphasis on other developmental programs began to cut down the relative expenditures on education. This did not mean, however, that expenditures on education in absolute terms were reduced. There were ex-

---

[37] Gilberto Loyo, *Población y desarrollo económico* (México, D.F., 1963), p. 46.
[38] Pablo González Casanova, *Democracy in Mexico* (New York, 1970), chapter 5 for discussion of illiteracy.

tensive additions to the system of federally supported schools both at primary and higher levels. Over the period 1946–1952, 5,069 new primary schools were added to the 12,000 already in existence; and there were 2,606 more added from 1952–1958.

From the 1940s on programs tended to proliferate without achieving substantial reductions in the proportionate level of illiteracy. The literacy campaign of *alfabetización,* a form of adult education begun in 1944 by Ávila Camacho, was continued by his successor as well as expanding post-primary studies.[39] There were 208 secondary and nine "preparatory" schools supported by the federal government in 1946. Ruiz Cortines continued development of a variety of programs: adult education, anti-illiteracy, mobile cultural missions, and so on. All of these programs, however, could not obscure the fact that there were three million children without an opportunity to go to school after the 38 years of the Revolutionary regime. This fact could not be erased by allusions to radio, television, and other cultural activities and their contributions to an overall improvement in the level of *cultura general.*[40]

The constant struggle of the Mexican government to cope with one of the highest birth rates in the world is nowhere better illustrated than in the field of education. In the latter 1950s and early 1960s the cost to education of the high rate of population growth (by then 3.5 percent) was clearly reflected in presidential reports to the nation. Between 1958 and 1964 in the federal school system the primary and pre-school levels alone doubled their teaching staff with the addition of 29,360 new "credential" teachers and 17,000 more from a shorter emergency program. The government issued 114 million texts in the Free Textbook Program. Enrollment climbed from 2,900,000 to 4,015,000.[41] Moreover, the growth in post-primary education was also striking. Between 1958 and 1964 post-primary enrollment went from 154,000 to 261,000. New programs for training industrial and rural workers were added, and federal budgetary support for universities was expanded 400 percent.[42]

This expansion continued after 1964. Total governmental expenditures on education during the year 1969–1970 alone amounted to 11.98 billion pesos; the government's portion was 8,218,000,000 pesos.

[39] Miguel Alemán, p. 5.
[40] Ruiz Cortines, p. 14.
[41] López Mateos, p. 20. López Mateos claimed he had invested enough to handle the population increase without a corresponding jump in illiteracy, and that this was the first time since 1950 that a president could say this. (See chapter 1.)
[42] López Mateos, pp. 20–21. He noted the increase in post-primary was unprecedented in Mexican history.

In 1970 the student population for pre-primary through university, whether or not in school, was estimated at over 11.5 million, an increase of 44 percent over the total six years earlier. The various cultural programs were expanded, and up to 50,000 students were receiving instruction through closed-circuit television programs.[43] The continuing pressure of population upon education and the budget was reflected in Echeverría's statement that his government had spent 23 percent more on education in 1972 than in 1971, and that in primary schools alone, there were 500,000 more students. The variety of training programs at various levels continued to increase. The number of students enrolled in education by 1974 had risen to 11.4 million elementary, 1.7 million secondary, and 400,000 higher education.[44]

The cumulative effect of the high birth rate, the decreasing infant mortality rate, and increasing emphasis on education was dramatically reflected by the end of the 1960s in a rapidly mounting number of students desiring enrollment in institutions of higher education throughout the country. In 1972 there were 286,000 students enrolled in federal and state universities. The National Polytechnic Institute reported nearly 100,000 students in contrast to 45,000 in 1964. The cost of the mushrooming student population of UNAM was indicated by the fact that it received more than double the expenditures allocated to all other institutions of higher learning with the exception of the Polytechnic Institute. The frustration of this continuing and expanding burden for policy makers was finally articulated explicitly by Echeverría in 1973:

> The federal government invested during the present cycle 3.75 billion pesos in higher education alone. This tripled the figure for 1970 . . . . The excessive enrollment in institutions of higher education and the high dropout rate which affects them is due in great part to the unjustified neglect of intermediate technical preparation. Our youth need to take note of new possibilities for professional training that are more adequate for their calling and with broader opportunities for employment. The disjunction between advanced education and employment opportunities is continuously greater. Many professionals upon leaving the campuses confront the grave problem of unemployment. To cope with this they take jobs that would have required less education, or they work at jobs for which they have no training. We ought to recognize that many educational insti-

[43] Díaz Ordaz, p. 38.
[44] Luis Echeverría, Fourth State of the Union Address, *Mexican Newsletter, Separata* (Sept. 1, 1974), pp. 8–9.

tutions resort too easily to the expedient of accrediting a little knowledge rather than undertaking the difficult commitment to teach in order to serve.

This distortion in values which is true for the entire society is traceable in large part to the fact that our youth attend classes not to learn, but to obtain a diploma. *The Constitution did not eliminate from our country titles of nobility, just to substitute them for titles in the professions* . . . . When the graduates do not obtain together with their university degree the advantages which the collective make-believe has promised them, nor succeed in being useful to the community in the degree to which they had hoped, there is provoked in our students a profound sense of frustration. In this disenchantment, among others, is one of the basic causes of the problems that plague our principal institutions of higher education.[45]

Echeverría went on to report that in the three years of his term 80 million textbooks had been distributed under the Free Textbook Program. Other programs related to primary and secondary education, particularly technical, agricultural, and teacher bilingual training, were being supported at a higher level than ever before. The students enrolled in the federal schools now involved a cost of 3.255 billion pesos for 1973, a 300 percent increase over 1970. There were 262,000 primary teachers being trained, 14,500 new teachers had been hired for 1974, more than the entire amount for the six-year term of Ruiz Cortines that ended in 1958. The costs were mounting as the population continued its rapid increase. Whether Mexico could educate all its people with other mounting needs was a real problem. (See Figure 9.)

## Essential Foodstuffs

Although education stands in a crucial position in relation to the transfer of information and mobilization of society for the purposes of industrialization and building a national identity, it is also critical that while rapid change is occurring some measures be taken to reduce the hardships that so often afflict the lower classes. One of Mexico's problems in this regard has been the efficient distribution of basic consumer products, especially foodstuffs. The supermarket techniques in merchandising that have developed over the last two decades have been of little benefit, generally speaking, to the poorer classes of the cities, nor have they benefited the *ejidatarios* and other

---

[45] Luis Echeverría, Third State of the Union Address, pp. 7–8. Author's italics added.

small-scale agriculturalists of the countryside. A well known figure historically on the Mexican scene has been the *acaparador,* the speculator who takes advantage of poor distributive facilities to buy cheaply in the countryside and sell for the highest possible price in the city. To deal with this situation, the Mexican government began to involve itself increasingly in the late 1940s in the field of merchandising and commerce through purchasing basic food commodities and selling them at lower-than-ordinary prices in the cities. This activity, which began primarily for reasons of welfare goals, has grown into an extensive set of operations which involve not only every segment of the food chain, but also other agencies for different reasons. Thus the government has developed modern plants for food processing and canning, its own trucking fleet, and even mobile grocery stores to bring low-cost products into low-income areas. It also has permanent retail outlets in all the larger cities. This is indeed business on an extensive scale. In its earlier days, it was criticized bitterly when the operation was known as *Compañía Exportadora y Importadora Mexicana, Sociedad Anónima (CEIMSA).* In more recent years the organization has been *Compañía Nacional de Subsistencias Populares* (CONASUPO).[46]

[46] See Kenneth F. Johnson, *Mexican Democracy: A Critical View* (Boston, 1972), pp. 100–107. Just about everything that can be said negatively about CONASUPO has been said by Johnson and others such as Manuel de la Isla, whose article in *Por Que,* April 10, 1968 Johnson quotes extensively. According to these views, CONASUPO wastes on a vast scale; it is a proliferation of bureaucracy that serves little purpose; food shortages occur where there should be none; and food prices often remain a good deal higher than they need be. Quoting de la Isla, Johnson's principal cause for all the evils he attributes is "... the fact that the true motive is political, not economic. CONASUPO is not producing wealth but suppressing it; and at the same time it acquires political power as a state-run monopoly." For a contrasting view, however, from an American scholar, see Marvin Alisky, "CONASUPO: A Mexican Agency Which Makes Low-Income Workers Feel Their Government Cares," *Inter-American Economic Affairs* (Winter 1973) pp. 45–79. Professor Alisky, who has been reporting on various aspects of Mexican government for the past two decades, views CONASUPO as an instrument subject to human error, but basically successful in easing the pressures of inflation and providing a better and fairer market for the small producer. For the official view, see Professor Carlos Hank González, editor, *Antecedentes de la Compañía Nacional de Subsistencias Populares* (México, D.F., 1969), pp. 3–4. However, a complex computer model reports that, "It should be noted that subsidies to agriculture, effected primarily through the national agency for price supports (CONASUPO), have not been extensive enough to alter basic trends." Louis M. Goreaux and Alan S. Manne, *Multi-level Planning: Case Studies in Mexico* (Amsterdam, 1973), p. 389. An unpublished paper "CONASUPO" by E. Ramírez, 1975, is very informative.

## Figure 9

### Population Pyramids (1950 and 1970)

(Population classified by age and sex)

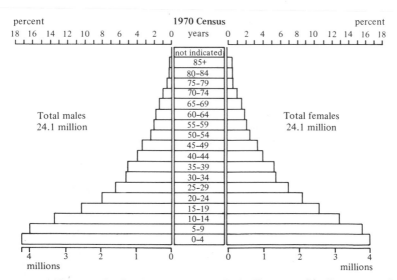

SOURCE: Thomas G. Sanders, "Mexico 1974: Demographic Patterns and Population Policy," *Fieldstaff Reports,* North America, Series Volume II, No. 1 [TGS–1–74], (July 1974), p. 19. © American Universities Field Staff, Inc.

The extent of the CEIMSA operations grew, and it reached the point where Ruiz Cortines reported in 1958 holdings of corn, wheat, rice, and beans to be worth approximately one billion pesos.[47] Under López Mateos, the CEIMSA operation was absorbed into a more extensive framework, CONASUPO. The government's avowed purpose continued to be that of purchase from the producer and sale to the consumer to maintain minimum guaranteed prices and cover internal needs. The growth of this operation and of the public sector in this field can be partially understood if one contrasts the report of López Mateos to the nation in 1964 with Ruiz Cortines' statement in 1958. In the term of López Mateos, CONASUPO bought and sold 19.6 million tons of assorted grains. The government subsidized these transactions in the amount of 3.4 billion pesos. CONASUPO storage facilities expanded by 1964 to accommodate 1.2 million tons of corn, 1 million tons of wheat, 170,000 tons of beans, and 11,000 tons of rice, amounts deemed "sufficient to regulate prices through the coming harvest."[48] In a single year, 1963–1964, Mexico exported 1.3 million tons of wheat, corn, and beans at a total value of one billion pesos. The extent of capital investment in storage facilities for *Almacenes Nacionales de Depósito, S.A.*, a subsidiary of CONASUPO, was to some degree indicated by its storage capacity, which had risen 100 percent since 1959 to 2,125,532 tons in 1964. In addition, the social capital of CONASUPO's subsidiary had grown from 85 million pesos in 1958 to 300 million in 1964. López Mateos emphasized welfare in addition to developmental aspects of CONASUPO's goals by connecting his report on CONASUPO with that on the *reforma agraria integral.*[49]

During the 1964–1970 period CONASUPO maintained its basic purpose and continued to grow in new directions. It acquired 2,364,-697 tons of basic commodities such as wheat, corn, beans, and rice, as well as other commodities of lesser importance. The combined value of these products was officially placed at 2.021 billion pesos. It expanded into processing, storing, and selling such items as dehydrated milk and hydrogenated oils. Transactions in wheat alone had accounted for 1.1 million tons with a total worth of 885 million pesos. Transactions in corn were a close second with 830 million pesos. *Almacenes Nacionales* had invested in storage facilities, port facilities, and equipment. In 1969 its budget was 5.9 million pesos with a 400 percent increase authorized for 1970, to 20.7 million pesos.[50] A new storage organization within CONASUPO had also been

[47] Ruiz Cortines, p. 17.
[48] López Mateos, p. 14.
[49] López Mateos, p. 14.
[50] Díaz Ordaz, p. 29.

created. This was the *Comisión Operadora CONASUPO de Graneros del Pueblo* ("the people's storage"), with, as its stated purpose, "to provide flexibility and autonomy for the activities of rural storage facilities." [51] The new program already in 1970 had facilities in 1,108 localities throughout 20 entities of the Republic serving over 432,000 *ejidatarios*. However, despite the emphasis on these (and other) programs, the president had to report in 1970 that it was necessary for Mexico to *import* 1.06 million pesos worth of agricultural products to permit supply of basic commodities "for the nourishment of our people, principally of the weakest economic classes, and to combat speculation and the rise in prices." [52]

The ramifications of CONASUPO operations now far exceeded the humble beginnings of the institution. CONASUPO, by the time of Díaz Ordaz, had 1,392 permanent stores throughout the country, and 32 regional warehouses. It served at least 20 million consumers, and the total value of the transactions had climbed over 700 million pesos. The various subsidiaries in milk, corn, vegetable oil, and other processing activities, and new facilities in the Federal District could turn out one billion bakery products per day. Expansion occurred into the merchandising of basic items such as clothing. The resources of CONASUPO had reached a level which made it possible to utilize this agency in relief of natural disasters, such as tornados, hurricanes, earthquakes, and the like.

In 1973 the government claimed that the value of CONASUPO operations reached 16 billion pesos, triple the amount for 1970 and almost equivalent to the six-year total announced by López Mateos for the period 1958–1964. One of CONASUPO's affiliated companies, *Bodegas Rurales CONASUPO,* managed 1240 grain and seed receiving centers in 28 states and had diversified the commodities operations to include wheat, sorghum, safflower, and aduki beans. By 1973, CONASUPO operated 2,515 retail outlets throughout the Republic. [53]

Education and governmental distribution of basic food commodities and clothing have always been visualized by policy-makers as serving a dual purpose, social welfare and economic development. Moreover, leaders of the Revolutionary coalition have never since the early 1930s expressed publicly any doubts concerning the compatibility of these goals. The official doctrine has been that an expanding range of public social services and a high rate of economic growth will work interdependently and harmoniously to facilitate overall social and economic change toward a more prosperous, hap-

[51] Díaz Ordaz, p. 31.
[52] Díaz Ordaz, p. 31.
[53] Luis Echeverría, Third State of the Union Address, pp. 7–8.

pier, and stronger Mexico. The satisfaction of welfare demands, as well as investment on infrastructure, basic industry, and all aspects of a modern industrial system were definite, Revolutionary pledges. The success of growth in all these spheres was sufficient to make Mexico a leader in Latin America and in the Third World, and a growing nation of global importance. Hopes for the future of the nation have been raised, and so the middle classes and workers, while frequently expressing cynicism, have also increasingly cherished expectations of more comfort and satisfactions. Governmental commitments have expanded to meet the growing new demands. The cost of meeting these has risen at an accelerating rate because of the corresponding increases in population and popular expectations.

## Social Services

In their welfare orientation the Mexican Revolutionary governments have experimented in ever-wider areas of concern. The complexity of the social services has been increased by corporativist demands by critical hierarchies such as the FSTSE, the armed forces, and select labor unions. The number of institutes and funds created by this has produced a confusing plethora of activities and programs. Despite this, the government has attempted to maintain a balanced view towards economic growth and social commitments, particularly since the 1940s. At times these welfare efforts have complemented policies directed toward growth of the economy. The Mexican Social Security Institute (IMSS), while still performing its primary purpose, eventually became a source of capital for investment in other public-sector segments, especially in infrastructure expansion and low-cost housing construction programs. Similarly, *Nacional Financiera,* at first the public-sector industrial development bank, later became involved with negotiation with multinational lending agencies for credits that clearly serve both welfare and development purposes. In both these areas, however, there has been a great proliferation of specialized government and quasi-public institutions in recent years.

A major impetus to both the IMSS and *Nacional Financiera* came from the policies of Miguel Alemán. During his presidency the IMSS expanded from serving 246,000 to over a million people. Not only did the population receiving benefits become more extensive, but the number of benefits available proliferated. Hospitalization, maternity care, and outpatient clinics of various kinds were incorporated into the basic concepts of Mexican social security.[54] Continuing the trend,

[54] *Tiempo* (September 5, 1952), pp. 5–7.

the IMSS increased its coverage by more than 100 percent from 1952 to 1958. The number of persons receiving benefits throughout all of the federal entities rose to 2,569,000. The coverage was mainly available to those in urban areas. Ruiz Cortines, for example, made a special point of the fact that 219,000 of the total in 1958 were peasants (*campesinos*), and represented less than 10 percent of the total. During this period resources at the disposal of the IMSS grew approximately 500 percent. Total value was placed at 290 million pesos in 1952 and 1.039 billion in 1958. The IMSS also became involved in low-cost housing while providing pensions, maternity care, hospitalization, and outpatient clinics. Along with the 161 million pesos invested by the IMSS in housing, the older National Mortgage Bank had expanded the value of its mortgages to 315 million pesos.[55]

In 1958 the IMSS was serving about 2.5 million persons. This coverage was increased about 600,000 per year during the following presidential term. The number of *municipios* with some IMSS services rose from 200 in 1958 to 510 in 1964. Of the 90 new medical units added to the IMSS, 84 were designed to serve the rural areas. Among the installations constructed by the IMSS were meeting halls, clubhouses for youth, classrooms, and shops for artisans. There were complementary programs of infant care, both medical and nutritional, and the construction of low-cost housing developments. At the same time, longstanding credit facilities such as the National Mortgage Bank were maintained.[56]

In recognition of their special status, bureaucrats were given their own institute, the ISSSTE. All members of this institute, furthermore, were to receive life insurance by a grant of the federal government in the amount of 40,000 pesos with "extremely low premiums." [57] Sometimes overlooked by outside observers was the fact that López Mateos placed in effect at the same time a social security law for the armed forces which would enable them, like the bureaucrats, to have their own social security institute. Some 6.27 million persons were covered by the IMSS by 1964, including the entire rural work force in the sugar industry.[58] During the Díaz Ordaz presidency, another million workers were added, and public policy seemed to be moving

[55] Ruiz Cortines, pp. 12–14.

[56] The *Banco Nacional Hipotecario* had become the *Banco Nacional Hipotecario, Urbano, y de Obras Públicas* (National Mortgage, Urban, and Public Works Bank). In 1973 it was called the National Bank of Public Works and Services.

[57] López Mateos, p. 19.

[58] Lopez Mateos, p. 19.

toward an "integrated" coverage to cover prenatal care, maternity benefits, outpatient clinics, hospitalization, special diseases, rehabilitation, workman's compensation and pensions, and unemployment insurance.[59]

By 1958, both the number and size of social service programs were growing. The new low-cost housing agency, National Housing Institute, had completed 4,000 dwellings at a cost of 24 million pesos. An agency often overlooked in discussions of the Mexican public sector, the Armed Forces Bank, made loans of 6 million pesos for housing, and also held 23 million pesos in mortgage loans. Other functions clearly were being shared by the military. Pensions amounted to 178 million for the period 1952–1958. The value of life insurance for military personnel increased from 2 million to 9 million pesos. For the armed forces, there were other services: maternity and child care and adult education. In fact, Ruiz Cortines spent a considerable amount of time in his last message to the nation discussing these benefits.[60]

By 1970 welfare services, and welfare institute lending and investment had far surpassed the administrative framework of the original IMSS. The number of federal government employees covered under the ISSSTE numbered over 1.4 million. A whole series of new agencies and institutes to cope with rising pressures of social change had been created. Continued political violence underlined the political necessity of closing the gap between Mexican reality and the welfare goals which had always been a part of the legitimizing mystique of the Revolutionary coalition. The Ministry of Health treated annually almost 8 million persons at the level of hospitalization or outpatient clinics. In addition, specialized institutes for treatment of particular diseases had been created with their own clinics, hospitals, and surgical facilities. Programs also existed to feed as many as 2 million persons in the most deprived rural areas, to provide housing for the elderly, and to shoulder many more of the whole range of welfare-state burdens.[61] (See Table 9 for the effect of these welfare goals on life expectancy.) There was evidence that the government intended to expand social welfare in line with Revolutionary goals when Echeverría announced in September 1973 that formerly unprotected rural workers in henequén, tobacco, as well as mining, along with many new urban groups living at subsistence had been brought under the protection of the IMSS. Some 1.5 million persons had been added to the rolls; the ISSSTE had reached an enrollment of 2 million and

[59] López Mateos, p. 37.
[60] Ruiz Cortines, pp. 12–14.
[61] Luis Echeverría, Third State of the Union Address, pp. 10–11.

bureaucrats with state and municipal governments were in the process of gaining coverage through agreements between the ISSSTE and their own local unions.[62]

Accelerated spending for low-cost housing was reflected in the activity of agencies such as FOVI, the Banking and Discount Housing Fund. FOVI underwrites credits to approved members of organizations such as the CTM, and private banks then do the actual lending. This accounts for part of the difficulty that will plague any analyst who attempts to survey accurately the extent of public and private lending. From 1965 to 1970 FOVI underwrote 53 housing projects in 26 different urban areas. But in addition to FOVI and the housing efforts of IMSS, another organization which underwrites or partially shares cost in low-cost housing is the Fund for Guaranteed Support of Housing Credit which underwrote 488 million pesos in private bank credits for the year 1969–1970 alone. The continuation and expansion of this kind of activity was reflected in the formation under Echeverría of still another housing fund representing inputs by employers and employees, the latter usually affiliated with CTM or another major industrial union. This organization, the National Workers' Housing Fund Institute, INFONAVIT, began with a 2 million-peso support fund from the government and was supposed to bring in about 3.54 billion pesos for the construction of 100,000 homes per year. During the first year, 1972–1973, over 3 billion pesos in construction projects and over 2 billion pesos were committed in housing credits to individuals, as distinct from projects. Once again, the governmental

*Table 9*

Changing Life Expectancy

| Year | Male | Female |
|------|------|--------|
| 1930 | 36.1 | 37.5 |
| 1940 | 40.4 | 42.5 |
| 1950 | 48.1 | 51.0 |
| 1960 | 57.6 | 60.3 |
| 1965 | 60.3 | 63.6 |

SOURCE: Thomas G. Sanders, "Mexico 1974: Demographic Patterns and Population Policy," *Fieldstaff Reports,* North America, Series Volume II, No. 1 [TGS–1–74], (July 1974), p. 16. © American Universities Field Staff, Inc.

[62] Luis Echeverría, Third State of the Union Address, pp. 10–11.

bureaucrats had their own housing fund, the Housing Fund of the Institute of Social Security and Services for Public Employees (FO-VISSSTE). In 1974 1.115 billion pesos were invested in housing by this agency.[63] The military forces also have their own housing fund. Greater emphasis is also given to the rural areas, through the National Institute for Development of Rural Communities and Popular Housing (INDECO). However, the efforts are comparatively small, and more emphasis has been given to railroad workers than other groups thus far. One further fund is the Fund for the Guarantee and Support of Housing Credits (FOGA). And in addition, the National Bank of Public Works and Service also possesses a low-cost housing fund.

These many funds and programs benefit selected groups as well as individuals. Another aspect of the housing situation, however, includes housing developments. INDECO and INFONAVIT together have extensive urban landholdings in the 50 largest cities which eventually will become housing developments. Developments are a vital part of the housing program, and are used to satisfy a sector's needs as well as the pressures on a specific locale. For example, the Federal District has been the recipient of many housing developments. But the very extensiveness of these programs has increased the burden on the budget and driven up the cost of construction because the demand for materials has increased faster than the supplies.[64]

## Development Financing

The expansion of these programs in the welfare field was exceeded by public sector expansion in the area of national economic development. In the late 1940s *Nacional Financiera* became a development bank for nationally owned industrial and commercial institutions as, well as some enterprises of the private sector. And although the entire Alemán administration invested more than 5 billion pesos in all types of business enterprises, the greater portion, some 3.5 billion pesos, was handled by *Nacional Financiera. Nacional Financiera* also became involved in international loans and the floating of international bond issues. Mexican industrial production rose by approximately 42 percent between 1946 and 1952, and *Nacional Financiera* provided the financial backing for the development of *Altos Hornos,* the beginning of a huge steel complex within the public sector.[65]

[63] Luis Echeverría, Fourth State of the Union Address, p. 23.
[64] Luis Echeverría, Third State of the Union Address, p. 11.
[65] Miguel Alemán, pp. 5–7.

Under Ruiz Cortines, lending through *Nacional Financiera* continued. Industrial production went up on the average of eight percent a year, and the national government invested 15 billion pesos in the year 1957 alone; the private sector in that year invested 10 billion. Altogether, public investment occurred without having the Ministry of the Treasury and *Banco de México* increase money in circulation. Foreign currency reserves, though smaller than desirable, constituted a positive balance of 28 million United States dollars. The total public debt was approximately 10 billion pesos divided into 4 billion for internal debt, 3.5 billion for credits charged to *Nacional Financiera,* and 2.5 billion for direct external debt, that is, credits from private foreign lenders and multinational agencies. In all, the total federal public debt amounted to ten percent of the gross national product.[66]

Success in achieving a high rate of growth — in part through use of *Nacional Financiera* and other agencies employing similar strategies on a lesser scale — led López Mateos to state that development could take place rapidly without penalizing lower income groups. Moreover, he claimed that though prices had gone up 14.1 percent, salaries and wages had gone up 97.7 percent.[67] He based his interpretation upon increases in the annual growth rate. López Mateos emphasized that planners had hoped for 5.4 percent, but a rate of seven percent was actually achieved. This growth was linked, according to the President, with public-sector lending and investment: 31.2 billion pesos by *Nacional Financiera,* 25 billion pesos through direct dependencies of the government (primarily the Ministry of the Treasury), and 8.1 billion pesos through enterprises lying mainly within the public sector.[68]

Such a high value of transactions attributed to *Nacional Financiera* only partially reflected its expansion as the principal public-sector development bank. Whereas in 1958 the total capital of *Nacional Financiera* stood at about 300 million pesos, in 1964 capital was 1.3 billion pesos "totally paid," and its total resources were placed at 13.59 billion pesos.[69] Although other lending and investment institu-

---

[66] Ruiz Cortines, pp. 8–10. Also, for the first time, one notes in Ruiz Cortines the feeling of "being burdened" that top policy-makers were beginning to feel from the annual population increase. Although the President made it clear that he regarded it as a challenge, more positive than negative, his preoccupation with the need for still further development in light of this increase was reflected in his discussion of the *bracero* program as indicative of the shortcomings of the Mexican economy.

[67] López Mateos, p. 19.

[68] López Mateos, p. 11.

[69] López Mateos, p. 12.

tions of the public sector showed striking increases in activity during this period, they were overshadowed by *Nacional Financiera*. Transactions of the National Bank of Public Works and Service (*Banco Nacional de Obras y Servicios Publicos*) increased over 200 percent from 1958 to 1964, as did that of agrarian-sector lending banks. The National Bank of Public Works and Service made loans that totaled 12.785 billion pesos while the loans of the *Ejidal* Bank and the government's Agriculture Bank increased from a value of 3 billion pesos in 1958 to 6 billion in 1964. A relative newcomer, the Small Merchants Bank (*Banco de Pequeño Comercio*), had lent 600 million pesos.[70]

By 1964, a basic change had taken place in the function of *Nacional Financiera*. Whereas in the time of Alemán this development bank had been used primarily for the direct promotion of new industries, it increasingly was becoming the primary stimulus in the negotiation of international financing from the International Monetary Fund, the World Bank, and the like. Much of this was done in connection with private capital, but a great deal of it was oriented towards development of publicly owned infrastructure rather than manufacturing enterprises. In earlier years *Nacional Financiera* was a major factor in capital investment such as the steel mill AHMSA, but in the later 1960s and the 1970s has been closely associated on the domestic scene with the National Bank of Public Works and Services.[71] *Nacional Financiera* has been lending to the Federal Electricity Commission for importation of capital equipment. This is the means that has been expanding Mexican infrastructure with increasing expenditures since 1962, and partially explains *Nacional Financiera*'s increase in loans outstanding of 73.8 percent for 1964–1970. *Nacional Financiera*'s credits outstanding reached 43.731 billion pesos and was reported by President Díaz Ordaz to have increased ten percent for the year 1969–1970 alone. He specifically named as beneficiaries of the increase such infrastructure elements as transportation, communications, roads and bridges, electrical energy, irrigation, agricultural investment, frontier development, dwellings, and other public works.[72] The ratio of investment was three to one for infrastructure over industry. (See Table 10 for investment data.)

In addition to *Nacional Financiera* there were a number of other development agencies. In contrast with the time of Miguel Alemán

---

[70] López Mateos, p. 12. These comparative values will give the reader perspective on the priorities of development.
[71] Díaz Ordaz, p. 28. George Blake, pp. 37–39.
[72] Díaz Ordaz, p. 29.

Table 10

Gross National Investment of the Major Sectors over Time

(Values expressed in millions of pesos)

| Year | Total | Government[a] | Public enterprise[b] | Private sector |
|------|-------|------------|------------------|----------------|
| 1940 | 747 | 147 | 143 | 457 |
| 1941 | 945 | 223 | 114 | 608 |
| 1942 | 988 | 319 | 145 | 524 |
| 1943 | 1227 | 384 | 184 | 659 |
| 1944 | 1673 | 408 | 249 | 1016 |
| 1945 | 2196 | 474 | 374 | 1348 |
| 1946 | 3155 | 591 | 408 | 2156 |
| 1947 | 4036 | 680 | 630 | 2726 |
| 1948 | 4456 | 796 | 743 | 2917 |
| 1949 | 5043 | 912 | 1044 | 3087 |
| 1950 | 5966 | 1123 | 1549 | 3294 |
| 1951 | 6691 | 1370 | 1466 | 3855 |
| 1952 | 8012 | 1649 | 1631 | 4732 |
| 1953 | 7676 | 1430 | 1646 | 4600 |
| 1954 | 9583 | 1898 | 2285 | 5400 |
| 1955 | 12,088 | 1917 | 2491 | 7600 |
| 1956 | 13,631 | 2025 | 2546 | 9060 |
| 1957 | 15,752 | 2609 | 3019 | 10,124 |
| 1958 | 16,960 | 2647 | 3543 | 10,770 |
| 1959 | 17,476 | 2866 | 3666 | 10,944 |
| 1960 | 22,834 | 2777 | 5599 | 14,458 |
| 1961 | 23,656 | 3656 | 6716 | 13,284 |
| 1962 | 24,275 | 3711 | 7112 | 13,452 |
| 1963 | 27,478 | 5435 | 8386 | 13,657 |
| 1964 | 36,620 | 6757 | 10,679 | 19,184 |
| 1965 | 39,258 | 5463 | 10,838 | 22,957 |
| 1966 | 44,902 | 6937 | 13,731 | 24,234 |
| 1967 | 52,291 | 8521 | 14,984 | 28,786 |

[a] Federal government and Federal District Department investments. Does not include states and territories.
[b] Includes decentralized organizations and public participation enterprises.

SOURCE: B. Griffiths, *Mexican Monetary Policy and Economic Development* (New York, 1972), table 6. © 1972 by Praeger Publishers, Inc.

(when there were at most seven banking and credit institutions in which the government had majority holdings), there were, by the time of Díaz Ordaz, a whole series of new development agencies generally called funds (*fondos*). These involved eleven new major lending outlets for different types of activity in the economy such as tourism, the fishing industry, the sugar industry, and the like.[73] There was also a host of cooperative lending agencies for specialized groups which were known as *fideicomisos*. There was a *Fideicomiso Pesquero* serving cooperatives of fishermen, which by 1970 had loans outstanding in the amount of 73 million pesos. Similar *fideicomisos* channeling government funds to complement membership dues were supporting cooperatives of small-scale artisans such as silversmiths and many other types of skilled small businessmen. Such *fideicomisos* also served associations of workers, as in the sugar and tobacco industries.[74] The government's cost of aid in such an extensive range of large and small development projects, as well as diverse programs involving frontier improvements, brought the total public debt to 56.439 billion pesos in 1970, in contrast to the 10 billion peso public debt at the end of the Ruiz Cortines administration eight years earlier.[75]

There was increasing evidence by 1970 that Mexico would have to borrow more heavily from external sources. There never had been such an inclusive discussion of borrowing from multinational agencies as was reported in the final address to the nation by Díaz Ordaz. At that time, *Nacional Financiera* had just negotiated a 272.5 million-peso loan with the World Bank. The country by this time already owed the World Bank 12.237 billion pesos. At the same time it was becoming for the first time deeply involved with the IMF. IMF credits together with other agreements made with the United States Treasury Department and Federal Reserve System brought the total amount of indebtedness to $600 million. Further dollar credits had been contracted with the IMF in the amounts of $35 million and $40 million for 1971–1972.[76] The government in the last two years of the Díaz Ordaz presidency contracted loans or credits with other multinational lending sources — the International Bank for Reconstruction and Development, the Inter-American Development Bank, and the Export-Import Bank — in the amount of 3.577 billion pesos.

[73] Miguel Alemán, pp. 4–5. Díaz Ordaz, pp. 29–30. George Blake, p. 40.
[74] Díaz Ordaz, pp. 29–30.
[75] Ruiz Cortines, p. 16. Presidents have avoided quoting the gross national product since López Mateos in 1964. Naturally it is difficult to obtain an adequate understanding of Mexico's economy with insufficient data.
[76] Díaz Ordaz, p. 27.

Credits were also being obtained in Europe. For example, 37.3 million pesos came from Instituto Mobiliare Italiano.[77] The greater amount of foreign borrowing from multinational agencies, according to official Mexican sources, was due to a government income policy that was too weak to support the desired public-sector investment goals.[78] This particular problem clearly emerged during the Díaz Ordaz years, and was accompanied by increasing costs of infrastructure development and the expansion of export industries. Borrowing from multinational agencies increased as inputs of private foreign investment capital dropped. (It must be noted that foreign investment in critical sectors is discouraged.) In 1970 these developments were accompanied by a trade deficit at $1.088 billion. This was the greatest balance-of payments-deficit ever suffered by a government of the Revolutionary regime. It dropped to $934 million in 1971, was up again in 1972 to $1.123 billion and rose again in 1973 to $1.69 billion. By February 1974 it was reported to have reached an all-time high of $2.46 billion despite a 35 percent increase in merchandise export for the year 1972–1973.[79]

The balance-of-payments difficulties were accompanied by a deterioration, at first scarcely noticeable, of the domestic growth rate. By the early 1970s this had dropped to 6 percent overall and only 7 percent for manufacturing industries, whereas the previous decade had experienced rates of 7 percent and 8.8 percent respectively.[80] This was accompanied by inflationary pressures which could no longer be ignored in the way that Díaz Ordaz had dismissed them in his final report to the nation.[81] For example, the National Consumer Price Index and the Mexico City Wholesale Price Index indicated that goods and services were up 21.4 percent and 25.2 percent re-

[77] Díaz Ordaz, p. 28. It could be argued that Díaz Ordaz was intentionally letting the world know that Mexico's credit was "top drawer." But it is also true that in earlier days spokesmen for the Revolutionary coalition had shown great pride in their independence of multinational lending agencies, especially the IMF.

[78] See "The Mexican Economy in 1973," Comercio Exterior (February 1974), p. 3. In 1974 the profits of state-affiliated companies were 3.4 billion pesos, a figure a little over 2 percent of the total amount of public investment. Luis Echeverría, Fourth State of the Union Address, pp. 12, 19.

[79] See "The External Sector of the Economy in 1972; A Preliminary Assessment," Comercio Exterior (April 1973), p. 3. See also International Monetary Fund, "Mexico's Foreign Trade Deficit," IMF Survey (March 22, 1974), p. 87. IMF sources were Secretaría de Industria y Comercio de México and the Wall Street Journal (February 28, 1974).

[80] Comercio Exterior (February 1974), p. 3.

[81] Díaz Ordaz.

spectively from December 1972 to December 1973.[82] More importantly, agriculture was experiencing a downward trend. Mean annual growth in agriculture from 1964–1972 was only 1.5 percent, and the first half of 1973 was termed "unfavorable." [83] (Keep in mind the mean annual population growth of over 3 percent.)

Another major challenge which has to be met is the disjunction between urban and rural enjoyment of the fruits of development. The level of production which had characterized non-subsistence agriculture was due largely to capital-intensive methods of farming. This has left many offspring of those who did benefit from land reform programs without productive employment. (See Tables 11 and 12 for the changing nature of employment.)

Table 11

Change in Economic Activities of Work Force (1960–1970)

(Percentage of total work force engaged in activity by year)

| Activity | 1960 | 1970 | Change 1960–1970 |
|---|---|---|---|
| Agriculture | 54.2 | 39.5 | −14.7 |
| Extractive industries and petroleum | 1.2 | 1.7 | .5 |
| Manufactures | 13.7 | 16.5 | 2.8 |
| Construction and electrical energy | 4.0 | 4.9 | .9 |
| Commerce | 9.6 | 9.3 | −.3 |
| Transportation | 3.1 | 2.8 | −.3 |
| Services (including government) | 13.5 | 19.6 | 6.1 |
| Other | 0.7 | 5.6 | 4.9 |
| (Total) | (100.0) | (100.0) | — |

SOURCE: *La dinámica de los sectores de la economía mexicana durante los decades de los cincuentas y sesentas,* Table 5.

[82] *Comercio Exterior* (February 1974), p. 5.

[83] *Comercio Exterior* (February 1974), p. 5. *Comercio Exterior* went on to say that "certain problems are immediately apparent: (a) agriculture was particularly affected by faltering public-sector investment, which the present Administration has partly, though not radically, remedied; (b) farm-credit behavior was similar to that of public investment; (c) the economy's unwieldy distribution apparatus is especially detrimental to farmers; (d) the *ejido* farm system continues to encounter many difficulties, and (e) price supports have been frozen too long."

Table 12

### Change in Employment by State (1960–1970)

(Percentage of change in work force by categories specified)

| State | Change in total employ-ment | Change in agricultural employ-ment |
|---|---|---|
| (Nation as a whole) | (14.7) | (−16.5) |
| Aguascalientes | 12.8 | −15.5 |
| Baja California | 32.7 | −25.1 |
| Baja California Sur | 34.3 | −15.6 |
| Campeche | 27.8 | 5.9 |
| Coahuila | 0.4 | −34.5 |
| Colima | 37.0 | 11.4 |
| Chiapas | 1.6 | −7.3 |
| Chihuahua | 10.6 | −19.4 |
| Distrito Federal | 27.3 | 5.7 |
| Durango | −4.4 | −25.1 |
| Guanajuato | 7.2 | −18.5 |
| Guerrero | 1.8 | −22.2 |
| Hidalgo | −4.6 | −17.9 |
| Jalisco | 18.7 | −22.1 |
| México | 69.4 | −16.5 |
| Michoacán | −5.3 | −24.9 |
| Morelos | 37.1 | −2.4 |
| Nayarit | 16.1 | −2.6 |
| Nuevo León | 35.3 | −27.3 |
| Oaxaca | −9.6 | −20.9 |
| Puebla | 2.9 | −14.2 |
| Querétaro | 14.4 | −21.3 |
| Quintara Roo | 52.2 | 17.6 |
| San Luis Potosí | 2.0 | −20.9 |
| Sinaloa | 34.5 | 6.8 |
| Sonora | 13.2 | −18.6 |
| Tabasco | 38.6 | 15.4 |
| Tamaulipas | 14.2 | −24.5 |
| Tlaxcala | −2.6 | −22.4 |
| Veracruz | 12.7 | −7.3 |
| Yucatán | 2.3 | −4.4 |
| Zacatecas | −12.4 | −29.8 |

SOURCE: *La dinámica de los sectores de la economía mexicana durante los decades de los cincuentas y sesentas*, Table 3.

The result was the *golondrinas,* the wandering youth of the countryside, and the mushrooming squatter settlements on the fringes of the great cities. This problem was intensified by the advantages provided in the Agrarian Code to the larger agriculturalists and live-stock-raisers who were able to use the capital-intensive methods so that rural unemployment increased. The deterioration of farming lands in various parts of Mexico and a trend toward increasingly uneconomic sizes of *ejido* plots all contributed to the impoverishment of the rural masses, a group who remained nearly 50 percent of the total population.[84]

Echeverría proposed an expansion of "integral agrarian reform," to diversify the agricultural activity of rural low-income groups, dispense simple and basic agricultural industries to the countryside, and integrate the rural areas into the national system of communication, distribution, and production through building a rural infrastructure. Policies directed towards labor-intensive, small rural improvement projects that would provide much-needed employment were given greater emphasis. This emphasis represented a major shift from the major projects employing a relatively small work force with major equipment that were characteristic of the presidency of Miguel Alemán and the following years. Under Echeverría emphasis was placed on the construction of badly needed feeder roads, bridges, earthen dams, and other small, basic items of development. Primary goals were provision for employment, reduction of discontent, and easier, increased flow of commodities to the urban areas. Under this program of rural development emphasizing labor-intensive methods, the government had invested approximately 3 billion pesos by the third year of Echeverría's term.

## Balancing Development and Welfare Goals

Increasing foreign trade deficits were partially indicative of the broader problems facing the Mexican leadership in the 1970s. The outlook for Mexico, the ruling coalition, and the existing political system was more stressful when Luis Echeverría took office in December 1970 than at any time since the inauguration of Cárdenas in the early 1930s. The potential for internal conflict had clearly emerged. On one hand there was the task of maintaining the rate

---

[84] See Chapters 8 and 1. Rodolpho Stavenhagen, "Seven Fallacies About Latin America," in James Petras and Maurice Zeitlin, eds., *Latin America, Reform or Revolution* 1968, and Pablo González Casanova, "Internal Colonialism and National Development," *Studies In Comparative International Development* (1967).

of growth and development in the economy without losing financial stability. There was also at the same time a broad range of welfare commitments, increasingly heavy with each year of rapid population growth, which needed further expansion to meet Revolutionary goals. Expectations associated with Revolutionary values could not be shattered without dangerously jeopardizing the legitimacy of the regime itself. Continuation of economic development was itself basic to the welfare commitment.

By 1970 the potential disjunction in these elements of Revolutionary values had become a reality. Mexico was suffering from inflation, a problem that plagued not only third-world countries, but also the industrialized nations of the West. Inflation seemed inevitably to come with production bottlenecks and economic deprivation of the lowest income classes. Expectations for the development of Mexico's export industries were not being met. The economic growth rate had placed Mexico in a favorable position for foreign borrowing but could not pull ahead of population growth. (See Table 13.) These trends were accompanied by evidence of political instability with the guerrillas in the countryside and the terrorists in the cities. A number of imbalances demanded attention. Among the more deeply rooted problems, for example, was lack of balance between local and central governments. The concentration both of public-sector

*Table 13*

**The Race Between Growth and Population**

| Period | Growth of GNP in % | Population growth in % | GNP growth per capita in % |
|---|---|---|---|
| 1930–1934 | –0.5 | 1.6 | –2.1 |
| 1935–1939 | 5.6 | 1.7 | 3.7 |
| 1940–1944 | 5.4 | 2.5 | 2.8 |
| 1945–1949 | 5.1 | 2.8 | 2.3 |
| 1950–1954 | 6.1 | 2.7 | 3.2 |
| 1955–1959 | 6.6 | 3.2 | 3.3 |
| 1960–1964 | 5.6 | 3.4 | 2.2 |
| 1965–1967 | 6.7 | 3.4 | 3.2 |

SOURCE: Thomas G. Sanders, "Mexico 1974: Demographic Patterns and Population Policy," *Fieldstaff Reports,* North America, Series Volume II, No. 1 [TGS–1–74], (July 1974), p. 25. © American Universities Field Staff, Inc.

and private-sector administrative headquarters was a key indicator, as was the mushrooming industrial plant and population growth of the Federal District. When Echeverría became President he began to attack this in several ways. He promised a definite diffusion of administrative functions, and in support of this policy he pledged housing- and cost-of-living allowances for bureaucrats moved from the Federal District to more peripheral locations. Also in the cause of decentralization, the President pledged his government to the construction of low-cost housing to attract poorer classes away from the Federal District. The possibility that the population of Mexico City could well reach 20 million by the year 2000 had finally been taken into consideration by policy-makers plagued with problems of providing municipal services. Decentralization might help resolve two basic problems: discontent in the outlying areas because of the necessity of journeying to Mexico City in order to resolve the most minute details of public policy and private business, and uncontrolled, costly urban sprawl. The decentralization to which Echeverría committed himself in both his second and third State of the Union Addresses, if carried out, would ameliorate these two major difficulties.[85]

A third major difficulty which had not been confronted at all by leaders of the Revolutionary coalition prior to 1970 was the stress caused by the rapidly expanding population. Under Article 123 of the Constitution of 1917, workers were promised not only collective-bargaining rights, but remunerative, sufficient and fair wages, maximum-hour laws, unemployment benefits, and the entire gamut of social welfare legislation. Under Article 3 of the Constitution, the leaders of the Revolution committed themselves to educating, through the primary grades at least, all Mexican children at public expense. The efforts made to implement both commitments have been impressive in absolute terms, but when assessed in relation to the demands created by population growth, they have been inadequate. (See Table 14.)

Policy-makers were still not prepared to face the incompatibility of welfare goals and the desire for large numbers of children when Echeverría took office. Rational policy would theoretically provide for all. By 1973 it was clear that the Revolutionary regime had been forced to face for the first time the fact that rapidly increasing population can be politically, economically, and socially detrimental. For the first time, official sources spoke of the problem,[86] and there was a

[85] Luis Echeverría, Second State of the Union Address, *Hispano Americano* (Sept. 11, 1972), p. 26; and Third State of the Union Address.
[86] Luis Echeverría, Third State of the Union Address, p. 31.

Table 14

The Changing Rural Population

(Values are expressed as percentage of total population)

|  | Year | | |
|---|---|---|---|
|  | 1940 | 1950 | 1960 |
| Rural population | 64.9 | 57.4 | 49.3 |
| School age children not in school | 13.0 | 11.5 | 8.9 |
| Habitually wear no shoes | 50.1 | 33.4 | 36.5 |
| Primary language is not Spanish | 12.7 | 9.5 | 8.7 |

SOURCE: Pablo González Casanova, *La democracia en México*, 2nd ed. (México, D.F., 1967), chapter 5.

public law which confronted the problem of excessive population growth.[87]

Mexico's population growth stems in part from the expansion of medical services, and from intangibles connected with the emphasis on family. (See Table 15.) In relation to welfare goals and the costs of various social services, population growth helps to bring into focus still another problem, that of inflation. A frequent argument is that a modest inflation benefits the masses because an increasing money supply enables debts to be paid more easily. However, it is a truism that high rates of inflation are definitely detrimental to the really poor. This deteriorating situation relative to the equitable distribution of wealth is reported by Roger D. Hansen in *The Politics of Mexican Development*.[88] Hansen found that in the period 1950–1963 in the lower half of the Mexican income scale, people "have clearly lost ground in a relative sense while shifts in the upper income brackets have benefited the emerging Mexican middle- and upper middle-class." The population growth rate along with spiraling inflation can only worsen this problem.

[87] *Hispano Americano* (Sept. 10, 1973), p. 1. See also "General Population Draft Bill," *Comercio Exterior* (Nov. 1973), p. 3.

[88] Roger D. Hansen, *The Politics of Mexican Development* (Baltimore, 1971), p. 76. See Table 4–2.

Population control, however, is still a very delicate topic to most Mexicans, including the highest national leaders. The program is termed the "Program of Responsible Parenthood," to be operated by the National Institute for the Protection of Infants in coordination with the Undersecretary of the Ministry of the Presidency (in charge of the Office of Special Programs). The President's wife heads the Foundation of the National Institute for the Protection of Infants. The program is to operate through other existing government agencies, especially the Ministry of Education and state governments. The heads of all other federal agencies (and their wives) are charged with informally assisting the program. Its initial aim is to emphasize the importance of the family while simultaneously through the Civil Registration Act requiring that every inhabitant be able to prove his name, age, civil status, nationality, parentage, and other aspects of civil status. The program is to utilize all means of modern communication — radio, television, press, pamphlets, flyers, billboards, sound trucks, etc. It was nationally initiated on December 1, 1974 with celebrations honoring the attainment of recognized legal status — both matrimonial and natal. There is also dissemination of information about birth-control and social hygiene, but it is specifically

*Table 15*

**Factors Associated with Changing Fertility in Women**

|  | Average Live Births |
| --- | --- |
| Working women | 2.4 |
| Nonworking women | 3.7 |
| No education | 4.44 |
| Incompleted primary | 4.02 |
| Completed primary | 3.13 |
| Secondary and Preparatory | 2.11 |
| Some university | 1.53 |
| National average | 3.1 |
| Federal District (highly urbanized) | 2.6 |

SOURCE: Thomas G. Sanders, "Mexico 1974: Demographic Patterns and Population Policy," *Fieldstaff Reports,* North America, Series Volume II, No. 1 [TGS–1–74], (July 1974), pp. 2, 18. © American Universities Field Staff, Inc.

stated that children will not be exposed to this type of information in the program.

The damage and demoralization caused by uncontrolled inflation on top of the population growth, and the threat they clearly posed to the goals as well as maintenance of the political life of the Revolutionary regime, were not confronted publicly by Mexican officialdom until 1973.

Both marginal and middle classes in Mexico in the 1970s were suffering from the rising inflation; also middle-class youths seeking jobs appropriate to their status could not fail to be affected by the slowdown in the economic growth rate. *Comercio Exterior* editorialized, "the cost in terms of balance of payments is so disproportionately high that growth cannot be sustained ... [without] certain severe correctives." [89] The Echeverría government was aware of the seriousness of the problem. On July 25, 1973, the government announced that immediate action had to be taken because, according to Bank of Mexico estimates, the general price index had gone up 11 percent during the first five months of the year. In his State of the Union Address of September 1973, Echeverría indicated that he would be willing to fight inflation whether or not his measures met the approval of the non-Communist industrial powers. He emphasized that he did not consider the inflation a result of either development or welfare policies followed by his government or his predecessors.

In 1974 Echeverría outlined his attack against inflation. There were policies aimed at promoting social justice as well as economic restructuring. Wages governed by minimum-wage laws would be adjusted annually by changes in the cost of living, and the government would continue its policy of protecting the costs of basic foodstuffs by controlling prices and increasing supplies, where necessary, by importation. But some notable changes were evident also, exemplified by new policies designed to bring about a "rational increase in State income." More efficient planning and control of public spending was emphasized, especially expenditures utilizing domestic resources and noninflationary domestic and foreign credit. Investments were to be channeled into only those activities which satisfy basic needs, are productive, help meet domestic demands, or help the substitution of imports or the expansion of imports. Finally, a system would be established to protect consumers by allowing only those price increases which represented real increases in the costs of production to occur.[90] The efficacy of these measures remained to be seen.

[89] *Comercio Exterior* (April 1973), p. 3.
[90] Luis Echeverría, Fourth State of the Union Address, pp. 28, 31, 32.

## Conclusion

A new Mexico is emerging. It is increasingly being unified with modern transportation and communication. Most of its people are literate, and possess a sense of loyalty to the nation. The new Mexico is based on the joining of the concepts of Mexicanism and development. The Revolutionary regime has progressed far beyond the days when it was easy to perceive and to achieve Revolutionary goals. The complexities of infrastructure, basic industries, agriculture, welfare goals, international financing, maintaining domestic peace, and balancing long-term investments and immediate needs confront the modern Mexican decision-maker.

Expectations have been raised to new heights in many segments of the population, but the scarcity of resources obstructs the realization of these hopes. Burdening the capability of Mexico to progress faster is the weakening international financial position. Credits obtained from abroad, although often invested, sometimes are used for immediate goals and do not go toward assisting development. And inflation, although not as high as in many nations of the world, bears heavily on the hopes and aspirations of masses that have begun to experience betterment of their condition.

Development is torn in different directions by conflicting loyalties and demands. First, demands of the competing corporate groups force decision-makers to choose which hierarchies will obtain what resources. Second, there are still those who do not directly make any demands, and their needs cannot be completely forgotten. Third, the overriding concern with Mexicanism means that development as a paramount goal cannot be abrogated. Fourth, welfare commitments must be met without too great a cost to much-needed investment. Finally, the resolution of the problems of inflation and balance of payments deficits cannot be made at the expense of Mexicanism.

The new and the old do not necessarily complement each other in this Mexico of the 1970s. The traditional patterns of culture still affect the political system and the development of the nation. The prevalence of *machismo* fires distrust and the extensive conflict in relationships. The prevalence of personalist ties facilitates continuism. Nevertheless, rapid circulation of the political elite is necessary, especially for the newer generations. And promises of reform in the direction of a competitive mass democracy do not seem promising in light of the orientations of most Mexicans and the unparalleled suppression of students at Tlatelolco and elsewhere. The future outcomes of the national order, of economic and social progress, and the growth of national power continue to hang in the balance.

# Epilog:
# The Prophecy of Betrayal

Political culture as defined in this work is not fixed or immutable. The experience of Mexico demonstrates this, because during the earlier part of this century a fundamental change in Mexican political culture occurred. In the critical period following the Revolution, roughly between the time that Obregón eliminated Carranza and the time that Cárdenas exiled Calles, there emerged for the first time a "national order" not dependent on the personalist following of one leader. For the first time also the Hispanic value of "order" became identified with the concept of Mexicanism. Tied to the emerging national identity was the possibility of a presidency which, even if affected by personal attributes of the President, stood apart from his personal following. The presidency came to have a legitimacy vis-à-vis political exigencies that was other than personalist. Thus, as a national order was forged there arose in company with it a presidency with legitimate standing at the peak of power, independent of the weaknesses or strengths of a particular man.

In Mexico the relatively new reality of a national order linked with the legitimacy of the presidential office is an important check upon certain historical patterns closely associated with Latin American republics: "barracks rebellions," coups d'état, and the more sweeping violence of civil rebellion and revolution. Relative order in the presidential succession is one outcome of the establishment of a national political order based on popular identity with Mexicanism. This regularized succession is now typical.

These qualities build a new kind of diffuse loyalty to the status quo supporting the rule of the Revolutionary coalition. This attachment was hard to build, and like most diffuse loyalties it is hard to attack. The order began to emerge after the cataclysm of 1910–1917, and does not provide specific loyalties and supports for policies and power contenders within the system. Diffuse loyalties, once developed, seem less vulnerable, and thus identification with Mexican nationality and the national order basically supports the political system and the ruling elite. The Revolutionary coalition thus takes care to use every available resource to continue its close association with nationalism and Revolutionary ideology, the necessary legitimizing bases of rule.

Another problem of the political culture rests in the many conflicts in Mexican society, especially the emphasis upon *machismo* and the distrust prevalent in personal and group relationships. These are related to recurrent, though segmented, violence and manifest popular cynicism towards politicans and government. These tendencies may be the reason why there is such a propensity for mass violence and destruction of the status quo. But cynicism, lack of confidence, and violent acts may also be perennial characteristics of the political culture that tend to divide the forces of potential rebellion. Instead of preparing a climate for revolutionary activity, skepticism may simply produce a general apathy to continued control by the existing rulers.

Similarly, the overlay of value symbols borrowed from the European revolutionary liberalism of the latter eighteenth and nineteenth centuries may provoke revolutionary violence. Cries of "effective suffrage — no re-election," invoked with demands for political rights have played their part in Mexican political cataclysms, but low priorities were assigned these values by the revolutionaries once they took power. The Revolutionary regime that emerged with the Constitution of 1917 pays tribute as a matter of form to the hallmarks of nineteenth-century liberalism, but the practice and the longevity of this regime indicate that groups seeking to appropriate nationalist, Revolutionary legitimacy, although invoking some symbols of liberalism, still adhere to the more deeply rooted guidelines of the Hispanic legacy.

In the Hispanic tradition order and anarchy are the extremes of good and evil between which there is no compromise. The values of order, hierarchy and dignity of the person remain critical. Order depends on hierarchy, the vertical distribution of status, deference and control by which each individual finds his proper place and plays his role according to his proper destiny. Dignity of the person resides in this inner sense of being unique, having a particular destiny, and a special status. The dignity of the person is jeopardized if hierarchy and order do not exist because these principles assure his claim to status, dignity, and identity.

Without order and hierarchy the individual is no longer assured of status nor of his right to appeal to a higher power in time of trouble.

Events that cause order and hierarchy to seem inadequate are threatening to the populace. When dignity is threatened, destiny is threatened. The rulers who allow these threats to exist are perceived as betrayers of the peoples' trust and illegitimate. A new order must then be created in which those who rule exercise their function properly and assure the necessary hierarchy that permits the dignity of the person.

The value of order so important to the nation and the political system is related to an old Hispanic theme: the great fear is the perversion or destruction of order, the betrayal of trust. Just as Spain was betrayed to the Moors, so Mexico was betrayed to the Spanish. Themes of betrayal are rife in the culture, and are reflected in the relationship of *maña* and *chingar,* the essence of *machismo.* Perversion of order is destruction by the betrayer. How does this happen? Those who disagree openly with the regime are not necessarily betrayers; betrayers are secret enemies within. It is the betrayers who must ultimately be destroyed, while dissenters must simply be controlled.

Nevertheless, since betrayal is a fundamental theme, there is a danger of it becoming a self-fulfilling prophecy. This can happen in either of two ways. First, it is the government's job to identify the betrayer and destroy him. The betrayer in this case can be a repressed group, such as the *cristeros* or the students at UNAM at the time of Tlatelolco. Second, it may fall to those who are governed to identify the betrayer and destroy him. The betrayer in this case has often been those who have ruled, who are suspected of destroying the national order or the paramount value of Mexicanism. The Revolutionary coalition's task is not to become identified with the figure of the betrayer.

The rulers have historically been the betrayers when the government has not complied with its obligations, when dignity of person has been denied. Dignity in interaction must be given: the access of the people to officials should not be denied. Dignity in status must be given: the aspirations of those who feel themselves eligible for political office and advancement should not be frustrated. Dignity in livelihood must be given: the material needs of individuals should be met. Dignity in life must be given: order must be maintained. If these essentials are not met, suspicions of betrayal are confirmed, and the Mexican may then act to redress the wrongs he suffers. Just as the Porfirian suppression of strikers at Río Blanco and Cananea heralded the Revolution of 1910–1917, so historians of the future might see the tragedy of Tlatelolco in 1968 and the widespread suppression of university students before and after it as the precursors of revolutionary upheaval. Tlatelolco and its accompanying events may not prove to be a sign of imminent collapse, but only an incident in a time of stress, though it is a landmark in its results.

With the emergence of a common identity and a national order the dignity of everyone is linked to the dignity of the nation. Thus the unforgiveable act against the nation and the dignity of all Mexicans must involve the betrayal of the national dignity. This betrayal comes about through the sale of Mexican patrimony (or pride) to non-Mexicans. This was exemplified prior to the Revolution by Díaz' policies of giving great land extensions, mineral rights, and preferential access to himself to non-Mexicans. The Revolutionary coalition, therefore, takes great care not to be too closely associated in the public's mind with the interests of the "Colossus of the North," the United States, as well as other major powers. Through this policy the dangers of being perceived as the betrayer of the nation in international affairs is kept minimal in a situation where territorial proximity poses great difficulties.

These considerations are fundamental to the stability of the political system. The problems we noted in previous chapters — continuism, access to authority, social welfare goals, and economic growth — present conflicting demands on the system. These stresses within sectors, groups, and individuals must be balanced, one against the other. Otherwise, violent change in the system will happen when a significant segment of the nation feels itself betrayed. The situation facing Mexico today is one in which the satisfaction of material and psychic needs is threatened by the nation's limited material resources. With limited resources and growing demands, the fulfillment of psychic needs assumes greater importance, yet this too depends increasingly on material resources. This is why it is critical to avoid the trap of continuism and to maintain open channels of access to the hierarchies in the political system. To do otherwise is to rely on coercive control. Inevitably this would discredit the Revolutionary coalition and jeopardize the Revolutionary goals gained through peaceful government. Yet perhaps merely avoiding continuism will not be adequate to deal with the newer generations of army officers. Their rewards are not equivalent to the responsibility they know they bear. They must combat continued terrorism, and their technical skills are essential to governing the nation. Although loyal to Mexico, an observer must wonder if the army's loyalty to the present leadership can be guaranteed.

It is important to reconsider here what the gains of peaceful government have been. The political system has permitted routinized, legal transfers of government since 1929. Until recently, careful observers agreed that institutionalization of political structures had occurred in the presidency, the PRI, existence of opposition parties, and even a functioning (though not powerful) Congress and judicial system. In contrast to every other Latin American country and parts of "politically developed" Western Europe, Mexico since the Revolution of 1910–1917 has had no attempted military coups. Yet Mexican political tradition and social history have been no less violent, no less full of *caudillos* and president-generals than other nations in Latin America. Mexico has been no less dependent than other Latin American nations on the United States, both economically and politically. Mexico has faced all the problems of a developing society: nation-building, integration of minority and ethnic groups, linguistic differences, regional conflicts, agrarian problems, and the dilemma of too rapid massive urbanization. There have been rising expectations by large segments of the population, yet some of these have not been met due to constraints on industrialization, the structure of the international economy, and the domestic environment. Despite its turbulent history and its growing stresses, the Mexican political system has generally been able to contain the regional, religious, and personal conflicts that at other times have degenerated into civil war.

On balance, this regime and its decision-makers have compiled a record of orderly progress scarcely equaled in the third world. If rural and urban workers have shouldered much of the burden of development, the cost has been no higher than that paid by immigrants in the United States, peasants in Western Europe, or the populations of socialist nations seeking to create modern industrial economies. The Mexican system has survived because of the widespread acceptance of powerful symbols: Mexicanism, agrarianism, national autonomy, and development. What makes these symbols so dangerous is the ever-present fear of their betrayal. Should they be widely perceived as betrayed, the specter of mass violence would again haunt the country.

# FOR FURTHER READING

These sources provide an introduction for the student to the complexities of the Mexican nation. They are not intended to be a complete or exhaustive bibliography. Three sections are provided: sources in English, in Spanish, and in newspapers and periodicals. An asterisk indicates particularly rich sources of numerical data that may benefit the growing number of students and professionals interested in the use of statistical techniques. However there are many sources for data of this type which have not been mentioned. For example, United Nations publications, International Monetary Fund publications, and the statistical publications of the Mexican government should be consulted.

## English Materials

Alba, Víctor. *The Mexicans: The Making of a Nation* (New York, 1967).

Alba, Víctor. *Politics and the Labor Movement in Latin America* (Stanford, Calif., 1968).

Alexander, Robert J. *Organized Labor in Latin America* (New York, 1965).

Alisky, Marvin. "CONASUPO: A Mexican Agency Which Makes Low-Income Workers Feel Their Government Cares," *Inter-America Economic Affairs* (Winter 1973).

American Chamber of Commerce of Mexico. *Business Mexico* (México, D.F., 1968).

Ames, Barry. "Bases of Support for Mexico's Dominant Party," *American Political Science Review* (March 1970).

Baerresen, Donald W. *The Border Industrialization Program of Mexico* (Lexington, Mass., 1971).

* Balán, Jorge, Harley L. Browning, and Elizabeth Jelin. *Men in a Developing Society: Geographic and Social Mobility in Monterrey, Mexico* (Austin, Texas, 1973).

Bernstein, Harry. *Modern and Contemporary Latin America* (Philadelphia, 1952).

Brandenburg, Frank R. *The Making of Modern Mexico* (Englewood Cliffs, N.J., 1964).

Brandenburg, Frank R. *Mexico: An Experiment in One-Party Democracy* (unpublished Ph.D. dissertation, University of Pennsylvania, 1955).

Clark, Marjorie R. *Organized Labor in Mexico* (Chapel Hill, N.C., 1934).

Cline, Howard F. *Mexico, Revolution to Evolution, 1940–1960.* (London, 1962).

Cline, Howard F. *The United States and Mexico* (Cambridge, Mass., 1953).

Cornelius, Wayne A., Jr. "Urbanization as an Agent in Latin American Political Instability: The Case of Mexico," *American Political Science Review* (September 1969).

Cumberland, Charles C. *Mexico: The Struggle for Modernity* (New York, 1968).

Díaz, May H. *Tonala: Conservation, Responsibility, and Authority in a Mexican Town* (Berkeley, Calif., 1970).

Everett, Michael David. *The Role of the Mexican Trade Unions, 1950–1963* (unpublished Ph.D. dissertation, Washington University, 1967).

Fagen, Richard R., and William S. Tuohy. *Politics and Privilege in a Mexican City* (Stanford, Calif., 1972).

Fehrenbach, T. R. *Fire and Blood: A History of Mexico* (New York, 1973).

Friedrich, Paul. *Agrarian Revolt in a Mexican Village* (Englewood Cliffs, N.J., 1970).

Fromm, Erich, and Michael Maccoby. *Social Character in a Mexican Village: A Sociopsychological Study* (Englewood Cliffs, N.J., 1970).

Fuentes, Carlos. *The Death of Artemio Cruz* (New York, 1964).

Glade, William P., Jr., and Charles W. Anderson. *The Political Economy of Mexico* (Madison, Wis., 1963).

Goldkind, Victor. "Another View of Social Stratification in the Peasant Community: Redfield's Chan Kom Reinterpreted," *American Anthropologist* (August 1965).

* Gonzalez Casanova, Pablo. *Democracy in Mexico* (New York, 1970).

* Griffiths, B. *Mexican Monetary Policy and Economic Development* (New York, 1972).

* Hansen, Roger D. *Mexican Economic Development: The Roots of Rapid Growth* (Washington, D.C., 1971).

* Hansen, Roger D. *The Politics of Mexican Development* (Baltimore, 1971).

Hawkins, Carroll. *Two Democratic Labor Leaders in Conflict: The Latin American Revolution and the Role of the Workers* (Lexington, Mass., 1973).

Hyman, Herbert H. *Political Socialization* (Glencoe, Ill., 1959).

James, Daniel. *Mexico and the Americans* (New York, 1963).

James, Dilmus. "Used Automated Plants in Less-Developed Countries: A Case Study of a Mexican Firm," *Inter-American Economic Affairs* (Summer 1973).

Johnson, Kenneth F. *Mexican Democracy: A Critical View* (Boston, 1971).

Kaufman, Susan. *Decision-Making in an Authoritarian Regime: The Politics of Profit-Sharing in Mexico* (unpublished Ph.D. dissertation, Columbia University, 1970).

Kern, Robert, ed. *The Caciques: Oligarchical Politics and the System of Caciquismo in the Luso-Hispanic World* (Albuquerque, 1973).

Kneller, George F. *The Education of the Mexican Nation* (New York, 1951).

Lewis, Oscar. *The Children of Sánchez* (New York, 1961).

Lewis, Oscar. *Five Families* (New York, 1959).

Mabry, Donald J. *Mexico's Acción Nacional: A Catholic Alternative to Revolution* (Syracuse, N.Y., 1973).

Mosk, Sanford A. *Industrial Revolution in Mexico* (Berkeley, Calif., 1950).

* Nacional Financiera, S.A. *Statistics on the Mexican Economy* (México, D.F., 1966).

X Needler, Martin C. *Politics and Society in Mexico* (Albuquerque, 1971).

Nelson, Michael. *The Development of Tropical Lands: Policy Issues in Latin America* (Baltimore, 1972).

O'Donnell, Guillermo A. *Modernization and Bureaucratic Authoritarianism* (Politics of Modernization Series, University of California, Berkeley, 1973).

Padgett, L. V. *Popular Participation in the Mexican "One-Party" System* (unpublished Ph.D. dissertation, Northwestern University, 1955).

Parkes, Henry Bamford. *A History of Mexico* (Boston, 1938).

Parsons, Elsie Clews. *Mitla — Town of Souls* (Chicago, 1936).

Paz, Octavio. *The Labyrinth of Solitude* (New York, 1960).

Paz, Octavio. *The Other Mexico: Critique of the Pyramid* (New York, 1972).

Pi-Sunyer, Oriol. *Zamora: Change and Continuity in a Mexican Town* (New York, 1973).

* Poleman, Thomas T. *The Papaloapan Project: Agricultural Development in the Mexican Tropics* (Stanford, Calif., 1964).

Price, John A. *Tijuana: Urbanization in a Border Culture* (Notre Dame, Ind., 1974).

Purcell, John F., and Susan Kaufman Purcell. "Machine Politics and Socioeconomic Change in Mexico" (to be published in *Contemporary Mexico: Papers of the IV International Congress of Mexican History*, ed. by James Wilkie, Michael Meyer, and Edna Monzon de Wilkie, Berkeley, Calif., 1975).

Purcell, Susan Kaufman. "Decision-Making in an Authoritarian Regime: Theoretical Implication from a Mexican Case Study," *World Politics* (October 1973).

Purcell, Susan Kaufman. *Public Policy and Private Profits: A Mexican Case Study* (to be published by University of California Press, 1975).

Ramos, Samuel. *Profile of Man and Culture in Mexico* (Austin, Texas, 1962).

* Reynolds, Clark W. *The Mexican Economy: Twentieth-Century Structure and Growth* (New Haven, Conn., 1970).

Romanucci-Ross, Lola. *Conflict, Violence, and Morality in a Mexican Village* (Palo Alto, Calif., 1973).

Ronfeldt, David. *Atencingo: The Politics of Agrarian Struggle in a Mexican Ejido* (Stanford, Calif., 1973).

* Sanders, Thomas G. "Mexico, 1974: Demographic Patterns and Population Policy," *Fieldstaff Reports* (July 1974).

Schers, David. *The Popular Sector of the Mexican PRI* (unpublished Ph.D. dissertation, University of New Mexico, 1972).

Scott, Robert E. *Mexican Government in Transition* (Urbana, Ill., 1959).
Scott, Robert E. "Nation-Building in Latin America," Karl W. Deutsch and William J. Polty, eds., *Nation-Building* (New York, 1966).
Scott, Robert E. "Politics in Mexico," Gabriel A. Almond, ed., *Comparative Politics Today: A World View* (Boston, 1974).
Shafer, Robert Jones. *Mexican Business Organizations: History and Analysis* (Syracuse, N.Y., 1973).
Simpson, Eyler N. *The Ejido: Mexico's Way Out* (Chapel Hill, N.C., 1937).
Stevens, Evelyn P. *Protest and Response in Mexico* (Cambridge, Mass., 1974).
Tannenbaum, Frank. *Peace by Revolution* (New York, 1933).
Tucker, William P. *The Mexican Government Today* (Minneapolis, Minn., 1957).
* Tuohy, William S., and Barry Ames. "Mexican University Students in Politics: Rebels Without Allies?" (Monograph Series in World Affairs, University of Denver, 1969–70).
Ugalde, Antonio. *Power and Conflict in a Mexican Community: A Study of Political Integration* (Albuquerque, 1970).
Vernon, Raymond. *The Dilemma of Mexico's Development* (Cambridge, Mass., 1963).
Walton, John, and Joyce Sween. "Urbanization, Industrialization, and Voting in Mexico: A Longitudinal Analysis of Official and Opposition Party Support," *Social Science Quarterly* (December 1971).
Whetten, Nathan L. *Rural Mexico* (Chicago, 1948).
* Wilkie, James W. *The Mexican Revolution: Federal Expenditure and Social Change Since 1910* (Berkeley, Calif., 1967).
Wilkie, James W. "New Hypotheses for Statistical Research in Recent Mexican History," *Latin American Research Review* (Summer 1971).
Wyckoff de Carlos, Ann. *Mexico's National Liberation Movement — The MLN* (unpublished paper from the Institute of Hispanic American and Luso-Brazilian Studies, Stanford University, 1963).

## Spanish Materials

Aguirre Beltrán, Gonzalo, y Ricardo Pozas. *Instituciones indígenas en el México actual* (México, D.F., 1954).
Anon. *Mi libro de tercer año* (México, D.F., 1960).
Barrón de Morán, Concepción. *Mi libro de cuarto año* (México, D.F., 1960).
Brun Martínez, Claudio. *Algunos aspectos importantes del pensamiento político de Luis Echeverría* (dissertation published by UNAM, México, D.F., 1972).
Burgoa, Ignacio. *El juicio de amparo*, 3rd. ed. (México, D.F., 1950).
Casillas H., Roberto. *Crisis en nuestra estructura política* (México, D.F., 1969).

Casillas H., Roberto. *Origen de nuestras instituciones políticas* (México, D.F., 1973).

* Centro de Estudios Economicos del Sector Privado, A.C. *La dinámica de los sectores de la economía mexicana durante las décadas de los cincuentas y sesentas* (México, D.F., 1971).

Confederación Nacional de Organizaciones Populares. *Bases constitutivas, principios, programa de acción estatutos* (México, D.F., 1952).

Confederación Patronal de la República Mexicana. *Franco dialogo entre gobierno y empresarios* (México, D.F., 1971).

Confederación Revolucionaria de Obreros y Campesinos. *Declaración de principios, programa de acción y estatutos* (México, D.F., 1952).

Cosío Villegas, Daniel. *El estilo personal de gobernar* (México, D.F., 1974).

Cosío Villegas, Daniel. *El sistema político mexicano: las posibilidades de cambio* (México, D.F., 1973).

Dana Montaño, Salvador M. *Las causas de la inestabilidad política en América latina* (Maracaibo, 1966).

de la Cerda Silva, Roberto. *El movimiento obrero en México* (México, D.F., 1961).

Echánove Trujillo, Carlos A. *Sociología mexicana* (México, D.F., 1963).

Fernández y Fernández, Ramón. *Economía agrícola y reforma agraria* (México, D.F., 1962).

Fernández y Fernández, Ramón, y Ricardo Acosta. *Política agrícola* (México, D.F., 1961).

Flores, Ana Maria. *Investigación nacional de la vivienda mexicana, 1961–1962* (México, D.F., 1963).

Fondo de Cultura Económica. *La industria petrolera mexicana* (México, D.F., 1958).

Galicia Ciprés, Paula. *Mi libro de segundo año* (México, D.F., 1960).

Guerra Utrilla, José Gabriel. *Los partidos políticos nacionales* (México, D.F., 1970).

Herzog, Jesús Silva. *Inquietud sin tregua* (México, D.F., 1965).

* Instituto Mexicano del Seguro Social Subdirección General Técnica. *Población amparadora por El Seguro Social: cifras estadísticas, 1944–1962* (México, D.F.).

Iturriaga, Jose E. *La estructura social y cultural de México*, (México, D.F., 1951).

*Ley electoral federal.* (México, D.F.).

López Aparicio, Alfonso. *El movimiento obrero en México* (México, D.F., 1952).

López Cámara, Francisco. *La génesis de la conciencia liberal en México* (México, D.F., 1954).

Loyo, Gilberto. *Población y desarrollo económico* (México, D.F., 1962).

Martínez de Navarette, Ifigenia. *La distribución del ingreso y el desarrollo económico de México* (México, D.F., 1960).

Mendieta y Lúñez, Lucio. *Efectos sociales de la reforma agrária en tres comunidades ejidales de la república mexicana* (México, D.F., 1960).

Mendieta y Lúñez, Lucio. *El problema agrário de México* (México, D.F., 1937).

\* *México: cincuenta años de revolución*, 4 vols. (México, D.F., 1961).

Molina Enriquez, Andres. *Esbozo de la história de los primeros diez años de la revolución agrária de México* (México, D.F., 1937).

Molina Enriquez, Andres. *Los grandes problemas nacionales* (México, 1909).

Monsiváis, Carlos. *Días de guardar* (México, D.F., 1970).

Moreno, Daniel. *Los partidos políticos del México contemporaneo (1926–1970)* (México, D.F., 1970).

Moreno Sánchez, Manuel. *Crisis política de México* (México, D.F., 1970).

*Nueva ley federal de reforma agrária* (México, D.F., 1972).

Pani, Alberto, J., ed. *Una envuesta sobre la cuestion democrática de México* (México, D.F., 1948).

Partido Revolucionario Institucional. *Declaración de principios del Partido Revolucionario Institucional* (VII Asamblea Nacional Ordinaria, México, D.F., 1972).

Partido Revolucionario Institucional. *Estatutos del Partido Revolucionario Institucional* (VII Asamblea Nacional Ordinaria, México, D.F., 1972).

Partido Revolucionario Institucional. *Programa de Acción del Partido Revolucionario Institucional* (VII Asamblea Nacional Ordinaria, México, D.F., 1972).

Ramírez Reyes, Manuel. "El desarrollo historico de los políticos mexicanos" (unpublished paper presented at the Sesión Academica Ordinaria of La Sociedad Mexicana de Geografía y Estadística, Oct. 8, 1963).

Sierra, Justo. *Evolución política del pueblo mexicano* (México, D.F., 1955).

Trueba Urbina, Alberto, y Jorge Trueba Barrera. *Nueva ley federal del trabajo reformada*, 23rd ed. (México, D.F., 1974).

Urquidi, Víctor, L., Ifigenia M. de Navarette, Leopoldo M. Solís, and David Ibarra. *El perfil de México en 1980*, vol. 1 (México, D.F., 1970).

Valdéz, Edmundo. "La muerte tiene permiso," in *Antología contemporánea del cuento mexicano* (México, D.F., 1963).

Velázquez, Manuel. *Revolución en la Constitución: perspectiva de la Constitución, la ideologia, y los grupos de presión en México* (México, D.F., 1969).

Yates, Paul Lamartine. *El desarrollo regional de México* (México, D.F., 1961).

## Newspapers, Periodicals, and Other Useful Periodic Sources

*Comercio Exterior* (México, D.F.) In English

*Excelsior* (México, D.F.) In Spanish

*Hispano Americano* (México, D.F.) In Mexico titled *Tiempo*. In Spanish.

*Insignia* (México, D.F.) In Spanish
*International Financial Statistics* (Washington, D.C.) In English
*The Los Angeles Times* (Los Angeles) In English
*Mexican Newsletter* (México, D.F.) In English
*The New York Times* (New York) In English
*Statesman's Yearbook* (London) In English
*Visión* (New York) In Spanish
*The Wall Street Journal* (New York) In English

# INDEX

ABM, *see* Bankers' Association
*acaparador,* defined, 290
*agostadero,* defined, 270
Agrarian Code, 38, 166, 244–245
agrarian reform: under Alemán,
  246–248; under Cárdenas, 40–42,
  245–246; historical background,
  29n–30n, 238–245; under Lopez
  Mateos, 250–256; recent problems
  of, 50, 54, 56–57, 258–273; under
  Ruiz Cortines, 248–250. *See also*
  certificates of inaffectability
Agrarian sector of PRI, *see* PRI
*agropecuaria,* defined, 269
Alamán, Lucas, 17
Alemán Valdés, Miguel, 4, 45, 46,
  124, 125, 174, 188, 195, 197, 198,
  220, 246–248, 280
*alfabetización,* 287; defined, 51
Almazán, Juan Andreu, 44, 93–96,
  98, 113
Altos Hornos, 226, 278–279
Álvarez, Juan, 16, 19
Álvarez, Luis H., 99
*amparo,* 201–203, 242, 244, 246–
  247; defined, 157
*amparo contra leyes,* defined, 202
*aparcero,* 271–272; defined, 270
Authentic Party of the Mexican
  Revolution, *see* PARM
Ávila Camacho, Manuel, 4, 40, 43–
  45, 48, 93–94, 169, 188, 245–246

Balán, Jorge, 235–237
*Banco de México, see* Bank of
  Mexico
*Banco Nacional de Comercio Ex-
  terior,* 207
Bank of Mexico, 207, 299
Bankers' Association (ABM), 179
Banking and Discount Housing Fund
  (FOVI), 297
Barragán, Juan, 103
*bracero,* defined, 249
Brandenburg, Frank, 97
Bravo, Nicolás, 17
Bucareli Agreements, 31

BUO, 126, 130, 135–136, 138, 148

*cacique,* 101, 152–153, 159–161.
  *See also continuismo*
Calles, Plutarco Elías, 4, 12, 27, 32–
  38, 75–76, 96, 121, 128, 242–244
*calpulli,* 216; defined, 56
*cámaras,* defined, 180
*camarilla,* 69–70, 114, 160, 185; defined, 37n
Cárdenas Lázaro, 4, 36–45, 76, 84–
  85, 96, 99, 110, 113, 177, 188,
  195, 245–246, 277, 280; and the
  CNC, 149–152, 163, 166–167; and
  labor, 118, 122–124, 128. *See
  also* agrarian reform and *ejido*
Carranza, Venustiano, 4, 25n, 26–29,
  32, 93, 96, 120–121, 208, 241–242
*Casa del Obrero Mundial,* 120
*casas de las aseguradas,* defined, 221
*categoría política,* defined, 241
*caudillo,* 75, 197
*causas de fuerzas major,* defined, 270
CCI, 113, 164–167
CEIMSA, 290, 292
certificates of inaffectability, 246–
  247, 250, 254–255, 269–272
CGT, 121–126, 128, 130, 135–136,
  139–143, 150
*China Nueva,* 111
*chingar,* 72; defined, 64
clergy, 11, 17, 18, 34, 108, 112
Cline, Howard F., 261–262
CNC, 81, 87, 150–154, 162–168,
  171, 174, 224
CNIT, 180–182, 228
CNOP, *see* Popular sector of the
  PRI
CNT (CNTM), 126–127, 130, 135–
  138
Coleman, James S., 10
*colonos,* 154
*Compañía Exportadora y Importa-
  dora Mexicana, S. A., see*
  CEIMSA
*Compañía Nacional de Subsistencias
  Popular, see* CONASUPO

327